ACTS

A Logion Press Commentary

Stanley M. Horton

LOGION
P R E S S

Springfield, Missouri
02-3040

3rd printing 2007

Library of Congress Cataloging-in-Publication Data

Horton, Stanley M.
Acts: a Logion Press commentary / Stanley M. Horton.
p. cm.
Rev. ed. of: The book of Acts. 1981.
Includes bibliographical references and indexes.
ISBN 0-88243-304-0
1. Bible. N.T. Acts—Commentaries. I. Horton, Stanley M.
Book of Acts. II. Title.
BS2625.3 H66 2001
226.6'077—dc21   2001034223

Printed in United States of America

CONTENTS

In-Depth, Spiritually Satisfying Bible Study without Hours of Research

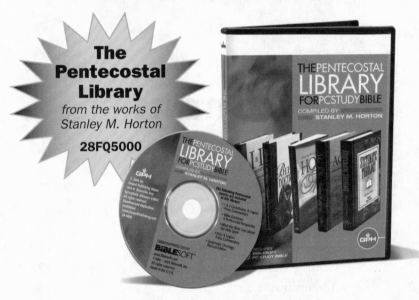

The Pentecostal Library
from the works of Stanley M. Horton

28FQ5000

From highly respected Pentecostal author and theologian Stanley M. Horton comes this digital treasury of outstanding systematic theology and biblical commentary. Combining extensive research with practical experience, each book in this collection offers solid teaching that will bring a deeper understanding of the Holy Spirit and His ministry to every believer.

Powerful and easy-to-use for study, research, and sermon preparation, **The Pentecostal Library** interfaces with the PC Study Bible®. These Pentecostal reference materials are searchable and can be easily cut and pasted into text documents or slide presentations. The content is also hyperlinked to other search tools within the PC Study Bible® library, such as dictionaries, lexicons, and encyclopedias for in-depth searches and results in seconds.

The following Pentecostal works are included in this library:

- *Acts*
- *1 & 2 Corinthians*
- *Systematic Theology*
- *Bible Doctrines: A Pentecostal Perspective*
- *What the Bible Says about the Holy Spirit*

REQUIREMENTS: This add-on module is only compatible with PC Study Bible® Version 4 or higher. It will not operate as a stand-alone unit or as an add-on for any previous version of PC Study Bible®.

Available at
www.GospelPublishing.com/PCStudyBible

FOREWORD

The Early Church of the Book of Acts is a model for the Pentecostal church of the twenty-first century. In Acts students discover the ingredients that caused the Early Church to grow and become a powerful force to affect their society. They were a people of prayer, the Word, fellowship, evangelism, and discipleship. They were committed to spreading the good news about Jesus. No wonder "the Lord added to their number daily those who were being saved" (Acts 2:47).

The growth of the Pentecostal and charismatic movement in recent years has encouraged many to turn to the Book of Acts, and their study has become an adventure in discovery. Many of the recent commentaries, however, look at the book from an anti-Pentecostal stance. Their authors have distanced themselves from the Pentecostal experience. They forget that Luke, the apostles, and all the early believers in Christ were Pentecostal. There is strong evidence that speaking in tongues and other gifts of the Spirit continued into the second and third centuries A.D. and only gradually died out. Revivals over the centuries brought refreshing restoration of the gifts. The past century has seen one of the greatest revivals and spread of the gospel in all of church history. The author of this commentary, Dr. Stanley M. Horton, writes from the perspective of one who has experienced the power and blessing of the Pentecostal revival.

Dr. Horton comes from a Pentecostal heritage where his grandmother was baptized in the Spirit in 1880 and his mother and father were baptized in the Spirit in 1906. He brings to this book insights from forty-six years of teaching in the seminary and colleges of the Assemblies of God. As a guest professor he has also observed the work of the Spirit in Canada, Ireland, Belgium, Germany, Lithuania, Russia, Kenya, Israel, Brazil, Singapore, and Korea. Other experiences of Dr. Horton include an archaeological dig at Dothan.

Dr. Horton's scholarship is unquestioned and thoroughly Pentecostal. He does not compromise his loyalty to Scripture as the infallible Word of God, inspired by the Holy Spirit. Students will find explanations in this verse-by-verse commentary that will encourage their faith and challenge them to proclaim the gospel in the power of the Holy Spirit. May you also apply its truths to practical Christian living. I highly commend this book to you.

Thomas E. Trask
General Superintendent
General Council of the Assemblies of God

PREFACE

The growth of the Pentecostal and charismatic movements has directed new attention to the Book of Acts. Many scholarly works have appeared since I wrote the first edition of this commentary in 1981. Most of them, however, neglect or bypass the Pentecostal distinctives that characterize Acts. I have taken note of recent literature and have sought to bring out what the Bible teaches.

In quoted Scripture, words I wish to emphasize are highlighted with italics.

For easier reading, Hebrew, Aramaic, and Greek words are all transliterated with English letters.

These abbreviations have been used:

Gk.: Greek
Heb.: Hebrew
Lat.: Latin
Beck: William F. Beck, *The New Testament in the Language of Today*
CEV: Contemporary English Version
JB: *Jerusalem Bible*
KJV: King James Version
NASB: *New American Standard Bible*
NCV: New Century Version
NEB: *The New English Bible*
NIV: New International Version
NKJV: New King James Version
NLT: New Living Translation
NRSV: New Revised Standard Version

Phillips: J. B. Phillips, *The New Testament in Modern English*
RSV: Revised Standard Version
TEV: Today's English Version
LXX: Septuagint
Acts: Greek Text: F. F. Bruce, *The Acts of the Apostles: The Greek Text with Introduction and Commentary,* 3d ed.

My special thanks go to Dr. Waverly Nunnally, Jr., Professor in Early Judaism and Christian Origins, Chair of Division of Biblical Education at Central Bible College, for reading the manuscript and making many valuable suggestions. Special thanks also to Glen Ellard, Paul Zinter, and Leta Sapp at Gospel Publishing House and to all who assisted in preparing this book. Thanks also to my wife, Evelyn, and to Dr. Dayton Kingsriter and the Pentecostal Textbooks Project Board for their encouragement.

INTRODUCTION
TO ACTS

The Book of Acts is special. No other book in the Bible is like it. Although there are historical books in the Old Testament, they emphasize the failures, the sins, and the idolatry that kept God's people from the fullness of His blessing.

In the Book of Acts, that failure is in the past. Israel has learned its lesson, and idolatry is no longer a problem among them. More importantly, Jesus has come. His death on Calvary has put the new covenant into effect (Heb. 9:15). By His resurrection He has brought blessing and great joy to His followers (Luke 24:51–52). A sense of both fulfillment and anticipation pervades the book.

1. Title And Content

Originally the book had no title. Since the middle of the second century A.D., however, it has been known as *The Acts of the Apostles.*[1] This title probably arose because the apostles are named in the first chapter (1:13) and in the first part of the book they preached in the temple. Yet, as we go through the Book of Acts we see that most of the apostles are not named again and some

[1]Because Marcion, about A.D. 144, declared that Paul was the only faithful apostle, the Muratorian list of New Testament books calls it *The Acts of All the Apostles.* See Kirsopp Lake and S. Lake, *An Introduction to the New Testament* (New York: Harper, 1937), 280; and F. F. Bruce, *The Acts of the Apostles: The Greek Text with Introduction and Commentary,* 3d ed. (Grand Rapids: Wm. B. Eerdmans, 1990), 1 (hereinafter cited as *Acts: Greek Text*).

are only barely mentioned.[2] Peter alone is prominent in the first part of the book; Paul alone is prominent in the latter part.

Actually, the Holy Spirit is more prominent than the apostles, though they have a place of honor. The book records how Jesus himself focused attention on the Holy Spirit (Acts 1:4–5). The outpouring of the Spirit (2:4) then sets the action of the book in motion. Acts mentions or refers to the Spirit fifty-one times. Consequently, many have suggested that *The Acts of the Holy Spirit* would be a better title.

However, the content of Acts is much broader.[3] Acts 1:1 suggests we might enlarge the title; notice the word "began." The "former book" (Luke's Gospel) recorded what Jesus "began to do and to teach." The Book of Acts, therefore, records what Jesus continued to do and teach through the Holy Spirit in the growing, spreading Church. Though Jesus is now in glory at the right hand of the Father's throne, He is still doing His work in the present world. Accordingly, an enlarged title for the Book of Acts might well be *The Acts of the Risen Lord by the Holy Spirit In and Through the Church.* I shall, however, refer to it simply as *Acts,* for it does not tell us details about all the apostles. Neither does it tell the full story of the growth of the Church.[4] In many cases it gives only brief summaries of what happened.[5] The churches in Galilee and Samaria are given very little attention (9:31). Important events such as the growth of a strong church in Egypt or even Rome during the first century are not even mentioned. On the other hand, some events are given in great detail (see chaps. 8; 10; 11; and 28).

The speeches and sermons that stand out so prominently in the book probably are also summaries. Paul, for example, sometimes preached until midnight (20:7). Other occasions obviously required a whole synagogue service, yet what is recorded can be read in a very few minutes. It is clear, however, that these

[2]James (Acts 12:2); John (Acts 4:13,19,23; 8:14,17).

[3]Simon J. Kistemaker, *Exposition of the Acts of the Apostles* (Grand Rapids: Baker Book House, 1990), 3.

[4]Everett F. Harrison, *Introduction to the New Testament* (Grand Rapids: Wm. B. Eerdmans, 1964), 228.

[5]See examples in 2:47; 5:42; 6:7; 8:4,40; 9:31; 12:24; 13:49; 16:5; 18:23; 19:20; 28:30–31.

speeches reflect the style and emphases of the apostles, as well as their actual words.[6] That they can be identified as different genres (deliberative, apologetic, and hortative)[7] also indicates that Luke did not compose these speeches out of his own imagination. Condensed accounts were necessary due to the limited space available in an ancient papyrus book or scroll. Someone has said that if we were to record the entire story of the growth and development of the Early Church, with all the signs and wonders given in detail, it would fill up several sets of books the size of the *Encyclopaedia Britannica* (cf. John 20:30–31; 21:25).

More than the limitations of space is involved, however. No one could write a history today by throwing together everything printed in the daily newspapers. The historian must choose events that are significant, events that show trends, turning points, and relationships. Luke does this by following a theme suggested by the words of Jesus: "'You will be my witnesses in Jerusalem, and in all Judea and Samaria, and to the ends of the earth'" (Acts 1:8). The first seven chapters center on events in Jerusalem, describing the initial growth and testing of the Church. Chapters 8 through 12 reveal how the Spirit broke down barriers in Judea and Samaria. Finally, chapters 13 through 28 show how the gospel began to move toward the ends of the earth. The latter chapters emphasize new centers for the spread

[6]For example, early tradition says Mark got his Gospel from Peter's preaching. We do see the same emphases in Mark's Gospel as we do in Peter's preaching in Acts. Compare also Acts 2:23 with 1 Pet. 1:2 and Acts 10:42 with 1 Pet. 4:5. In comparing Paul's sermons in Acts with his epistles, however, keep in mind that in Acts he was speaking to people who had never heard the gospel. In his epistles he was dealing with Christians and the problems that arose among people who already knew and believed the gospel. See Richard Heard, *An Introduction to the New Testament* (New York: Harper & Row, 1950), 139–40. Compare, however, Acts 20:24 with 2 Tim. 4:7 and with Col. 4:17. Some modern writers say "these speeches are not a record of what was actually said, but at best a recollection of what might have been said" or were composed by Luke. Gerhard A. Krodel, *Acts* (Minneapolis: Augsburg Publishing House, 1986), 35–36. Williams, however, gives reasons for considering them "a reliable guide to what was actually said." David John Williams, *Acts* (Peabody, Mass.: Hendrickson Publishers, 1990), 10–11. F. F. Bruce points out that the speeches of Paul "suit Paul's changing circumstances and are well adapted to the varying audiences addressed." *Acts: Greek Text,* 38–39.

[7]Bruce, *Acts: Greek Text,* 38, 39.

of the gospel at Antioch, Ephesus, and, finally, Rome, the center of the Roman Empire. Then, because Acts has no formal conclusion, we are left with the assurance that the gospel will continue to spread toward "'the ends of the earth.'"

Luke's clarity and logical progression lead most Bible-believing scholars to agree that Luke is a first-class historian, not only because of what he included in Acts, but also because of what he left out.[8] (Bible-believing scholars agree, of course, that the Holy Spirit directed and inspired the writing of the Scriptures.)

The events Luke does include are both significant and typical. At the time he wrote, churches in various areas were in communication with each other and were familiar with many of the events he describes. Thus the first readers of Acts would not have had any difficulty seeing the relationship of their own local church to the course of events described in Acts.[9] We too can see in Acts a new way for us to live in relationship to the Lord, the Church, and the Holy Spirit. It will affect our values and help us be disciples who claim God's promises and bring Christ glory. Acts is more than "a chronicle of the past. Rather, the past becomes the platform from which to preach to the present."[10] We need to do more than study the Book of Acts, we need to live it![11]

2. Genre, Authorship, and Date

GENRE

Many consider the genre of the Book of Acts to be historical monograph.[12] Luke-Acts has "much in common with the sacred

---

[8]See Charles W. Carter and Ralph Earle, *The Acts of the Apostles* (Grand Rapids: Zondervan Publishing House, 1959), 6. This is also the view of the British historian Sir William Ramsay.

[9]Heard, *Introduction to the New Testament*, 136.

[10]William H. Willimon, *Acts* (Atlanta: John Knox Press, 1988), 5.

[11]C. Peter Wagner, *Spreading the Fire: Book 1: Acts 1–8* (Ventura, Calif.: Gospel Light, Regal Books, 1994), 11.

[12]Darryl W. Palmer, "Acts and the Ancient Historical Monograph," in *The Book of Acts in Its Ancient Literary Setting*, ed. Bruce W. Winter and Andrew D. Clarke, vol. 1 of *The Book of Acts in Its First Century Setting*, ed. Bruce W. Winter (Grand Rapids: Wm. B. Eerdmans, 1993), 3, 28. See Also Charles B. Puskas, *An Introduction to the New Testament* (Peabody, Mass.: Hendrickson Publishers, 1989), 113–18.

historiography of ancient Israel, and even with the secular historiography of the Greco-Roman world."[13] The formal prefaces of Luke and Acts indicate that "Luke deliberately places his work into the context of sophisticated Greek literature."[14] However, two features "distinguish Acts from the genre of Hellenistic historical writings. One is the absence of chronology in Acts and the second is the presence of the perspective of God, Christ, the Holy Spirit, and the chosen witnesses."[15] Its author, Luke, the only Gentile New Testament writer, focuses consistently on the progress and development of the Church as a missionary body, fulfilling the command of Jesus to spread the gospel.[16] "By recognizing the invincible rise of Christianity, Luke was a better historian than anyone else among his contemporaries."[17] The first section follows Peter who is a prophet as well as an apostle. The remainder of the book follows Paul. His call is prominent (chap. 9, and retold in chaps. 22 and 26). It inspired his mission and the repetition keeps his mission and its importance before the reader. Another important emphasis is his prison experiences that reflect his own declaration that he was a prisoner, not of Rome, but of his Lord, Jesus Christ (Eph. 3:1; 4:1; 2 Tim. 1:8; Philem. 1,9,23).

As I. Howard Marshall points out, it seems best to view the Gospel of Luke and the Book of Acts as "two parts of the one unified work."[18] He points out that the prologues of the two books uphold this. So does the material in the Gospel and its ending. He notes especially that the prophetic elements in the Gospel point forward to Acts.[19] Therefore, "Acts should be read

---

[13]Roger Stronstad, *The Prophethood of All Believers: A Study in Luke's Charismatic Theology* (Sheffield, England: Sheffield Academic Press, 1999), 13.

[14]S. John Roth, *The Blind, the Lame, and the Poor: Character Types in Luke-Acts* (Sheffield, England: Sheffield Academic Press, 1997), 89.

[15]Gerhard Krodel, *Acts* (Philadelphia, Fortress Press, 1981), 2.

[16]Talbert takes Acts to be a "*bios* ('biography')" of a people group, the Church, analogous to *bioi* of peoples written by Greek writers. Charles H. Talbert, *Reading Acts: A Literary and Theological Commentary on the Acts of the Apostles* (New York: Crossroad Publishing, 1997), 14.

[17]Krodel, *Acts,* 41.

[18]I. Howard Marshall, "Acts and the 'Former Treatise'," in *Acts in Its Ancient Literary Setting,* ed. Winter and Clarke, 172. As a student, I heard this from Henry J. Cadbury at Harvard Divinity School in 1945.

[19]Ibid., 174–76.

in the light of the Gospel."[20] In Luke, "conceived, empowered, and guided by the Holy Spirit, Jesus both embodies the Way and makes provision for others to follow in it, thereby fulfilling the divine plan."[21] In Acts, believers "empowered by the Holy Spirit . . . bear an unstoppable, universal witness to Jesus by word and deed, thereby fulfilling the divine plan."[22] Thus, Luke and Acts have the same genre "because Luke's term *diēgēsin*/narrative (Lk. 1.1) applies to his entire two-volume history."[23] This is confirmed further by parallel structure, both Luke and Acts having similar thematic elements. Also, Luke shows careful design in Acts when he "reports each of Paul's three evangelistic tours according to the same structure: (1) introductory episode(s); (2) a major report about one city; and (3) a series of summary reports."[24]

Some writers see apologetic motifs in Acts as well, noting how Acts brings out the political innocence of Jesus and the apostles.[25] Earl Richard points out, however, that "the theme of innocence is subordinate to that of righteousness and so motivated more by religious than by political concerns."[26] Another concern is "relations between Jesus and his followers on the one hand and . . . non-believing Jews on the other."[27] Some have used negative images of unbelieving Jews in Acts to justify Christian anti-Judaism. However, that is based on a misreading of the texts. Even though there are negative images of Judaism and Jewish

[20]Luke T. Johnson, *The Acts of the Apostles* (Collegeville, Minn.: Liturgical Press, 1992), 13.

[21]Talbert, *Reading Acts,* 4.

[22]Ibid. It should be noted that Luke's Gospel and the Book of Acts were never connected in any canonical list. The speeches and matters of tone and attitude, and the fact that Acts is more Hellenic, cause some to challenge the generic unity of Luke and Acts. Mikeal C. Parsons and Richard I. Pervo, *Rethinking the Unity of Luke and Acts* (Minneapolis: Fortress Press, 1993), 8, 38–40, 53.

[23]Stronstad, *Prophethood of All Believers,* 19 n. 2; see also 23–24.

[24]Ibid., 14, 15.

[25]Dr. Henry J. Cadbury stressed this in a 1945 class I took studying the Greek text of Acts in Harvard Divinity School.

[26]Earl Richard, "Luke: Author and Thinker," in *New Views on Luke and Acts,* ed. Earl Richard (Collegeville, Minn.: Liturgical Press, 1990), 17.

[27]Joseph B. Tyson, *Images of Judaism in Luke-Acts* (Columbia, S.C.: University of South Carolina Press, 1991), 3.

leaders, "Aspects of Jewish religious life are often portrayed in positive ways."[28] Paul and the early Jewish believers were faithful to their Jewish heritage and to the God of their fathers.

Another concern of Luke's is to give a clear picture of the plan of God for the spread of the gospel. "God's providential guidance" is an important focus of the missionary speeches recorded in Acts 2 through 17.[29] As a "world Christian . . . he shows how the walls of separation between Jews and Gentiles were broken down and, thus, writes more about true missiology than any other biblical author."[30]

AUTHORSHIP

Though the Book of Acts does not name its author, it is evident that Acts 1:1 refers to the same Theophilus mentioned in Luke 1:1–4. What we find in Acts is the outworking of the Gospel of Luke, though the Gospel does not name its author either. Good evidence, however, connects both the Gospel and Acts with the person Paul calls "our dear friend Luke, the doctor" (Col. 4:14).[31] The Muratorian Canon attributes them to Luke the physician,[32] as did Irenaeus and many of the early church fathers.

One important evidence of Luke's authorship is the "we" passages in Acts 16:10–17; 20:5 to 21:18; 27:1 to 28:16.[33] These passages "are written in a style indistinguishable from the rest of the book" and indicate that Luke "was using his own material."[34] In these passages the author indicates he was with Paul on parts of the second and third missionary journeys as well as the jour-

---

[28]Ibid., 187.

[29]John T. Squires, *The Plan of God in Luke-Acts* (Cambridge, England: Cambridge University Press, 1993), 63.

[30]Wagner, *Spreading the Fire*, 19.

[31]F. Scott Spencer, "Acts and Modern Literary Approaches," in *Acts in Its Ancient Literary Setting*, ed. Winter and Clarke, 407.

[32]See Bruce, *Acts: Greek Text*, 1, 2.

[33]Acts mentions Silas and Timothy in these passages, but in the third person. Titus is not mentioned in the greetings of Paul's epistles. Paul speaks of Luke as his fellow worker (Col. 4:14; 2 Tim. 4:11; Philem. 24). "Luke is the most likely person to have composed the books attributed to him." Kistemaker, *Acts*, 21.

[34]Williams, *Acts*, 4. Note that the "we" passages are all sea journeys, but the writer does not use "we" in every sea voyage. That is, he doesn't use it for someone else's sea voyages, only for those where Luke was with Paul.

ney to Rome.[35] To parts of the Book of Acts, then, Luke was an eyewitness. He was also able to talk to eyewitnesses, such as Philip the evangelist in Caesarea (21:8) and John Mark.[36]

The fact that Luke was with Paul on his last visit to Jerusalem and also accompanied him on the journey to Rome indicates Luke was in Palestine during the two years Paul was imprisoned in Caesarea (24:27). Archaeological evidence shows Luke checked his facts carefully. Though the titles and statuses of Roman officials changed frequently in the first century, Luke never made a mistake. Nor did he make mistakes in what he says about geography and history. His "exact information about the cities of the coastal Plain, the Road from Jerusalem to Caesarea, and the relation between the Temple and the Antonia fortress in Jerusalem is striking."[37] It would not be wrong to assume, therefore, that Luke spent those two years checking facts and talking to eyewitnesses of the events of his Gospel and the first part of Acts.[38]

For example, in Luke's Gospel he tells the story of the birth of Jesus from Mary's viewpoint, while Matthew gives it from Joseph's. Joseph most probably was dead before Luke came to Jerusalem, but Mary was still alive. Luke tells how Mary treasured the events surrounding Jesus' birth in her heart (Luke 2:51). That is, she remembered them carefully. Luke also tells us that Mary was present in the Upper Room on the Day of Pentecost. Paul confirmed that many who saw the risen Christ were still alive when he wrote 1 Corinthians (15:6). Consequently, Luke was able to confirm the events that, under the guidance and inspiration of

---

[35]The church historian Eusebius (about A.D. 330) and Jerome who translated the Latin Vulgate version (about A.D. 400) believed Luke was from Antioch. One ancient manuscript (Codex Bezae, or D) adds to Acts 11:28, "When we came together." If this is correct it would indicate Luke was present in Antioch about A.D. 42.

[36]In Luke 1:3, "investigated" is a perfect participle, *parēkolouthēkoti,* that is never used of research of documents or legal search. It always means being in possession of firsthand information. That is, Luke talked to people who witnessed these events.

[37]Martin Hengel, "The Geography of Palestine in Acts," in *The Book of Acts in its Palestinian Setting,* ed. Richard Bauckham, vol. 4 of *Acts in Its First Century Setting,* ed. Winter (Grand Rapids: Wm. B. Eerdmans, 1995), 27.

[38]George E. Ladd, *A Theology of the New Testament* (Grand Rapids: Wm. B. Eerdmans, 1983), 313.

the Holy Spirit, he included in Acts.[39]

He is accurate also "in his reproduction of the local color of widely differing places. . . . He gets the atmosphere right every time. Jerusalem, with its excitable and intolerant crowds, stands in contrast with the intellectually and religiously hospitable metropolis of Antioch on the Orontes."[40] What we read of Philippi, Athens, Ephesus, the shipwreck, and Malta, all reflect the fact that Luke was personally present or acquainted with each situation.

The fact Paul calls Luke "our dear friend . . . the doctor" (Col. 4:14) also fits what we find in Luke and Acts. Luke gives special attention to healing and often gives additional details or a more specific diagnosis. When Jesus said it was easier for a camel to go through the eye of a needle than for a rich man to enter the kingdom of heaven, the other Gospels use the common word for a sewing needle (Gk. *raphidos,* Matt. 19:24; Mark 10:25). Luke uses instead the more classical Greek word that the Greeks used for a surgeon's needle (Gk. *belonēs,* Luke 18:25). (Some have tried to press this further by looking for medical terms in Luke and Acts. However, doctors in New Testament times used everyday language. There was no such thing as a "medical language" at that time.)[41]

DATE

Since Acts concludes with Paul's first imprisonment in Rome, A.D. 60–62 is the earliest date it could have been written.[42]

---

[39]These include the miracles. Even some who have not been brought up to believe in miracles admit that the miracles are not tacked on to the Book of Acts. They are part of its very framework and structure. Take them out and the whole book falls apart. Since Luke was so meticulous in verifying everything else, we can be sure he did not fail to verify these miracles also.

[40]Bruce, *Acts: Greek Text,* 33.

[41]Dr. William K. Hobart in *The Medical Language of St. Luke* (Dublin, Ireland: Hodges, Figgis, 1882) went too far in this direction. About ninety percent of his "medical terms" have been found in the works of nonmedical writers such as Josephus and even in the Septuagint (LXX).

[42]As Johannes Munck says, "Since certain points in Luke's work clearly indicate an early date of composition—at the beginning of the sixties—there is good reason to favor that date." *The Acts of the Apostles,* rev. William F. Albright and C. S. Mann, vol. 31 of *Anchor Bible Series* (Garden City, N.Y.: Doubleday & Co., 1979), LIV.

Moreover, "Acts devotes so much space to events of A.D. 58–60 (chapters 20–28) that it is like the events had just occurred. We best explain the accuracy of geographical, political and sociocultural details, humanly speaking, if the work was produced close to the events it describes."[43] In A.D. 64 Rome burned and Nero began persecuting Christians. This brought a complete change in the relation between the Christians and the empire. Therefore, the latest date for the writing of Acts would be about A.D. 62[44] or 63.[45] Note also that Acts gives no hint of the Jewish revolt of A.D. 66, or of the destruction of the temple in A.D. 70. We have in the book a record of the first generation of believers, the first thirty years of the growth of the Church that began at Pentecost.

3. Luke As A Theologian

Acts is clearly a Church book, giving us important theological teaching concerning the nature, growth, life, and purpose of the Church. Some, claiming Acts is only history, deny it can provide us with doctrine; consequently, we must go to the Epistles for doctrine. This categorization of Scripture sounds like "a canon within a canon."[46] They overlook the fact that the Bible does not give us history to satisfy our historical curiosity but rather to teach truth. Even the Epistles refer to both Old and New Testament history in order to teach doctrine or theology. When Paul wanted to explain justification by faith in Romans 4, he went back to the history of Abraham in Genesis. When he wanted to show what God's grace can do, he went back to the history of David. Acts does more than give a mere transition, or "shifting of gears," between the Gospels and the Epistles. It pro-

[43]William J. Larkin, Jr., *Acts* (Downers Grove, Ill.: InterVarsity Press, 1995), 18.

[44]E. M. Blaiklock, *Acts: The Birth of the Church* (Old Tappan, N.J.: Fleming H. Revell, 1980), 10.

[45]Harrison, *Introduction,* 226. Some German scholars (esp. Conzelmann and Käsemann) suppose delay in Christ's second coming influenced Luke and this means Luke wrote near the end of the first century. However, this "has no compelling reason in its favor." Everett F. Harrison, *Interpreting Acts: The Expanding Church* (Grand Rapids: Zondervan Publishing House, Academie Books, 1986), 24.

[46]William W. Menzies and Robert P. Menzies, *Spirit and Power: Foundations of Pentecostal Experience* (Grand Rapids: Zondervan Publishing House, 2000), 38.

vides a background to the Epistles and is necessary for a better understanding of the truths they teach.

I am not alone in emphasizing the theological importance of Acts.[47] Recent scholars have recognized that Luke is not just a historian but a theologian. His use of the Old Testament[48] shows he is a biblical theologian who knew the Scriptures well and who believed in their inspiration and authority. They influenced his use of language, giving the book "a certain Semitic colouring."[49] Luke also sees the gospel and its spread as fulfilling Old Testament promises and prophecies. As I. Howard Marshall points out, "Throughout Acts Luke seizes the opportunity to show . . . that the Christian faith and witness are not contrary to the laws and true interests of Judaism."[50] Rather, the Christian faith and witness continue the work of God, building on the covenants and promises given to Israel in the past. Luke also uses this relation to the Old Testament as a political polemic to indicate to the Romans that Christians were still part of a legitimate religion (that is, Judaism). Even the inclusion of the Gentiles is presented as fulfillment of promises given to Israel.[51] This is in contrast to the Qumran community, "which centered its attention on the Mosaic Law" and whose influence on the Early Church "was largely peripheral."[52]

It is important to recognize therefore that Luke uses the past to present divine truth. He sees God directing the events of history (2:23; 3:21; 10:42; 17:31; 19:21; 23:11; 27:24,26) and he often speaks of the will of God (2:23,31; 4:28; 13:22,36; 20:27; 21:14; 22:14). God and Jesus act in history and the Holy Spirit

[47]For a good summary of the theology of Acts see Larkin, *Acts*, 23–33.

[48]Cited thirty-five times. See G. L. Archer and G. C. Chirichigno, *Old Testament Quotations in the New Testament* (Chicago: Moody Press, 1987), xx. Seventeen of these quotations reflect the Heb. rather than the LXX. See Brian S. Rosner, "Acts and Biblical History," in *Acts in Its Ancient Literary Setting*, ed. Winter and Clarke, 69.

[49]Rosner, "Acts and Biblical History," 69. This would seem to contradict Roth's statement that "Luke-Acts presupposes an audience that is not familiar with Hebrew terminology, but is familiar with the LXX." Roth, *Blind*, 213.

[50]I. Howard Marshall, *An Introduction to Acts* (Sheffield, England: JSOT Press, 1992), 46.

[51]Willimon, *Acts*, 15.

[52]Harrison, *Interpreting Acts*, 34.

gives direction (2:32–33; 8:29,39; 11:17; 15:8–9; 16:6–7). As Marshall says, "Throughout Acts the church remains subject to the guidance of the Spirit and its work is done through the power of the name of Jesus. It does not 'possess' these gifts. It is a church under the Word and subject to its Lord."[53] Angels also carry out God's will (5:19; 8:26; 10:30; 12:7–10; 12:23; 27:23).

Though the kingdom (rule, reign) of God is mentioned only six times in Acts (1:3; 8:12; 14:22; 19:8; 28:23,31), it is an important feature of the Book. What is involved in the rule, or reign, of God "is spelled out in detail throughout the book."[54] In the Church "as the community of the Spirit" we see "the purpose to both reflect and witness to the values of the Reign of God, by the power of the Spirit to the world."[55] This, we can be sure, must always be connected with teaching "about the Lord Jesus Christ" (28:31; cf. 8:12; 19:8,10; 20:25,28).[56]

Luke draws attention also to the way the Holy Spirit promoted the unity of the Body. Notice how often he mentions being "in one accord."[57] More than once the Church were in danger of being split but the Spirit brought them together. The world tends to disrupt, divide, and build barriers. The Holy Spirit broke down barriers as the Church prayed together, worked together, evangelized together, suffered together. Nature tends to disperse, scatter, and break down. It takes a higher energy to unite, and more wisdom and power to build up, than to tear down. Consequently, an important theme of *The Acts of the Risen Lord Through the Holy Spirit* is church building; the acts of the Risen Lord are carried forward by the believers as "a community of charismatic prophets" and by "the ministry of six charismatic prophets . . . Stephen, Philip, Barnabas, Agabus, Peter and Paul."[58]

---

[53]I. Howard Marshall, *Luke: Historian and Theologian,* enl. ed. (Grand Rapids: Zondervan Publishing House, Academie Books, 1989), 214.

[54]Howard Clark Kee, *To Every Nation Under Heaven: The Acts of the Apostles* (Harrisburg, Pa.: Trinity Press International, 1997), 20.

[55]Eldin Villafañe, *The Liberating Spirit* (Grand Rapids: Wm. B. Eerdmans, 1993), 187.

[56]Ladd, *Theology of the New Testament,* 333.

[57]Gk. *homothumadon,* "with one mind or purpose"; see Acts 1:14; 2:1 (Textus Receptus); 2:46; 4:24; 7:57; 8:6; 12:20; 18:12; 19:29. The NIV often translates it "together."

[58]Stronstad, *Prophethood of All Believers,* 54.

Notice further that just as in the Gospels and Epistles, Jesus is central in Acts. The books complement each other and exalt Him. Acts shows that the total life of the Church continued to revolve around the living Christ (not just the suffering Messiah, though that is an emphasis)—the One risen, ascended, and seated at the right hand of the Father interceding for us. In 1 Corinthians chapters 12 through 14, Paul has something to say about the Holy Spirit, but in chapter 15 he returns the focus of attention to the Christ who died for our sins and rose again. So, though Acts gives teaching and shows us much of the work of the Holy Spirit, it focuses attention primarily on Jesus. He is the Prince of Life, the One who has come, who is present through the Spirit, and who will come again. His resurrection life and power flow through the book. Luke also shows "as clearly as Paul or John that salvation is through faith in Christ alone (Acts 15:11)."[59] The Gospels, Acts, the Epistles, and the Book of Revelation are all one revelation of Christ, who is himself the Word of God. What a tragedy if any part is neglected.[60]

One more thing should be kept in mind. Unlike many other books of the New Testament, the Book of Acts has no formal conclusion. It simply breaks off. Some suppose that this came about because Luke was martyred shortly after the apostle Paul. However, several ancient traditions claim he lived longer. It seems, rather, that the abrupt ending is intentional. The book had to come to an end, just as that first generation had to come to an end. But the acts of the Risen Lord through the Holy Spirit did not end then. They continued on into the second and third centuries with the same spiritual gifts[61] and manifestations. Further, they continue today wherever God's people gather in one accord with an earnest desire to search His Word, seek His gifts, and do His work.

---

[59]Marshall, *Luke: Historian and Theologian,* 190.

[60]"Both Chrysostom and Jerome note a general neglect of Acts." Parsons and Pervo, *Rethinking,* 1. Sadly, that neglect continued over much of church history.

[61]It should be noted that the Gk. *charismata,* "gifts," refers to ministries, not abilities. See Kenneth Berding, "Confusing Word and Concept in 'Spiritual Gifts'; Have We Forgotten James Barr's Exhortations?" *Journal of the Evangelical Theological Society* 43, no. 1 (March 2000): 51.

4. Text

The NIV text we are using is based on what most Bible scholars accept as the oldest and best Greek manuscripts (recognized as a neutral text), collated by the American Bible Society. In a few cases it accepts readings from what is called the Western Text, represented by the Codex Bezae (D)[62] and the Old Latin and Syriac versions.[63] The Book of Acts in Codex Bezae is ten percent longer than the neutral text. Some of this may be genuine Lukan material (e.g. 12:10; 19:9; 20:4,15; 27:5).[64] Most of the additions are either specific statements, possibly coming from early tradition, such as found in Acts 12:10 where it states that Peter and the angel "went down six steps." Others are later, non-Lukan revisions or explanations (commentary) intended to clarify and smooth the text;[65] for example, in Acts 14:2 Codex Bezae adds "but the Lord gave peace quickly."[66] Because some readings of the Western Text were copied into the late manuscripts used by the King James Version, you will find that the NIV text leaves them out. However, none of these omissions affects the truth of God's Word, since whatever is true that was in these Western texts is found elsewhere in the New Testament. Thus, we can have confidence in the text we are using in this commentary.[67]

STUDY QUESTIONS

1. What would be a better title for the Book of Acts, and why?
2. What evidence indicates that Luke was a first-class historian?

[62]Codex Bezae is a sixth-century manuscript now in Cambridge, England.

[63]For a discussion of significant variant readings see Bruce Metzger, *A Textual Commentary on the Greek New Testament,* 3d ed. (New York: United Bible Societies, 1971).

[64]W. A. Strange, *The Problem of the Text of Acts* (Cambridge, England: Cambridge University Press, 1992), 2. Many church fathers, beginning with Irenaeus, agree often with the Western Text.

[65]Ibid., 50; see also Peter Head, "Acts and the Problem of Its Texts," in *Acts in Its Ancient Literary Setting,* ed. Winter and Clarke, 417.

[66]Munck, *Acts of the Apostles,* lxxxv.

[67]For "a critical comparison of the various types of text current in the early Christian centuries," see Bruce, *Acts: Greek Text,* 69–80.

3. Why should we consider the genre of Acts to be historical monograph?
4. What can be said about the relationship between the Gospel of Luke and Acts?
5. What evidence is there for Luke's authorship of Acts?
6. What does Luke as a theologian emphasize?
7. What is the significance of the abrupt ending of Acts?
8. How is the Western Text of Acts different from the neutral text?

ACTS OUTLINE

I. The Church Established 1:1–2:47

  A. The promise of the Father 1:1–8
    1. What Jesus continued to do and teach 1:1
    2. Jesus gives final instructions 1:2–3
    3. Jesus promises baptism in the Holy Spirit 1:4–5
    4. Jesus promises power for witness 1:6–8

  B. Jesus ascends to heaven 1:9–11
    1. Disciples see Him taken up 1:9
    2. Angels promise His return 1:10–11

  C. The witness of the apostles 1:12–26
    1. Prayer in the Upper Room 1:12–14
    2. Matthias chosen as an apostolic witness 1:15–26

  D. The Church recognized and empowered 2:1–40
    1. The Day of Pentecost 2:1
    2. The signs of wind and fire 2:2–3
    3. All filled with the Spirit 2:4
    4. The crowd amazed and confused 2:5–13
    5. Peter manifests the gift of prophecy 2:14–40
      a. Joel's prophecy fulfilled 2:14–21
      b. Jesus exalted 2:22–36
      c. Peter calls for repentance 2:37–40

  E. The Church growing and loving 2:41–47
    1. Three thousand added 2:41
    2. Continuing as disciples 2:42
    3. Apostolic miracles 2:43

    4. Fellowship and worship 2:44–46
    5. Continued growth 2:47

II. Ministry in Jerusalem 3:1–8:4

  A. The lame man healed 3:1–4:31
    1. A gift of healing 3:1–10
    2. Peter exalts Jesus 3:11–26
      a. The Prince of Life 3:11–21
      b. A prophet like Moses 3:22–26
    3. Peter and John arrested 4:1–4
    4. Peter and John brought to trial 4:5–12
    5. Peter and John speak boldly 4:13–22
    6. Peter and John return to assembled believers 4:23–31
      a. Praying for boldness and miracles 4:23–30
      b. A fresh filling with the Holy Spirit 4:31

  B. Apostles tested and triumphant 4:32–5:42
    1. A united, caring Church 4:32–37
    2. A purified, growing Church 5:1–16
      a. Judgment on Ananias and Sapphira 5:1–10
      b. Fear and continued growth 5:11–16
    3. The twelve apostles arrested 5:17–26
    4. The verdict to kill the apostles 5:27–33
    5. Gamaliel's advice not to kill the apostles 5:34–39
    6. The apostles disobey the Sanhedrin's command 5:40–42

  C. Seven chosen to serve 6:1–7
    1. A conflict resolved 6:1–6
    2. Continued growth in Jerusalem 6:7

  D. Stephen martyred 6:8–8:4
    1. Stephen's ministry stirs opposition 6:8–11
    2. Stephen brought before the Sanhedrin 6:12–7:1
    3. Stephen's defense 7:2–53
      a. Joseph rejected 7:2–16
      b. Moses rejected 7:17–37
      c. God rejected 7:38–43
      d. The temple insufficient 7:44–50
      e. The Holy Spirit rejected 7:51–53
    4. Stephen stoned 7:54–60
    5. Resulting persecution spreads the gospel 8:1–4

III. Ministry in Samaria and Judea 8:5–11:18

    A. Philip's ministry 8:5–40

        1. Philip's preaching and miracles in Samaria 8:5–13

        2. Peter and John minister in Samaria 8:14–25

           a. Samaritans receive the Holy Spirit 8:14–17

           b. Simon offers to buy the gift 8:18–24

           c. Peter and John preach in Samaria 8:25

        3. The Ethiopian eunuch 8:26–40

    B. Saul's conversion 9:1–31

        1. Saul threatens the disciples 9:1–2

        2. Jesus appears to Saul in blinding light 9:3–9

        3. Jesus sends Ananias to Saul 9:10–19

        4. Saul preaches in Damascus 9:20–25

        5. Barnabas befriends Saul 9:26–31

    C. Peter's ministry in Judea 9:32–11:18

        1. Peter ministers in Lydda 9:32–35

        2. Peter brought to Joppa 9:36–43

        3. Cornelius sends for Peter 10:1–8

        4. Peter's visions 10:9–22

        5. Peter meets Cornelius 10:23–33

        6. Peter announces good news for Gentiles 10:34–43

        7. Gentiles baptized in the Holy Spirit 10:44–48

        8. Peter explains to the apostles and the church in Jerusalem 11:1–18

IV. Antioch: a New Center 11:19–18:22

    A. The gospel reaches Antioch 11:19–30

        1. Gentiles believe in Antioch 11:19–21

        2. Barnabas sent to Antioch 11:22–26

        3. Agabus prophesies a famine 11:27–30

    B. Peter's Deliverance 12:1–24

        1. Herod kills the apostle James 12:1–2

        2. Herod arrests Peter 12:3–6

        3. An angel rescues Peter 12:7–19

        4. Herod's death 12:20–24

    C. Paul's first missionary journey 12:25–14:28

        1. Barnabas and Saul return to Antioch 12:25

        2. Sent out by the Spirit and the church 13:1–3

I. THE CHURCH ESTABLISHED 1:1–2:47

A. The Promise Of The Father 1:1–8

1. WHAT JESUS CONTINUED TO DO AND TEACH 1:1

[1]In my former book, Theophilus, I wrote about all that Jesus began to do and to teach

The "former book" is Luke's Gospel.[1] Did Luke plan a third volume? Some say the word "former" and the abrupt ending of the Book of Acts call for this. Luke may have planned one. However, his ministry may have been cut short by martyrdom, as Gregory of Nazianzen states; at least, Luke stayed with Paul when he was imprisoned for the second time and others deserted him to save themselves (2 Tim. 4:11). But the word "former" (or "first," NASB) need not imply another volume. The content of Luke's Gospel and the content of the Book of Acts complement each other perfectly. Luke's Gospel gives the good news of the life, death, and resurrection of Jesus. Acts shows the outworking of the gospel in the first generation of the Church. This work of the Holy Spirit was never intended to come to a conclusion in this age.

Theophilus ("friend of God," "dear to God") was the first recipient of this book, as he was of Luke's Gospel. The Bible tells us practically nothing about him, so he has been the subject of much speculation. Was he a lawyer who was to handle Paul's case in Rome? This is unlikely. Paul rose to his own defense in all previous trials. Was he a Greek nobleman converted under Luke's ministry?[2] Was he a philosopher searching for the truth? Was *Theophilus* a personal name, or a title? We do not know for sure, though it was a common personal name.[3] Another theory is that Luke, like most doctors in ancient days, was a slave of Theophilus. Luke's skill brought Theophilus back from the brink

---

[1]See Luke 1:1–4 for the primary preface of Luke-Acts.

[2]Luke 1:3 calls him "most excellent." The same phrase is used of officials such as Felix and Festus (Acts 23:26; 24:3; 26:25). Simon J. Kistemaker, *Exposition of the Acts of the Apostles* (Grand Rapids: Baker Book House, 1990), 46.

[3]F. F. Bruce, *Commentary on the Book of Acts* (Grand Rapids: Wm. B. Eerdmans, 1954), 32.

of death, so he set Luke free.[4] Most likely, however, Theophilus was a Roman official of high rank, a personal friend whom Luke could count on to read the book and to have copies made and circulated.[5] The title "most excellent" (Luke 1:3) fits this view.

That Luke's Gospel dealt with what Jesus "began[6] to do and to teach" shows us three things. First, the Church had its beginning in the Gospel. Luke's Gospel ends with a convinced group of believers. Jesus "opened their minds so they could understand the Scriptures" (Luke 24:45). They were no longer an easily scattered group of disciples but a commissioned body: united, worshiping, waiting to be "'clothed with power from on high'" (Luke 24:49). In other words, they were already the Church. As Hebrews 9:15–17 makes clear, Christ's death and the shedding of His blood put the new covenant into effect. Thus, the believers who were daily in the temple, especially at the hours of prayer (Acts 3:1), praising God, were already a new covenant Body. They were already "the Church that carries on the life of Christ."[7]

Second, the work of Jesus did not end when He ascended.[8] As has already been noted, the Book of Acts shows what Jesus continued "to do and to teach" by the Holy Spirit through the Church (cf. 2:47; 9:5,10,34; 11:7–9; 12:11; 14:3; 16:14; 18:9–10; 22:8–21; 23:11; 26:23). "Jesus is at the centre of the narrative. . . . The Christianity of Acts is characterized by mission . . . , by the effectiveness and expansion of the word. . . . Its direction and success is dependent on and enabled by the Holy Spirit."[9]

---

[4]William Barclay, *The Acts of the Apostles,* 2d ed. (Philadelphia: Westminster Press, 1955), xv.

[5]Johannes Munck, *The Acts of the Apostles,* rev. William F. Albright and C. S. Mann, vol. 31 of *Anchor Bible Series* (Garden City, N.Y.: Doubleday & Co., 1979), xvi; see also James D. G. Dunn, *The Acts of the Apostles* (Valley Forge, Pa.: Trinity Press International, 1996), xi. Juel compares him to the wealthy Epaphroditus who was Josephus's patron and was able to "underwrite copying and distribution of 'Against Apion.'" Donald Juel, *Luke-Acts: The Promise of History* (Atlanta: John Knox Press, 1983), 11.

[6]"Began" is emphatic.

[7]Barclay, *Acts of the Apostles,* 2.

[8]"Taken up" (Luke 24:51) is the kind of phraseology used of Elijah's translation in the LXX of 2 Kings 2:9–11. It was the occasion of the beginning of Elisha's ministry, just as Christ's ascension was the occasion of the beginning of the Church's ministry.

[9]Dunn, *Acts of the Apostles,* xix.

Third, Luke "carefully investigated everything" (Luke 1:3). He was concerned about historical accuracy. Unlike most other religions, "Christianity is a historical religion . . . not based primarily on an idea or philosophy."[10] What Jesus did, how He lived and died for us, how He rose again and ascended to God the Father's right hand, are all essential. You cannot reduce Christianity "to a religion of mere ethics or ideas."[11]

2. Jesus Gives Final Instructions 1:2–3

[2]until the day he was taken up to heaven, after giving instructions through the Holy Spirit to the apostles he had chosen.

Clearly, Jesus did not ascend until "after [He had given] instructions through the Holy Spirit to the apostles he had chosen" for himself to carry out His work (Luke 6:13–16).[12] The word "apostles" ("sent ones") here may not be limited to the Twelve but include other "sent ones" commissioned by Jesus (as seventy-two were in Luke 10:1).[13] The Holy Spirit was already working, making Jesus' instructions clear to the apostles and impressing them on their memories.[14] They were the chosen recipients and custodians of the body of teaching we have in the New Testament. Jesus did not give "secret teachings," special additional teachings, to others, as Gnostics, Mormons, and many false cults claim.

[3]After his suffering, he showed himself to these men and gave many convincing proofs that he was alive. He

[10]James M. Boice, *Acts* (Grand Rapids: Baker Book House, 1997), 15.

[11]Ibid.

[12]Codex Bezae (D) and some Syriac manuscripts add that He commanded them to preach the gospel. Luke seems to assume that the command of Matt. 28:19 was known to his readers. See H. B. Hackett, *A Commentary on the Acts of the Apostles* (Philadelphia: American Baptist Publication Society, 1882), 30.

[13]Although the KJV uses "seventy," most recent versions accept manuscript evidence that indicates seventy-two.

[14]Some scholars connect "through the Holy Spirit" with "the apostles he had chosen" rather than with "giving instructions": "he gave orders to the apostles he had chosen with the help of the Holy Spirit" (CEV). Jesus did spend the night in prayer before choosing the apostles (Luke 6:12–14). See Gerhard A. Krodel, *Acts* (Minneapolis: Augsburg Publishing House, 1986), 54–55.

appeared to them over a period of forty days and spoke
about the kingdom of God.

Apparently the apostles included those to whom Jesus
"showed" (Gk. *parestēsen*, "presented") himself in definite ways
and at definite times[15] for forty days after His suffering, that is,
after the Passion Week and Crucifixion. To them He gave "many
convincing proofs" (positive proofs, decisive proofs, sure signs,
unmistakable evidence) that He was alive (cf. Luke 24:36–43).[16]
He also spoke to them about God's kingdom, that is, His rule
and plan. It also refers to His restoration of His kingdom under
Jesus' rule in the Millennium (as v. 6 indicates). This gospel message "can be trusted: the apostles received it from Jesus."[17]

3. JESUS PROMISES BAPTISM IN THE HOLY SPIRIT
1:4–5

**[4]On one occasion, while he was eating with them, he gave
them this command: "Do not leave Jerusalem, but wait for
the gift my Father promised, which you have heard me
speak about. [5]For John[18] baptized with water, but in a
few days you will be baptized with the Holy Spirit."**

Luke's Gospel condenses the forty days after the Resurrection
and jumps to the final exhortation for the 120 to wait in
Jerusalem until they were "'clothed with power from on high'"
(Luke 24:48–49; cf. John 14:16; 15:26; 16:7,13).[19]

[15]Jesus presented himself at least ten times: (1) Matt. 28:9–10; (2) Mark
16:9–11; John 20:11–18; (3) Mark 16:12; Luke 24:13–32; (4) Luke 24:34;
1 Cor. 15:5; (5) Luke 24:36–43; John 20:19–23; (6) John 20:24–29; 1 Cor.
15:5; (7) John 21:1–23; (8) Matt. 28:16–20; Mark 16:14–18; (9) 1 Cor. 15:6;
(10) 1 Cor. 15:7. See Kistemaker, *Acts*, 48.

[16]"The fact of the resurrection . . . was the core of the apostle's first preaching. . . . It was revealed in Jerusalem . . . in the presence of those who, with horror or with awe, knew the tomb was empty. The King James Version is justified
in adding 'infallible' in verse 3." E. M Blaiklock, *Acts: The Birth of the Church*
(Old Tappan, N.J.: Fleming H. Revell, 1980), 11. For a good discussion of His
resurrection see George E. Ladd, *A Theology of the New Testament* (Grand Rapids:
Wm. B. Eerdmans, 1983), 315–27.

[17]William J. Larkin, Jr., *Acts* (Downers Grove, Ill.: InterVarsity Press, 1995), 39.

[18]Gk. *Iōannēs*, equivalent of the Heb. *yochanan*, "The Lord has shown favor."

[19]See J. A. Alexander, *A Commentary on the Acts of the Apostles*, 3d ed. (1875;
reprint, London: Banner of Truth Trust, 1956), 1:7.

In Acts 1:4 Luke again goes to the time immediately preceding the Ascension. Jesus was "eating with them."[20] At that time He repeated the command, emphasizing that they were not to leave Jerusalem. This was very important. The Day of Pentecost would have had little effect if only two or three of them had remained in Jerusalem. Further, Jesus began His ministry in the power of the Spirit (Luke 4:14); so must they.

There is no conflict here with the command given on the resurrection day to go away into Galilee (Matt. 28:10; Mark 16:7). By comparing the Gospels we can see that Jesus initially commanded the women to tell the disciples to go to Galilee. Because Peter and John did not really believe, they went to the tomb. Two of the other disciples (not of the twelve apostles) decided to go home to Emmaus, while the rest stayed where they were in the Upper Room. Jesus appeared on the evening of the resurrection day and reproved them for their unbelief. Thomas[21] was not present when Jesus appeared, however, and refused to believe the report of His appearance. Jesus appeared again the following week and called Thomas to the place of faith. Then the disciples, along with Peter, met Jesus in Galilee (Matt. 28:16). There was a delay, but Jesus needed to deal with Peter. He still carried the guilt of his denial of Jesus and needed a special humbling and a special recommissioning (John 21). Since Jesus spent much time in Galilee during His ministry, He probably made other appearances there, including the one to more than five hundred (1 Cor. 15:6). Then, toward the close of the forty days, the apostles and others returned to Jerusalem where Jesus gave His final teaching.

Luke does not mention the visit to Galilee, possibly because it was described elsewhere and his purpose was to focus attention

[20]The Gk. *sunalizomenos* is probably from *sun*, "together with," and *'als*, "salt." Thus, it meant originally "eating salt with"; cf. Luke 24:42–43. See Richard B. Rackham, *The Acts of the Apostles* (1901; reprint, Grand Rapids: Baker Book House, 1964), 5; P. C. H. Lenski, *The Interpretation of the Acts of the Apostles* (Columbus, Ohio: Wartburg Press, 1940), 26. See also Acts 10:41 where Peter tells Cornelius that chosen witnesses "ate and drank" with the risen Jesus.

[21]Meaning "Twin." "Strong early tradition" says "his formal name was Judas." Margaret H. Williams, "Palestinian Jewish Personal Names in Acts," in *The Book of Acts in Its Palestinian Setting*, ed. Richard Bauckham, vol. 4 of *The Book of Acts in Its First Century Setting*, ed. Bruce W. Winter (Grand Rapids: Wm. B. Eerdmans, 1995), 103.

on the coming Day of Pentecost.

It is especially significant to the "promise of the Father" (Acts 1:4, KJV) that Jesus gave His instructions through the Holy Spirit (v. 2). The resurrected Jesus was still full of the Spirit, as He had been during all His previous ministry (see Luke 4:14, for example). Just as the Father bore witness to His Son when the Spirit came upon Him (and into[22] Him) in a special way, so the Father bore witness to the faith of the believers by pouring out the promised Holy Spirit giving them power for service.

That the gift of the Spirit is the Father's promise also relates it to the Old Testament promises. The idea of promise is one of the bonds that unite the Old and New Testaments. The promise to Abraham was not only so he and the nation of Israel would be blessed, but so "'all peoples on earth will be blessed through'" him (Gen. 12:3) and through his offspring (22:18). When Abraham believed (trusted) God's promise, his faith was put down on the credit side of his account for righteousness (15:6).

The story of God's dealings with His people is a step-by-step revelation: First, He promised defeat of Satan through the seed of the woman (Gen. 3:15; cf. Rev. 12:9). Then he gave His promise of blessing for the offspring (seed) of Abraham, of Isaac, of Jacob, of Judah, and of David. Finally, Jesus appeared as David's greater Son, God's David or Beloved (David means "beloved").

Along with the promises that led to the coming of Jesus we find promises of the outpouring of the Holy Spirit (Isa. 32:15; 44:3–5; Ezek. 11:19–20; 36:26–27; Joel 2:28–32; Zech. 12:10). Paul also referred to what must have been these promises (Gal. 3:14; Eph. 1:13).

Jesus had already promised this mighty outpouring of the Spirit to His followers (John 7:38–39; and especially chaps. 14 through 16). So had John the Baptist, whose baptism was limited to baptizing in water.[23] Now Jesus, John promised, would

---

[22]Some ancient manuscripts of Mark and Luke say the Spirit as a dove descended *into* Him. Stanley M. Horton, *What the Bible Says About the Holy Spirit* (Springfield, Mo.: Gospel Publishing House, 1976), 90.

[23]"*In* water" is preferable to "*with* water." Baptize means "to immerse, to dip under." They went down into the water and came up out of the water (Matt. 3:16; Mark 1:10; Acts 8:38–39).

baptize them in the Holy Spirit (Mark 1:8; John 1:33).[24] Jesus further promised that it would occur soon ("in a few days"; the Western Text adds, "even unto Pentecost").[25] This promise that Jesus would baptize in the Spirit indicates that "the Pentecost narrative is programmatic for their ongoing ministry in the Spirit. In other words, from the day of Pentecost onwards they are the eschatological community of Spirit-baptized, Spirit-empowered and Spirit-filled prophets."[26]

Note that Jesus made a clear distinction between baptism in water and baptism in the Holy Spirit.[27] The fact that in church history theologians eventually tied baptism in the Spirit to water baptism was "devastating. . . . And then when baptisms eventually transferred from adult converts to infants in Christian homes, which meant that they, too, had now received the Spirit, the phenomenological, experiential dimension to life in the Spirit was all but eliminated."[28] The Pentecostal revival has brought needed restoration. As Pentecostals and charismatics, we find that the baptism in the Spirit is still an overwhelming experience that initiates a new level of life in the Spirit. We find too that this baptism is

[24]Since Jesus is the Baptizer, "It is a baptism *by* Jesus *in* the Holy Spirit." Anthony D. Palma, *Baptism in the Holy Spirit* (Springfield, Mo.: Gospel Publishing House, 1999), 12–13, Palma's emphasis.

[25]Note that Jesus did not add "and in fire" as John the Baptist did (Matt. 3:11) when speaking to a group including hypocrites. See Horton, *What the Bible Says,* 84–89. Note also that Jesus had already breathed on them and said, "'Receive the Holy Spirit'" (John 20:22), that is, in the way we receive Him at the new birth. They had the Holy Spirit present in them, but they still needed the promised mighty outpouring and empowering that came at Pentecost. See Horton, *What the Bible Says,* 127–33.

[26]Roger Stronstad, *The Prophethood of All Believers: A Study in Luke's Charismatic Theology* (Sheffield, England: Sheffield Academic Press, 1999), 15.

[27]Menzies points out that this distinction, "while not specifically articulated by Paul, is consistent with (and complementary to) his theological perspective" since he "alludes to the power of the Spirit enabling his own ministry (Rom. 15.19; 1 Cor. 2.4; 1 Thess. 1.5). And he also refers to special anointings which energize the ministry of others (1 Tim. 4.14; 2 Tim.1.6–7; cf. 1 Thess. 5.19)." Robert P. Menzies, "Spirit-Baptism and Spiritual Gifts," in *Pentecostalism in Context,* ed. Wonsuk Ma and Robert P. Menzies (Sheffield, England: Sheffield Academic Press, 1997), 55.

[28]Gordon D. Fee, *Gospel and Spirit: Issues in New Testament Hermeneutics* (Peabody, Mass.: Hendrickson Publishers, 1991), 118–19.

the gateway "to a special cluster of gifts described by Paul . . . prophetic type gifts,"[29] including the message of wisdom, the message of knowledge, prophecy, distinguishing between spirits, different kinds of tongues, and the interpretation of tongues.

4. JESUS PROMISES POWER FOR WITNESS 1:6–8

6So when they met together, they asked him, "Lord, are you at this time going to restore the kingdom to Israel?" 7He said to them: "It is not for you to know the times or dates the Father has set by his own authority.

In Acts and the Epistles we find a great deal more about the Holy Spirit and the Church than we do about the Kingdom. But the Kingdom was an important part of Jesus' teaching. Mark 10:32–40 speaks both of Jesus' suffering and James[30] and John's request to sit on His right hand and on His left in the Kingdom. This shows that the Cross carries with it the promise of the Kingdom.

Jesus in Luke 12:32 also assured the disciples that the "'Father has been pleased to give you the kingdom.'" The word "kingdom" in the New Testament deals primarily with the king's power and rule. "Righteousness, peace and joy in the Holy Spirit" are evidence that God is ruling in our lives, and that we are in His kingdom (Rom. 14:17). But that does not exclude a future kingdom.

When the disciples were questioning Jesus about the restoration of the kingdom to Israel, they were thinking of the future rule. They knew the prophecies of Ezekiel 36:24–27 and 37:12–14 that promised restoration of Israel to the Promised Land and the outpouring of God's Spirit. They knew also that God's promise to Abraham included not only his seed and blessing on all nations but also the land. All through the Old Testament the hope of God's promise to Israel is connected with the Promised Land. Ezekiel, in chapters 36 and 37, saw that God would reinstate Israel in the land, first in unbelief and then in spiritual renewal. He would do this not because they deserved

---

[29]William W. Menzies and Robert P. Menzies, *Spirit and Power: Foundations of Pentecostal Experience* (Grand Rapids: Zondervan Publishing House, 2000), 101–2.

[30]Gk. *Iakobos;* Heb. *Ya'aqov,* see Gen. 25:26 and 27:36.

it but to reveal His own holy name and character. Since Ezekiel also prophesied God's Spirit to be poured out on a restored and renewed Israel,[31] the promise of the Spirit called this to their minds. Thus, it was more than mere curiosity that caused the disciples to ask about that part of God's promise.[32]

Jesus did not rebuke the disciples, nor did He deny that it was still in God's plan to restore the Kingdom (the rule of God, the theocracy) to Israel. But here on earth they would never know the times (specific times) and the dates (proper occasions) of that restoration (cf. Matt. 24:36; Mark 13:32-33). These the Father "has set by his own authority [Gk. *exousia*]." He is the only One who knows all things and has the wisdom to take all things into account. Therefore, the times and dates are His business, not ours.[33]

In Old Testament times, God did not reveal the time span between the first and second comings of Christ. Even the prophets sometimes jumped from one to the other and back again in almost the same breath. Notice how Jesus stopped in the middle of Isaiah 61:2 when He was reading it in Nazareth (Luke 4:19). Isaiah jumps ahead to the Second Coming there. John the Baptist did not recognize this time difference either. Because Jesus did not bring the judgments John foresaw, he wondered if Jesus was the Messiah or simply another forerunner like himself (Matt. 11:3). But Jesus did the works of the Messiah, and His disciples accepted the revelation that He is the Messiah: God's anointed Prophet, Priest, and King, the Son of the Living God (Matt. 16:16-20).

From time to time Jesus warned the disciples that no one on earth knows the day or the hour of His return. Mark 13:33 adds "'You do not know when that *time* will come.'" (We will not know the season, the month, or the year either.) Then, when the

---

[31]By "a restored and renewed Israel" I mean national Israel, not the Church. Luke always uses the term "Israel" to mean the Jews. See Acts 2:22,36; 3:12; 4:10,27; 5:21,31,35; 7:42; 9:15; 10:36: 13:16-17,23-24; 21:28; 28:20.

[32]Compare Luke 24:21, "'We had hoped that he was the one who was going to redeem Israel.'" Dr. Waverly Nunnally of Central Bible College suggested to me that the disciples' question was more nationalistically inspired than Old Testament theologically inspired (cf. the attitude of the disciples in Mark 10:32-45).

[33]See Lenski, *Interpretation of the Acts*, 30.

people on that last journey to Jerusalem before the Crucifixion "thought that the kingdom of God was going to appear at once" (Luke 19:11), Jesus gave them a parable to show them that it would be a long time before He would return in kingly power to rule on earth. In the parable Jesus spoke of a man of noble birth going to a "distant" country, thus indicating a long time. Even so, the disciples obviously had a hard time comprehending this. They did not want to accept the fact that the times and dates were none of their business.[34] Date setting has been a continuing problem down through church history, and date setters are still hurting the gospel witness.

> **8But you will receive power when the Holy Spirit comes on you; and you will be my witnesses in Jerusalem, and in all Judea and Samaria, and to the ends of the earth."**

What was their business? Verse 8 gives the answer: They were to "receive power" (Gk. *dunamin,* "mighty power")[35] when the Holy Spirit came on them (Gk. *epelthontos . . . eph humas,* "having come on them," i.e., after coming on them). Then their business was to be witnesses to tell what they had seen, heard, and experienced of Jesus (1 John 1:1). This program for witnessing also gives us a virtual table of contents for the Book of Acts:[36] Beginning in Jerusalem (chaps. 1 through 7)[37] they would carry their witness through Judea and Samaria (chaps. 8 through 12) and would continue "to the ends of the earth" (chaps. 13 through

[34]See Donald Guthrie, *The Apostles* (Grand Rapids: Zondervan Publishing House, 1975), 18.

[35]This term for power occurs ten times in Acts (1:8; 2:22; 3:12; 4:7,33; 6:8; 8:10,13; 10:38; 19:11). In all but 4:33 (where it may refer to powerful preaching) it refers to "miracle-working power." See Wayne Grudem, "Should Christians Expect Miracles Today?" part 2, *Pneuma Review* 3, no. 2 (spring 2000): 23. He points out that miracles attest the truthfulness of the gospel and also the power to witness brings conviction and activates faith.

[36]Jesus did not mention Galilee here, but there is evidence that Luke at times includes Galilee with Judea. See Everett F. Harrison, *Acts: The Expanding Church* (Chicago: Moody Press, 1975), 40–41. Acts 9:31 indicates churches were established in Galilee.

[37]Dunn suggests that beginning at Jerusalem is theologically important, showing that though the movement is toward Rome, "it is still 'the hope of Israel' (28:20) which is at stake." Dunn, *Acts of the Apostles,* 2.

28). It also indicates that Luke, inspired by the Holy Spirit, selected and limited the content of Acts, with the major portion of the book showing Paul's mission to the Gentiles, climaxing in his ministry in Rome.[38] Luke did not mean, however, that when Paul reached Rome the commission to be witnesses was fulfilled. Rome was the center of the empire, not the ends of the earth. "The ends of the earth were yet to be reached, and thus Acts ends in an open-ended way"[39] so that we are drawn into the mandate to continue to be witnesses everywhere.

God always wanted His people to be His witnesses. In Isaiah 44:8 He called Israel to quit being afraid. But though they were commissioned to be His witnesses, fear hindered. Thus, as a whole, the nation of Israel failed to be the witnesses God really wanted. But God did not give up on His plan. In Isaiah 49:6 He again looks ahead and sees His Servant, the Messiah, bringing the restoration of Israel. The Messiah also is appointed to be "'a light for the Gentiles.'" He is to *be* (not merely *bring*) God's salvation to the ends of the earth.[40] The call to be His witnesses then makes us Spirit-empowered ambassadors whose lives and ministries are extensions of the Spirit-empowered life and ministry of Jesus (Luke 4:14; cf. Isa. 61:1–2). Through the Spirit we have met Him. We know Him. We live by Him, with Him, and in Him.

As Christians we need not fail. The baptism in the Spirit is available as an empowering experience. "You will receive power" (Gk. *dunamis,* "mighty power"). Here again, the power is related to the promise given to Abraham that all the families (of all nations) of the earth would be blessed. Jesus, in Matthew 24:14, told His disciples that "'this gospel of the kingdom [the good news of God's power and rule] will be preached in the whole world as a testimony to all nations.'" He also emphasized that His followers could not wait for ideal conditions before spreading the gospel to the nations. This age would be characterized by wars, rumors of wars, famines, and earthquakes. The Greek word

[38]Martin Hengel, "The Geography of Palestine in Acts," in *Acts in Its Palestinian Setting,* ed. Bauckham, 35.

[39]Krodel, *Acts,* 13; William H. Willimon, *Acts* (Atlanta: John Knox Press, 1988), 20.

[40]See Stanley M. Horton, *Isaiah* (Springfield, Mo.: Logion Press, 2000), 335, 368.

for witness, *marture,* is the word from which we get "martyr." As His witnesses, believers must go out and spread the gospel to all nations in the midst of all these natural calamities and political upheavals, regardless of the cost. How would this be possible? They would receive power as a result of being filled with the Spirit. This would be their key to success in the Church Age until its final consummation, when Jesus returns. This puts the great responsibility of being Christ's witness on all who have a personal knowledge of Jesus and are filled with the Spirit.[41] "God wants a community that, like Jesus, gets caught up in the transformation of the world."[42] There was a marvelous, rapid spread of the gospel in the first century. The tremendous spread of the Pentecostal revival around the world in the twentieth century is evidence that the power of the Spirit is still working today, evangelizing the world and building the body of Christ.[43] Also, more witnesses are becoming martyrs than at any time since the early centuries.[44] But there is still a great challenge, for many cultural groups are yet unreached.

That Luke sees the Holy Spirit as the Spirit of prophecy "is the one point on which there is broad consensus among scholars."[45] Robert Menzies gives a "concise definition of Luke's understanding of the gift of the Spirit . . . 'a prophetic enabling which empowers one for participation in the mission of God.'"[46] He explains further that "Luke does *not* present reception of the

[41]See Guthrie, *Apostles,* 19.

[42]Clark H. Pinnock, *Flame of Love: A Theology of the Holy Spirit* (Downers Grove, Ill.: InterVarsity Press, 1996), 141.

[43]See Benjamin Sun, "The Holy Spirit: The Missing Key in the Implementation of the Doctrine of the Priesthood of Believers," in *Pentecostalism in Context,* ed. Ma and Menzies, 181–82.

[44]In Canterbury's chapel it states that "already in the 1930s it was clear that" the twentieth century "was becoming a century of Christian martyrdom without parallel since the early centuries of the Church. Since then this fact has become steadily more evident." William Purcell, *Martyrs of Our Time* (St. Louis: CBP Press, 1983), 2.

[45]William H. Shepherd, Jr., *The Narrative Function of the Holy Spirit as a Character in Luke-Acts* (Atlanta: Scholars Press, 1994), 15.

[46]Robert P. Menzies, "The Spirit of Prophecy, Luke-Acts and Pentecostal Theology: A Response to Max Turner," *Journal of Pentecostal Theology* 15 (October 1999): 52.

Spirit as necessary for one to enter into and remain within the community of salvation: the source of cleansing, righteousness, intimate fellowship with and knowledge of God."[47] As we go on in the Book of Acts we see also that the activity of the Spirit includes not only witness and prophecy, but "[j]oy, discernment, miracle power . . . boldness,"[48] and, I would add, the fear of God, comfort, guidance, and spiritual gifts—all of course "primarily associated with the missionary enterprise of the church."[49]

STUDY QUESTIONS

1. In what ways do Luke's Gospel and Acts complement each other?
2. What is the significance of the mention of Theophilus?
3. What instructions did the risen Jesus give to His apostles?
4. What previous instructions had Jesus given the apostles with regard to the Holy Spirit?
5. What is the meaning of the word "kingdom" and how does Acts use it?
6. What should we say to people who set dates for Christ's return?
7. How is the baptism in the Holy Spirit theologically distinct from the born-again experience in its purpose?

B. JESUS ASCENDS TO HEAVEN 1:9–11

1. Disciples See Him Taken Up 1:9

[9]**After he said this, he was taken up before their very eyes, and a cloud hid him from their sight.**

Christ's ascension climaxed Luke's Gospel. Luke 24:50 indicates Jesus led His followers out to the Mount of Olives to the

---

[47]Ibid., Menzies' emphasis.

[48]James B. Shelton, review of *Power From on High: The Spirit in Israel's Restoration and Witness in Luke-Acts,* by Max Turner, *Pneuma* 21, no. 1 (spring 1999): 167.

[49]Menzies, "Spirit of Prophecy," 53.

vicinity of Bethany. As He blessed them He was "taken up"[1] into heaven (that is, taken gradually, not abruptly). Then a cloud, not an ordinary cloud but undoubtedly a glory cloud like the Shekinah in the Old Testament, took him up.[2] The Greek could well mean that the cloud swept under Him and He rode it up out of their sight. But not only did He leave the surface of the earth, He ascended to the right hand of the Father, and He is still bodily present as the God-Man in heaven (Heb. 9:24). Stephen saw Him there (Acts 7:55).

2. ANGELS PROMISE HIS RETURN 1:10–11

[10]They were looking intently up into the sky as he was going, when suddenly two men dressed in white stood beside them. [11]"Men of Galilee," they said, "why do you stand here looking into the sky? This same Jesus, who has been taken from you into heaven, will come back in the same way you have seen him go into heaven."

Jesus ascended as they were "looking intently." They were not dreaming; they actually saw Him go. After He disappeared, the disciples still stood there in amazement with their gaze fixed on the heavens where He had gone. Suddenly, two men "dressed in white" stood beside them. The white symbolizes purity.[3] Though the Bible does not call them angels here, most Bible students assume they were.[4] Angels are spirits, but they generally appear in the Bible as young men. The white clothing also reminds us of the angels who appeared at the tomb on the resurrection day. Luke calls them men (Luke 24:4), while John refers to them as angels (John 20:12).

---

[1]"The word *up* does not express a 'three-tiered universe.'" The Greeks knew the earth was round, "and we, who know the same, still go 'up' and 'down' in meteorological phraseology." E. M. Blaiklock, *Acts: The Birth of the Church* (Old Tappan, N.J.: Fleming H. Revell, 1980), 13.

[2]See Exod. 40:34; also the cloud of the Transfiguration (Mark 9:7).

[3]Or "purity and joy." Simon J. Kistemaker, *Exposition of the Acts of the Apostles* (Grand Rapids: Baker Book House, 1990), 56.

[4]According to James D. G. Dunn, "Johnson . . . thinks that Luke intended an allusion rather to Moses and Elijah." *The Acts of the Apostles* (Valley Forge, Pa.: Trinity Press International, 1996), 14, citing Luke T. Johnson, *The Acts of the Apostles* (Collegeville, Minn.: Liturgical Press, 1992).

The angels asked why these disciples, "men of Galilee" (only Judas[5] was of Judea), stood gazing into heaven. This implies they were straining their eyes as if they hoped to see into heaven where Jesus had gone. Christ's first coming was fulfilled. His work of redemption was complete. It would be a long time before His return, but He would be with them as truly as He had been before (Matt. 28:20; cf. Heb. 13:5). Now, He had left them a commission, a work to do. He had given them instructions to wait in Jerusalem for the promise of the Father and for power to be witnesses. They must obey with the assurance that He would come again.

The promise of His return is as emphatic as it could possibly be. "This same Jesus . . . will come back in the same way you have seen him go into heaven." He had already told them He would return in the clouds (Mark 13:26). At His trial He identified himself with the Son of Man of Daniel 7:13–14 whom Daniel speaks of as coming with clouds. No wonder the fact of His return continues to be one of the most important motivations for Christian living and service (see 1 John 3:2–3). It should encourage the Church to be what it must be—a missionary Church!

STUDY QUESTIONS

1. Why did the angels emphasize the promise of Christ's return?
2. How is Christ's return related to the Great Commission?

C. The Witness Of The Apostles 1:12–26

1. PRAYER IN THE UPPER ROOM 1:12–14

¹²Then they returned to Jerusalem from the hill called the Mount of Olives, a Sabbath day's walk from the city. ¹³When they arrived, they went upstairs to the room where they were staying. Those present were Peter, John,

---

[5]Heb. *yᵉhudah,* "[God] be praised."

James and Andrew;[1] Philip[2] and Thomas, Bartholo-
mew[3] and Matthew;[4] James son of Alphaeus[5] and
Simon[6] the Zealot, and Judas son of James. [14]They all
joined together constantly in prayer, along with the
women and Mary[7] the mother of Jesus, and with his
brothers.

Luke's Gospel describes the return of Jesus' followers to
Jerusalem as being "with great joy" (Luke 24:52). It was only "a
Sabbath day's walk" (about a thousand yards; cf. Exod. 16:29
and Num. 35:5) from the Mount of Olives[8] back to the city.
There, in a large upstairs room, the eleven apostles were staying.[9]
This may have been the same upper room of the Last Supper
and of the resurrection appearances. Some believe it was the
home of Mary, the mother of John Mark mentioned in Acts
12:12, though there is no proof of this.[10]

Luke draws attention to five things here.

1. They all joined "together" ("with one accord," KJV). What
a contrast this was to the jealousy exhibited before the Cross,
where each wanted to be the greatest (Matt. 20:24).

As was mentioned before, Jesus dealt with them all after the
Resurrection, and especially Peter (John 21). Now all were
restored and recommissioned, harboring no conflict or jealousy.

[1]Gk. *Andreas,* "manly."

[2]"Lover of horses."

[3]"Son of Tolmai."

[4]"Gift of the LORD."

[5]"God has replaced."

[6]Or Simeon, "[The LORD] has heard."

[7]Gk. *Maria* or *Mariam;* Heb. *Miryam.* Some take it to mean "beloved."

[8]Luke 24:50 is not a contradiction. Jesus "had led them out to the vicinity of
Bethany," which may mean in that direction. This may be "intentionally vague."
See John R. W. Stott, *The Spirit, the Church, and the World: The Message of Acts*
(Downers Grove, Ill.: InterVarsity Press, 1990), 46.

[9]Though the order is different here, the list of disciples is the same as that in
Luke 6:14–16 with the omission of Judas. Judas the son of James is called
Thaddaeus in Matt. 10:3 and Mark 3:18. Simon the Zealot was converted from
a group of Jewish nationalists who believed in using force against the Romans.
This group was called in Aramaic *Kannaya* or *Kann'ana* (Gk. *Kananaios* in Matt.
10:4; Mark 3:18; "Canaanite," KJV).

[10]See Simon J. Kistemaker, *Exposition of the Acts of the Apostles* (Grand Rapids:
Baker Book House, 1990), 58–59.

All were with one mind united together. "Together" or "one accord" ("with one mind," NASB) in the Greek is *homothumadon,* "with one purpose," and is one of Luke's favorite words. Being united in one accord with one purpose is surely still an important key to getting God's work done. This is what Christian fellowship is all about.

2. "They all joined . . . constantly in prayer." This included faithfulness to the temple at the morning and evening hours of prayer (Acts 2:15 indicates 9 A.M. and 3:1 indicates 3 P.M.) and also persistence in the Upper Room, which was their "headquarters."[11] They kept an atmosphere of prayer and, as Luke 24:53 shows, united prayer and joyful praise with expectation of the outpouring of the Spirit were their chief occupation during these days (see also Luke 11:9–13; 18:1; they were asking for the promised gift of the Spirit). United prayer and praise with expectation that God will fulfill His promise was common in Acts and is still important if we want to see fresh outpourings of the Spirit. (This does not rule out the fact that times of divine visitation in the providence of God may surprise us, as in the case of Cornelius and his household; Acts 10.)

3. The women joined with them in prayer with the same steadfastness. Actually, the women were present all along, supporting Jesus and His ministry (Matt. 27:55; Mark 15:41; Luke 8:2–3; 23:49,55; 24:1–11). In those days, if one man was present the masculine pronoun was used for the mixed group. Even when Peter called them "brothers" (v. 16) this included the women. The Jews understood this. But Luke wanted Theophilus (and other Gentiles) to know the women were present and praying, so he mentioned them specifically.[12] They included Mary Magdalene, Salome, Joanna, Mary and Martha of Bethany, John Mark's mother, Susanna, and others who had followed Jesus,

---

[11]We cannot be certain of its location because the Romans leveled Jerusalem in A.D. 134 and rebuilt it as a Gentile city, renamed Aelia Capitolina. The "Upper Room" in today's Jerusalem is probably on or near the site of the house of Mark's mother.

[12]Codex D adds "and children." Johnson points out that this would demand "the translation 'with their wives and children,' a domestic touch Luke probably did not intend!" Luke T. Johnson, *The Acts of the Apostles* (Collegeville, Minn.: Liturgical Press, 1992), 34.

supported Him financially (Luke 8:1–3), and witnessed His death, burial, and resurrection (Luke 23:49, 54–56; 24:1–10).

4. Mary the mother of Jesus is given special mention. She was present because John was fulfilling Jesus' request to take care of her. She was not there as a leader, but simply joined the others in humble prayer and in waiting for the promise of the Father. We can be sure she received the Spirit even though this is the last time she is mentioned in Acts. Some traditions say she died in Jerusalem. Others say she went with John to Ephesus and died there.

5. The brothers of Jesus were present, though prior to the Cross they did not believe on Him (Mark 3:21; John 7:5). Jesus, however, made a special appearance to the eldest of His brothers, James (1 Cor. 15:7). Both James and Jude became leaders in the Jerusalem church (see Acts 12:17; 15:13; 21:18; Gal. 2:9; James 1:1; Jude 1). Now these brothers were joined in one accord with the others and waiting for the promise of the Father as well.[13]

2. MATTHIAS CHOSEN AS AN APOSTOLIC WITNESS
1:15–26

15In those days Peter stood up among the believers (a group numbering about a hundred and twenty)

Apparently not all of the more than 500 who saw Jesus in Galilee followed Him back to Jerusalem. About 120 men and women united in an atmosphere of prayer and praise (Luke 24:53).[14] Among them[15] Peter stood up and took the initiative to take care of a felt need.

---

[13]Some say these "brothers" were cousins, or children of Joseph by a previous marriage. However, Matt. 1:25 makes it clear that Joseph did enter into the physical marriage relation with Mary after Jesus was born. Thus, there is every reason to believe these brothers were actual children of Mary and Joseph. Mark 6:3 names them. No doubt His sisters were present as well.

[14]Jewish tradition indicated that 120 males could form a synagogue with its own council able to make decisions. Thus the 120 formed a legitimate Jewish community. William H. Willimon, *Acts* (Atlanta: John Knox Press, 1988), 22. (Twelve males could form a synagogue for worship and teaching, but it could not have its own council.)

[15]Most ancient manuscripts have *adelphōn*, "brothers." Codex D has *mathētōn*, "disciples" (possibly because the brothers of Jesus are also mentioned). The NIV has "believers" because women are also included.

¹⁶and said, "Brothers, the Scripture had to be fulfilled which the Holy Spirit spoke long ago through the mouth of David concerning Judas, who served as guide for those who arrested Jesus—¹⁷he was one of our number and shared in this ministry." ¹⁸(With the reward he got for his wickedness, Judas bought a field; there he fell headlong, his body burst open and all his intestines spilled out.

The "brothers"¹⁶ did more than pray. They also gave attention to the Scriptures. God talks to us through the Bible. What God showed Peter in the Scriptures (Ps. 69:25; 109:8) caused him to stand up and draw attention to the fulfillment of David's prophecy¹⁷ spoken by the Spirit,¹⁸ concerning Judas who acted "as a guide for those who arrested Jesus." Peter recognized that the Holy Spirit is the real author of God's Word and that what David said about his enemies applied to the enemies of Jesus, since David is a type pointing to Jesus.¹⁹

The tragedy was that Judas was one of the twelve apostles and received an assigned portion in their ministry (cf. Luke 22:3). Jesus sent him out with the others with authority to drive out evil spirits (demons) and to heal all kinds of diseases and sicknesses (Matt. 10:1). Further, he was present when Jesus promised the disciples they would sit on thrones judging (ruling) the twelve tribes of Israel—that is, in the Millennium (Luke 22:29–30).

In this connection Peter (or Luke) adds a parenthetical note about the death of Judas that seems to differ from the description in the Gospels. Matthew 27:5 says Judas went away and

---

¹⁶The term "brothers" includes the 120, both men and women. Acts often uses "brothers" for the whole group of believers. This was a cultural expression, a matter of language usage, not meant to omit women or their ministry. It was also very Jewish. In the OT it is used primarily as a familial term. In the intertestamental period it moved toward being a covenantal term—which became fully realized in the NT. It is not used of Gentiles until Acts 15.

¹⁷In v. 16 Codex Bezae (D) and the Latin Vulgate have "it was necessary," thus putting the emphasis on Ps. 109:8 and the necessity of replacing Judas Iscariot.

¹⁸Cf. 2 Pet. 1:20–21.

¹⁹See David Guthrie, *The Apostles* (Grand Rapids: Zondervan Publishing House, 1975), 22; see also David Peterson, "The Motif of Fulfilment and the Purpose of Luke-Acts," in *The Book of Acts in Its Ancient Literary Setting*, ed. Bruce W. Winter and Andrew D. Clarke, vol. 1 of *The Book of Acts in Its First Century Setting*, ed. Bruce W. Winter (Grand Rapids: William B. Eerdmans, 1993), 95.

hanged himself. Since Luke had searched out all that was written, he knew this and obviously did not see a contradiction.

People were not hanged by a rope in those days. Crucifixion and impalement through the belly over a sharp stake were the two common methods of hanging. Judas, of course, could not crucify himself. But he could set up a sharp stake and fall headlong over it, causing his body to burst open and his intestines to spill out. Peter, however, does not emphasize what Judas did as much as God's judgment.

> [19]Everyone in Jerusalem heard about this, so they called that field in their language Akeldama, that is, Field of Blood.) [20]"For," said Peter, "it is written in the book of Psalms, "'May his place be deserted; let there be no one to dwell in it,' and, "'May another take his place of leadership.'

Apparently, the field became known as *Akeldama,* Aramaic for "Field of Blood," for two reasons. Matthew 27:6–8 says that the priests bought the field. Since it was bought with the money they gave Judas, they undoubtedly bought it in Judas's name. They called the field Akeldama because the thirty pieces of silver was the price of blood, that is, of Jesus' death. They also named it so because of Judas's violent death there, since blood in the New Testament usually refers to violent death.

Peter's emphasis, however, was on Psalm 69:25[20] and 109:8,[21] with special attention to the latter: "May another take his place of leadership."

> [21]Therefore it is necessary to choose one of the men who have been with us the whole time the Lord Jesus went in and out among us, [22]beginning from John's baptism to the time when Jesus was taken up from us. For one of these must become a witness with us of his resurrection."

Jesus chose the Twelve as primary witnesses to His teaching and His resurrection (cf. Luke 6:12–16; Acts 4:33; 13:30–31; 1 Cor. 15:5). They would have positions of authority in the coming kingdom as well (Matt. 19:28; Luke 22:29–30). Judging,

[20]In the LXX, Ps. 68:26.
[21]In the LXX, Ps. 108:8.

or ruling, the twelve tribes would require twelve apostles. So they needed someone to replace Judas. It must be someone who had been with them "the whole time," from Jesus' baptism to His ascension.[22]

Arrington suggests that the term "apostle" may be related to what rabbinic sources call a *shaliach,* "a person who acts in behalf of another . . . similar to what we call the power of attorney."[23] The New Testament speaks of other apostles such as Paul and Barnabas (Acts 14:14; Rom. 16:7; cf. Phil. 2:25, where the NIV translates *apostolos* as "messenger"), but the twelve are a special, restricted group.

> **23So they proposed two men: Joseph called Barsabbas (also known as Justus) and Matthias. 24Then they prayed, "Lord, you know everyone's heart. Show us which of these two you have chosen 25to take over this apostolic ministry, which Judas left to go where he belongs."**

Peter laid down the conditions, but the people made the choice. Two men met the conditions best. One was Joseph,[24] named Barsabbas,[25] who, like so many Jews, had a Roman name, Justus.[26] The other was Matthias (a short form of Mattathias, "gift of the Lord"). Eusebius, the third-century church historian, says he was one of the seventy-two sent out by Jesus in Luke 10:1.

To make the choice between the two, the apostles first prayed, recognizing that the Lord (Jesus) knew which one He wanted as the twelfth apostle. Jesus is the "Heart Knower" (see John 2:24-25; cf. Acts 15:8). They also recognized that Judas fell away by his own choice and went to the place he had chosen, that is, to the place of punishment.

> **26Then they cast lots, and the lot fell to Matthias; so he was added to the eleven apostles.**

[22]Many followed Jesus. Jesus specifically called some; others simply followed Him (John 1:35-47). Later, Jesus spent a night in prayer, and then out of the crowd of disciples chose twelve to be apostles ("sent ones"). Jesus refers to this latter calling in John 15:16—a choosing for a particular service.

[23]French L. Arrington, "The Acts of the Apostles," in *Full Life Bible Commentary to the New Testament,* ed. French L. Arrington and Roger Stronstad (Grand Rapids: Zondervan Publishing House, 1999), 540.

[24]"May [God] add."

[25]"Son of the Sabbath," that is, born on the Sabbath.

[26]"Righteous man."

After prayer they used the Old Testament method of casting lots, probably following the precedent of Proverbs 16:33.[27] They believed Jesus would overrule the laws of chance and show His choice by this means. The Book of Acts never mentions this method again. After Pentecost they relied on the Holy Spirit for guidance (see Acts 15:8, for example).

Some modern writers question whether Peter and the others were right in choosing Matthias. They say Paul was the Lord's choice. But Matthias was the Lord's choice, the answer to their prayer to Him. Jesus chose Paul to be the apostle to the Gentiles (Acts 9:15; 22:21; Gal. 1:16). Paul never anticipated ruling one of the tribes of Israel. He was an apostle equal in calling and authority to the others (Gal. 2:8); he was a true witness to the resurrection and teachings of Jesus (Acts 1:22; cf. 1 Cor. 9:1; 15:8–9; Gal. 1:12)—but he never included himself with the Twelve (1 Cor. 15:7–8).

The 120 were in prayer when the choice was made. Surely, they were in touch with God. The Bible states without adverse comment that Matthias "was added to the eleven apostles." In Acts 6:2 he is still included with the Twelve. Though he is not mentioned again by name, neither are most of the other apostles.[28]

It is important to notice also that the fact Judas became a lost soul made his replacement necessary. When King Herod[29] had James the brother of John put to death, no one was chosen to take his place (Acts 12:2). James would rise again to judge and rule with the Twelve in the coming kingdom.[30]

STUDY QUESTIONS

1. What are the five things Luke mentions in Acts 1:12–14 and why is each important?

---

[27]See also Lev. 16:7–10; Num. 26:55; 1 Sam. 14:41–42.

[28]See H. B. Hackett, *A Commentary on the Acts of the Apostles* (Philadelphia: American Baptist Publication Society, 1882), 40–41. Tradition says Matthias was martyred in Ethiopia. E. M. Blaiklock, *Acts: The Birth of the Church* (Old Tappan, N.J.: Fleming H. Revell, 1980), 17.

[29]Gk. *Herodes,* from *heros,* "hero."

[30]Thus, there is no such thing as "apostolic succession" that the Roman Catholic church teaches.

2. Why and how was Matthias chosen to be a member of the twelve apostles?

3. Are there apostles today who fit the qualifications demanded by the Early Church?

D. The Church Recognized And Empowered 2:1–40

1. THE DAY OF PENTECOST 2:1

¹When the day of Pentecost came, they were all together in one place.

The 120 continued in prayer and praise about ten days after the ascension of Jesus, until the Day of Pentecost.[1] This was a harvest festival among the Jews. It was also called the Feast of Weeks (Exod. 34:22; Num. 28:26; Deut. 16:10,16; 2 Chron. 8:13)[2] as there was a week of weeks (seven weeks) between it and Passover. Pentecost means "fiftieth," and it was so-called because on the fiftieth day after the waving of the sheaf of firstfruits (Lev. 23:15–16) they waved two loaves for firstfruits (Lev. 23:17).[3] When the Day of Pentecost came (Gk. *en tō sumplērousthai,* "in the being completed") the period of waiting was coming to an end.[4] The Old Testament prophecies and the promise of the

---

[1]Some have used these days of waiting to insist that there must be an extended time of "tarrying" (see Luke 24:49, KJV) for the baptism in the Holy Spirit. However, most Pentecostals recognize that there is no evidence in Acts of any necessary time gap between regeneration and the baptism in the Holy Spirit. Most Pentecostals emphasize theological separability and subsequence, "not temporal subsequence." Douglas A. Oss, "A Pentecostal/Charismatic View," in *Are Miraculous Gifts for Today?* ed. Wayne A. Grudem (Grand Rapids: Zondervan Publishing House, 1996), 255.

[2]In the LXX it is called *pentecostē* in Tob. 2:1; 2 Macc. 12:32.

[3]The Sadducees, who controlled the temple, took the Sabbath of Lev. 23:15 to be the weekly Sabbath after the Passover. This made Pentecost occur on a Sunday. See F. F. Bruce, *Commentary on the Book of Acts* (Grand Rapids: Wm. B. Eerdmans, 1954), 53.

[4]Many scholars believe this Pentecost took place in the last week of May, A.D. 30. See Simon J. Kistemaker, *Exposition of the Acts of the Apostles* (Grand Rapids: Baker Book House, 1990), 75.

Father (proclaimed by Jesus, Acts 1:4) were about to be fulfilled. The 120 were still in one accord and all were "together in one place."[5] None were missing. We are not told where the place was; but most take it to be the Upper Room, which was their head-quarters (Acts 1:13). Others, in view of Peter's statement that it was the third hour of the day (nine o'clock in the morning), believe they were in the temple for prayer, probably in the Court of the Women (see 3:1). We have already seen that the believers were habitually in the temple at the hours of prayer (Luke 24:53). One of the porticoes, or roofed colonnades on the edge of the court, would have provided a good place for them to gather and join in worship. This would help explain the crowd that gathered after the Holy Spirit was outpoured.[6] Those who believe they were in the Upper Room suggest they went down to an open-air marketplace, but there is no evidence to support this idea.

2. THE SIGNS OF WIND AND FIRE 2:2–3

[2]Suddenly a sound like the blowing of a violent wind came from heaven and filled the whole house where they were sitting. [3]They saw what seemed to be tongues of fire that separated and came to rest on each of them.

"Suddenly," surprisingly and without warning, a sound came from heaven like "the blowing of a violent wind," or tornado. But it was not an actual wind; it was only its sound that filled

[5]Codex Bezae (D) leaves out "with one accord" (v. 1, KJV), and simply states they were "together" in one place. Clearly, the majority of ancient manuscripts are right. They were indeed in one accord—as they had been during all the pre-ceding period.

[6]Though the temple is called a "house" in Acts 7:47, some believe "the whole house" (2:2) cannot mean the temple. They suggest that either the 120 left the Upper Room when the Spirit fell or else the Upper Room was open to the street. See P. C. H. Lenski, *The Interpretation of the Acts of the Apostles* (Columbus, Ohio: Wartburg Press, 1940), 58. Others say the fact they were sitting (v. 2) would be against their being in the temple, because rabbinical literature notes that only the true king was ever allowed to sit in the temple. However, Luke 2:46 tells of the twelve-year-old Jesus sitting among the teachers in the temple. I believe it is more likely that they were in the Court of the Women in the temple. See Martin Hengel, "The Geography of Palestine in Acts," in *The Book of Acts in Its Palestinian Setting*, ed. Richard Bauckham, vol. 4 of *The Book of Acts in Its First Century Setting*, ed. Bruce W. Winter (Grand Rapids: Wm. B. Eerdmans, 1995), 37.

the house[7] where they were sitting,[8] overwhelming them. That the sound came "suddenly" and "from heaven" highlights "divine, not human, control of the Spirit's action."[9]

The sound of wind would remind them of powerful Old Testament divine manifestations. God spoke to Job out of a storm, probably a windstorm (Job 38:1; 40:6). A mighty east wind dried out the path through the Red Sea, enabling the Israelites to escape from Egypt on dry ground (Exod. 14:21). Wind was also a frequent symbol of the Spirit in the Old Testament (Ezek. 37:9–10,14, for example).[10] Jesus also referred to wind in speaking of the Spirit (John 3:8). The sound was undoubtedly loud enough to attract the attention of the crowds that filled Jerusalem at the Pentecost season.

The sound of the wind indicated to those present that God was about to manifest himself and His Spirit in a special way. That it was the sound a wind with carrying power would make also spoke of the empowering Jesus promised in Acts 1:8, an empowering for service.

Just as suddenly, "what seemed to be tongues of fire" appeared and "separated" (were distributed). That is, something that looked like a ball or mass of flames appeared over the whole group. Then it broke up,[11] and a single tongue that looked like a flame of fire settled on the head of each one of them, both men and women. There was, of course, no actual fire, and no one was burned. But fire and light were common symbols of the divine presence, as in the case of the burning bush that Moses saw (Exod. 3:2), and also the Lord's appearance in fire on Mount Sinai after the people of Israel accepted the old covenant (Exod. 19:18).[12] The Spirit coming in power charred the ropes that

[7]Cf. Anthony D. Palma, *The Holy Spirit: A Pentecostal Perspective* (Springfield, Mo.: Logion Press, 2001), 58.

[8]The same word is used in Luke 24:49, where it is translated "stay."

[9]William H. Shepherd, Jr., *The Narrative Function of the Holy Spirit as a Character in Luke-Acts* (Atlanta: Scholars Press, 1994), 160.

[10]Also in the Apocrypha, Bel and the Dragon, 36.

[11]H. B. Hackett, *A Commentary on the Acts of the Apostles* (Philadelphia: American Baptist Publication Society, 1882), 42.

[12]J. W. Packer, *Acts of the Apostles* (Cambridge, England: Cambridge University Press, 1975).

bound Samson (Judg. 15:14). The "fire of the Lord" burned up
Elijah's sacrifice and even the stones of the altar and the soil
(1 Kings 18:38). Fire is also connected with the Old Testament
prophecies of the outpouring of the Spirit in Isaiah, Ezekiel, Joel,
and Zechariah. Tongues also indicated speech—the fiery, powerful, prophetic witness that the Holy Spirit would give.[13]

Some suppose these tongues constituted a baptism of fire
bringing cleansing and fulfilling John the Baptist's prophecy.[14]
However, the hearts and minds of the 120 were already open to
the resurrected Christ, already cleansed, already filled with praise
and joy (Luke 24:52–53), already responsive to the Spirit-
inspired Word (Acts 1:16), already in one accord. Rather than
cleansing or judgment, the fire here signified God's acceptance[15]
of the Church body as the new temple, or sanctuary, of the Holy
Spirit (1 Cor. 3:16; Eph. 2:21–22).[16] Then when the single
flames rested on the heads of each individual, it signified accepting them as also being temples of the Spirit (1 Cor. 6:19). Thus,
the Bible makes clear that the Church was already in existence
before the Pentecostal baptism.[17] Hebrews 9:15,17; 12:24 show
that it was the *death* of Christ that put the new covenant into
effect. From the resurrection day when Jesus breathed on the disciples, the Church was constituted as a new covenant Body.[18]

It is important to notice that these signs preceded the
Pentecostal baptism, or gift of the Spirit. They were not part of

[13]Oss, "Pentecostal/Charismatic View," 254 n. 25. Waverly Nunnally of
Central Bible College disagrees, however, and says that the phrase "tongues of
fire" here is an idiom for "flames of fire" and has nothing to do with the gift of
tongues; the similarity is accidental.

[14]René Pache, *The Person and Work of the Holy Spirit*, rev. ed. (Chicago:
Moody Press, 1966), 23. See also Kistemaker, *Acts*, 76–77.

[15]Fire often indicates God's acceptance also in the Apocrypha, Pseudepig-
rapha, and rabbinic literature.

[16]See Stanley M. Horton, *I and II Corinthians* (Springfield, Mo.: Logion Press,
1999), 45.

[17]As Roger Stronstad points out, the pouring out of the Spirit on the Day of
Pentecost was "neither the birth of the Church, nor merely a blessing for God's
people. Rather . . . it is vocational, that is, it baptizes and empowers the company
or community of God's people." *The Prophethood of All Believers: A Study in Luke's
Charismatic Theology* (Sheffield, England: Sheffield Academic Press, 1999), 70.

[18]Stanley M. Horton, *What the Bible Says About the Holy Spirit* (Springfield,
Mo.: Gospel Publishing House, 1976), 140–42.

it, nor were they repeated on other occasions when the Spirit was outpoured. Peter, for example, identified the filling of the Gentile believers at the house of Cornelius with Jesus' promise that they would be baptized in the Spirit, calling it the "'same [Gk. *isēn*, "identical"] gift'" (Acts 11:17; cf. 10:44–47). But the wind and fire were not present. They seem to have been needed only once.

3. ALL FILLED WITH THE SPIRIT 2:4

⁴All of them were filled with the Holy Spirit and began to speak in other tongues as the Spirit enabled them.

Now that God had acknowledged the Church as the new temple, the next thing was to pour out the Holy Spirit on the members of the Body.

What Jesus promised as a baptism is pictured here as a filling, that is, a full, satisfying experience. Some try to make a distinction between being baptized in the Holy Spirit and being filled.[19] Actually, the Bible uses a variety of terms.[20] It was also a pouring out of the Spirit as Joel prophesied (Acts 2:17–18,33); a receiving (and active taking) of a gift (Acts 2:38); a falling upon (Acts 8:16; 10:44; 11:15); a pouring out of the gift (Acts 10:45); and a coming upon. With this variety of terms it is impossible to suppose that the baptism is any different from the filling.

Remember, too, that since the Holy Spirit is a Person, we are talking about an experience that brings a relationship. Each term brings out some aspect of the Pentecostal experience, and no one term can bring out all the aspects of that experience.

It is clear also, since they were all together and in one accord, that when Acts 2:4 says, "all of them were filled," the entire 120 is meant.[21] Some writers suppose that only the 12 apostles were

---

[19]Some say that the baptism in the Spirit took place only once—on the Day of Pentecost. They call other occurrences in Acts and later just "fillings." Peter, in Acts 11:16, however, recognizes that the gift of the Holy Spirit outpoured on the house of Cornelius also fulfilled Jesus' promise that He would baptize in the Spirit. Therefore, all believers who are *filled with* the Spirit can be said to be *baptized in* the Spirit. The Pentecostal experience today is still the baptism in the Spirit.

[20]Anthony D. Palma, *Baptism in the Holy Spirit* (Springfield, Mo.: Gospel Publishing House, 1999), 10–12.

[21]Homer G. Rhea, "Symbols of the Holy Spirit," in *The Holy Spirit in Action,* comp. Homer G. Rhea (Cleveland, Tenn.: Pathway Press, 1996), 34.

filled.[22] However, more than twelve languages were spoken. Moreover, Peter, speaking in the gift of prophecy, quotes Joel, who wrote of sons and daughters prophesying (v. 17; see Joel 2:28). Later, when Peter spoke before a large group in Jerusalem, he said, "'God, who knows the heart, showed that he accepted them [the Gentiles] by giving the Holy Spirit to them, just as he did to us'" (Acts 15:8). This suggests that the Spirit fell in the same way not only on the 12 but also on the 120 and also on the 3000 who believed on the Day of Pentecost. Clearly, the experience was and is for all. This, however, was a New Testament experience. In the Old Testament, only selected individuals were filled.[23]

As soon as they were filled, the 120 began to speak (and continued speaking) in other tongues (languages). This also was a new thing.[24] Speaking in tongues (Gk. *glōssais lalein*, which gives us the term "glossolalia") "was entirely unknown in Judaism, and its appearance would be regarded as a remarkable *novum* marking an equally remarkable new phase in God's dealings with His people."[25] "Began" is significant. It shows, as in Acts 1:1, that what was begun was to continue. This indicates that speaking in other tongues was the normative accompaniment of the baptism in the Holy Spirit.[26] It continued to be a gift that brought edifi-

[22]Howard Clark Kee, *To Every Nation Under Heaven: The Acts of the Apostles* (Harrisburg, Pa.: Trinity Press International, 1997), 43–44, 49.

[23]Horton, *What the Bible Says,* 26–29.

[24]"No one can say they were psychologically conditioned for such an experience. It happened without their expecting it. It was a sovereign and supernatural manifestation of the Holy Spirit." Hardy W. Steinberg, "Initial Evidence of the Baptism in the Holy Spirit," in *Conference on the Holy Spirit Digest,* ed. Gwen Jones (Springfield, Mo.: Gospel Publishing House, 1983), 1:39.

[25]Max Turner, *Power From on High: The Spirit in Israel's Restoration and Witness in Luke-Acts* (Sheffield, England: Sheffield Academic Press, 1996), 357. Turner rejects the initial evidence doctrine. For evidence upholding it see Palma, *Baptism in the Holy Spirit.*

[26]J. A. Alexander, *A Commentary on the Acts of the Apostles,* 3d ed. (1875; reprint, London: Banner of Truth Trust, 1956), 1:44. Note also that other evidences of the baptism in the Holy Spirit will follow as the Spirit continues to immerse us and affect every part of our lives (John 7:37–39; Acts 4:8). See William W. Menzies and Stanley M. Horton, *Bible Doctrines: A Pentecostal Perspective* (Springfield, Mo.: Logion Press, 1994), 122, 129.

cation and blessing on other occasions (1 Cor. 14:4).[27]

This speaking came "as the Spirit enabled them" (Gk. *edidou apophthengesthai autois,* "proceeded to give and kept on giving them to speak out loudly and boldly").[28] That is, they used their tongues, their muscles; they spoke. However, the words did not come from their own minds or thinking. The Spirit gave them what to speak—and they expressed it boldly, loudly, and with obvious anointing and power. This was the one sign of the baptism in the Holy Spirit that was repeated.

Some writers call these tongues "ecstatic" utterance. "Ecstatic," as the word is used today, implies a state beyond both reason and self-control. It also suggests a trance, or mystic state, that makes it nearly impossible for one to move. This sort of ecstatic state or trance was common among the pagans, but "ecstatic" is really an improper term and does not apply either here or in other passages where speaking in tongues is mentioned.[29] There is no evidence that any believer spoke as if forced to do so. They retained their senses and spoke in willing cooperation with the Holy Spirit.

With this in mind we must also recognize that the tongues here and the tongues in 1 Corinthians 12 to 14 are the same.[30] Tongues at Pentecost were a sign to unbelievers. God used them to draw a crowd as well as to edify the believers. But when they continued speaking in tongues, the crowd said of them that they were drunk. This corresponds to what 1 Corinthians 14:23 says about uninterpreted tongues.[31] We should also note that there are about four thousand languages now and many more existed in the past (cf. 1 Cor. 14:10). But in a local church, as at

[27]"The phenomenon that both Luke and Paul refer to is essentially the same." Palma, *Baptism in the Holy Spirit,* 41.

[28]The same verb is used in the LXX of speaking out supernaturally, or of claims to do so (1 Chron. 25:1; Ezek. 13:9,19; Mic. 3:11; Zech. 10:2).

[29]Jack Hayford points out that the Gk. verb *eksistēmi* is used of the observers in Acts 2:12. They were the ones who were "stunned, ecstatic." *The Beauty of Spiritual Language* (Dallas: Word Publishing, 1992), 198–99.

[30]Some refer to tongues-speaking in Acts 2 as *xenolalia* because the languages were understood. However, the Bible makes no distinction between *xenolalia* and *glossolalia.* "They are two sides of the same coin." Charles H. Talbert, *Reading Acts: A Literary and Theological Commentary on the Acts of the Apostles* (New York: Crossroad Publishing, 1997), 43.

[31]See Horton, *I and II Corinthians,* 138.

Corinth, there are not likely to be many foreigners present. Therefore, the messages in tongues need interpretation (1 Cor. 14:6–13). The fact that they can be interpreted shows also that the speaking in tongues is real language, not gibberish.[32]

In the 1906 Azusa Street revival, people were coming from all over the world. When my grandmother spoke in tongues a man from Denmark told her she was speaking Danish. When my mother spoke in tongues a black woman from one of the French-speaking islands told her she was speaking French. There was enough of that type of evidence to let them know that what was happening was the same as on the Day of Pentecost. A number of missionaries have told me of people in recent times speaking in tongues that were languages the missionaries understood but the people who were speaking did not.[33]

4. The Crowd Amazed And Confused 2:5–13

[5]Now there were staying in Jerusalem God-fearing Jews from every nation under heaven.

Jerusalem was a cosmopolitan center in that many of the Jews from the Dispersion returned and settled there (cf. 6:9). "Staying" (Gk. *katoikountes*) usually means something more than a temporary stay or visit. In any case, because it was the Feast of Pentecost—one of the three feasts for which the Law required attendance in Jerusalem (Deut. 16:16)—we can be sure that perhaps as many as one million Jews from all over the known world were in Jerusalem.[34] These were devout, "God-

[32]See Hayford, *Beauty of Spiritual Language,* 74–75.

[33]Rev. Randy Hurst as a boy with his missionary father in inland China heard a Chinese girl speak in perfect English when the Lord baptized her in the Spirit. The girl had no knowledge of English and had no foreign contact prior to this. See C. Peter Wagner, *Spreading the Fire: Book 1, Acts 1–8* (Ventura, Calif.: Gospel Light, Regal Books, 1994), 95, for a more recent example of a monolingual British pastor praying in tongues in Iranian and then in Ugaritic. See also Harold Carpenter, *Mandate & Mission: The Theory and Practice of Assemblies of God Missions* (Springfield, Mo.: CBC Press, 1988).

[34]"Every nation under heaven" was a common idiom used to speak primarily of those in the known world or even in the Roman Empire. The word "nation" (people) was often used of the people of a Roman province. About one million Jews would be present at the pilgrimage feasts of Passover, Pentecost, and Tabernacles. Wolfgang Reinhardt, "The Population Size of Jerusalem and the

fearing" people, sincere in their worship of the Lord. Probably more of them would be in Jerusalem at this time than at Passover, since travel on the Mediterranean Sea was safer at this season.[35]

> **[6]When they heard this sound, a crowd came together in bewilderment, because each one heard them speaking in his own language. [7]Utterly amazed, they asked: "Are not all these men who are speaking Galileans? [8]Then how is it that each of us hears them in his own native language?**

As the sound of the 120 speaking in tongues rose and became heard, a crowd came together from all directions. All were bewildered because each one kept hearing them speak "in his own language." "Own" is emphatic: his very own language that he used as a child. The tongues here were distinct languages. They were not speaking merely in a variety of Galilean or Aramaic dialects but in a variety of entirely different languages.[36]

The result among the hearers was total amazement. They were astonished. They were filled with awestruck wonder, for they recognized that the 120 (probably by their clothing) were Galileans. And they simply could not understand how they could hear the language of their home countries being spoken by Galileans.

Some writers take verse 8 to mean that the 120 were all really speaking the same language and by a miracle of hearing the multitude were made to hear it in their mother tongues. But verses 4, 6, and 7 are too specific for that. They "began to speak." Each man heard them "speak" in his own dialect without any Galilean accent.[37] There would have been no surprise if the 120 spoke in Aramaic or Greek.

A few commentators have supposed that the 120 really spoke in tongues, but no one understood them. They propose that the Spirit interpreted the unknown tongues in the ears of the hear-

Numerical Growth of the Jerusalem Church," in *Acts in Its Palestinian Setting*, ed. Bauckham, 262. See also Josephus *Antiquities* 4:204 and *War* 1:253.

[35]Ralph Earle, *The Acts of the Apostles* (Kansas City, Mo.: Beacon Hill Press, 1965), 273.

[36]Lenski, *Interpretation of the Acts*, 65.

[37]Hackett, *Commentary on the Acts*, 42–43, points out that these were clearly unacquired languages different from the native language of the Galileans, which was Aramaic. (They also knew Greek.)

ers into their own language—as a miracle of hearing. But verses 6 and 7 rule that out too. They spoke real languages that were understood by a variety of people from a variety of places.[38] This gave witness to the universality of the gift of the Spirit and to the unity of the Church.[39]

> [9]Parthians, Medes and Elamites; residents of Mesopotamia, Judea and Cappadocia, Pontus and Asia, [10]Phrygia and Pamphylia, Egypt and the parts of Libya near Cyrene; visitors from Rome [11](both Jews and converts to Judaism); Cretans and Arabs—we hear them declaring the wonders of God in our own tongues!"

The places named where these godly Jews were born were in all directions, but Luke gives them in a general order (with exceptions) beginning in the northeast.[40] Parthia was east of the Roman Empire between the Caspian Sea and the Persian Gulf; Media was east of Assyria;[41] Elam was north of the Persian Gulf in the southern part of Persia; Mesopotamia was the ancient Babylonia, mostly outside the Roman Empire. Babylon had a large Jewish population in New Testament times and later became a center for orthodox Judaism (1 Pet. 5:13).

Judea is mentioned because Jews there still took pride in speaking Hebrew and would have been amazed at the lack of a Galilean accent. It is also possible that Luke includes with Judea all of Syria, in fact, all the territory of David and Solomon from the Euphrates River to the "'river of Egypt'" (Gen. 15:18).[42]

---

[38]Alexander, *Commentary on the Acts*, 1:45; Earle, *Acts of the Apostles*, 278.

[39]Many writers see a reversal of what happened at the Tower of Babel here (Gen. 11:1,7). See Stanley M. Horton, *Genesis*, vol. 1 of *The Complete Biblical Library: The Old Testament* (Springfield, Mo.: World Library Press, 1994), 81, 95. At Babel, God miraculously brought about what would have otherwise taken a long time. All of nature shows that God loves variety. Paul recognized that variety is essential to the Church, not uniformity (1 Cor. 12).

[40]The areas outside the Roman Empire were not Greek speaking.

[41]Some of the exiles from the ten northern tribes were settled in Media (2 Kings 17:6). There is evidence that these and others of the ten tribes joined in with the synagogues of the Jews, so that all twelve tribes were represented among the Jews of the Dispersion.

[42]Earle, *Acts of the Apostles*, 279, citing K. Lake and H. J. Cadbury, *The Acts of the Apostles* (London: Macmillan, 1933).

Cappadocia was a large Roman province in the central part of Asia Minor. Pontus was a Roman province in northern Asia Minor on the Black Sea. Asia was the Roman province comprising the western third of Asia Minor. Phrygia was an ethnic district, part in the province of Asia and part in Galatia.[43] Paul later founded many churches in this area.

Pamphylia was a Roman province on the south coast of Asia Minor; Egypt to the south had a large Jewish population. The Jewish philosopher Philo said in A.D. 38 that about a million Jews were there, many in Alexandria. Cyrene was a district in Africa west of Egypt on the Mediterranean coast (Acts 6:9; 11:20; 13:1).

Others present in Jerusalem were visitors (temporary residents), citizens of Rome, including both Jews and Gentile converts to Judaism.[44] Still others were from the island of Crete and from Arabia, the district east and southeast of Judea.[45]

All these kept hearing in their own languages "the wonders [the mighty, magnificent, sublime deeds] of God." These may have been in the form of exclamations of praise to God for these wonders. No discourse or preaching is implied, though preaching would surely have brought the salvation of some (1 Cor. 1:21). There is no record here or elsewhere, however, of the gift of tongues being used as a means of preaching or teaching the gospel.

12Amazed and perplexed, they asked one another, "What does this mean?" 13Some, however, made fun of them and said, "They have had too much wine."

Instead, the hearers were "amazed" (astounded) and "perplexed" (confused, at a loss, completely unable to understand

---

[43]Antiochus III of Syria deported two thousand Jewish families to Phrygia in the second century B.C. See Josephus *Antiquities of the Jews* 12.3.4.

[44]Gk. *prosēlutoi,* "proselytes" (v. 10, KJV). Full proselytes took circumcision, performed a self-baptism, and offered a sacrifice to declare their purpose to keep the law of Moses and live as Jews. The Talmud adds that conversion must be supervised by three Jews (*The Talmud of Babylonia,* trans. Jacob Neusner, vol. 13B: Tractate Yebamot [Atlanta: Scholars Press, 1992], 68–78). Some believe both Jews and proselytes were found among all fifteen nations. See Earle, *Acts of the Apostles,* 280.

[45]Rome did not conquer Arabia until after NT times.

what this was all about). "What does this mean?" expresses their total confusion as well as their extreme amazement. They understood the meaning of the words, but not the purpose. That is why they were confused by what they heard.

Others in the crowd took it all as the ravings of people who were drunk. Because they did not understand the purpose, they jumped to the conclusion that it had *no* purpose.[46] Therefore they proceeded to make fun of them in a mocking, scornful way,[47] saying that the 120 had "had too much wine." "Wine," Gk. *gleukous* (from which we get our word "glucose"), is not the ordinary word for wine, and some say it represents an intoxicating wine made from a very sweet grape.[48] However, there is definite evidence that *gleukous* designates "sweet new wine,"[49] that is, sweet, unfermented grape juice. Samuele Bacchiocchi points out, "In view of the meaning of *gleukos* as unintoxicating grape juice, the irony of the charge is self-evident. What the mockers meant is 'These men, too abstemious to touch anything fermented, have made themselves drunk on grape juice.' . . . The inadequacy of the cause, grape juice, to produce the effect, drunkenness, is designed to add point to the derisive jest."[50]

The Greek indicates there were mocking gestures as well as words. Some drinkers become noisy and this may be what the mockers were thinking of. We must not suppose there was any sign of the kind of frenzy that marked heathen drunken debauchery. The detractors were wrong. The disciples' chief emotion was still joy. They had been thanking and praising God in their own

[46]Donald Guthrie, *The Apostles* (Grand Rapids: Zondervan Publishing House, 1975), 27.

[47]The Gk. indicates continued, intense action. Compare what Jesus' enemies said in Luke 7:34.

[48]Luke T. Johnson, *The Acts of the Apostles* (Collegeville, Minn.: Liturgical Press, 1992), 44.

[49]Bauer, Arndt, Gingrich, and Danker, *A Greek-English Lexicon of the New Testament and Other Early Christian Literature* (Chicago: University of Chicago Press, 1979), 161.

[50]Samuele Bacchiocchi, *Wine in the Bible: A Biblical Study on the Use of Alcoholic Beverages* (Berrien Springs, Mich.: Biblical Perspectives, 1989), 180. See also Ernest Gordon, *Notes From a Layman's Greek Testament* (Boston: W. A. Wilde, 1941), 121–22; and David John Williams, *Acts* (Peabody, Mass.: Hendrickson Publishers, 1990), 46.

language (Luke 24:53); now the Holy Spirit had given them new languages to praise God in. We can be sure the hearts of the 120 were still going out to God in praise for His wonderful works, even though they did not understand what they were speaking.

5. PETER MANIFESTS THE GIFT OF PROPHECY 2:14–40

a. Joel's Prophecy Fulfilled 2:14–21

[14]Then Peter stood up with the Eleven, raised his voice and addressed the crowd: "Fellow Jews and all of you who live in Jerusalem, let me explain this to you; listen carefully to what I say. [15]These men are not drunk, as you suppose. It's only nine in the morning!

When Peter and the 11 other apostles (including Matthias) stood to their feet, the 120 immediately ceased speaking in tongues. Then the whole crowd gave their attention to Peter. Still anointed by the Spirit, he "raised his voice" and proceeded to address (Gk. *apephthenxato,* "speak out to") the crowd. The word used for this speaking is from the same verb used of the speaking in tongues in Acts 2:4.[51] It suggests that Peter spoke in his own language (Aramaic) as the Spirit enabled him.[52] In other words, what follows is not a sermon in the ordinary sense of the word. Certainly, Peter did not sit down and figure out three points. Rather, this was a spontaneous manifestation of the gift of prophecy (1 Cor. 12:10; 14:3).[53]

Peter directed his address to the Jews and to all who lived in Jerusalem. This was a polite way to begin and followed their custom. It included both men and women. Even when they mentioned only men, they were not ruling out the women. This would be true also of verses 22 and 29. By calling them "fellow Jews" he also recognized that the Spirit-baptized believers were still true Jews. Their faith in Jesus had not removed them from the congregation of Israel.

Apparently, as the 120 continued to speak in tongues, the mocking increased until most were making fun of them. Peter did

[51]In the LXX the same verb is used of prophesying (1 Chron. 25:1).
[52]See Williams, *Acts,* 49.
[53]See Horton, *What the Bible Says,* 144.

not draw attention to the fact that some did not understand the purpose or were perplexed. He answered only those who mocked.

The 120 were not drunk, as the crowd supposed, for it was only about "nine in the morning" (lit. "the third hour of the day"). Actually, even fermented wine was not very strong. In those days they had no way of distilling alcohol or fortifying drinks. Their strongest drinks were wine and beer, and they made it a practice to dilute the wine with several parts of water. It would have taken a great deal to get them drunk that early in the morning. We are sure also that anyone drinking at that hour would not be in a public place. Thus Peter showed that the words of those making fun of the 120 were absurd.

> [16]No, this is what was spoken by the prophet Joel: [17]"'In the last days, God says, I will pour out my Spirit on all people. Your sons and daughters will prophesy, your young men will see visions, your old men will dream dreams. [18]Even on my servants, both men and women, I will pour out my Spirit in those days, and they will prophesy.

Peter then turned to the Word of God. As James D. Brown pointed out, "The authority of the Word is over both private and corporate experience."[54] Peter did not refer to Ezekiel 36:26 which speaks of "inward renewal of the heart."[55] So Peter declared that what they saw and heard (Acts 2:33) was a fulfillment of Joel 2:28-32 (Joel 3:1-5 in the Heb. Scriptures). Because the context of Joel goes on to deal with the coming judgment and the end of the age, some writers today believe that Joel's prophecy did not have a fulfillment on the Day of Pentecost. One writer actually says Peter did not really mean "This is that" (v. 16, KJV) but rather "This is something like that." In other words, he thinks the Pentecostal outpouring was only similar to what will happen when Israel is restored at the end of the age.[56]

[54]James D. Brown, "The Authority of the Word," in *Conference on the Holy Spirit Digest,* ed. Gwen Jones (Springfield, Mo.: Gospel Publishing House, 1983), 1:17.

[55]French L. Arrington, "The Acts of the Apostles," in *Full Life Bible Commentary to the New Testament,* ed. French L. Arrington and Roger Stronstad (Grand Rapids: Zondervan Publishing House, 1999), 537.

[56]A. C. Gabelein, *The Holy Spirit in the New Testament* (New York: Our Hope, n.d.), 34.

Peter, however, did say, "This is what was spoken by the prophet Joel." Joel, like the other Old Testament prophets, did not see the time span between the first and second comings of Christ. Even Peter himself probably did not see how long it would be. He did see, however, that the Messianic Age is coming, and probably hoped it would be soon.

Peter makes one apparent change in the prophecy. Under the inspiration of the Holy Spirit he specified what the word "afterward" in Joel 2:28 means: the outpouring is "in the last days." Thus he recognized that the "last days" began with the ascension of Jesus (Acts 3:19-21). From this we can see that the Holy Spirit recognizes the entire Church Age as "last days" to be characterized by His powerful working.[57] We are in the last age before the rapture of the Church, the restoration of Israel, and Christ's millennial reign on earth—the last age before Jesus "is revealed from heaven in blazing fire" to "punish those who do not know God and do not obey the gospel" (2 Thess. 1:7-10).

Peter's inclusion of "God says" in the introduction "identifies the prophecy of Joel as 'the promise of the Father' . . . (Lk 24.49; Acts 1.4; 2.33)."[58]

The first part of the quotation from Joel has an obvious application to the 120. The many languages highlight God's purpose to keep pouring out His Spirit or to pour out His Spirit again and again[59] on "all people" (Gk. *pasan sarka,* "all flesh"). In the Hebrew "all flesh" usually means all humankind, as in Genesis 6:12. "Flesh" can also speak of frailty, and this fits with the fact that the baptism in the Holy Spirit is an empowering experience. The Spirit wants to give us power and make us strong.

Whether any dreams or visions were seen while they were speaking in tongues, we do not know. Perhaps there were. But the repeated emphasis (vv. 17-18) is on the pouring out of the Spirit so that those filled would prophesy. Evidently, Peter, through the Spirit, saw that tongues when understood are the

---

[57]Oss, "Pentecostal/Charismatic View," 266-67.

[58]Robert P. Menzies, "The Spirit of Prophecy, Luke-Acts and Pentecostal Theology: A Response to Max Turner," *Journal of Pentecostal Theology* 15 (October 1999): 64-65.

[59]Both the Gk. and the Heb. indicate action that is continuing or repeated.

equivalent of prophecy (1 Cor. 14:5–6).[60] In the Bible, to prophesy means to speak for God as His spokesman, or "mouth" (cf. Exod. 4:15–16; 7:1).

"All people" (v. 17) is then broken down to sons and daughters. There is no distinction in the Pentecostal experience with regard to gender. This is another indication that all the 120 were baptized in the Spirit, including the women.[61] Later we read of Philip's daughters who prophesied (Acts 21:9).

Young men would "see visions" and old men "dream dreams" (v. 17). No division with respect to age would exist. Nor does there seem to be any real distinction here between dreams and visions. The Bible often uses the words interchangeably (cf. Dan. 7:1,2). Here they are at least parallel. (See Acts 10:17; 16:9–10; and 18:9 for examples of visions.) Some writers, however, take "visions" to be supernatural visitations—actually seen while awake—not a fantasy, not a product of human imagination. "Dream dreams" then would mean to have supernatural visions in dreams.

Even upon male and female slaves, which is what "servants" (v. 18; Gk. *doulous, doulas*) actually means, God would pour out His Spirit. In other words, the Spirit would pay no attention to social distinctions. Though there were probably no slaves among the 120, twenty percent of the population of the Roman Empire were slaves[62] and in many areas slaves composed as high as eighty percent of the population. Fulfillment of the prophecy would come: Slaves would be saved and, of course, filled with the Holy Spirit (cf. Eph. 6:5–9; Col. 3:22 through 4:1; 1 Tim. 6:1–2; Titus 2:9–10; 1 Pet. 2:18–21).

It is also possible to take verse 18 as a summary statement: "upon my church of slaves," parallel to the Israelite slaves delivered from Egypt by God's mighty power. All the Epistles refer to the believers as servants (Gk. *douloi,* "slaves"), rather than disciples ("learners"). They asked nothing for themselves, claimed no rights, and gave everything in the service of their Master and

[60]Roger Stronstad emphasizes that "the pouring out of the eschatological gift of the Spirit is the Spirit of prophecy" and it is "for the community of God's people." *Prophethood of All Believers,* 68–70.

[61]Harrison, *Acts,* 58.

[62]Keith Crim, ed., *The Interpreter's Dictionary of the Bible,* Supplementary Volume (Nashville: Abingdon, 1976), 830.

Lord. Even the brothers of Jesus, James and Jude, call themselves servants, or "slaves," of the Lord Jesus (James 1:1; Jude 1).

The fact that we read "my servants" also "highlights what is implicit in the Joel text: The gift of the Spirit is given only to those who are members of the community of salvation,"[63] that is, to those who are already born-again believers.

[19]I will show wonders in the heaven above and signs on the earth below, blood and fire and billows of smoke. [20]The sun will be turned to darkness and the moon to blood before the coming of the great and glorious day of the Lord.

Many interpret verses 19 and 20 symbolically.[64] Others suppose they were somehow fulfilled during the three hours of darkness when Jesus hung on the cross. It seems, rather, that the mention of the signs indicates that the outpouring and the prophesying would continue until these signs come at the end of the age. Peter also means that these signs can just as confidently be expected.[65]

We may also see the gift of the Spirit as the firstfruits of the age to come (Rom. 8:23). The unregenerate human heart and mind has no conception of "'what God has prepared for those who love Him'—but God has revealed it to us by his Spirit" (1 Cor. 2:9–10). The inheritance that will be fully ours when Jesus comes is no mystery to us. We have already experienced it, at least in a measure. As Hebrews 6:4–5 points out, all who have "tasted [really experienced] the heavenly gift" and are "made partakers of the Holy Spirit" (NASB) have already experienced "the good word [promise] of God" (NASB) and "the powers [mighty powers, miracles] of the coming age."[66]

---

[63]William W. Menzies and Robert P. Menzies, *Spirit and Power: Foundations of Pentecostal Experience* (Grand Rapids: Zondervan Publishing House, 2000), 77.

[64]Harrison, *Acts,* 58.

[65]Wonders and signs are mentioned nine times in chaps. 2 through 15. Robert Wall suggests that this repeated formula "is a narrative commentary on Joel's prophecy . . . which interprets the prophetic 'Day of the Lord' as having dawned." "'Purity and Power' According to the Acts of the Apostles," *Pneuma* 21, no. 2 (fall 1999): 216.

[66]Jans Conzelmann, *An Outline of the Theology of the New Testament,* trans. John Bowden (New York: Harper & Row, 1969), 37.

Some writers also take the "fire and . . . smoke" as a reference to the signs of God's presence at Mount Sinai (Exod. 19:16–18; 20:18) and consider Pentecost as the giving of a new law or the enacting of the new covenant. However, as Hebrews 9:15–18, 26,28 indicates, the death of Christ put the new covenant into effect and there is no need for anything further.

The signs here also include "blood" and refer to the increasing bloodshed, wars, and smoke from wars that will cover the sun and make the moon appear red. These things will happen "before the coming of the great and glorious day of the Lord"; they are part of this present age. The Day of the Lord in the Old Testament includes both the judgments on the present nations of the world and the restoration of Israel with the establishment of the messianic millennial kingdom. But Peter is not concerned with these prophecies as such here. He wants his hearers to understand that the Pentecostal power of the Spirit will continue to be poured out throughout this present age. The age of the Church is the age of the Holy Spirit. The gift of the Spirit will still be available even in the midst of coming wars and bloodshed.[67]

21And everyone who calls on the name of the Lord will be saved.'

This verse gives the purpose of the outpouring. Through this empowering the Holy Spirit will do His convicting work in the world, not just in the end but throughout the age—right down to the great Day of the Lord. All during this period, whoever calls on the name of the Lord for help, that is, for salvation, will be saved. "The Lord" is Jesus (cf. Rom. 10:9,13). The Greek *pas hos,* "everyone whoever," is strong. No matter what happens or what forces oppose the Church, the door of salvation will remain open. The Greek also indicates that we can expect many to respond and be saved. John confirms this, for he saw "a great multitude . . .

---

[67]Roger Stronstad identifies the "wonders in the heaven above" with "the sound like the blowing of a violent wind," and the "signs on the earth below" with "the tongues of fire." He adds, "Joel announced a scene with the morning sun to the east and the late-setting moon to the west which, when viewed through the unreported but implied smoke of the 'fire' of Pentecost, not only darkens these celestial luminaries but also makes them appear blood red to those on the Temple Mount." *Prophethood of All Believers,* 56.

from every nation, tribe, people and language standing before the throne" (Rev. 7:9). These come out of "'the great [long] tribulation'" (Rev. 7:14) that Jesus mentioned in John 16:33.[68]

b. Jesus Exalted 2:22–36

22"Men of Israel, listen to this: Jesus of Nazareth was a man accredited by God to you by miracles, wonders and signs, which God did among you through him, as you yourselves know.

The main body of Peter's manifestation of the gift of prophecy (vv. 22–36) centers not on the Holy Spirit but on Jesus.[69] The Pentecostal experience was intended to bear powerful witness to Jesus, the one who poured out the Spirit (Acts 1:8; John 15:26–27; 16:14).

Peter first drew attention to the fact that the people of Jerusalem knew the *man* of Nazareth,[70] Jesus. They also knew how God had "accredited," "attested" (NASB), "approved" (KJV), Him for their benefit "by miracles [Gk. *dunamesin*, "works of mighty power"], wonders and signs." These are the three words the Bible uses for supernatural miracles. They refer to the variety of miracles God did through Jesus, especially in the temple at the feast times (John 2:23; 4:45; 11:47). The people needed to be reminded of what Jesus did for them.

23This man was handed over to you by God's set purpose and foreknowledge; and you, with the help of wicked men, put him to death by nailing him to the cross.

Peter did not hesitate to identify the people of Jerusalem as responsible for the death of Jesus on the cross,[71] noting that they did it "with the help of wicked men" (Gk. *anomōn*, "lawless men,

---

[68]Stanley M. Horton, *The Ultimate Victory: An Exposition of the Book of Revelation* (Springfield, Mo.: Gospel Publishing House, 1991), 117–18.

[69]Some writers consider this part of the Holy Spirit's message to be "programmatic" for the preaching throughout Acts. Mark L. Strauss, *The Davidic Messiah in Luke-Acts* (Sheffield, England: Sheffield Academic Press, 1995), 133.

[70]Nazareth (Heb. *Netsereth*) is derived from the word "branch" (Heb. *netser*) used in Isa. 11:1 of the greater Son of David, the Messiah.

[71]Waverly Nunnally stresses that the Cross is the centerpiece of apostolic proclamation.

men outside the Law"), that is, Pilate and the Roman soldiers. However, the cross was not an accident. Peter made it clear that Jesus was handed over to the Jews "by God's set purpose [Gk. *boulē*, "designated will, definite plan," as revealed in the OT prophecies] and foreknowledge"—which Jesus himself recognized (Luke 24:25–27,46), giving himself of His own accord (Gal. 1:4; 2:20; Eph. 5:2,25; 1 Tim. 2:6; Titus 2:14). This did not lessen their guilt, however.[72] The word "foreknowledge" (Gk. *prognōsis*) is found only here and in 1 Peter 1:2—another indication that Luke got the account of this message from Peter or from someone who wrote it down as he gave it. (This was a literate age and people were careful to record what was going on.)[73]

It should be emphasized also that Peter was speaking here to Jerusalem Jews, many of whom were involved in the cry "Crucify Him!" The Bible never puts this kind of responsibility or guilt on the Jews in general. For example, in Acts 13:27–29, Paul, speaking to Jews in Pisidian Antioch, is careful to attribute the crucifixion to the people and rulers of Jerusalem, saying "they," not "you." Further, Gentiles had a hand in the crucifying, so the sins of all people nailed Him to the cross.[74]

24But God raised him from the dead, freeing him from the agony of death, because it was impossible for death to keep its hold on him.

Quickly Peter adds, "God raised him from the dead." The resurrection of Christ took away the stigma of the Cross and reversed the decision of the Jewish leaders and Pilate. It also indicated God's acceptance of Jesus' sacrifice. By the resurrection also God released Jesus "from the agony of death." "Agony" (Gk. *ōdinas*) usually means "birth pangs," so that the death here is

[72]Jack T. Sanders, *The Jews in Luke-Acts* (Philadelphia: Fortress Press, 1987), 234. Claire Amos points out that what Acts really attacks "is a false religiosity which believes that power, security and control are more important than traveling where the Spirit might lead." "Acts," in *Sowers and Reapers,* ed. John Parr (Nashville: Abingdon Press, 1994), 388–89.

[73]E. M. Blaiklock, *Acts: The Birth of the Church* (Old Tappan, N.J.: Fleming H. Revell, 1980), 26.

[74]Jon A. Weatherly, *Jewish Responsibility for the Death of Jesus in Luke-Acts* (Sheffield, England: Sheffield Academic Press, 1994), 54, 56, 97.

perceived as labor. Just as labor pains are relieved by the birth of a child, so the resurrection brought an end to the pains of death.

Why was it "impossible for death to keep its hold on him"? Since "the wages of sin is death" (Rom. 6:23), some writers say death could not hold Him because He had no sin of His own for death to claim. In this context, however, it is because of God's purpose to resurrect His anointed One, the Messiah, and because the prophetic Scriptures concerning Him must be fulfilled.

> 25David said about him: "'I saw the Lord always before me. Because he is at my right hand, I will not be shaken. 26Therefore my heart is glad and my tongue rejoices; my body also will live in hope, 27because you will not abandon me to the grave, nor will you let your Holy One see decay. 28You have made known to me the paths of life; you will fill me with joy in your presence.'

Peter bases his whole argument on the Word of God. Under the inspiration of the Spirit he says that David was speaking of Jesus in Psalm 16:8–11. Jewish tradition of the time also applied this to the Messiah.[75]

The central point is the promise that God would not abandon Him "to the grave" (Gk. *eis hadou*, "into Hades," the place of punishment for the wicked, translating the Heb. *Sheʾol*).[76] He did go into the grave, but this does not necessarily imply that He went into Hades or Sheol.[77]

---

[75]"My body also will live in hope" is from the LXX. The traditional Heb. text of Ps. 16:9 has "My body will also rest secure." But the security does imply a future hope.

[76]Dr. R. Laird Harris of Covenant Theological Seminary, a member of the NIV translation team, told me that it was through his influence that the NIV translates *Sheʾol* as "the grave." Nevertheless, careful examination of such passages as Job 26:6; Pss. 30:3; 49:13–15; 55:15; 88:11–12; Prov. 5:5; 7:27; 9:18; 15:10–11; 27:20; Isa. 38:18 shows it means "hell," the place of punishment for the wicked, as does *Hadēs* in the NT.

[77]Wayne Grudem, *Systematic Theology* (Grand Rapids: Zondervan Publishing House, 1994), 586–94. He gives strong biblical opposition to a "descent into hell" and points out that the Apostles' Creed did not contain the phrase "he descended into hell" until Rufinus added it in A.D. 390 and others did not include it until 650. It seems also that Rufinus understood *Hadēs* to mean the grave rather than what we call hell. However, Frank D. Macchia says, "[I]t would seem that Christ did descend into hell at His death to proclaim the victory of the

29"Brothers, I can tell you confidently that the patriarch David died and was buried, and his tomb is here to this day.

Peter declared that it was proper[78] for him to say "confidently" (freely and openly)[79] of "the patriarch"[80] (chief father and ancestral ruler) David that the psalm could not possibly apply to him. He not only died and was buried, his tomb was still there in Jerusalem.[81] Obviously David's flesh did "see corruption" (v. 31, KJV). But Jesus' did not. Though Peter did not say it, he clearly implies that Jesus' tomb was empty.

30But he was a prophet and knew that God had promised him on oath that he would place one of his descendants on his throne. 31Seeing what was ahead, he spoke of the resurrection of the Christ, that he was not abandoned to the grave, nor did his body see decay.

Because David was a prophet (a speaker for God), and because he knew God had sworn an oath that one of his descendants would sit on his throne, he foresaw and spoke of the resurrection of the Christ (the Messiah, God's Anointed One). The reference here is to the Davidic covenant. In it God promised David there would always be a man from his descendants for the throne. God gave this first with respect to Solomon (2 Sam. 7:11–16). But He warned that if any of David's descendants sinned He

---

Cross over the forces of darkness." "Created Spirit Beings," in *Systematic Theology,* ed. Stanley M. Horton, rev. ed. (Springfield, Mo.: Logion Press, 1995), 199. He adds, "But we must be cautious not to fantasize about battles between Jesus and demons in hell, since Christ completed His work of redemption on the cross. We should also avoid claiming that Jesus won the keys of hell and death from Satan, since Jesus received all authority from the Father (Matt. 28:18)."

[78]The Gk. implies that Peter did not want them to be offended by what he was about to say: "It is right for me to speak to you about our ancestor David" (CEV).

[79]Gk. *parrēsias,* translated "boldly" in 28:31; see also 4:13,29,31. The Spirit enables us to spread the gospel with boldness. See Earl Richard, "Pentecost as a Recurrent Theme in Luke-Acts," in *New Views on Luke and Acts,* ed. Earl Richard (Collegeville, Minn.: Liturgical Press, 1990), 136.

[80]Called "the patriarch" because he was founder of the Davidic dynasty that led to Christ, the greater heir of David.

[81]According to Josephus, Herod the Great broke into the tomb to get the treasure Solomon buried there. The tomb fell into ruins by the time of the emperor Hadrian.

would punish him just as He would punish anyone else. God, however, would never turn His back on David's line and substitute another as He had in the case of King Saul. This promise was unusual. All the surrounding nations had one dynasty (ruling family) after another. Later, in the northern kingdom of Israel they had nine ruling families (two of them lasting only a very short time). Psalms 89:4–5 and 132:11–12 reaffirm the Davidic covenant. Queen Athaliah tried to wipe out the line, but Joash was saved and Athaliah punished (2 Kings 11:1–21).

Because the kings of David's line did not follow the Lord, God finally had to bring an end to their kingdom and send them into Babylonian exile (2 Chron. 36:11–20). His purpose in doing this was to rid them of their idolatry. But the promise to David still stood. The Anointed One to come would some day sit on David's throne and make it eternal (cf. Luke 1:32–33). The resurrection of this Anointed One was necessary to fulfill what the Old Testament prophesied.

32God has raised this Jesus to life, and we are all witnesses of the fact.

Peter thus declared that Jesus is the Messianic King. Because God raised Him to life, He was not abandoned to Hades nor did His flesh "see decay" (v. 27). Furthermore, Peter and the 120 were "all witnesses" to His resurrection (cf. 1 Cor. 15:3–6).

33Exalted to the right hand of God, he has received from the Father the promised Holy Spirit and has poured out what you now see and hear.

Christ's resurrection, however, was only part of a process whereby God, by His powerful right hand, raised Jesus to an exalted position of power and authority at His right hand.[82] This is also the place of triumph and victory. By paying the full price, Jesus won for us the battle against sin and death. Thus He remains at God's right hand throughout this age (See Mark 16:19; Rom. 8:34; Eph. 1:20–21; Col. 3:1; Heb. 1:3; 8:1; 10:12; 12:2; 1 Pet. 3:22). This means also that He is always there to intercede for us (Heb. 7:25; 1 John 2:1).

---

[82]The Gk. indicates both "by" and "at" God's right hand.

In Christ we also are seated at the right hand of God (Eph. 2:6). Because this is our position in Christ we do not need our own works of righteousness to claim His promise of the baptism in the Holy Spirit. Nothing we could do could give us a higher position than we already have in Christ.

Next, Peter uses Christ's exalted position to explain the Pentecostal experience. Now at the Father's right hand, Jesus received from the Father "the promised Holy Spirit," and in turn "poured out" the Holy Spirit. The results of this outpouring the crowd now saw and heard: the 120 speaking in other tongues.[83]

Jesus had said it was necessary for Him to go away in order for the "Counselor" (Gk. *paraklētos,* "Helper") to come (John 16:7). Thus, though the baptism in the Holy Spirit is the promise of the Father, Jesus is the One who pours it out (cf. Luke 3:16–17). We see here also a clear distinction between the Persons of the Triune God. God is the Giver, but Jesus is the Baptizer.

The outpouring of the Spirit was also evidence that Jesus actually was exalted to the Father's right hand. This means something to us who now believe and receive the baptism in the Holy Spirit. This baptism becomes evidence to us personally that Jesus is there and that He is still working. Therefore we can be first-hand witnesses to where Jesus is and what He is doing.

[34]For David did not ascend to heaven, and yet he said, "'The Lord said to my Lord: "Sit at my right hand [35]until I make your enemies a footstool for your feet.'"

Peter uses another quotation from Scripture to give further evidence that none of this could apply to David. David did not "ascend to heaven" as Jesus did, but he did prophesy that exaltation in Psalm 110:1. Again, David could not be speaking of

---

[83]Some scholars compare Moses' ascent on Sinai (to meet God and bring the Law to establish the old covenant) to Christ's ascension (and His pouring out the Spirit to establish the new covenant). However, the new covenant was put into effect by the death of Jesus and the shedding of His blood. As Robert Menzies says, "[I]t is . . . illegitimate to assume that the mere mention of" the Day of Pentecost (Acts 2:1) "would have evoked images of Moses, Sinai or the covenant renewal ceremony in the minds of Luke's readers." Robert P. Menzies, *The Development of Early Christian Pneumatology: With Special Reference to Luke-Acts* (Sheffield, England, Sheffield Academic Press, 1991), 235.

himself, since he prophesied that his Lord would sit on the Father's right hand until the Father made for Him a footstool of His enemies; that is, until the Father gave Him complete and final victory (cf. Josh. 10:24; Heb. 1:13). Jesus also referred to this in Luke 20:41–44, recognizing that David called his greater Son "Lord" (see also Matt. 22:42–45; Mark 12:36–37).

36"Therefore let all Israel be assured of this: God has made this Jesus, whom you crucified, both Lord and Christ."

The conclusion Peter drew is that all Israel needed to know that God had made this Jesus, whom the Jerusalem residents crucified, "both *Lord* and Christ" (Messiah).

From this also we see that, in fulfillment of Joel's prophecy, Jesus is the Lord on whom all must call for salvation. Paul also recognized that "God exalted him to the highest place and gave him the name that is above every name, that at the name of Jesus every knee should bow, in heaven and on earth and under the earth, and every tongue confess that Jesus Christ is *Lord,* to the glory of God the Father" (Phil. 2:9–11). "*The* Name" in Old Testament Hebrew always means the Name of God. (Heb. has other ways of referring to the name of a human being without using the definite article, "the.") The Name stands for the authority, person, and especially the character of God in His righteousness, holiness, faithfulness, goodness, love, and power. "Lord" (Gk. *kurios*) is used in the New Testament for the Name of God. Mercy, grace, and love are part of the holiness, the holy Name by which Jesus is recognized as "Lord," the full revelation of God to humankind. That Jesus is in heaven as our reigning Lord, and that "'all authority in heaven and on earth'" has been given to Him (Matt. 28:18), assures us that God will see to it that His plan is carried out whatever happens to this world.

God's enthronement of Jesus declared Him Christ as well as Lord. However, that does not mean that Jesus only then became the Messiah. He was already the Messiah, the "Anointed One" who ministered "in the power of the Spirit" (Luke 4:14). As the Messiah He suffered and died for us (Rom. 5:6,8; 14:15; 1 Cor. 8:11; 2 Cor. 5:14–15; 1 Thess. 5:9–10).[84]

---

[84]Strauss, *Davidic Messiah in Luke-Acts,* 67.

French L. Arrington adds, "Speaking in tongues is a sign to the unbelieving hearers (cf. 1 Cor. 14:22). The words of praise on the lips of the disciples serve as a sign of judgment to unbelievers. On the basis of the miraculous manifestation Peter declares 'Let all Israel be assured of this: God has made this Jesus, whom you crucified, both Lord and Christ.'"[85]

c. Peter Calls For Repentance 2:37–40

[37]When the people heard this, they were cut to the heart and said to Peter and the other apostles, "Brothers, what shall we do?"

The response to this Spirit-inspired prophetic word was immediate. The people were "cut [pierced] to the heart." No longer were they saying "What does this mean?" The Holy Spirit's message stung their consciences. They recognized their guilt and spoke to Peter and to the other apostles (who were evidently still standing with him), wanting to know what they must do.

They did not feel completely cut off, however. Peter had called them "brothers" (v. 29), and they responded by calling the apostles "brothers." Their sin in rejecting and crucifying Jesus was great, but their response shows that they believed there was hope, there was something they could do. We can see in this a fulfillment of John 12:32, where Jesus said, "'But I, when I am lifted up from the earth [on the cross], will draw all men to myself.'"

[38]Peter replied, "Repent and be baptized, every one of you, in the name of Jesus Christ for the forgiveness of your sins. And you will receive the gift of the Holy Spirit.

Peter answered by calling on them to repent, that is, to change their minds and fundamental attitudes by accepting the forgiveness and the will of God revealed in Christ. As in Romans 12:1–2, this change means more than being sorry for one's sins. It requires a renewing of one's mind with an accompanying change in attitude toward sin and self. People who truly repent abhor sin (Ps. 51). They humble themselves, recognize their dependence on Christ, and realize they have no good thing in themselves enabling them to stand before the Holy God.

[85]Arrington, "Acts of the Apostles," 543.

The repentant ones can then declare their change of heart and mind by being baptized "in the name" (Gk. *epi to onomati,* "upon the name") of Jesus Christ, that is, upon the authority of Jesus, for "the name" here means the authority. Luke does not explain further; but he often does not explain what is made clear elsewhere. The authority of Jesus points to His own command given in Matthew 28:19. Thus, the actual baptizing was done "into the Name" (Gk. *eis to onoma,* meaning "into the worship and service") of the Father, the Son, and the Holy Spirit.

This baptism would also be "for the forgiveness of . . . sins." How marvelous! What earthly king, president, or ruler has ever forgiven a traitor? But Christ did and does. This is pure grace and matchless love (see Rom. 5:8,10). "For [Gk. *eis,* "unto," "because of"] the forgiveness of your sins," however, is better translated "because of the release from and forgiveness of your sins." Our sin and guilt is removed as far from us as "the east is from the west" (Ps. 103:12)—an infinite distance. They are not only forgiven, they are really gone, out of existence, never to be brought up against us any more.

"Because of" is better than "for" or "unto" since it is the same type of Greek construction used where John baptized people in water "'for repentance'" (Matt. 3:11). It is clear that John baptized no one to produce repentance. When the Pharisees[86] and Sadducees came to him he demanded that they produce "'fruit in keeping with repentance'" (Matt. 3:8), in other words, demonstrating true repentance. That is, they must repent first, then he would baptize them. We are saved by grace through faith, not through baptism (Eph. 2:8). After repentance, water baptism becomes the "pledge," or testimony, of a good conscience that has already been cleansed by the blood and by the Spirit's application of the Word concerning Christ's atoning death and resurrection (Rom. 10:9–10; 1 Pet. 3:21).

---

[86]"Pharisees" probably means "separated ones," from Heb. *parash,* possibly referring to their emphasis on washings and ceremonial purity. Another meaning of *parash,* "to inform precisely," also fits. They were sticklers for the details of the Law. They probably developed from the *Chasidim* ("Holy Ones") who opposed the attempts of Antiochus Epiphanes to Hellenize the Jews. F. S. Hewitt, *The Genesis of the Christian Church: A Study of Acts and the Epistles* (London: Edward Arnold, 1972), 10.

Some writers argue wrongly that there was not enough water in Jerusalem to baptize three thousand people by immersion. However, the pool of Bethesda alone was a large double pool, and remains of other pools have been excavated. In fact, the facilities for baptism by immersion were much greater in Jerusalem then than they are now.

The forgiveness of sins would be followed by a distinct impartation of the gift of the Spirit. This too was indicated in Old Testament prophecies (Ezek. 36:25–27; 37:14).

39The promise is for you and your children and for all who are far off—for all whom the Lord our God will call."

Next, Peter spoke of the promise of the Father (see 1:4). Believers would also receive the Holy Spirit as a distinct gift after the forgiveness of their sins. This gift, of course, is the baptism in the Holy Spirit. It must be distinguished from the gifts of the Spirit that are given by the Spirit (1 Cor. 12 through 14). Jesus, the mighty Baptizer, gives the gift of the Spirit.[87]

Peter goes on to emphasize that this promise of the baptism in the Spirit was not limited to the 120.[88] It would continue to be available, not only to them but also to their children (including all their descendants), and to all who are far away, "for all whom the Lord our God will call." Thus, the only condition for receiving the promise of the Father is repentance and faith. It is therefore still available to all who respond to the Father's call to salvation today.

The "call" may refer to Joel 2:32 but cannot be limited to the Jews. In Isaiah 57:19 God speaks peace "'to those far and near.'" Ephesians 2:17 applies those "far away" to the preaching of the gospel to the Gentiles. Acts 1:8 also speaks of witnessing "'to the ends of the earth.'" Though Peter may not have understood this fully until his experience at the house of Cornelius (Acts 10; 11), it is clear that the Gentiles are included. It is also clear that as long as God is calling people to himself, the promised baptism

[87]See Horton, *What the Bible Says*, 159–61, 173, 258; John W. Wyckoff, "The Baptism in the Holy Spirit," in *Systematic Theology*, ed. Horton, 427–33; Anthony D. Palma, *The Holy Spirit: A Pentecostal Perspective* (Springfield, Mo.: Logion Press, 2001).

[88]Note that the outpouring of the Spirit at the house of Cornelius is also referred to as their being baptized (see Acts 10:44–45 with 11:16–17).

in the Spirit is available to all who come.

This promise is foundational for the entire message of the Book of Acts. "Joel's prophecy continues to be fulfilled or implemented as the message of salvation is proclaimed and received in a variety of contexts."[89]

40With many other words he warned them; and he pleaded with them, "Save yourselves from this corrupt generation."

Luke does not record the rest of Peter's witness and exhortation. But in this warning and pleading Peter may have been exercising another of the gifts of the Spirit—exhortation or encouraging (Rom. 12:8). Peter became the agent through whom the Holy Spirit carried out the work foretold by Jesus in John 16:8, to "'convict the world of guilt in regard to sin and righteousness and judgment.'" As Paul later said, "Our gospel came to you not simply with words, but also with power, with the Holy Spirit and with deep conviction" (1 Thess. 1:5).

The essence of Peter's pleading was that they should save themselves (rather, "be saved")[90] or "let yourself be saved"[91] "from this corrupt [Gk. *skolias,* "perverse, crooked, twisted, vicious"] generation." Namely, they should turn away from the perversity and corruptness of those around them who were rejecting the truth about Jesus and living for self. (See Deut. 32:5; Ps. 78:8 and the words of Jesus in Matt. 12:39; 16:4; 17:17; 23:33–36; Mark 8:38; Luke 9:41; 11:29; 17:25.) There is no other antidote to the perversity and corruptness of contemporary society.

STUDY QUESTIONS

1. What does Pentecost as a harvest festival suggest as a reason for waiting for the outpouring of the Spirit?

[89]David Peterson, "The Motif of Fulfilment and the Purpose of Luke-Acts," in *The Book of Acts in Its Ancient Literary Setting,* ed. Bruce W. Winter and Andrew D. Clarke, vol. 1 of *Acts in Its First Century Setting,* ed. Winter (Grand Rapids: Wm. B. Eerdmans, 1993), 97.

[90]This "picks up the 'will be saved' of the Joel citation (2:21)." Johnson, *Acts of the Apostles,* 58.

[91]William H. Willimon, *Acts* (Atlanta: John Knox Press, 1988), 37.

2. Do believers need to wait a specified length of time today in order to be filled with the Spirit? Why or why not?

3. What was the purpose of the signs of wind and fire?

4. What made the 120 different from the crowd in the temple?

5. What terms does the Bible use of the Pentecostal experience and what is their significance?

6. What is wrong with calling speaking in tongues "ecstatic utterance"?

7. What did the visitors to Jerusalem hear when the 120 spoke in tongues?

8. What Old Testament Scriptures did Peter's prophecy use and how were they applied?

9. What was the chief emphasis of Peter's prophecy and how was it developed?

10. What other gift of the Spirit did Peter manifest and with what result?

E. The Church Growing and Loving 2:41–47

1. Three Thousand Added 2:41

⁴¹Those who accepted his message were baptized, and about three thousand were added to their number that day.

Those who "accepted" ("welcomed," Phillips) Peter's message (because they believed it, cf. TEV, CEV) then testified to their faith by being baptized by immersion in water.

Again, Luke does not always specify details that are clear elsewhere; he does not have the space to do it in this one book. Therefore, though Luke does not mention it, we can be sure that all three thousand new believers who were added to the Church received the promise of the Father as Peter said they would and were filled with the Spirit, speaking in other tongues as in Acts 2:4.

The mention of the "three thousand" is significant. One of the themes in Acts is the spread of the Word and the numerical increase of the believers (see 2:47; 4:4; 5:14; 6:1,7; 13:49; 18:9–10; 19:10; 21:20; 28:31). God "added" them. He was carrying out His purpose and plan by the power of the Holy Spirit.

The apostles and believers never tried to carry out some program of their own devising. They followed step-by-step as the Holy Spirit guided them.

2. Continuing As Disciples 2:42

42They devoted themselves to the apostles' teaching and to the fellowship, to the breaking of bread and to prayer.

At the beginning most of the responsibility for the work of the Church fell upon the shoulders of the apostles. They were the pastors, evangelists, teachers, and counselors for the whole body. They were concerned for the well-being of all, not only spiritually but physically and materially as well.

The Spirit had baptized the three thousand into the body of Christ (see 1 Cor. 12:13). God never saves us to wander off by ourselves. Consequently the three thousand new believers did not scatter but remained together and "devoted themselves" continuously to the apostles' "teaching and . . . fellowship," continuing together also in "the breaking of bread and . . . prayer."

From this we see further evidence of their faith and their being filled with the Spirit: Not only did they take a firm stand for Christ with the apostles, they also had a persistent desire for instruction. Their acceptance of Christ and the gift of the Spirit was more than a mystical experience. It opened up to them a whole new understanding of God's plan and purpose. With joy they became hungry to learn more. This also shows that the apostles had a body of teaching (which came to be included in the four Gospels), and they were obeying Jesus and making disciples as He had commanded (Matt. 28:19). It also shows that discipleship includes this kind of eager desire to learn more of Jesus and of God's Word. We can be sure the baptism in the Holy Spirit made the Spirit their great Teacher as they listened intently to their human teachers, the apostles. The Spirit made the truth real and helped them apply it in their own lives. He increased their joy as well.

Fellowship was experienced in the process of teaching. It was more than getting together. It was a partnership in the purposes of the Church and a sharing in its message and work. As in 1 John 1:3, the Word, as witnessed to by the teaching of the apostles, brought this fellowship, a fellowship not only with the apostles but also "with the Father and with his Son."

The "breaking of bread" (Gk. *tou artou*, "of the bread")[1] some writers take to mean only the Lord's Supper, but it also includes table fellowship. Believers could not observe the Lord's Supper in the temple, so this was done in their homes, at first in connection with a meal (since Jesus instituted it at the close of the Passover meal). Paul would later have to deal with the problems caused by the way the Corinthian believers ate the meal and observed the Lord's Supper, so we do not observe it in connection with a meal today (see 1 Cor. 11:17–34; the breaking of bread was intended to foster unity; instead, it was promoting division).

As Spirit-filled believers they also devoted themselves to prayer. Prayer was an integral part of their daily life. It kept them connected with the Lord of the Church and was necessary to the work He had for them.

3. APOSTOLIC MIRACLES 2:43

43Everyone was filled with awe, and many wonders and miraculous signs were done by the apostles.

The continuing witness of the apostles to the resurrection of Jesus brought an awe, a reverential response to the presence of the supernatural, on every one of the believers. This was further enhanced by the "many wonders and miraculous signs" done by the apostles, that is, done by God through the apostles. The Greek indicates secondary agency. God really did the work (cf. 1 Cor. 3:6).

Later, God gave miracles through many others. But here the apostles had the teaching from Jesus and the background of His encouragement of their faith. The miracles were not for display but rather to confirm the Word, the teaching (see Mark 16:20). They also helped the faith of the new Pentecostal church members to be established in the Word and in the power of God (see 1 Cor. 2:4–5). In all missionary advances in the Book of Acts, the Word was accompanied by miraculous signs and wonders

---

[1]See Simon J. Kistemaker, *Exposition of the Acts of the Apostles* (Grand Rapids: Baker Book House, 1990), 111.

(cf. 4:30; 5:12; 14:8–10; 15:12; 19:10–12; cf. 1 Thess. 1:5).[2]
Signs and wonders should still be normative wherever the gospel
is being spread. Though "signs and wonders by themselves never
saved anyone . . . healing and deliverance make many more open
to consider the claims of Jesus."[3]

4. FELLOWSHIP AND WORSHIP 2:44–46

**[44]All the believers were together and had everything in
common. [45]Selling their possessions and goods, they
gave to anyone as he had need.**

The believers remained together in fellowship and had things
"in common." Many sold pieces of land they owned and personal property as well. The money was distributed to those in
need. "Anyone as he had need" is a key statement: They did not
sell property until there was a need.

This was not communism in the modern sense, or even com-
munal living. It was just Christians caring and sharing with love.
They all realized the importance of becoming established in the
apostles' teaching. Some of those visiting Jerusalem for Pentecost
soon ran out of money, so those who were able simply sold what
they could to make it possible for them to stay. Later Peter made
it clear that no one was under any compulsion to sell anything or
give anything (Acts 5:4; cf. 2 Cor. 9:7). But the fellowship, joy,
and love made it easy to share what they had (cf. 1 John 3:17).

**[46]Every day they continued to meet together in the tem-
ple courts. They broke bread in their homes and ate
together with glad and sincere hearts,**

The picture, then, is of a loving body of worshiping believers
meeting daily in the temple, probably in Solomon's Colonnade
(see Acts 3:11; 5:12)—with one accord, one mind, one purpose,

---

[2]See Johannes Munck, *The Acts of the Apostles,* rev. William F. Albright and C.
S. Mann, vol. 31 of *Anchor Bible Series* (Garden City, N.Y.: Doubleday & Co.,
1979), 22. See also William W. Menzies and Robert P. Menzies, *Spirit and Power:
Foundations of Pentecostal Experience* (Grand Rapids: Zondervan Publishing
House, 2000), 149.

[3]C. Peter Wagner, *Spreading the Fire: Book 1, Acts 1–8* (Ventura, Calif.: Gospel
Light, Regal Books, 1994), 27.

and sharing table fellowship "in their homes." Each house became a center of Christian fellowship and worship. Mark's mother's home was one such center (12:12). Undoubtedly the home of Mary and Martha in Bethany was another. Jerusalem was not able to hold such a multitude, and many certainly stayed in surrounding villages.

The table fellowship was also very important. They took their food "with glad and sincere hearts." This means there was delight and great joy, and yet a simplicity of heart. Because of the influence of the Holy Spirit[4] there was no jealousy, no criticism, no wrangling, no attempt to outdo each other, just joy and hearts full of praise to God.

5. Continued Growth 2:47

[47]praising God and enjoying the favor of all the people. And the Lord added to their number daily those who were being saved.

We can be sure that the believers' praise found expression also in "psalms, hymns and spiritual songs" with gratitude to God in their hearts (Col. 3:16). The result was that they found favor (were well liked and enjoyed good relations) with the whole of the people of Jerusalem (cf. 4:33; 5:13). Others saw their unity, their devotion to God, their daily worship in the temple, and their love for one another. From Acts 1:8 we can be sure they continually witnessed to others in the power of the Spirit. Thus the Lord kept adding to the Church day by day "those who were being saved."[5] These the Church joyfully accepted, we may be sure.

It should be noted here that no predestination of individuals is intended by the last part of verse 47. The Greek is a simple statement that every day some were being saved and the saved ones were added to the Church. Notice, too, that no great pres-

---

[4]Note how the Book of Acts emphasizes that the Holy Spirit brings joy (8:8,39; 13:48,52; 15:3; 16:34). See also Rom. 14:17; 15:13.

[5]As James D. G. Dunn points out, "Salvation was understood from the beginning as a process, of which conversion, baptism and the gift of the Spirit was only the start." *The Acts of the Apostles* (Valley Forge, Pa.: Trinity Press International, 1996), 37. We are being saved now and the ultimate salvation will be ours when Jesus returns and we receive new immortal and incorruptible bodies.

sure was placed on the people of Jerusalem who were not yet saved. They just saw the joy and the power and they opened their hearts to the Word, the truth about Jesus.

STUDY QUESTIONS

1. What evidences of the work of the Spirit were present in the three thousand who were saved?
2. What gave the believers favor with all the people?
3. What contributed to the increase of the number of believers?

II. MINISTRY IN JERUSALEM 3:1–8:4

A. The Lame Man Healed 3:1–4:31

1. A GIFT OF HEALING 3:1–10

¹One day Peter and John were going up to the temple at the time of prayer—at three in the afternoon.

Luke often makes a general statement and then gives a specific example. Acts 2:43 states that "many wonders and miraculous signs were done by the apostles." Now Luke proceeds to give one example to illustrate this point and at the same time show how the miracle brought both persecution and further growth of the Church. The "terse, factual, and slightly rugged style" of the Greek is like that of Mark's Gospel (who "had his narrative from Peter") and indicates Luke got this account from Peter.[1]

On this occasion Peter and John[2] were going up the temple hill into the temple[3] to join the others for the hour of evening

[1]E. M. Blaiklock, *Acts: The Birth of the Church* (Old Tappan, N.J.: Fleming H. Revell, 1980), 32.

[2]Some suggest that Peter and John were sent together when Jesus sent the apostles out two by two (Mark 6:7). Cf. Acts 8:14; Gal. 2:9. Simon J. Kistemaker, *Exposition of the Acts of the Apostles* (Grand Rapids: Baker Book House, 1990), 120.

[3]Gk. *hieron,* the temple with its courts (*naos* is used of the central sanctuary itself).

prayer, about 3 P.M. ("the ninth hour," KJV).[4] They had not rejected their Jewish roots and Old Testament background. They continued "devotedly serving God in the Temple."[5] The priests regularly offered sacrifice and incense at the hours of prayer (Exod. 29:28–41; Num. 28:2–8; Ps. 141:2).

> [2]Now a man crippled from birth was being carried to the temple gate called Beautiful, where he was put every day to beg from those going into the temple courts. [3]When he saw Peter and John about to enter, he asked them for money.

Between the Court of the Gentiles and the Court of the Women was a beautifully carved Corinthian-style bronze gate with gold and silver inlays. It was worth more than if it had been made of solid gold.[6] Later, tradition connected it to miraculous occurrences.

As Peter and John approached the Beautiful Gate a man crippled from birth confronted them. He was carried and laid outside of it daily to ask for money (alms, a gift of charity). Later we read that the man was over forty years old (4:22). Jesus had passed this way many times, but apparently the man never asked Him for healing. Because he was born crippled he probably never imagined that he could be healed. Possibly also, Jesus, in divine providence and timing, "reserved" this man so that he could become a greater witness when he was healed later.

---

[4]"In contrast to the synagogue, numerous sources depict the Second Temple as a focus for prayer . . . twice daily . . . morning and evening." Daniel K. Falk, "Jewish Prayer Literature and the Jerusalem Church in Acts," in *The Book of Acts in Its Palestinian Setting,* ed. Richard Bauckham, vol. 4 of *The Book of Acts in Its First Century Setting,* ed. Bruce W. Winter (Grand Rapids: Wm. B. Eerdmans, 1995), 267, 285, 296.

[5]Jack T. Sanders, *The Jews in Luke-Acts* (Philadelphia: Fortress Press, 1987), 33.

[6]Most scholars agree that this "Nicanor Gate," east of the Court of the Women, was the Beautiful Gate. The Court of the Gentiles was as far as Gentiles could go. The Court of the Women was as far as women could go. Israelite men could go into the Court of Israel and take part in the offering of the sacrifices (Lev. 1:2–5). See Martin Hengel, "The Geography of Palestine in Acts," in *Acts in Its Palestinian Setting,* ed. Bauckham, 39, 41. For the possibility that it was the Shushan Gate that led into the Court of the Gentiles near Solomon's Colonnade see David John Williams, *Acts* (Peabody, Mass.: Hendrickson Publishers, 1990), 66.

⁴Peter looked straight at him, as did John. Then Peter said, "Look at us!" ⁵So the man gave them his attention, expecting to get something from them.

When this man asked for money, Peter, together with John, fastened his eyes intently on him. What a contrast this is to the jealousy the disciples once showed toward each other (Matt. 20:24). Now they acted together in complete unity of faith and purpose. Then Peter as the spokesman said, "Look at us!" This riveted the man's full attention on them and aroused an expectation that he would receive something.

⁶Then Peter said, "Silver or gold I do not have, but what I have I give you. In the name of Jesus Christ of Nazareth, walk." ⁷Taking him by the right hand, he helped him up, and instantly the man's feet and ankles became strong.

Peter, however, did not do what the man expected. What money he had was probably already given to needy believers.[7] But he did have something better to give. His emphatic statement, "Silver or gold I do not have, but what I have I give you," took faith on Peter's part. He undoubtedly said it under the prompting of the Holy Spirit who had given him a gift of healing for this man (1 Cor. 12:9,11).[8]

As a positive command, Peter then said, "In the name [including the authority] of Jesus Christ of Nazareth, [rise up and] walk."[9] At the same time Peter put his own faith into action by taking hold of the man's right hand and lifting him up. Immediately the man's feet and ankle bones received strength (and the shrunken, useless muscles were made firm). It is quite possible also that the man's faith was stirred at the mention of the name of Jesus the Messiah of Nazareth (see v. 16). To Jews of that day one's name was more than a label. It connoted "both identity and authority," and in Acts the name of Jesus is "the instru-

[7]He did not use religion "as a means of acquiring wealth." James M. Boice, *Acts* (Grand Rapids: Baker Book House, 1997), 65.

[8]See Stanley M. Horton, *What the Bible Says About the Holy Spirit* (Springfield, Mo.: Gospel Publishing House, 1976), 273–74.

[9]A few ancient manuscripts omit "rise up and," so the NIV omits these words; but even these manuscripts clearly imply "rise up," so it is a proper reading.

ment of healing and authority."[10] Perhaps some of the three thousand saved at Pentecost had already witnessed to him. He surely had heard of others healed by Jesus. The ministry, suffering, death, and resurrection of Jesus were well known (see Acts 26:23,26; they were "not done in a corner").

8He jumped to his feet and began to walk. Then he went with them into the temple courts, walking and jumping, and praising God.

When strength came into the man's feet and ankles, Peter no longer had to lift. The man jumped to his feet, stood for a moment, and started walking. Since he was crippled from birth, he had never learned to walk. No act of human will could have accomplished this instantaneous, complete healing.

Now that the man was healed he could go into the temple. Since he had always been laid at the gate of the temple, this would be the first time in his life for him to enter.[11] He went in, walking normally, with Peter and John. Every few steps he would jump for pure joy, shouting God's praises continually (cf. Isa. 35:6a). God had touched him and he could not hold in the joy and praise.

9When all the people saw him walking and praising God, 10they recognized him as the same man who used to sit begging at the temple gate called Beautiful, and they were filled with wonder and amazement at what had happened to him.

Verse 11 indicates the man still held on to Peter's hand and took hold of John's as well. What a scene this must have been as the man came walking and jumping into the temple court, dragging Peter and John along with him.

All the people saw him and recognized him as the man who was born crippled and was always sitting begging for money at the Beautiful Gate. His healing, therefore, filled them with won-

[10]Howard Clark Kee, *To Every Nation Under Heaven: The Acts of the Apostles* (Harrisburg, Pa.: Trinity Press International, 1997), 63.

[11]Lame priests could not enter the temple (Lev. 21:16–18). Some Jews of that day may have applied this to others who were lame. (Cf. Dead Sea Scrolls, 1QSa 2:5–6.)

der (Gk. *thambous,* "astonishment, awe") and amazement (Gk. *ekstaseōs,* "confused, bewildered amazement"). They were in a state of shock.

2. PETER EXALTS JESUS 3:11-26

a. The Prince Of Life 3:11-21

11While the beggar held on to Peter and John, all the people were astonished and came running to them in the place called Solomon's Colonnade.

By this time the healed cripple, still holding the hands of Peter and John, was in Solomon's Colonnade, a roofed portico formed by a double row of white-marble Corinthian columns, fifty feet high, on one side of the temple court (probably the eastern side). From all over the temple courts the greatly amazed people ran together to see the three. There could easily have been ten thousand people in the temple at the hour of prayer.

12When Peter saw this, he said to them: "Men of Israel, why does this surprise you? Why do you stare at us as if by our own power or godliness we had made this man walk?

This was Peter's opportunity, and he was quick to answer the unspoken questions on their wondering faces. His message follows the same general pattern given by the Spirit on the Day of Pentecost, but adapted to this new situation. This time there was no skepticism or ridicule as there had been on the Day of Pentecost.

Addressing them as Israelite men, as was the custom even though women were in the crowd,[12] he asked why they were surprised by this (Gk. *thaumazete epi touto,* "marveled in surprise at this"). The people were staring intently at Peter and John as if the man's ability to walk had its source in the apostles' own power or godliness. But the apostles "never regarded themselves as sources of power but only as channels of power."[13]

---

[12]This was typical in the Mishnah and other Jewish literature.

[13]William Barclay, *The Acts of the Apostles,* 2d ed. (Philadelphia: Westminster Press, 1955), 30.

¹³The God of Abraham, Isaac and Jacob, the God of our fathers, has glorified his servant Jesus. You handed him over to be killed, and you disowned him before Pilate, though he had decided to let him go. ¹⁴You disowned the Holy and Righteous One and asked that a murderer be released to you.

Peter, speaking by the Spirit's gift of prophecy (see Matt. 10:19–20), continually bore witness to Jesus. The one true God that the Scriptures describe as the "God of Abraham, Isaac and Jacob," the God of the ancestors of the Jews (Exod. 3:6,15; cf. Matt. 8:11; 22:32; Mark 12:26–27; Luke 20:37–38; Acts 7:32; 22:14), had glorified His Servant[14] Jesus. Peter was not preaching a new religion but the fulfillment of the one God had revealed from Abraham's time on.

Again he reminds them that they were responsible for arresting Jesus and disowning Him before Pilate, even when Pilate had decided to release Him (Luke 23:16,22). The One they knew and disowned is "the Holy and Righteous One." Again, this is a reference to the Suffering Servant in Isaiah (53:11; cf. Jer. 23:5; 33:15; Zech. 9:9), a major apostolic emphasis. But they turned from Him so completely that they asked for a murderer to be released to them instead. (See Luke 23:18–19,25; cf. Matt. 27:20; Mark 15:7; John 18:40).

¹⁵You killed the author of life, but God raised him from the dead. We are witnesses of this.

They were guilty of killing the author[15] of life. What a con-

---

[14]The Gk. word here (*paida*) may mean "servant" or "child," but it is never used of Jesus when the emphasis is on His divine sonship. Here Peter's words undoubtedly identify Jesus with the Suffering Servant of Isa. 52:13 through 53:12. The Servant of the Lord is the one who does the Lord's work. This healing was the result of the fulfillment of Isaiah's prophecy. That prophecy spoke of the sufferings of Jesus in our behalf. See P. C. H. Lenski, *The Interpretation of the Acts of the Apostles* (Columbus, Ohio: Wartburg Press, 1940), 133; Everett F. Harrison, *Acts: The Expanding Church* (Chicago: Moody Press, 1975), 72–73; Ralph Earle, *The Acts of the Apostles* (Kansas City, Mo.: Beacon Hill Press, 1965), 293; Kistemaker, *Acts*, 128–29.

[15]Gk. *archēgon*, "originator, author, founder, leader, prince." The same word is used in Heb. 2:10 and 12:2. He is "the Davidic crown prince of life" and salvation. William J. Larkin, Jr., *Acts* (Downers Grove, Ill.: InterVarsity Press, 1995), 67.

trast! They gave death to the One who gave them life. "Author" speaks of Jesus' part in creation. As John 1:3 says of Jesus, the living Word, "Through him all things were made; without him [apart from Him] nothing was made that has been made." In other words, the preincarnate Jesus was the living Word who spoke the worlds into existence. Through Him God breathed life into the man He had formed from moist dust of the earth (Gen. 2:7). This Jesus, the very source of life, the giver also of eternal life (John 10:28), and therefore of healing, they had killed. But God raised Him from the dead. Peter and John were witnesses to this. The man's healing was also a witness that Jesus is alive.

> **[16]By faith in the name of Jesus, this man whom you see and know was made strong. It is Jesus' name and the faith that comes through him that has given this complete healing to him, as you can all see.**

Notice the repetition of "the name" of Jesus in this verse. "By faith" (on the ground of faith, on the basis of faith) in His name this man was made strong. The crowd saw the man. They knew the man. They had seen his shriveled feet and ankles many times before. Now they saw them firm and strong. Jesus' name made him strong. The man's faith that came through Jesus gave him this complete healing, this freedom from all bodily defect, in the presence of them all.[16]

"The name," of course, refers to the character and nature of Jesus as the Healer, the great Physician. The healing came on the ground of faith in Jesus for what He is. But it was not their faith as such that brought the healing. It was the Name,[17] that is, the fact that Jesus is true to His nature and character. He is the Healer. Faith did have a great part, of course, but it was the faith that was "through him [Jesus]." The faith Jesus himself had imparted (not only to Peter and John, but also to the man) gave complete freedom from defect before their very eyes.[18] Jesus had

---

[16]It is also possible that the apostles' faith is meant here, and that the healing caused the man to put his faith in Jesus.

[17]"Name" in the Bible often means one's nature and character.

[18]Gk. *holoklērian,* "complete freedom from defect," is the same term used of the freedom from defect necessary for animals used in sacrifices.

healed cripples during His ministry. He was still healing cripples through His followers.

17"Now, brothers, I know that you acted in ignorance, as did your leaders. 18But this is how God fulfilled what he had foretold through all the prophets, saying that his Christ would suffer.

Peter calls them "brothers" in the sense of fellow Jews. Then he adds that he knew that through ignorance they and their leaders killed Jesus. As Jesus himself said on the cross, "'Father, forgive them, for they do not know what they are doing'" (Luke 23:34). Paul later confessed that he had persecuted the Church because of his own ignorance and unbelief (1 Tim. 1:13). This implies that they did not really know Jesus is the Messiah, nor did they know He is God's Son. This ignorance did not lessen their guilt. Yet even in the Old Testament forgiveness was always available for sins done in ignorance (Num. 15:22–29).[19]

The sufferings and death of Jesus also fulfilled the prophecies God had revealed through all the prophets, that is, through the body of prophets as a whole. Their message, taken as a whole, had for a focal point the rejection and death of Christ. Even so, this did not lessen the guilt of the Jerusalemites either.

19Repent, then, and turn to God, so that your sins may be wiped out, that times of refreshing may come from the Lord, 20and that he may send the Christ, who has been appointed for you—even Jesus. 21He must remain in heaven until the time comes for God to restore everything, as he promised long ago through his holy prophets.

As on the Day of Pentecost, Peter then called on them to repent, that is, to change their minds and attitudes about their sin and about Jesus. There was still hope for them. Let them renounce their old ways and "turn" (Gk. *epistrepsato*, "turn back, return") to God so that their sins might be "wiped out," obliterated, in order that "times" (seasons, occasions) of refreshing "from the Lord" (from the face, that is, the presence of the Lord)

[19]Some theologians today claim that when the Jews had Jesus crucified, God cut them off forever so that they have no more place in His plan. But the Bible says, "God did not reject his people, whom he foreknew" (Rom. 11:2).

might come. And to you who repent, the Lord (God the Father) will send the "appointed for you" Messiah, Jesus. Jesus was God's choice to be Israel's anointed Prophet, Priest, and King. He alone is the true Messiah, the true Christ.

There will, however, be a delay. Jesus must stay in heaven until the time of restoration (reestablishment) of everything that God promised, speaking through His holy (dedicated, consecrated) prophets. "Long ago" (Gk. *ap' aiōnos*) is a paraphrase that means "from earliest times," or "from ages long past." The sense is "all the prophets ever since there were prophets."

From this passage we see that repentance and a radical turning to God bring not only obliteration of sins but "times of refreshing" (v. 19) from the Lord. Nor do we have to wait until Jesus comes back before we can enjoy these seasons of revival and blessing. We can have such times now, and as the Greek especially indicates, we can have them until Jesus comes back to earth again.

Too many writers put all their emphasis on the warnings of terrible times to come, times hard to live in, and the statement that there will be a rebellion, or "falling away" (2 Thess. 2:3, KJV; cf. 2 Tim. 3:1). These things will come. The "falling away" may mean spiritual falling away from Christ and from the truth of the gospel, though the Greek word *(apostasia)* ordinarily means revolt or revolution and war (possibly referred to in Ezek. 38 and 39). Though these warnings are necessary, Christians do not need to make this the focus of their attention. Repentance (a change of mind and attitude) and a turning to God will still bring times of refreshing from the presence of God. The day of spiritual blessing, the day of miracles, the day of revival, is not past. In the midst of terrible times we can still get our eyes on the Lord and receive mighty, refreshing outpourings of the Holy Spirit.[20]

The time of restoration refers to the coming age, the Millennium, when God will restore and renew, and Jesus will

[20]See Wayne Grudem, "Should Christians Expect Miracles Today?" part 1, *Pneuma Review* 3, no. 1 (winter 2000): 48. He points out that "the New Testament encourages miraculous answers to prayer. . . . See also the entire pattern of gospel proclamation in the evangelism carried on in Acts: 3:6,12ff.; 4:29,30; 5:12–16,20,21,28,42; 6:8,10; 8:4–7,12; 9:17,18[cf. 22:13],34,35; 14:3,8–10,15ff.; 15:12,36; 18:5,11[cf. 1 Cor. 2:4–5; 2 Cor. 2:12]; 19:8–12; cf. Heb. 2:4; James 5:13–18."

reign personally on the earth. The prophesied restoration includes a further outpouring of the Spirit on the restored kingdom.

Some writers take "restore everything" (v. 21) out of context and try to make the phrase assert that even Satan and all those in the lake of fire will ultimately be saved. But "everything" must be taken with God's promise through the prophets. Only those things prophesied will be restored.[21]

The prophets also show that the Kingdom must be brought in through judgment. Daniel 2:34–35,44–45 describes an image that represents the whole world system from Babylon to the end of the age. Not until it is hit in the feet (in the last days of this age) will the present world system be destroyed and crushed to powder. Even the good in the present world system will have to be destroyed to make way for the better things of the coming millennial kingdom—which will fill the earth after Jesus comes again in power and glory.

We do not know when that will be. But, most importantly, we do not have to wait for the future kingdom before we experience God's blessings and power. The Holy Spirit brings us a deposit (Gk. *arrabōna,* "first installment," NLT) guaranteeing that we shall receive more of the same blessings when Jesus comes (2 Cor. 1:22; 5:5; Eph. 1:14). And we can have these promised times of refreshing even now if we fulfill the conditions of repentance and turning to God. It is implied also that repentance speeds the Lord's return (see 2 Pet. 3:12).[22]

b. A Prophet Like Moses 3:22–26

[22]For Moses said, 'The Lord your God will raise up for you a prophet like me from among your own people; you must listen to everything he tells you. [23]Anyone who does not listen to him will be completely cut off from among his people.'

Peter next goes back to Moses to show that God's saving purpose and plan of redemption for Israel and the Gentiles would be fulfilled in Jesus. He quotes the promise that God would raise

[21]Stanley M. Horton, *Our Destiny: Biblical Teachings on the Last Things* (Springfield, Mo.: Logion Press, 1996), 238.

[22]Kistemaker, *Acts,* 135.

up a prophet like Moses (Deut. 18:15–16,18–19; see also Lev. 26:12; Acts 7:37). The people had this promise in mind also when they asked John the Baptist if he were "'the Prophet'" (John 1:21,25). Some writers believe the Deuteronomy passage calls for a partial fulfillment in Joshua ("'a man in whom is the spirit,'" Num. 27:18), Samuel, and the rest of the line of Old Testament prophets. But it had its complete fulfillment in Jesus.[23]

In what way was Jesus like Moses? God used Moses to bring in the old covenant; Jesus brought in the new covenant. Moses led the nation of Israel out of Egypt and brought them to Mount Sinai where God brought them to himself—into a covenant relation with himself (Exod. 19:4–5). Jesus, by shedding His blood, became the new and living (resurrected) way whereby we can enter into the very holiest presence of God (Heb. 10:19–20). Moses gave Israel the command to sacrifice a lamb; Jesus is himself the Lamb of God. God used Moses to perform great miracles and signs. Jesus performed many more miracles and signs—but most of His were signs of love rather than of judgment. (See Heb. 3:3–6, which proclaims the superiority of Christ to Moses.)

Since Jesus is the Prophet whom Moses promised, the people must listen and obey—or suffer the consequences: They will be cut off from the true Israel.

24"Indeed, all the prophets from Samuel on, as many as have spoken, have foretold these days.

Samuel was the next great prophet after Moses (1 Sam. 3:20). From that time on, all the prophets "foretold these days," that is, the days of God's work through Christ. Some may not have given specific prophecies in their writings, but all of them gave prophecies that led up to or prepared for these days.

25And you are heirs of the prophets and of the covenant God made with your fathers. He said to Abraham, 'Through your offspring all peoples on earth will be blessed.'

The Jews Peter was addressing were the literal descendants of the prophets. They were heirs also of the Abrahamic covenant

---

[23]See Earle, *Acts of the Apostles*, 296.

with its promise that in and through Abraham's "offspring"[24] (Christ) all the families of the earth will be blessed (Gen. 22:18; Gal. 3:16). The promised blessing is for all nations.

> **26When God raised up his servant, he sent him first to you to bless you by turning each of you from your wicked ways."**

The blessing brought by God's Suffering Servant (Isa. 53) and promised to all the families of the earth (Gen. 12:3) came first to these Jews in Jerusalem. What a privilege! Yet this was not favoritism on God's part. It was their opportunity to receive the Abrahamic blessing by repenting and by letting Him turn them away from their "wicked ways" (their evil or malicious acts). They needed salvation—and salvation includes forgiveness, blessing, and righteousness. God wanted their lifestyle to be different from the world's lifestyle (2:40). Receiving the blessing is also an opportunity for service.

Actually, someone had to be first to carry the message. (See Rom. 1:16; 2:9–10; 3:1–2.) Paul always went to the Jew first because they had the knowledge of God through His dealings with them and through His Word (which included the promise of the coming Messiah). But they could not carry the message of the blessing to others without first repenting and experiencing the blessing for themselves. God had prepared the Jews for this. All the first evangelists[25] (spreaders of the good news) were Jews. They were the first to begin to fulfill the Great Commission by making disciples (Matt. 28:19). But the word "first" implies that the blessing should be carried to others besides Jews. Peter speaking by the Spirit said more than he fully understood, as chapter 10 shows.

3. Peter And John Arrested 4:1–4

1The priests and the captain of the temple guard and the Sadducees came up to Peter and John while they were speaking to the people. 2They were greatly disturbed

---

[24]The Gk. term translated "offspring" is singular.

[25]"Evangelist" is the transliteration of the Gk. *euangelistēs,* a spreader of the *euangelion* (the "good news," the "gospel").

because the apostles were teaching the people and proclaiming in Jesus the resurrection of the dead.

While Peter and John were still speaking,[26] the priests (chief
priests), the captain (the priest next in rank to the high priest)
who commanded the temple guard of chosen Levites, and a
group of their Sadducee supporters came upon them suddenly
and unexpectedly. As verse 3 indicates, it was now evening
(about sundown), and since the miracle took place about 3 P.M.,
Peter and John had continued to talk to the crowd about three
hours. Undoubtedly they explained the full gospel further and
probably had time to answer questions from the crowd.

The high priest was a Sadducee, as were many of the priests in
Jerusalem. They claimed to be religious but did not accept the
traditions of the Pharisees and did not consider the Old
Testament prophetical books or the Writings (the third division
of the Hebrew canon) to be on the same level as the Law (the
Torah, the Pentateuch).[27] They also denied the existence of
angels and spirits and said there was no resurrection (Matt.
22:23; Luke 20:27; Acts 23:8).[28]

They were not excited about the miracle, but they were disturbed because there was such a great crowd around Peter and
John. Then they were "greatly disturbed" (upset, deeply
annoyed, exasperated) because the apostles proclaimed in Jesus
"the resurrection of [out from among] the dead." As James D. G.
Dunn points out, "Jesus is the defining centre of the new movement; and . . . his resurrection is the key point of emphasis and
differentiation in its preaching (cf. 4:33)."[29]

**3They seized Peter and John, and because it was evening,
they put them in jail until the next day. 4But many who
heard the message believed, and the number of men
grew to about five thousand.**

[26]The verb "speaking" is a plural participle indicating continuous action. It
shows also that John did some speaking and that more was said than Luke had
space to record; see Harrison, *Acts,* 79.

[27]Ibid., 80. See Josephus *Antiquities* 13.10.6.

[28]See Josephus *Antiquities* 18.1.3.

[29]James D. G. Dunn, *The Acts of the Apostles* (Valley Forge, Pa.: Trinity Press
International, 1996), 50.

Peter was preaching a resurrected Jesus, and the Sadducees understood that this was evidence for the truth of the resurrection of all believers. Because this teaching was against their doctrine, the Sadducees felt they could not tolerate it.

They therefore "seized Peter and John" (arrested them) and threw them in jail overnight. "It was evening," too late to call the Sanhedrin together.[30] But it was too late, also, to stop the gospel from having its effect.[31] "Many who heard the message believed." We can be sure they were soon baptized in water (probably the next day) as well as in the Holy Spirit. The number is given as "about five thousand" men. The Greek may be translated "*became* about five thousand," so some take this to mean the total number of believers was now up to five thousand. But the way it is stated here indicates the number was so large that they counted only men (Gk. *andrōn,* "men, males"). There must have been a large number of women and children who believed also. Acts 3:9 says all the people saw the crippled man, and 4:1–2 indicates they were teaching all the people, both men and women.

It is clear that though the officials were now hostile toward what the apostles were doing, the apostles were still held in high esteem by the people. It is also clear that the gospel kept spreading among the Jews and the number of Jewish believers kept growing. It would eventually become the "myriads" of Acts 21:20 (NKJV).

4. Peter And John Brought To Trial 4:5–12

⁵The next day the rulers, elders and teachers of the law met in Jerusalem. ⁶Annas the high priest was there, and so were Caiaphas, John, Alexander and the other men of the high priest's family.

The next day the "rulers" (the executives or official members of the Sanhedrin, the Jewish Senate and Supreme Court)[32] with the "elders and teachers of the law" (experts in the interpretation

---

[30]Pharisaic law called night meetings illegal.

[31]Cf. 2 Tim. 2:9.

[32]The Sanhedrin was also called the *Gerousia* (Assembly, Senate; see 5:21) and the *Presbuterion* (the Body of Elders; see 22:5). The high priest was always its president and it consisted of seventy other members.

of the law of Moses; professional teachers of the Law)[33] who were in Jerusalem assembled. With them came, specifically, Annas, Caiaphas, John, Alexander, and all the rest of the relatives of the high priest who happened to be in the city. This was probably not an official meeting of the Sanhedrin, but "may simply have been a rather *ad hoc* gathering instigated by the family of Annas."[34]

Annas here is called the high priest. He was officially high priest from A.D. 6–15. Then his son Jonathan[35] was appointed for about three years. Next Caiaphas, the son-in-law of Annas, was made the official high priest (A.D. 18–36). But Annas remained the power behind the position and kept his honorary title. The people did not accept his deposition by the Romans and still considered him to be the true high priest. In the Old Testament, Aaron and each of his successors was made high priest for life. The Law made no provision for the secular governors to change this. Consequently, Jesus was taken to Annas's house first (John 18:13), then to Caiaphas (who probably occupied a portion of the same building around the same courtyard). Annas and Caiaphas, along with some of the rest of the relatives of Annas, formed something of a "closed corporation" that ran the temple and controlled its vast income and wealth.

John here may have been Jonathan the son of Annas.[36] Alexander was probably one of the leading Sadducees.

7They had Peter and John brought before them and began to question them: "By what power or what name did you do this?"

They made Peter and John stand in the midst of the assembled court, which was basically the same one that convicted Jesus. (Their meeting place, according to Josephus, was just west of the temple area.)[37] Then they began their inquiry by asking them, "By what [sort of] power [*dunamis,* "mighty power"] or

---

[33]According to Josephus, these teachers were all Pharisees; cf. Acts 23:6.

[34]Dunn, *Acts of the Apostles,* 52.

[35]"The Lord has given."

[36]Codex Bezae (D) has "Jonathan" instead of "John" here. Others take this John to be Johanan ben Zaccai who became the president of the Great Synagogue after A.D. 70, but this is not a likely identification.

[37]Josephus *Wars of the Jews* 5.4.2.

what name ["authority"] did you [plural, emphatic] do this?"

"What" (power, name) is used here in a derogatory way. The emphasis on "you" shows contempt.[38] They were trying to awe the disciples or even scare them. Perhaps they remembered how the disciples had fled in fear when Jesus was arrested. Verse 13 shows the reason for the Sanhedrin's contempt—the disciples were "unschooled, ordinary men," not educated in their schools.

> [8]**Then Peter, filled with the Holy Spirit, said to them: "Rulers and elders of the people!**

Peter had indeed once cringed before a girl in the courtyard when this same group was gathered around Jesus. Now there was a difference. Peter, as he began to speak, was filled with the Holy Spirit. The form of the Greek verb here indicates a new, fresh filling.[39] This does not mean he had lost any of the power and presence of the Spirit he received on the Day of Pentecost. In view of the pressures of this critical situation, the Lord simply enlarged his capacity and gave him this fresh filling to meet this new need for power to witness.

We can see here also a practical application of Jesus' instructions and promise given in Matthew 10:19–20; Mark 13:9–11; and Luke 12:11–12; 21:12–15. They were not to worry or take any advance thought of what they should speak. The Spirit of their Heavenly Father would speak in (and by) them. Thus instead of trying to defend themselves, the Spirit would make their words a witness. We may be sure Peter and John had slept well the night before and awoke refreshed.

Peter, filled anew with the Spirit and sensing His presence in a powerful way, did not let the Jewish leaders frighten him. As Paul told Timothy (2 Tim. 1:7), God has not given us a spirit of timidity (cowardly fear), but "of power, of love, and of self-discipline." Politely, Peter addressed them as "rulers [official members of the Sanhedrin] and elders."

---

[38]Larkin, *Acts,* 72.

[39]Gk. aorist. See J. A. Alexander, *A Commentary on the Acts of the Apostles,* 3d ed. (1875; reprint, London: Banner of Truth Trust, 1956), 1:137; H. B. Hackett, *A Commentary on the Acts of the Apostles* (Philadelphia: American Baptist Publication Society, 1882), 30; Earle, *Acts of the Apostles,* 300.

⁹If we are being called to account today for an act of kindness shown to a cripple and are asked how he was healed, ¹⁰then know this, you and all the people of Israel: It is by the name of Jesus Christ of Nazareth, whom you crucified but whom God raised from the dead, that this man stands before you healed.

Then, in a dignified way, he told them that if they were making a judicial examination concerning the good deed done for a weak human being, by what means the man had been (and still was) "healed" (saved, restored),[40] then Peter had the answer.

Peter proclaimed that by the name of Jesus—whom they crucified ("you" is plural) and whom God raised from the dead—by Him this man stood before them restored to health. What a contrast Peter makes between what these leaders did to Jesus and what God did through Him! Notice also how he emphasizes the significant name of Jesus, not only here but also throughout this response.

¹¹He is "'the stone you builders rejected, which has become the capstone.'

Then Peter quoted a passage that most of these same chief priests and elders had heard from Jesus himself. On one occasion they had challenged Jesus' authority to teach. He gave them parables and then quoted Psalm 118:22. (See Matt. 21:23,42,45; 1 Pet. 2:7.)[41] Peter, however, makes it personal. "This one [emphatic] is 'the stone treated with contempt [ignored, despised, scorned] by you [plural] the builders, who has become the head of the corner'" (my translation). He became "the capstone"[42] because He is exalted to the Father's right hand (2:33; 5:31). God had accomplished His purpose in spite of their opposition.

---

[40]Usually translated "saved," the Gk. *sesōstai* ("has been [and still is] healed") also includes the ideas of saving from danger, disease, illness, sin, and sin's effects.

[41]Since Ps. 118 is set in the temple, these words challenged "those who regarded the temple as their personal prerogative and power base." Clare Amos, "Acts," in *Sowers and Reapers,* ed. John Parr (Nashville: Abingdon Press, 1994), 399.

[42]Some take it to be the "stone at the base of the corner where two walls meet and take their line from it." Larkin, *Acts,* 74. Others take it to be the keystone or capstone above the door or the one at the top joining the two sides of an arch. Either interpretation shows Jesus is essential to all of God the Father's purposes.

¹²Salvation is found in no one else, for there is no other name under heaven given to men by which we must be saved."

Then Peter explains what this means: There is no salvation in anyone else (the salvation which they hoped to be brought by the Messiah is not in anyone other than Jesus), "for there is no other name under heaven given to men [human beings] by which we must be saved."[43] "Must"(Gk. *dei*) is an emphatic word indicating compelling necessity. If we do not find salvation through the name (Person) of Jesus, we shall never find it. Nowhere in the entire world is there another Savior—there never has been and never will be.

The healing of the lame man thus witnessed to Jesus as the only Savior. The Jewish leaders could see no use in Jesus; yet God had made Him of unique and supreme value. In Him, as Isaiah chapter 53 also shows, is (the promised) salvation. There is only one salvation, only one way (Heb. 10:12–22). Jesus said, "'I am the way. . . . No one comes to the Father except through me'" (John 14:6). There will never be another Messiah sent from God, or another Savior.

Many have claimed to be Messiahs or Saviors; many have presented other ways of salvation. The Sanhedrin also claimed to declare the good works that would help the Jews to obtain salvation. However, Peter considers all other "ways" to salvation as having no value when compared to our Lord Jesus Christ. We have only one choice when we face the claims of Christ: We can accept or reject. Other ways which may seem right can only lead to destruction (Prov. 14:12; Matt. 7:13).

It is not popular to be so exclusive. Most unbelievers who are not atheists want to think that there are many ways to find God. Some cults, the Baha'i, for example, even try to combine what they suppose is the good in various religions.[44] But all this is in vain. God has rejected all other ways. In Christ alone is hope. It is this that places the heavy responsibility of the Great Com-

---

[43]A few ancient manuscripts have "you" instead of "we."

[44]I heard the rabbi of our local Reform Jewish community say, "All religions are just different paths going up the same mountain." Liberal theologians would agree.

mission upon us. If there were any other way of salvation, we could afford to take it easy. But there is no hope for anyone apart from the salvation through Christ.[45] This may sound intolerant. "But it is also true."[46] Only through Him can we enter into the inheritance and glory God has promised to those who love Him.

5. PETER AND JOHN SPEAK BOLDLY 4:13–22

13When they saw the courage of Peter and John and realized that they were unschooled, ordinary men, they were astonished and they took note that these men had been with Jesus.

The priests and elders were "astonished" (marveled, wondered) when they saw the "courage" (Gk. *parrēsian,* confident openness and freedom in speech) of Peter and John; they perceived they were "unschooled," not having attended a rabbinical school[47] or having sat under a great rabbi like Gamaliel,[48] and were "ordinary men," nonprofessionals, laymen, amateurs. This does not mean they were totally unschooled. They had gone to the synagogue schools in their hometowns, but they were not professional teachers or trained speakers like the scribes and lawyers. Ordinary laymen did not speak with authority like this.

It must have been hard for Peter and John to face such snobbishness. But the key to their courage and freedom in speaking was not their own talent or ability. It was, of course, the new fresh filling with the Spirit (as in 4:31). He gave them the words to say.

Then something else struck these Jewish leaders. The phrase "took note" does not mean they inquired further of them. Rather, the Greek simply means they gradually recognized that they "had been with Jesus" (cf. NASB). Perhaps the words of Peter jogged their memory of what Jesus had said (see v. 11). As they thought about their confrontation with Jesus, they remembered He had had disciples with Him. Now they recog-

---

[45]Even in the OT one of the things the prophets condemn most strongly is the worship of the Lord *plus* other gods.

[46]Boice, *Acts,* 78.

[47]The word "unschooled" (Gk. *agrammatoi*) sometimes means illiterate, but scholars agree that this is not the meaning here. See F. F. Bruce, *Commentary on the Book of Acts* (Grand Rapids: Wm. B. Eerdmans, 1954), 122.

[48]"My reward is God."

nized Peter and John as having been among them.

The Jewish leaders must have been shocked, for they had believed they would be rid of Jesus by crucifying Him. Jesus had spoken with authority; and now His disciples, trained by Him, spoke with that same authority. Jesus had done miracles as signs; now His disciples were doing the same. Their use of the name of Jesus was not just repeating a formula. They had known Him personally. Jesus had commissioned them and was with them as He had promised (Matt. 28:20). Later, the sons of Sceva found that simply repeating a formula does not work (Acts 19:13–17).

14But since they could see the man who had been healed standing there with them, there was nothing they could say.

Now the elders were confronted with something else. The man who was healed was standing erect and strong with Peter and John.[49] Suddenly, the priests and elders had nothing else to say. What could they say against such a miracle? (Cf. Luke 21:15.)

15So they ordered them to withdraw from the Sanhedrin and then conferred together. 16"What are we going to do with these men?" they asked. "Everybody living in Jerusalem knows they have done an outstanding miracle, and we cannot deny it.

The leaders then commanded Peter and John to go out of the room where the Sanhedrin was meeting. The Sanhedrin then engaged in a discussion among themselves.[50] They did not know what to do with Peter and John. They could not deny that "an outstanding miracle" (Gk. *gnōston sēmeion*, a known supernatural sign) had been done by (through) them, visible to all the inhabitants of Jerusalem.[51]

---

[49]Some believe this man was arrested also and brought in with Peter and John. Others believe he was let go and came back in the morning to observe the questioning. The man himself was not questioned, nor does he speak. Thus, the latter is probable. The man himself was not on trial.

[50]Emil Schürer, *A History of the Jewish People in the Time of Jesus Christ* (Edinburgh: T & T Clarke, 1885), 2:i, 193–94, cited by Earle, *Acts of the Apostles,* 303, suggests that Saul (Paul) was in this session of the Sanhedrin and later told Luke what was said behind the scenes here.

[51]The number of graves and other sources indicate a resident population of about 120,000 in Jerusalem. Wolfgang Reinhardt, "The Population Size of

This could imply that they did not deny the resurrection of Jesus. The thing that bothered them was the fact that the apostles were using it to teach a future resurrection for all believers. In order to avoid this problem earlier, they had bribed the soldiers to say the body of Jesus had been stolen (Matt. 28:12–13). Some, even today, contend that the women and the disciples looked in the wrong tomb. But the women paid special attention to where Jesus was laid (Luke 23:55).

Actually, these Jewish leaders were neither stupid nor unsophisticated. They knew how difficult it is to get rid of a body and, so, would have made an intensive search for the body if they had not known He was risen from the dead. But it takes more than mere knowledge, or a mental acceptance, of the truth of Christ's resurrection for a person to be saved (Rom. 10:9–10).

17But to stop this thing from spreading any further among the people, we must warn these men to speak no longer to anyone in this name." 18Then they called them in again and commanded them not to speak or teach at all in the name of Jesus.

Even though they had no logical reply to Peter and John, the Sanhedrin did not return a verdict in line with the facts of the case. Instead, they sidestepped their responsibility and decided the best course was to suppress the disciples' teaching about Jesus and the resurrection—which the Sanhedrin contemptuously called "this thing." They knew they could not bribe the disciples. They would therefore threaten them to speak no longer "in [on the ground of, by the authority of] this name" to anyone. By this the Sanhedrin recognized that the name of Jesus included the message of the gospel.[52]

When they called Peter and John back into the room, they tried to use their own authority to impress the apostles and commanded them "not to speak [open their mouth, utter a word] or teach at all in [or concerning] the name of Jesus." This probably implied that they were also not to use the name of Jesus in healing the sick.

Jerusalem and the Numerical Growth of the Church," in *Acts in Its Palestinian Setting,* ed. Bauckham, 237.

[52]Kistemaker, *Acts,* 159.

¹⁹But Peter and John replied, "Judge for yourselves whether it is right in God's sight to obey you rather than God. ²⁰For we cannot help speaking about what we have seen and heard."

But these threats did not intimidate the two apostles. Calmly and courteously, but very firmly, they put the responsibility back on the Jewish leaders to "judge" (or decide) whether it was right before God to listen to them rather than to Him. Then Peter and John boldly declared that they were not able to stop talking about what they had "seen and heard." They were not hearsay witnesses. They were firsthand witnesses (see 1 John 1:1,3). As He had for Jeremiah, the Holy Spirit made the truth like a fire in their hearts and within their bones, so they could not stop (Jer. 20:9; cf. Amos 3:8). Because they were filled with the Spirit, they were fulfilling Jesus' command to be His witnesses (Acts 1:8). As Turner points out, "The Spirit is the God who cannot be gagged."[53]

²¹After further threats they let them go. They could not decide how to punish them, because all the people were praising God for what had happened. ²²For the man who was miraculously healed[54] was over forty years old.

The Sanhedrin members wanted to find some way to punish Peter and John. The implication is that they did try to find some punishable offense, but they could not because of the people: Everyone kept glorifying God for what was done, especially since this man who was born crippled was now "over forty years old."[54] Therefore, they simply added more threats to their previous warning and let them go.

This was a big mistake on their part, for it let the people know God could deliver from the Sanhedrin. It illustrated that the Jewish leaders had no case against these apostles, nor did they have any way to refute their message. However, the Jewish elders, chief priests, and teachers of the Law who rejected Jesus (Luke

---

[53]Max Turner, *Power From on High: The Spirit in Israel's Restoration and Witness in Luke-Acts* (Sheffield, England: Sheffield Academic Press, 1996), 439.

[54]"The man who was miraculously healed" is literally "the man on whom this sign of healing had taken place." The healing was a sign showing that the apostles were indeed continuing what Jesus did and taught (see Acts 1:1 and comments).

9:22) remained "uniformly hostile" to the followers of Jesus.[55]

6. PETER AND JOHN RETURN TO ASSEMBLED BELIEVERS 4:23-31

a. Praying For Boldness And Miracles 4:23-30

23On their release, Peter and John went back to their own people and reported all that the chief priests and elders had said to them.

As soon as they were released, Peter and John "went back to their own people," the assembled believers who most certainly had gathered to pray for them.[56] The Early Church was a close-knit body. When one of their members was in trouble or having difficulty they did more than say a brief prayer. They learned on the Day of Pentecost that the Holy Spirit works powerfully through a body of believers who are in one accord in one place. So Peter and John reported all the high priest and elders had said to them, holding nothing back.

24When they heard this, they raised their voices together in prayer to God. "Sovereign Lord," they said, "you made the heaven and the earth and the sea, and everything in them.

The threats of the Sanhedrin did not scare the believers. No one groaned or complained. Instead they responded immediately by raising "their voices" ("voice" is actually singular, indicating they prayed in unison) in one accord, with one purpose, praying to God. Probably the prayer the Bible records here was given, however, by one of them who became the spokesman for them all.

We can learn much from this prayer. First, as in the case of most prayers in the Bible, they recognized who God is. They

[55]Sanders, *Jews in Luke-Acts,* 19.

[56]Since the believers numbered over 5,000 men, "their own people" may mean the 120 who gathered in the Upper Room; see Kistemaker, *Acts,* 165. Stronstad, however, points out that the believers were still meeting in Solomon's Colonnade (Acts 5:12) and the entire body of believers were filled with the Spirit and prophesied—speaking the Word of God boldly. Roger Stronstad, *The Prophethood of All Believers: A Study in Luke's Charismatic Theology* (Sheffield, England: Sheffield Academic Press, 1999), 74.

addressed Him as *Despota* (Gk.), a different word from that translated "Lord" in most other Bible passages, this one meaning "Master" (CEV, JB), "Owner," "Sovereign Lord" (NEB, NIV). Then they recognized that He alone is God, the Creator of the universe and all that is in it. He therefore has all power and authority.

> [25]You spoke by the Holy Spirit through the mouth of your servant, our father David: "'Why do the nations rage and the peoples plot in vain? [26]The kings of the earth take their stand and the rulers gather together against the Lord and against his Anointed One.'

Second, they based their petition on the inspired Word of God, "spoke by the Holy Spirit" through the mouth of David. Again, most of the prayers of the Bible are based on the Word of God already given. In Psalm 2:1–2[57] they saw a word from the Lord that was fulfilled in the opposition of these Jewish leaders. The Psalm speaks of the "nations" (the Gentiles) raging, and the "peoples" plotting (planning, devising and pursuing) "in vain": It is empty, "foolish" (CEV), ineffective.[58] The kings of the earth and their rulers who gather together against the Lord and His Christ (His Messiah, His Anointed One) are also Gentiles. Thus, this prayer inspired by the Spirit recognized that the Jewish leaders were in the same class as the outside nations who were always raging, always conspiring, against God and against Jesus. There is precedent for this in the Old Testament prophets who sometimes used the word *goi* for Israel when Israel would turn from God (e.g. Isa. 1:4; Ezek. 2:3; Mal. 3:9).

> [27]Indeed Herod and Pontius Pilate met together with the Gentiles and the people of Israel in this city to conspire against your holy[59] servant Jesus, whom you anointed. [28]They did what your power and will had decided beforehand should happen.

The believers recognized that what was happening was not strange. Nor was it a temporary outbreak of hostility. Rather,

[57]From the LXX.

[58]"Vain" is emphatic. All the plotting against God and Christ is futile.

[59]"Holy" (separated to God and His service) emphasizes Christ's consecration and dedication to the work His Father gave Him to do. See John 10:36; 17:4,18,19; see also Isa. 53.

they were seeing an expression of the continued hostility against God, Christ, and God's kingdom that has marked the world since Adam's fall. Just as the nations rage (Ps. 2), Herod (Herod Antipas), Pilate, the Gentiles, and the people (lit. "peoples") of Israel truly were gathered together (in a hostile way) against God's "holy servant Jesus." As before, "servant" here means the dedicated, consecrated Servant of the Lord (as in Isa. 52:13 through 53:12). Yet they could do only what God's "power" (Gk. *cheir*, "hand," meaning active power) and God's "will" (Gk. *boulē*, "purpose, plan") had "decided beforehand" to be done. They were, however, responsible for their deeds, for they had chosen freely to do them.

Third, the believers based their petition on what God did through Jesus. God's hand was in control when He permitted the death of Jesus; Jesus was indeed God's Servant who accomplished God's will in their behalf (cf. 2:23). They could come to God on the basis of what was fully accomplished through Jesus' death and resurrection (1 Cor. 1:23–24; 3:11; 2 Cor. 1:20).

29Now, Lord, consider their threats and enable your servants to speak your word with great boldness.

The Jewish authorities' threats and plots against Jesus were now being turned on the apostles. Their petition was that the Lord would now look on the threats of the Sanhedrin and give His servants (Gk. *doulois*, "slaves") opportunities to keep on speaking His Word "with great boldness" (Gk. *parrēsias;* see v. 13). They probably felt less confident now, after they left the courtroom, than while they were in it, and felt they needed renewed courage. Even after a spiritual victory, Satan may suggest to us that we are fools; so we must pray for continued boldness. Abraham, too, became afraid during the night after boldly testifying before the king of Sodom; God came to reassure and comfort him (Gen. 15:1).

30Stretch out your hand to heal and perform miraculous signs and wonders through the name of your holy servant Jesus."

What opportunities they would have! The healing of the lame man was just a beginning. There would be more such opportunities provided by God as He stretched out His hand for healing and for signs and wonders to be done "through the name of [His] holy servant [Gk. *paidos*, "child" or "servant"] Jesus," and through prayer in accordance with the Word (Mark 16:17–18).

In effect, they were praying for boldness to keep on doing the same thing that had brought their arrest and the threats of the Sanhedrin.[60] They did not want God to do miracles for miracles' sake, however; they saw miracles as opportunities to preach the gospel and as signs for people to recognize that Jesus was indeed risen from the dead. By glorifying the risen Jesus they would get results.

b. A Fresh Filling With The Holy Spirit 4:31

[31]After they prayed, the place where they were meeting was shaken. And they were all filled with the Holy Spirit and spoke the word of God boldly.

God did not fail them. After they prayed[61] the place where they were gathered "was shaken" (by the Spirit, not by an earthquake),[62] indicating a mighty move of God. At the same time they were all "filled with the Holy Spirit," and in His power they all continued speaking the Word of God "with boldness" (KJV et al.; Gk. *parrēsias;* see v. 13 and 28:31). This was as great a work of the Spirit as the miracles. That they continued to speak with great boldness is further emphasized in 5:42.

The Greek (of v. 31) indicates again a new, fresh filling of the Spirit. Some writers contend that only the new believers (the five thousand mentioned in 4:4) were filled at this time. But the Greek does not uphold this. All the believers, including the apostles, received this fresh filling, empowering them to meet

---

[60]French L. Arrington says this prayer is a model for us. "The Acts of the Apostles," in *Full Life Bible Commentary to the New Testament,* ed. French L. Arrington and Roger Stronstad (Grand Rapids: Zondervan Publishing House, 1999), 557.

[61]Douglas A. Oss notes that the Spirit's "empowering work is closely linked to prayer" (cf. Luke 3:21; Acts 13:1–3). "A Pentecostal/Charismatic View," in *Are Miraculous Gifts for Today?* ed. Wayne A. Grudem (Grand Rapids: Zondervan Publishing House, 1996), 253.

[62]Some see this as parallel to Isa. 6:4 and as directing "forward to Stephen's speech (Acts 7:48ff.)." Clare Amos, "Acts," in *Sowers and Reapers,* ed. John Parr (Nashville: Abingdon Press, 1994), 400.

the continued need and the pressures upon them.[63] New, fresh fillings of the Holy Spirit are part of God's wonderful provision for all believers. Just as we can give more of ourselves to Him, He can give more of himself to us.

STUDY QUESTIONS

1. Identify changes in the cripple other than physical healing.
2. How does Peter's message in chapter 3 compare with that in chapter 2?
3. What was it about Peter's preaching that bothered the Sadducees and why?
4. How did the arrest of Peter and John affect those who had been listening to Peter's preaching in the temple?
5. How was Matthew 10:17–19 fulfilled in Peter's witness to the Sanhedrin?
6. What were the chief points of Peter's witness to the Sanhedrin?
7. How did Peter and John respond to the threats of the Sanhedrin?
8. What helped to give the apostles courage against compromise?

B. Apostles Tested And Triumphant 4:32–5:42

1. A UNITED, CARING CHURCH 4:32–37

³²All the believers were one in heart and mind. No one claimed that any of his possessions was his own, but they shared everything they had.

The increasing number of believers continued "one in heart and mind." That is, they formed a community of believers who

---

[63]Douglas A. Oss points out that "Luke uses precisely the same language here as we observed in 2:4 to describe the initial 'filling' (cf. also similar language in 4:8; 9:17; 13:9,52). Luke consistently emphasizes the empowering experience of the Spirit." "Pentecostal/Charismatic View," 255–56.

were transformed and guided by the Holy Spirit and who were in one accord with a unity of mind, purpose, and desire. None of them said, "What I have is mine and I am afraid I might need it myself." Instead, they felt a love and responsibility for each other that made them want to share everything. God was supplying their needs and they believed He would continue to provide. The same attitude that sprang up after they were first filled with the Spirit on the Day of Pentecost still prevailed (Acts 2:44–45). Again, there was no compulsion.[1] Their sharing was simply an expression of their love and their unity of mind and heart in the one body of Christ (cf. Gal. 6:10).[2]

33With great power the apostles continued to testify to the resurrection of the Lord Jesus, and much grace was upon them all.

At the same time, the apostles "continued to testify," kept on giving witness, to the resurrection of the Lord Jesus. But the work of the Spirit was not limited to the apostles, for "much grace was upon them all."[3] They all enjoyed God's gracious favor in their lives and witness.

34There were no needy persons among them. For from time to time those who owned lands or houses sold them, brought the money from the sales 35and put it at the apostles' feet, and it was distributed to anyone as he had need.

Verse 34 shows an important way this grace was expressed. No one was "needy" (Gk. *endeēs*, "in want, impoverished," cf. Deut. 15:4), that is, lacked what was needed for food, clothes, and shelter, for as many as were owners of fields or houses were selling them and kept contributing the proceeds from the things that were sold. The Greek here does not mean that everyone sold

---

[1]This was quite different from the common ownership of property in the Qumran community. See Simon J. Kistemaker, *Exposition of the Acts of the Apostles* (Grand Rapids: Baker Book House, 1990), 173–74.

[2]This is not mere repetition of Acts 2:44–45. It gives background for what Barnabas did and for what Ananias and Sapphira did.

[3]God's blessing is implied. However, since "grace" (Gk. *charis*) also means "favor," some commentators take this to mean that the majority of the people of Jerusalem looked with favor on the believers: "all held in high esteem" (NEB); "all given great respect" (JB). Kistemaker, *Acts*, 174.

his or her property at once. Rather, "from time to time" this was done as the Lord brought needs to their attention.[4] Then the money was "put at the apostles' feet" (i.e., put under their authority, cf. Pss. 8:6; 47:3; 110:1); then they distributed to each one in proportion to his or her need.

> [36]Joseph, a Levite from Cyprus, whom the apostles called Barnabas (which means Son of Encouragement), [37]sold a field he owned and brought the money and put it at the apostles' feet.

After this general statement Luke gives a specific example, chosen because it gives background for the events at the beginning of the next chapter and for the mission of spreading the gospel toward the ends of the earth (1:8).

It is not clear whether Barnabas was given the name "Son of Encouragement" because of this action or previous actions. From what we see of Barnabas later, he had a character that fitted the meaning of the term. "Son of" was often used in Hebrew and Aramaic to indicate a person's character, or nature. The name "Barnabas" is probably derived from an Aramaic phrase meaning "son of prophecy or encouragement or exhortation."[5] The name stuck. He is never called Joseph again (cf. 9:27; 11:22,25,26,30; 12:25; 13:1,2,7,42,43,46,50; 14:1,3,12,14,23; 15:12,22,35,36, 37,39; 1 Cor. 9:6; Gal. 2:1,9,13; Col. 4:10). "Son of prophecy" also indicates it was the wonder-working Holy Spirit who prompted Barnabas to sell his field and give the money to the apostles to distribute to the poor (cf. Deut. 15:7–8).

Barnabas was a Levite[6] from the country of Cyprus, a large island off the south coast of Asia Minor with a large Jewish population.[7] He was a good example of those Spirit-filled believers

---

[4]P. C. H. Lenski, *The Interpretation of the Acts of Apostles* (Columbus, Ohio: Wartburg Press, 1940), 189–90.

[5]Luke calls Barnabas a prophet (Acts 13:1) and "reports several dimensions of Barnabas' ministry as a charismatic prophet." Roger Stronstad, *The Prophethood of All Believers: A Study in Luke's Charismatic Theology* (Sheffield, England: Sheffield Academic Press, 1999), 93–94.

[6]Though Levites were not assigned a specific tribal territory, they were assigned cities scattered among the other tribes and did own property. See Lev. 25:32–33; Num. 35:2; 1 Chron. 9:2; Ezek. 45:5.

[7]Josephus *Antiquities of the Jews* 13:285–88.

who were concerned about the needy believers and also about Christian stewardship.[8]

2. A PURIFIED, GROWING CHURCH 5:1–16

a. Judgment On Ananias And Sapphira 5:1–10

[1]Now a man named Ananias, together with his wife Sapphira, also sold a piece of property. [2]With his wife's full knowledge he kept back part of the money for himself, but brought the rest and put it at the apostles' feet.

"Now" (Gk. *de*) is better translated "but" (KJV, NASB, NEB, et al.) to bring out the contrast that follows. With the example of Barnabas the Encourager before them, two members of the believing community conspired to get for themselves the same kind of attention given to him. It is clearly implied that they were believers enjoying the blessings of God. They knew what it was to be filled with the Spirit. They listened to the teaching of the apostles, saw the miracles, and shared the fellowship.[9] But their actions were guided by selfish motives,[10] not by the Holy Spirit, as Barnabas's actions had been.

Apparently they were a little jealous of Barnabas, perhaps since he was from "out of town." So they, like he, sold a field, a piece of farm property. But in every other way, what they did was in strong contrast to him.

Ananias "kept back part"[11] of the price for himself. Sapphira[12] shared the knowledge of this and was therefore in accord with him and equally guilty. Then he brought a certain part of it and "put it at the apostles' feet," giving the impression he had done

---

[8]Ralph Earle, *The Acts of the Apostles* (Kansas City, Mo.: Beacon Hill Press, 1965), 307.

[9]See Everett F. Harrison, *Acts: The Expanding Church* (Chicago: Moody Press, 1975), 93.

[10]Compare with the greed and hypocrisy of Achan (Josh. 7:10–26).

[11]The same verb is translated "steal" (NIV) and "purloining" (KJV) in Titus 2:10 (in the sense of embezzling). The LXX of Josh. 7:1 uses it of Achan's sin. Unfortunately, it is not impossible for believers to become liars and deceivers.

[12]"Ananias" is used in the LXX for both *Chananiah* ("the Lord is gracious [or, "shows favor"]") and *Ananiah* ("the Lord protects"). "Sapphira" may mean a sapphire stone or may be an Aramaic word meaning "fair" or "beautiful." Someone has said both names were too good for them.

just as Barnabas had done. Thus, he not only lied, he was really robbing God.

> ³Then Peter said, "Ananias, how is it that Satan has so filled your heart that you have lied to the Holy Spirit and have kept for yourself some of the money you received for the land? ⁴Didn't it belong to you before it was sold? And after it was sold, wasn't the money at your disposal? What made you think of doing such a thing? You have not lied to men but to God."

Peter, acting as representative and spokesman for the twelve apostles, knew immediately what had been done. He did not have spies out to report to him; but he had the Holy Spirit. Perhaps this was revealed to him through one of the gifts of revelation such as the "message [Gk. *logos*, "word"] of wisdom" or the "message ["word"] of knowledge" (1 Cor. 12:8).

Peter asked Ananias how it was that (or, "why," KJV, NASB, et al.) Satan ("the Adversary")[13] had filled his heart to lie to the Holy Spirit and keep back for himself part of the price of the land. The question "Why?" draws attention to the fact that their action was voluntary; there was no excuse for what they did. Before they sold it, it remained theirs, and they were under no compulsion to sell it. After they sold it, it was still "at [their] disposal" (in their power or authority). There was nothing compelling them to give it all (cf. 2 Cor. 9:7, "God loves a cheerful giver"—one who is glad to give, delights to give). What Ananias had conceived in his heart was a lie, "not . . . to men but to God."

Satan was behind the hypocrisy and lie of Ananias and Sapphira. It seems that because of their jealousy, unbelief, and love of money, the Spirit of the Lord was grieved, and they lost out with God (cf. Matt. 6:24; Luke 16:13; 1 Tim. 6:10). These things did not happen overnight. But by the time they conspired together, Satan had filled their hearts (their whole inner beings) and there was no room for the Holy Spirit to remain there. Thus they became willing agents of Satan—who is a thief determined

---

[13]Cf. Rev. 12:9–10. Stott points out that Satan's activity was behind all the opposition in chaps. 3 through 6. John R. W. Stott, *The Spirit, the Church, and the World: The Message of Acts* (Downers Grove, Ill.: InterVarsity Press, 1990), 88.

to "'steal and kill and destroy'" (John 10:10).[14]

They could have submitted to God and resisted Satan (James 4:7; 1 Pet. 5:8–9). But they let pride, self, and the love of money possess them. The love of money is "a root of all kinds of evil" (1 Tim. 6:10; cf. Heb. 13:5). That is, once the love of money takes possession of a person, there is no evil that he cannot or will not do. With the love of money in control, a person will do things he never would do otherwise, including murder and every other sin. It is clear also that if a person is filled with the love of money he cannot love God (Matt. 6:24).

Keeping back part of the price was also a sign of unbelief and failure to trust God fully. Perhaps they feared the Church might collapse and thought they had better save back a good portion in case that happened.

It is clear also that in lying to the Holy Spirit (who was guiding the Church, the believers, and the apostles), they were lying to God, for sin is always against God. This identification of the Holy Spirit with God in verses 3 and 4 also makes it clear that the Holy Spirit is a divine Person.[15]

⁵When Ananias heard this, he fell down and died. And great fear seized all who heard what had happened. ⁶Then the young men came forward, wrapped up his body, and carried him out and buried him.

While Ananias was still listening to Peter, "having fallen down, he expired."[16] That is, he breathed out his last breath. This was indeed severe punishment. But God brought this judgment near the beginning of the Church's history to let the Church know what He thinks of unbelief, greed, and self-seeking hypocrisy that lies to God (see 1 Pet. 4:17). In times of beginnings God is often more severe.[17] When the sons of Aaron offered "unauthorized [foreign, pagan] fire" before the Lord, fire came out from the manifest presence of the Lord in the Holy of Holies and struck

---

[14]One of the themes in Acts is the underlying conflict between the Holy Spirit and Satan.

[15]Stott, *Spirit, the Church, and the World,* 110.

[16]My translation.

[17]H. B. Hackett, *A Commentary on the Acts of the Apostles* (Philadelphia: American Baptist Publication Society, 1882), 76–77.

them down (Lev.10:1–2). After that the people were more careful to seek God for His way to do things. When Israel first went into the Promised Land, Achan was made an example (Josh. 7:24–26). Severe judgment also came when David first attempted to bring back the ark to Jerusalem on a cart, just as the Philistines had sent it; death resulted when Uzzah touched the ark of the covenant (2 Sam. 6:6–8). The second time, David was careful to bring it on the shoulders of the Levites as God had commanded (1 Chron. 15:12–15).

It should be emphasized also that Ananias's lie was premeditated. When he died, "great fear" (including terror and awe) seized all who heard about the miracle. They knew then that the Holy Spirit is a mighty power. He is indeed holy, and it does not pay to lie to Him. This encouraged holiness and undoubtedly kept others from the same kind of sin.

Burial was done quickly in those days. Also, because Ananias was under God's judgment they believed he should be buried immediately (cf. Deut. 21:23). So the "young men"[18] quickly wrapped him up in a linen winding sheet, or shroud, took him out of the city, and without the usual expressions of mourning, buried him in a tomb, either above ground or in a cave.

> **7About three hours later his wife came in, not knowing what had happened. 8Peter asked her, "Tell me, is this the price you and Ananias got for the land?" "Yes," she said, "that is the price."**

About three hours later, Sapphira came in, not knowing what had happened to her husband. She obviously was looking for commendation and praise. Peter answered her inquiring look by asking her if she and her husband had sold the land for the amount he had brought in. Peter thus gave her an opportunity to confess the truth. But she too lied.

> **9Peter said to her, "How could you agree to test the Spirit of the Lord? Look! The feet of the men who buried your husband are at the door, and they will carry you out**

---

[18]Some commentators consider these a class of younger men who assisted the elders of the Church. They were probably just some of the younger believers who were present.

also." ¹⁰At that moment she fell down at his feet and
died. Then the young men came in and, finding her
dead, carried her out and buried her beside her husband.

Peter was just as severe with her. His question clearly indicated
he knew she and her husband had "agreed together"¹⁹ (KJV) to test
the Spirit of the Lord. They were deliberately trying to see how far
they could go in disobedience without provoking God's wrath. (Cf.
Exod. 17:2; Num. 15:30–31; Deut. 6:16; Luke 4:12.)²⁰

Then Peter directed her attention to the feet of the young
men at the door who had now returned from burying her husband. They would carry her out too. Thus, by the same kind of
miracle of divine judgment, Sapphira fell down immediately at
Peter's feet and breathed out her last breath. The young men
then came in, found her dead, carried her out, and buried her
beside Ananias in the tomb.

b. Fear And Continued Growth 5:11–16

¹¹Great fear seized the whole church and all who heard
about these events.

Once more the Bible emphasizes that great fear came on "the
whole church"²¹ and on all who heard these things. But the fear
was a holy fear and did not split up the Church or hinder the
work of God. Some people imagine we must lower God's standards for the Church to make progress in today's world. But this
has never been true. The Church has always been strengthened
when it catches a vision of the holiness of God and seeks practical holiness in individual lives.

¹⁹The verb is a passive form of *sumphōne*, "harmonize." Note the irony.

²⁰Rabbinic Judaism did not accept a woman's testimony and would not have
found Sapphira guilty. In the NT community, however, women were equal to
men; so with equality came greater responsibility.

²¹Or, "congregation," "assembly." The Gk. word (*ekklēsia*) was normally used
in NT times for an assembly of free citizens (see Acts 19:39; Eph. 2:19). Here it
is used of all the believers in Jerusalem and the surrounding area. It shows that
the believers now considered themselves a distinct body, though they still
thought of themselves as Jews. It should be noted, however, that Greek-speaking
Jews used the same word (*ekklēsia*) for the congregation (nation) of Israel (see
Deut. 4:10; 9:10; 18:16 in the LXX).

12The apostles performed many miraculous signs and wonders among the people. And all the believers used to meet together in Solomon's Colonnade. 13No one else dared join them, even though they were highly regarded by the people.

We see the ongoing answer to the prayer of Acts 4:30 as the apostles continued to be full of the Spirit and power and kept right on doing many miraculous signs and supernatural wonders—even more than before. These miracles were never done for display. Instead, they all pointed to the truth of the gospel and to the fact that Jesus cared about His people and their needs. The Greek, *dia de tōn cheirōn tōn apostolōn*, "through the hands of the apostles" (NKJV), again emphasizes that the apostles were secondary agents. God was performing the signs and wonders. It may also imply that the apostles were laying their hands in faith on the people who needed the miracles.

The Church also remained in "one accord" (KJV; Gk. *homothumadon* indicates singleness of purpose), meeting daily at the hours of prayer in Solomon's Colonnade of the temple[22] (and probably overflowing into the temple court beside it). The fear and awe that resulted from the deaths of Ananias and Sapphira also affected the unbelievers, so that "no one else dared join them."[23] That is, no unbelievers dared to mix in with the crowd of believers as if they were one of them (whether out of curiosity or in hopes of an overflow of the blessings).

14Nevertheless, more and more men and women believed in the Lord and were added to their number.

The fear engendered by the deaths of Ananias and Sapphira, however, did not mean that the Church's growth was slowed. When the people saw how God dealt with sin among the believers, they realized that the Church as a whole was pleasing God and held high standards of honesty and righteousness. Therefore they regarded them highly. The actual result was that more and

[22]Jesus ministered here (John 10:23).

[23]Harrison, *Acts*, 96, suggests it was the believers who did not dare join the apostles lest they be judged as Ananias and Sapphira were. But there is no evidence that there was any less fellowship with the apostles; therefore this interpretation seems unlikely.

more believers were being added to their number—crowds both
of men and of women. "More and more" indicates women had
been part of the fellowship all along. It has been suggested that
the number of believers was over ten thousand by this time.[24]

> [15]As a result, people brought the sick into the streets and
> laid them on beds and mats so that at least Peter's shad-
> ow might fall on some of them as he passed by. [16]Crowds
> gathered also from the towns around Jerusalem, bring-
> ing their sick and those tormented by evil spirits, and all
> of them were healed.

Because the believers had confidence in the Lord they "brought
the sick," including the lame, the crippled, and the infirm, out
into the streets (into wide streets or into public squares) and laid
them on beds (stretchers) and mats (pallets), so that when Peter
passed by even his shadow "might fall on some of them." That is,
they believed the Lord would honor Peter's faith and theirs even if
Peter was not able to stop and lay hands on each one of them.

Word of what God was doing spread to the surrounding towns
of Judea (the next step fulfilling Acts 1:8). Soon, because of their
newfound faith, a crowd came from these towns "bringing their
sick" and "those tormented [troubled] by evil [Gk. *akatharton*,
"unclean"] spirits."[25] "All of them," probably including those in
verse 15, were healed. This was a critical point in the history of
the Church, and God did special things that demonstrated the
power of the gospel and the presence of the Holy Spirit.

Nothing indicates that "shadow healing" continued after this.
As in the ministry of Jesus, the Holy Spirit continued to use a variety of ways to encourage people's faith. (Compare the use of Paul's
sweatcloths and work aprons, which functioned in "*extraordinary
miracles,*" in 19:11–12; cf. also Matt. 9:20.) We should not make
exceptional occurrences a test of our spirituality. For example, if
some today would not be satisfied until their shadow brought
healing they would probably be dissatisfied and perhaps eventually disillusioned. As Waverly Nunnally said to me, "The issue is not

---

[24]Earle, *Acts of the Apostles,* 312.

[25]As in the Gospels, the Book of Acts makes a clear distinction between the
sick and the demon possessed. Obviously, the majority of the sick were not
demon possessed.

the method, but ministry and the love of God."

3. THE TWELVE APOSTLES ARRESTED 5:17–26

17Then the high priest and all his associates, who were members of the party of the Sadducees, were filled with jealousy. 18They arrested the apostles and put them in the public jail.

Once again the Sadducees (most of whom were based in Jerusalem and the temple), including the high priest and his close friends, were upset. This time they were "filled with jealousy" ("indignation," KJV). The Greek word *(zēloō)* can mean zeal or enthusiasm in a good sense, or it can mean the worst kind of jealousy. It is not hard to see how the word is used here. It also implies a factional spirit and a zeal for their Saducean teachings against the resurrection of the dead. We can be sure they hated to see the crowds gathering around the apostles. They were probably jealous also because the name of Jesus "rather than theirs . . . was being proclaimed."[26]

Jealous indignation, then, caused these Sadducees to go into action: arresting the twelve apostles and throwing them into the "public jail." "Public" here is actually an adverb meaning publicly. That is, this was done with a crowd looking on. Apparently the priests and Sadducees had become desperate. This time they dared to risk the disapproval of the crowds.

19But during the night an angel of the Lord opened the doors of the jail and brought them out. 20"Go, stand in the temple courts," he said, "and tell the people the full message of this new life."

The Sadducees, who did not believe in angels and "who believed all history was the result of human decisions[,] . . . were in for a surprise."[27] During the night "an angel"[28] of the Lord opened the jail doors, took the apostles past the guards without their knowing it (v. 23), and told the apostles to go and take their stand. They were to continue speaking in the temple to the peo-

[26]James M. Boice, *Acts* (Grand Rapids: Baker Book House, 1997), 106.
[27]William J. Larkin, Jr., *Acts* (Downers Grove, Ill.: InterVarsity Press, 1995), 90.
[28]The Gk. does not have the definite article (as in KJV, JB).

ple "the full message" (Gk. *panta ta rhēmata,* "all the words") of this "new life," that is, the words that are life-giving to those who believe (see John 6:68). The gospel is more than a philosophy or a set of precepts. It, through the work of the Holy Spirit, gives life (and salvation is implied; cf. 3:19; 13:26).

> 21At daybreak they entered the temple courts, as they had been told, and began to teach the people. When the high priest and his associates arrived, they called together the Sanhedrin—the full assembly of the elders of Israel—and sent to the jail for the apostles.

Because of this angel's command, the apostles went to the temple "at daybreak" and proceeded "to teach the people" publicly. They were full of the boldness they had prayed for (4:29). This must have astonished the people who had seen them arrested and thrown in jail the night before. It must also have helped them to see that God was still with the apostles and behind their message.

Some time later that morning "the high priest and his associates" called the Sanhedrin together. The Sanhedrin is further identified as "the full assembly of the elders of Israel." This seems to mean that all seventy members were present.

It also implies that on the previous occasion when Peter and John were arrested (and on some other occasions such as the trial of Jesus) only those who were Sadducees under the domination of the high priest were called. This included the major portion of the Sanhedrin and constituted a quorum. But this time, because they knew they were going against most of the people in Jerusalem, they brought in the full body, expecting them to concur in their decision and uphold punishment of the apostles by the full weight of their authority.

> 22But on arriving at the jail, the officers did not find them there. So they went back and reported, 23"We found the jail securely locked, with the guards standing at the doors; but when we opened them, we found no one inside."

When they sent the "officers" (not high officers, but servants, attendants of the temple) to the jail to bring in the apostles, they were not there. Returning, the officers reported that they found the prison doors still locked with full security, "with the guards standing at the doors." However, when they opened the doors, they "found no one."

24On hearing this report, the captain of the temple guard and the chief priests were puzzled, wondering what would come of this.

"This report" caused the high priest and his associates to be "puzzled" (in doubt and troubled) concerning them, wondering "what would come of this." ("Come" here translates a form of the Gk. word for "become" or "happen.") Further, this implies they were worried and wondered about what would happen next (rather than how the apostles were set free).

25Then someone came and said, "Look! The men you put in jail are standing in the temple courts teaching the people." 26At that, the captain went with his officers and brought the apostles. They did not use force, because they feared that the people would stone them.

About this time someone arrived and reported that the men who were supposed to be in the jail were in the temple, standing in its courts openly "teaching the people." Then the commander of the temple guard went with the attendants of the temple and brought the Twelve "without using force" (NEB), because they were afraid the people would turn on them and stone them. They had dealt with mobs before and knew what a mob spirit and mob violence could do.

Actually, the temple guard did not need to use force. The apostles went willingly even though they also knew they had but to say the word and the mob would have stoned the officers as enemies of God and as blasphemers of God's servants. The apostles, however, undoubtedly hoped this arrest would become another opportunity to witness for their Messiah and Savior.

4. The Verdict To Kill The Apostles 5:27–33

27Having brought the apostles, they made them appear before the Sanhedrin to be questioned by the high priest. 28"We gave you strict orders not to teach in this name," he said. "Yet you have filled Jerusalem with your teaching and are determined to make us guilty of this man's blood."

The high priest avoided asking the disciples how they got out of the prison. It was obviously something supernatural, and it may be he did not want to hear about angels he did not believe in. So he began by reminding the apostles that they had been given "strict orders" not to teach in "this name" (a derogatory reference to the name [i.e., the authority] of Jesus).[29] Then he accused them of not only filling Jerusalem with their teaching, but also desiring to bring on the Jewish leaders the guilt of "this man's blood."[30] Probably they remembered the words of Pilate, "'I am innocent of this man's blood. . . . It is your responsibility!'" (Matt. 27:24).

The statement that they had "filled Jerusalem with [their] teaching" was a great admission of the effectiveness of the apostles' witness. Yet the high priest totally misunderstood the apostles' purpose, probably because, in spite of himself, he felt guilty for what had been done to Jesus. His statement that the apostles wanted to bring vengeance on the Sanhedrin for the death of Jesus was nothing but pure slander, being completely false.

[29]Peter and the other apostles replied: "We must obey God rather than men!

Peter and the apostles (with Peter as spokesman) did not apologize. Without hesitation they answered, "We must obey God rather than men [human beings]!" "Obey" (Gk. *peitharchein*) is a word used of obedience to one in authority, as in Titus 3:1. With a consciousness of Christ's authority, they said, "We must obey." Before, in Acts 4:19, they had said, "You judge." But the Sanhedrin did not judge that the apostles were under divinely appointed necessity to spread the gospel. They attributed to human effort what the apostles were doing. Therefore, the apostles had to declare themselves very strongly here.

[30]The God of our fathers raised Jesus from the dead—whom you had killed by hanging him on a tree. [31]God exalted him to his own right hand as Prince and Savior

[29]KJV makes this a question. NLT construes it as a rhetorical question. It is better to take it as a statement, as NIV, NCV, RSV, and many others.

[30]I.e., make them answerable for this man's death (murder). "This man" is another derogatory reference to Jesus. It also shows they wanted to avoid mentioning the name of Jesus if possible.

that he might give repentance and forgiveness of sins to Israel.

Peter didn't hesitate to remind them how "the God of [their] fathers"—the covenant-keeping God, the God who gave the promise to Abraham and commissioned Moses (Gen. 12:3; Exod. 3:15)—"raised Jesus from the dead."[31] Then, once again, he contrasted the way God treated Jesus with the way the Jewish leaders treated Him, "hanging Him on a tree."[32] That is, they tried to put Him under God's curse (see Deut. 21:23; Gal. 3:13; 1 Pet. 2:24).

Contrary to their fears, it was not the apostles' desire nor was it God's purpose to punish them for this. Rather, God had exalted Jesus, the very One they crucified, to His right hand to be a Prince (Gk. *archēgon*, "author, founder, leader, chief") and a Savior (a title used for God; Isa. 45:21; Luke 1:47), in order to give repentance (that is, the opportunity for repentance) to Israel and forgiveness of sins (cf. Matt. 1:21).

Peter, of course, does not mean to restrict this offer of forgiveness to Israel but simply to apply it to those he was speaking to. God's purpose was to give forgiveness and salvation to all sinners. Their guilt would be cancelled if they would repent. By exalting Jesus, God put Him in a position where it should have been easy to repent or change their attitude toward Him.

[32]We are witnesses of these things, and so is the Holy Spirit, whom God has given to those who obey him."

As before, the apostles emphasized that they were Christ's witnesses to "these things" (or, "these words," Gk. *rhēmatōn*, used of the "words" of this life in v. 20). Then Peter adds that the Holy Spirit himself also witnesses (cf. 1 Pet. 1:11; 2 Pet. 1:21). In fact, He is the One whom God has given (and still gives just as on the Day of Pentecost) to those who obey Him (recognizing His authority), thus enabling them to witness (Matt.10:20; John

---

[31]"From the dead" is added by the NIV translators (cf. other contemporary versions, e.g., NLT, TEV, NCV) in order to clarify what the Gk. *ēgeiren*, "raised up," means. Some commentators take the Gk. to mean "raised up as the Messiah." See David John Williams, *Acts* (Peabody, Mass.: Hendrickson Publishers, 1990), 109.

[32]The Gk. word for "tree" also means wood or certain things made of wood, e.g., a post, a pole, a beam, and so includes the cross. The cross was made of rough-hewn wood; the central stake may have been a section of a tree trunk.

14:26). God is the Giver (John 15:26–27). It is quite clear that the giving of the Spirit was not to be limited to the apostles or to their era.

[33]When they heard this, they were furious and wanted to put them to death.

Apparently the majority of the Sanhedrin took Peter's words to mean that the apostles considered them not only guilty of Christ's death, but also guilty of a refusal to accept God's authority and obey Him. (The apostles did link their witness to the Spirit's witness.)[33] But instead of accepting the offer of repentance,[34] they were furious (Gk. *dieprionto,* "sawn through," and so, cut to the heart, cut to the quick with anger, indignation, and jealousy). Immediately they started proceedings to kill the apostles. (The same word for "put to death" is used of killing Jesus in Acts 2:23.)

5. GAMALIEL'S ADVICE NOT TO KILL THE APOSTLES 5:34–39

[34]But a Pharisee named Gamaliel, a teacher of the law, who was honored by all the people, stood up in the Sanhedrin and ordered that the men be put outside for a little while.

As before, the Sadducees took the lead against the apostles. But this time they had the entire Sanhedrin together; and it included some prominent Pharisees.[35] Among them was Gamaliel,[36] an authoritative teacher of the Law, valued highly by all the people.[37] In the Jewish Talmud he is said to be the grandson of Hillel, the most influential teacher of the liberal wing of

---

[33]Donald Guthrie, *The Apostles* (Grand Rapids: Zondervan Publishing House, 1975), 52–53.

[34]See Matt. 3:7–8. These leaders did not believe they needed repentance.

[35]Sadducees dominated the temple and priesthood at this time. But Pharisees had the most influence in the synagogues and among the majority of the Jews. Pharisees were generally careful not to exceed the demands of justice in administering the Law. See Harrison, *Acts,* 101.

[36]"Reward of God."

[37]The Babylonian Talmud repeatedly refers to him as Rabban Gamaliel the Elder (to distinguish him from his grandson who was also a rabbi). He was the first to be given the title of "Rabban" ("our master"). Only five others were ever given it.

the Pharisees (in contrast to Shammai). Hillel was held in high esteem by all later orthodox Jews. Paul was trained by Gamaliel[38] and became one of his most prominent students (22:3).

Standing up, Gamaliel took charge of the situation and ordered that the apostles be taken outside for a little while.[39]

> **35Then he addressed them: "Men of Israel, consider carefully what you intend to do to these men. 36Some time ago Theudas appeared, claiming to be somebody, and about four hundred men rallied to him. He was killed, all his followers were dispersed, and it all came to nothing.**

Then Gamaliel proceeded to warn the Sanhedrin to "consider carefully" ("be cautious in," NEB; give careful attention to) what they were intending to do (or, were about to do) to the apostles.

By two examples he reminded them that individuals in the past had gathered a following but came to nothing. The first example was Theudas[40] who said of himself that he was "somebody."[41] Theudas was a common name, and he was probably one of the rebels who arose after Herod the Great died in 4 B.C. (Josephus speaks of a later Theudas. However, Luke was a careful historian who checked his facts, so we can be sure Gamaliel was speaking of a different Theudas.[42]) About four hundred men attached themselves to this Theudas. He was murdered, and all who had "rallied to him" (obeyed him and believed in him) were dispersed and "came to nothing." Gamaliel implies that with Jesus crucified, His followers will also come to nothing. He also implies that Jesus was no different from those previous false leaders, who failed.

> **37After him, Judas the Galilean appeared in the days of the census and led a band of people in revolt. He too was killed, and all his followers were scattered.**

---

[38]Gamaliel was one of the few who did not forbid his students to study Greek culture and literature.

[39]He was the leading Pharisee in the Sanhedrin and served almost as a "co-chair" with the high priest.

[40] Short for Theodotus, "given by God."

[41]Codex Bezae (D) has "something great."

[42]Luke was a better historian than Josephus. Stott, *Spirit, the Church, and the World,* 118.

After Theudas, Judas the Galilean rose up "in the days of the census [for the purpose of taxing]."[43] He drew away a considerable number of people after him. But the Romans smashed his revolt, and all who obeyed him were scattered. However, some of them became Zealots[44] (cf. Matt. 10:4). In this way, Gamaliel may have been implying that since the Sanhedrin did not fight the Zealots, they should not fight the Christians.

> **[38]Therefore, in the present case I advise you: Leave these men alone! Let them go! For if their purpose or activity is of human origin, it will fail. [39]But if it is from God, you will not be able to stop these men; you will only find yourselves fighting against God."**

Gamaliel's conclusion was that they should withdraw from these men and let them go, for if this counsel or this work was from a mere human source it would be "overthrown" (NASB), destroyed. But if it was "from God" they would not be able to suppress or overthrow it or them; "you will only find yourselves [be proved unexpectedly to be] fighting against God."[45]

We must keep in mind that this was a Pharisee saying this.[46] That is, the inspired record makes it clear that Gamaliel said this; his recorded words were the conclusions of his own thinking, human reasoning, not God's truth. In a sense, Gamaliel was a hypocrite, for he did not accept Jesus as Lord, nor did he admit that the signs and wonders done by the apostles showed Jesus was different from the former leaders who died.

It is true, of course, that what is from God cannot be overthrown (2 Chron. 13:12). It is true also that it is foolish to try to use physical means to overthrow spiritual forces. But it is not true that everything of human origin is soon overthrown and its followers scattered. There are many pagan religions, false doctrines,

---

[43]The Romans ordered the first census of the people and their property in 10–9 B.C.; it reached Palestine about 6 B.C. (Luke 2:2). There was another census every fourteen years after that. The second census reached Palestine, however, in A.D. 6 when this Judas arose and, according to Josephus (*Jewish War* 2.8.1), taught the people not to pay taxes to Caesar.

[44]R. Allan Killen, "Judas," in *Wycliffe Bible Encyclopedia* (Chicago: Moody Press, 1975), 1:966.

[45]One word in the Gk., meaning "God-fighting," or "God-fighters."

[46]Contrast Gamaliel's counsel with that of Caiaphas (John 11:49–53).

evil movements, and modern cults that maintain a following after many years. The judgments at the end of this age will bring them all to an end and the things of God will continue.

6. THE APOSTLES DISOBEY THE SANHEDRIN'S COMMAND 5:40–42

⁴⁰His speech persuaded them. They called the apostles in and had them flogged. Then they ordered them not to speak in the name of Jesus, and let them go.

Though we must be careful not to press the words of Gamaliel too far, they did have their effect on the Sanhedrin. The rulers were "persuaded" (convinced) by him.

Then they called in the apostles and "had them flogged" (with whips that took skin off their backs). The Greek word *(deirantes)* basically meant "skinned," though it came to mean this type of beating. Thus the council still took out their spite and indignation on the apostles, probably by the usual thirty-nine stripes (see Deut. 25:3; 2 Cor. 11:24). (Jesus had warned them this would happen, Mark 13:9.) Then the Sanhedrin "ordered them not to speak in the name of Jesus" and set them free. They recognized that "the name of Jesus," His character and authority, was central to the apostles' message, that without this focus on who Jesus is, the new movement would die out.

⁴¹The apostles left the Sanhedrin, rejoicing because they had been counted worthy of suffering disgrace for the Name.

They went away from the presence of the Sanhedrin "rejoicing because they had been counted worthy of suffering disgrace for the Name" (cf. Matt. 5:11–12; 1 Pet. 1:6–9; 4:13–16). That is, they suffered for the sake of all that "the Name,"[47] and therefore Christ's character and nature, includes, especially His messiahship, deity, saviorhood, and lordship (see Phil. 2:9–10).

⁴²Day after day, in the temple courts and from house to house, they never stopped teaching and proclaiming the

[47]In the OT, "the Name" (Heb. *hashshem*) always refers to the name of God. Later rabbis used it as a Heb. circumlocution for "God." Waverly Nunnally stresses that this is another very important statement of Jesus' divinity.

good news that Jesus is the Christ.

In spite of their strict warnings, the Jewish leaders did not pursue the apostles further at this time. So the apostles freely continued their ministry. Every day "in the temple courts and from house to house"[48] they never ceased teaching and preaching the good news (the gospel) that the Messiah is Jesus.[49] They boldly defied the orders of the Sanhedrin and paid no attention to their threats. This, however, is the last time Acts mentions ministry in the temple. It was time for the believers to expand their horizons in order to carry out the Great Commission.

STUDY QUESTIONS

1. How did the Church react to the death of Ananias and Sapphira?
2. What caused the high priest and Sadducees to persecute the apostles?
3. How did the apostles answer the charge that they sought revenge for the death of Jesus?
4. In what ways is the Holy Spirit a witness to what Peter and the other apostles said?

C. Seven Chosen To Serve 6:1–7

1. A CONFLICT RESOLVED 6:1–6

¹In those days when the number of disciples was increasing, the Grecian Jews among them complained against the Hebraic Jews because their widows were being overlooked in the daily distribution of food.

---

[48]"From house to house" indicates what will be an increasing use of house churches as "the basic social organization through which the gospel advances from Palestine to Rome . . . (Acts 20:20)." John H. Elliott, "Temple Versus Household in Luke-Acts: A Contrast in Social Institutions," in *The Social World of Luke-Acts: Models for Interpretation,* ed. Jerome H. Neyrey (Peabody, Mass.: Hendrickson Publishers, 1991), 226.

[49]Some ancient manuscripts have "the good news of Christ Jesus." This would include the good news He taught.

Acts 4 tells of the first attack on the Church from the outside. Acts 5 describes a problem on the inside. In both cases the Holy Spirit took care of the situation and the Church kept growing. Now we see in Acts 6 that the number of the "disciples" (or, "learners," so-called because they were all believers desiring to learn more about Jesus and the gospel; 2:42) was still increasing.

What happens when a community of people grows? All those newcomers crowding in cause problems. In this case the growing Church was a cross section of society as it was in Jerusalem and Judea.[1] Some of them had been born there and spoke Hebrew[2] in their homes; they knew Greek as a second language, for Greek had been the language of trade, commerce, and the government since the days of Alexander the Great. However, the Jews born outside of Palestine did not know Hebrew well and normally spoke Greek. Since the community of believers represented many countries, Greek was the one language they all understood.

In previous chapters we saw that believers contributed to a common fund distributed by the apostles for the benefit of the needy. As time went on, most people found jobs and no longer needed this help. Widows, however, could not go out and get a job. It was not uncommon in those days, especially among the Gentiles, for widows to starve to death.[3] By the time this chapter begins, the widows were the only ones left who needed help from this fund. Apparently, believers who could do so still brought money to the apostles for the fund. Then the apostles were responsible to see that the widows' needs were supplied.

Tension had probably been building up for some time between the "Grecian Jews" (Greek-speaking Jews who were probably born in other lands) and the "Hebraic Jews" (local Hebrew-speaking believers) before it surfaced. Language is always a serious barrier

[1]David A. Fiensy, "The Composition of the Jerusalem Church," in *The Book of Acts in Its Palestinian Setting,* ed. Richard Bauckham, vol. 4 of *The Book of Acts in Its First Century Setting,* ed. Bruce W. Winter (Grand Rapids: Wm. B. Eerdmans, 1995) 213.

[2]Most take this to mean Aramaic, though there is evidence that Jerusalem Jews kept alive the biblical Hebrew.

[3]The law of Moses shows God's special concern for widows and others who have no one to help them. (See Exod. 22:22–24; Deut. 10:18; 14:29; 24:19–21; see also Ps. 68:5; 146:9; Jer. 49:11; Luke 7:11–17; 1 Tim. 5:3–16.)

between peoples. It is easy for a minority group to feel neglected, especially if they do not understand the language of the majority population. In fact, the Greek-speaking widows' inability to understand could have caused them to be reticent and thus be overlooked.

Finally, a "complaining" (CEV; Gk. *gongusmos,* a grumbling, half under their breath)[4] arose among the Greek-speaking believers against the Hebrew-speaking believers because their widows were being neglected in the "daily distribution of food."[5] These complaints threatened the spiritual unity of the Body. The Holy Spirit and the gospel brought a variety of people together. Now a problem on the natural level was about to split them apart.

[2]So the Twelve gathered all the disciples together and said, "It would not be right for us to neglect the ministry of the word of God in order to wait on tables.

Then "the Twelve" (the apostles, including Matthias) recognized the problem and called "the multitude of the disciples" (KJV) to themselves and gave them what was a manifestation of the Spirit's gift of a message of wisdom (1 Cor. 12:8). They told them "it would not be right" (pleasing, satisfactory, acceptable, appropriate) for them to abandon the "ministry" (Gk. *diakonia,* "service"), that is, the teaching and preaching of the Word of God to "wait on" (serve)[6] tables. (The Gk. word for tables *[trapezais]* in this passage means money tables as in Matt. 21:12; 25:27; Mark 11:15; Luke 19:23; John 2:15.)

Up to this point the apostles were the pastors, evangelists, teachers, and counselors for the growing body of believers. They were concerned over the spiritual, physical, and material well-being of all. But the great need here made them aware of the

[4]A term used by the LXX for the grumbling of the Israelites against God (Exod. 16:7–12; Num. 11:1; 17:5).

[5]Gk. *diakonia,* "service, ministry." Codex Bezae (D) adds that it was administered by the Heb. speakers. "Of food" is not in the Gk. but is the interpretation of some scholars. I believe it is more likely that money rather than food was distributed (see TEV, "funds").

[6]Gk. *diakonein,* a verb used in early Gk. of keeping wine glasses full by a special waiter called a *diakonos* ("deacon"). In NT times the verb was used of any type of serving.

importance of delegating authority and responsibility. The people also needed to come to a new degree of cooperation in the work of the Lord.

³Brothers, choose seven men from among you who are known to be full of the Spirit and wisdom. We will turn this responsibility over to them

They told the believers to choose from among themselves "seven men . . . full of the Spirit and [practical] wisdom." These would oversee this need. In other words, the apostles laid down the qualifications and the people looked over the congregation to see who met them. The apostles thus trusted the Holy Spirit to give the congregation collectively the wisdom needed. Then the people chose the seven through some kind of an election. "Turn . . . over" means simply "put in charge." This was not arbitrary appointment. The congregation did the choosing, not the apostles—not even Peter.[7]

The seven are not called deacons here, though the verb is a form of *diakoneō*, "serve," from which "deacon" is derived. Most probably, this election gave precedent for what we find as an office in local churches later. (See 1 Tim. 3:8–12; and Rom. 16:1, where Phoebe is a deacon, not deaconess.[8])

Some see a special significance in the number seven here. It may signify a "complete" number. More likely the only reason for having seven was because seven were needed to keep the accounts and give out the money to the widows.

⁴and will give our attention to prayer and the ministry of the word."

Choosing the seven enabled the apostles to give themselves constantly "to prayer and the ministry[9] of the word." That is, the apostles prayed in order to more effectively serve the Word. They disbursed the Word, while the seven disbursed the money.

---

[7]In other words, no apostle is acting in the capacity of a pope exercising powers of appointment, setting precedents for church polity, etc.

[8]"Servant" (Rom. 16:1) is Gk. *diakonon*, a masculine word because it refers to the office of deacon.

[9]Ministration; Gk. *diakonia*, the same word translated "distribution" in v. 1. The corresponding verb is used in v. 2, "wait on."

This set a pattern for ministry that is truly apostolic.

> [5]This proposal pleased the whole group. They chose
> Stephen, a man full of faith and of the Holy Spirit; also
> Philip, Procorus, Nicanor, Timon, Parmenas, and Nicolas
> from Antioch, a convert to Judaism.

There was no dissent to this, for the "proposal" (or "word," Gk. *logos*) pleased all the believers. They must have been pleased as well that the whole assembly would have a voice. They proceeded to choose Stephen (Gk. for "victor's crown" or "wreath"), a man full of faith and the Holy Spirit; "also" Philip ("lover of horses"); Procorus ("leader of a chorus or choir"); Nicanor ("victorious" or "conqueror"); Timon ("one showing honor"); Parmenas ("steadfast"); and Nicolas ("victor over the people"), a Gentile convert to Judaism from Antioch (of Syria).[10]

All of these men had Greek names and were undoubtedly from among the Greek-speaking believers. Surely this shows the grace of God and the work of the Holy Spirit in the hearts of the Hebrew-speaking believers. Although in the majority, they chose all the deacons from the minority group. These seven would have charge of the administration of the fund for the needy in both groups. Thus, the Greek-speaking believers could lodge no possible complaint any more. We can be sure that not only Stephen but all of the seven were full of the Holy Spirit, as the word "also" indicates.[11] The problem was not just the distribution of money, not just business; relationships within the Church needed the continuing wisdom and direction of the Spirit as well.

> [6]They presented these men to the apostles, who prayed
> and laid their hands on them.

The people set the seven before the apostles, who prayed and laid their hands on them. This was wisdom. It also shows how the Holy Spirit broke down this first barrier that rose up in the

[10]Later traditions tried to connect this Nicolas with the Nicolaitans of Rev. 2:6,15, but there is no real evidence for this.

[11]Roger Stronstad calls them "charismatic deacons" with Stephen as an example to let us know that all were inspired and empowered by the Holy Spirit. *The Prophethood of All Believers: A Study in Luke's Charismatic Theology* (Sheffield, England: Sheffield Academic Press, 1999), 87–88.

Church. This laying on of hands was probably like the public recognition of Joshua in Numbers 27:18–19,23.[12] It did not confer anything spiritual on him, for he was already a man "'in whom is the Spirit'" (v. 18). But it inaugurated a new level of service. Stephen and the others were all full of the Spirit before this. The laying on of hands also symbolized prayer for God's blessing on them. They probably prayed also that the Spirit would give them whatever gifts and graces would be necessary to carry out this ministry.

This choosing of the seven was the first step in the organization of a local church. God intends the Church to be a living organism, but nothing in nature is more highly organized than a living cell. When it loses its organization, it dies. Likewise the church must have organization, with a division of labor and delegation of authority and responsibility. A mark of true leadership is the ability to find ways to put others to work using their Spirit-given gifts.[13] The ideal is to have one hundred percent of the people engaged in some kind of ministry.

2. CONTINUED GROWTH IN JERUSALEM 6:7

7So the word of God spread. The number of disciples in Jerusalem increased rapidly, and a large number of priests became obedient to the faith.

Luke concludes this incident with another summary statement saying that "the word of God spread" (Gk. *ēuxanon,* "was increasing, kept on growing"). That is, God's blessing was on this step of organization. It allowed greater freedom for the Spirit and the Word. So the proclaiming of the Word increased, implying that others in addition to the apostles were involved in spreading it. The number of disciples "increased rapidly" (Gk. *eplēthuneto,*

---

[12]The Gk. can mean that the people prayed and laid hands on them, just as the Israelites laid hands on the Levites (Num. 8:10). See James D. G. Dunn, *The Acts of the Apostles* (Valley Forge, Pa.: Trinity Press International, 1996), 84; David John Williams, *Acts* (Peabody, Mass.: Hendrickson Publishers, 1990), 123.

[13]Turner points out that Luke's position is close to Paul's view "that the one charismatic Spirit creates a community with different gifts and ministries." Max Turner, *Power From on High: The Spirit in Israel's Restoration and Witness in Luke-Acts* (Sheffield, England: Sheffield Academic Press, 1996), 443.

"was being multiplied") in Jerusalem and "a large number of priests" were also obedient to the gospel.[14] The Greek indicates priests kept coming. This was a major breakthrough, since most of the priests were Sadducees, who did not believe in the resurrection of the dead.[15] They probably continued in their priestly office, since the Jewish Christians were all faithful to the worship in the temple.[16] With the conversion of the priests the gospel had now reached every segment of society in Jerusalem.

STUDY QUESTIONS

1. What problem did the growth of the Church bring and how did the apostles solve it?
2. How do the qualifications of the seven chosen to serve tables compare with the qualifications of deacons given in 1 Timothy 3:8–13?

D. Stephen Martyred 6:8–8:4

1. STEPHEN'S MINISTRY STIRS OPPOSITION 6:8–11

⁸Now Stephen, a man full of God's grace and power, did great wonders and miraculous signs among the people.

The fact that the seven had been chosen to carry out a rather routine service did not limit their ministry. The anointing of the

[14]Josephus said there were twenty thousand priests at that time. *Against Apion* 2.8. They were the most Hellenized part of Jerusalem's society. The choosing of the seven who were Greek speaking may have helped to attract these priests. Luke seems to suggest this by putting the two assertions side by side.

[15]Some say that those priests who were converted did not include any of the Sadducees but were humble priests like the father of John the Baptist. See Everett F. Harrison, *Interpreting Acts: The Expanding Church* (Grand Rapids: Zondervan Publishing House, Academie Books, 1986), 107. However, it is more likely that Luke wants us to see that the gospel was successful even among its most determined opponents.

[16]Some writers suppose priests from the Qumran community were included, but there is no evidence for this. Johannes Munck, *The Acts of the Apostles,* rev. William F. Albright and C. S. Mann, vol. 31 of *Anchor Bible Series* (Garden City, N.Y.: Doubleday & Co., 1979), 56.

Holy Spirit was on their obedience and faithfulness. Soon they were stepping out in new ministries. Stephen is the first example of one who did this. Full of God's "grace"[1] and mighty "power," he began to do (and kept on doing) "great [Gk. *megala,* "magnificent, sublime"] wonders" and startling, supernatural "signs" among the people. The people were not merely spectators but experienced the miracles as God's gifts to meet their needs.[2]

This is the first time we read of miracles being done by those who were not apostles. The important thing, however, is that the Holy Spirit was working *through* Stephen. The supernatural power of the Spirit was doing the work. The phrase "full of [God's] grace" is found in only one other passage in the New Testament (John 1:14), and there it describes Jesus. The Holy Spirit could use Stephen because he reflected the character of Jesus.

But Stephen did nothing to deserve the mighty power manifested through him. Luke-Acts often connects the word "power" (Gk. *dunamis*) with the baptism in the Holy Spirit, which is a gift, not a reward for merit. *Dunamis* also suggests the fearlessness of Old Testament prophets such as Micah, who said, "I am filled with *power,* with the Spirit of the LORD" (Mic. 3:8).

> [9]**Opposition arose, however, from members of the Synagogue of the Freedmen (as it was called)—Jews of Cyrene and Alexandria as well as the provinces of Cilicia and Asia. These men began to argue with Stephen, [10]but they could not stand up against his wisdom or the Spirit by whom he spoke.**

The Word of God is the sword of the Spirit (Eph. 6:17; Heb. 4:12), and the Spirit used Stephen to wield it with telling effect. Soon "opposition arose." This time it came from Greek-speaking Jews, who, like Stephen, had returned to live in Jerusalem. They had their own synagogue (or synagogues),[3] and included Jews

[1]"Grace," rather than "faith" (KJV), seems to be the correct reading here. Stephen was both the recipient and the channel of God's unmerited favor.

[2]Codex Bezae (D) and some other ancient manuscripts and versions add that Stephen did these miracles through the name of the Lord Jesus Christ.

[3]The word is singular, but many take it as distributive and apply it to each group, for the Jerusalem Talmud says there were about four hundred synagogues

who were "Freedmen,"[4] probably captured in war, taken as slaves to Rome, and later set free by their Roman masters. Some were Cyrenians (from Cyrene, west of Egypt on the Mediterranean coast of Libya) and Alexandrians (from Alexandria in Egypt). Others were from Cilicia (Paul's home province in southeastern Asia Minor) and from the province of Asia (in western Asia Minor).

Most of the Jews in the Dispersion had to face many threats to their teaching, living as they did surrounded by Gentiles. Consequently, they were quicker to defend themselves against anything different from what their rabbis taught them. But, though they kept trying to "argue with" (or "debate," NLT) Stephen, they did not have the strength or power "to stand against the wisdom and Spirit by which [he] spoke" (NLT). In other words, Stephen was not depending on his own wisdom but on the anointing and gifts of the Holy Spirit. No wonder all their arguments fell flat!

[11]Then they secretly persuaded some men to say, "We have heard Stephen speak words of blasphemy against Moses and against God."

In spite of Stephen's argument, they still refused to believe and were determined to stop him. So they secretly "persuaded" (instigated and incited in some unfair way, probably by bribery[5]) some men to say they had heard Stephen speaking abusive, scurrilous words against Moses and against God—a sin calling for

---

in Jerusalem at this time. See F. F. Bruce, *Commentary on the Book of Acts* (Grand Rapids: Wm. B. Eerdmans, 1954), 153; Everett F. Harrison, *Acts: The Expanding Church* (Chicago: Moody Press, 1975), 109; Ralph Earle, *The Acts of the Apostles* (Kansas City, Mo.: Beacon Hill Press, 1965), 328. Simon J. Kistemaker suggests there were two synagogues, one for Jews from Egypt and Libya, the other for Jews from Asia Minor. *Exposition of the Acts of the Apostles* (Grand Rapids: Baker Book House, 1990), 228. See also Rainer Riesner, "Synagogues in Jerusalem," in *The Book of Acts in Its Palestinian Setting*, ed. Richard Bauckham, vol. 4 of *The Book of Acts in Its First Century Setting*, ed. Bruce W. Winter (Grand Rapids: Baker Book House, 1995), 192–205.

[4]A translation of the Lat. *libertini*, "freed from slavery." The term was applied especially to descendants of those who had been taken prisoner by Pompey's forces in 63 B.C. and made slaves but later freed.

[5]John R. W. Stott, *The Spirit, the Church, and the World: The Message of Acts* (Downers Grove, Ill.: InterVarsity Press, 1990), 126.

death by stoning under the Law (Lev. 24:16; cf. John 10:33). Probably what they did was twist and misinterpret the teachings of Jesus that Stephen repeated. They refused to recognize that their human traditions had emptied the law of Moses of its true meaning. They closed their eyes to the prophecies of a new covenant (Jer. 31:31–32). They would not admit that Jesus' treatment of customs and traditions was in line with the revelation of the will of God in the prophets. For the same reasons Jesus was also accused of blasphemy (Mark 14:64; John 10:33).[6]

2. STEPHEN BROUGHT BEFORE THE SANHEDRIN
6:12–7:1

12So they stirred up the people and the elders and the teachers of the law. They seized Stephen and brought him before the Sanhedrin.

Then they violently "stirred up the people" into a vicious mob that included "the elders and the teachers of [experts in] the law" of Moses. With all these supporting them, they came upon Stephen suddenly and unexpectedly, seized him (took hold of him violently and kept a firm grip on him), put him under arrest, and brought him to the Sanhedrin (or to the place where the Sanhedrin was meeting).

13They produced false witnesses, who testified, "This fellow never stops speaking against this holy place and against the law.

Then they set up "false witnesses," who misrepresented Stephen's words, putting them in as bad a light as possible: They took the stand and said that this man did not cease to speak words "against this holy place" (i.e., the temple) and "against the law" of Moses.

14For we have heard him say that this Jesus of Nazareth will destroy this place and change the customs Moses handed down to us."

They also claimed they heard Stephen say that "this Jesus of Nazareth[7] will destroy [break up] this place and change the cus-

[6]See Bruce, *Commentary*, 134–35.

[7]Or, "this 'Jesus the Nazarene.'" "This" is used in a contemptuous way here, as in 5:28 and 6:14.

toms [including the rites and institutions] Moses handed down to us." This, of course, refers to Matthew 26:61, Mark 14:58, and John 2:19–21, where Jesus was really speaking of the temple of His body and of His death and resurrection. (See also Matt. 12:42 where Jesus said, "'Now one greater than Solomon is here.'") Stephen may have referred also to the prophecy Jesus gave of the destruction of the temple (Matt. 24:2)—a prophecy that was fulfilled in A.D. 70. More likely, he emphasized the positive message: The Law and the temple pointed to, and found their fulfillment in, Jesus.[8]

15All who were sitting in the Sanhedrin looked intently at Stephen, and they saw that his face was like the face of an angel. 1Then the high priest asked him, "Are these charges true?"

After these false accusations all those who were seated in the Sanhedrin fixed their eyes on Stephen and "saw that his face was like the face of an angel." This probably means there was a glow, or brightness, that was more than human and came from heaven. Possibly it was similar to the appearance of Moses when he came down from the presence of God on the mountain (Exod. 34:29,35) or, better, of Jesus when He was transfigured and the inner glory showed through (Luke 9:29). "So full of the Spirit, so full of wisdom, faith, grace, and power is Stephen that the glory of God shines from his face."[9]

Then the high priest (probably Caiaphas) gave Stephen opportunity to respond to the charges.

3. STEPHEN'S DEFENSE 7:2–53

a. Joseph Rejected 7:2–16

2To this he replied: "Brothers and fathers, listen to me! The God of glory appeared to our father Abraham while he was still in Mesopotamia, before he lived in Haran. 3'Leave your country and your people,' God said, 'and go to the land I will show you.' 4"So he left the land of the Chaldeans and settled in Haran. After the death of his

---

[8]Stott, *Spirit, the Church, and the World,* 129, 143.
[9]William J. Larkin, Jr., *Acts* (Downers Grove, Ill.: InterVarsity Press, 1995), 105.

father, God sent him to this land where you are now living.

After politely addressing the Sanhedrin, recognizing their dignity and authority, Stephen began a review of the history of Israel, a history they all knew well.[10] He was not trying to defend himself. His purpose was to defend the gospel against false charges and to show a parallel between the way Old Testament Jews treated their prophets and the way the Jewish leaders treated Jesus. In doing this he recognizes himself as a faithful member of the community of Israel, calling Abraham "our father" (see also vv. 11,12,19,38,44,45).

The false witnesses said that Stephen had blasphemed Moses and God. Stephen met this charge by reminding them that the "God of glory" (the God who revealed himself in glory, giving instruction and promises) appeared to Abraham[11] while he was in Mesopotamia (in Ur of the Chaldees)[12] before he lived in Haran[13] (Gk. *Charrhan,* a spelling that is closer to the Heb. pronunciation). Genesis does not mention this directive to Abraham in Ur, but Nehemiah 9:7 confirms that he received it.

God commanded him to leave his country (Ur) and his people (relatives, countrymen) and "go to the land" (whatever land) God would show him.[14] After stopping in Haran until his father died (Gen. 11:31-32),[15] he was sent by God to the land that later became Israel's (Gen. 12:5).

5He gave him no inheritance here, not even a foot of ground. But God promised him that he and his descen-

[10]The literary form of "recounting redemptive history" being done here by Stephen was also used by Moses in Deut., by Joshua in chaps. 23 and 24, by Samuel, by Nehemiah, by the Psalmists, and by Peter and Paul. The Holy Spirit emphasizes that Bible history is told from God's point of view.

[11]Note that the same glory appeared to Stephen (7:55).

[12]Some archaeologists, such as Cyrus Gordon, believe this was a northern Ur rather than the Ur east of Babylon. There is some evidence that the Chaldeans did come from the north and did not come into Babylonia until after Abraham's time.

[13]In western Mesopotamia, now Turkey.

[14]Stephen is using the language of the LXX.

[15]Terah's age given in Gen. 11:26 is his age at the birth of his eldest son. Abraham was actually born sixty years later but is mentioned first because he was the most important.

dants after him would possess the land, even though at that time Abraham had no child.

But God gave him no inheritance in it, "not even a foot of ground."[16] Yet God—while Abraham still "had no child"—promised to give it to him and to his descendants for "'an everlasting possession'" (Gen. 17:8). So Abraham trusted God's word, accepted the promise, and put his life in God's hand.

> [6]God spoke to him in this way: 'Your descendants will be strangers in a country not their own, and they will be enslaved and mistreated four hundred years. [7]But I will punish the nation they serve as slaves,' God said, 'and afterward they will come out of that country and worship me in this place.'

God also spoke of Abraham's descendants living temporarily as resident aliens in a land belonging to a people who would make them slaves and treat them badly for "four hundred years."[17] But He also promised to judge the nation that made them slaves. After that they would come out and "worship" ("serve," NASB) God "in this place" (i.e., the Promised Land).

> [8]Then he gave Abraham the covenant of circumcision. And Abraham became the father of Isaac and circumcised him eight days after his birth. Later Isaac became the father of Jacob, and Jacob became the father of the twelve patriarchs.

Another thing God gave Abraham was the "covenant of circumcision"—as a covenanted assurance of His faithful love (Gen. 17:10–14)—so that Isaac was circumcised the eighth day after his birth (Gen. 21:4). Then came Jacob and the "twelve patriarchs" (tribal heads or tribal rulers).[18]

---

[16]Abraham *bought* the cave of Machpelah to bury Sarah in; God did not *give* it to him (Gen. 23:13–18).

[17]See Gen. 15:13–14 in the LXX. Four hundred is a round number here and is given exactly as 430 in Exod. 12:40–41. Paul seems to understand the 430 years as including all the time from Abraham to Moses (Gal. 3:17). The rabbis, however, understood the 400 years to be from Isaac's birth to the Exodus.

[18]The emphasis here is that they were all born under the covenant of circumcision. This was a change from the situation before Abraham.

⁹"Because the patriarchs were jealous of Joseph, they sold him as a slave into Egypt. But God was with him ¹⁰and rescued him from all his troubles. He gave Joseph wisdom and enabled him to gain the goodwill of Pharaoh king of Egypt; so he made him ruler over Egypt and all his palace.

The patriarchs, moved with jealousy, sold Joseph into Egypt (Gen. 37:11,28). "But God was with him." God rescued this rejected person out of all his "troubles" (tribulations, distressing circumstances) and gave him favor and wisdom before Pharaoh. Because of a divinely inspired interpretation of dreams, Pharaoh made Joseph "ruler" (leader, leading man) over Egypt and all his household (including all his business affairs; Gen. 41:38–40). Stephen strongly contrasts the way Joseph's brothers treated him and the way God treated him. Stephen is leading also to a comparison with the way the Jewish leaders treated Jesus and the way God exalted Him.

¹¹"Then a famine struck all Egypt and Canaan, bringing great suffering, and our fathers could not find food. ¹²When Jacob heard that there was grain in Egypt, he sent our fathers on their first visit. ¹³On their second visit, Joseph told his brothers who he was, and Pharaoh learned about Joseph's family.

When the famine came, the patriarchs (now identified as "our fathers") were not exempt from the "great suffering" (tribulation, distress) it brought. Jacob, hearing there was "grain"[19] (or, bread) in Egypt, sent them there. The second time they came, Joseph, now thirty-seven years old and in appearance an Egyptian, made himself known and revealed his "family" (Gk. *genos,* "race, stock, nation") to Pharaoh.

¹⁴After this, Joseph sent for his father Jacob and his whole family, seventy-five in all. ¹⁵Then Jacob went down to Egypt, where he and our fathers died. ¹⁶Their bodies were brought back to Shechem and placed in the tomb that Abraham had bought from the sons of Hamor at Shechem for a certain sum of money.

[19]KJV "corn" is from Old English for grain; hence NIV, "grain." The Heb. means both wheat and bread (cf. Gen. 42:2).

Then Joseph sent for Jacob and all his relatives, "seventy-five in all."[20] So Jacob went down and died, as did the "fathers" (i.e., Jacob's sons), and they were transferred to Shechem, placed in the tomb bought for "a hundred pieces of silver" from the sons of Hamor, the "father of Shechem," prince of the town of Shechem (Gen. 33:19).[21]

In all this there is a subtle emphasis on the way Joseph was sold by his jealous brothers yet was used by God to save their lives. There is also emphasis on the faith of Abraham and his immediate descendants who believed God's promise even when they saw absolutely no evidence that it would be fulfilled.

These members of the Sanhedrin were refusing to believe God even though He had provided evidence of the fulfillment of His promise through the resurrection of Jesus. The treatment of Joseph by his brothers and the contrast to the way God treated him also parallels the way the Jewish leaders had treated Jesus.

b. Moses Rejected 7:17–37

17"As the time drew near for God to fulfill his promise to Abraham, the number of our people in Egypt greatly increased. 18Then another king, who knew nothing about Joseph, became ruler of Egypt. 19He dealt treacherously with our people and oppressed our forefathers by forcing them to throw out[22] their newborn babies so that they would die.

Stephen next deals with the accusation that he had blasphemed Moses. He begins by recounting the way the Israelites "greatly

[20]The LXX and one of the Dead Sea Scrolls give 75 in Gen. 46:27; Exod. 1:5; and in some copies of Deut. 10:22. The Heb. has the number 70, for it does not include the grandsons of Joseph as the LXX does. See Gleason L. Archer, *Encyclopedia of Bible Difficulties* (Grand Rapids: Zondervan Publishing House, Regency Reference Library, 1982), 378.

[21]The reference here is to the burial of the twelve patriarchs. Jacob was buried in Machpelah near Hebron (Gen. 23:17,19; 50:13). Joseph was buried in Shechem (Josh. 24:32). Stephen believed the other brothers were also buried there. Gen. 33:19 and Josh. 24:32 indicate Jacob did the actual buying. However, Abraham was still alive and it was undoubtedly done in the name of the head of the clan.

[22]Gk. *ektithēmi,* a form of infanticide. The same verb is used in v. 21.

increased" in Egypt (Gen. 47:27) as the time came for the fulfillment of the promise God had sworn to Abraham, the promise that
his descendants would possess the land of Canaan (Gen. 15:18).

This increase continued until a king arose (belonging to a new
dynasty) who "did not know about Joseph" (Exod. 1:8). He vic-
timized the Israelites by trickery and treated them badly. He even
made them "throw out" their newborn infants. ("Throw out" is
a term used for exposing babies in some place where the elements
or wild animals would cause them to die. In this case boys were
thrown into the Nile River; Exod. 1:22.)

**20"At that time Moses was born, and he was no ordinary
child. For three months he was cared for in his father's
house. 21When he was placed outside, Pharaoh's daughter took him and brought him up as her own son.
22Moses was educated in all the wisdom of the Egyptians
and was powerful in speech and action.**

At this time Moses was born and was "no ordinary child" (Gk.
asteios tō theō, lit. "beautiful [lovely, fine] to God"). This may
mean he was made so by God or considered so by God (cf. Heb.
11:23). In either case, we know God was with Moses from his
birth. God's care was shown when Moses was exposed after
"three months . . . in his father's house." Pharaoh's daughter took
him and "brought him up as her own son" (Exod. 2:5–10). Thus
Moses was instructed in all the wisdom of Egypt and was powerful in both his words and deeds. This was significant, for
Egyptians had already made great advances in science, engineer-
ing, mathematics, astronomy, and medicine.

**23"When Moses was forty years old, he decided to visit
his fellow Israelites. 24He saw one of them being mistreated by an Egyptian, so he went to his defense and
avenged him by killing the Egyptian. 25Moses thought
that his own people would realize that God was using
him to rescue them, but they did not.**

At forty Moses "decided to visit" (Gk. *episkepsasthai,* "look
after, relieve, protect"; cf. CEV) his Israelite brothers (Heb.
11:24–25). Seeing "one of them being mistreated," he "avenged
him [did justice to him] by killing the Egyptian" (Exod.
2:11–12).

Stephen's point in this part of the history was that Moses did this because he supposed his Israelite brothers would understand that God was "using him to rescue them" (give them deliverance[23]). But they did not, and Stephen saw a clear parallel to the way the Jewish leaders failed to understand what God had done through Jesus in providing salvation. They rejected Jesus just as their fathers, for a time, had rejected Moses.

> [26]The next day Moses came upon two Israelites who were fighting. He tried to reconcile them by saying, 'Men, you are brothers; why do you want to hurt each other?' [27]"But the man who was mistreating the other pushed Moses aside and said, 'Who made you ruler and judge over us? [28]Do you want to kill me as you killed the Egyptian yesterday?'

Stephen reminded his audience how Moses, wanting to reconcile the fighting Israelites and have them be at peace (Exod. 2:13–14), said, "Men, you are brothers; why do you want to hurt [injure unfairly] each other?" But the one harming his neighbor pushed Moses away. By his question he was really denying that Moses had any right to be a ruler or judge over his fellow Israelites. Then he asked Moses if he wanted to kill him as he had the Egyptian the day before. In this way Moses was "misunderstood and denounced by his own people"[24] (cf. 7:35).

> [29]When Moses heard this, he fled to Midian, where he settled as a foreigner and had two sons. [30]"After forty years had passed, an angel appeared to Moses in the flames of a burning bush in the desert near Mount Sinai.

At this, Moses fled[25] and became a resident alien in Midian, a district on the east side of the Gulf of Aqaba, populated by a Semitic people (Exod. 2:15). There his two sons were born. He

---

[23]Gk. *sōtērian,* "salvation," a word that is used of deliverance, health, well-being, as well as salvation. This term draws attention to the parallel between the work of Moses and the work of Jesus. See v. 35.

[24]Howard Clark Kee, *To Every Nation Under Heaven: The Acts of the Apostles* (Harrisburg, Pa.: Trinity Press International, 1997), 95.

[25]The evidence fits the time after Queen Hatshepsut of Egypt died. Her successor even chiseled her name off monuments. Since Moses was Queen Hatshepsut's favorite, his position in Egypt was precarious. He fled because he knew the Pharaoh was looking for an excuse to get rid of him.

stayed there forty years. Then "an angel"[26] appeared to him in the desert of Mount Sinai in the flame of fire in a thornbush (Exod. 3:2).[27]

> [31]When he saw this, he was amazed at the sight. As he went over to look more closely, he heard the Lord's voice: [32]'I am the God of your fathers, the God of Abraham, Isaac and Jacob.' Moses trembled with fear and did not dare to look. [33]"Then the Lord said to him, 'Take off your sandals; the place where you are standing is holy ground.

Moses was amazed at the sight. As his curiosity drew him "to look more closely" at the burning bush, God spoke, declaring himself to be "the God of Abraham, Isaac and Jacob" (Exod. 3:6). Then "Moses trembled" and no longer dared to look. This shows he knew about God's dealings with Abraham, Isaac, and Jacob; he knew what a holy God they served. He knew too that God had made covenant promises. No doubt his mother had told him these things (see Exod. 2:8–9).

Then[28] the Lord told him to take off his shoes because the place where he was standing was "holy ground" (even though it was far from the Promised Land). By doing this he would be recognizing God's holiness and would be taking his place as a worshiper of the Lord. He would be making Abraham's God his God.

> [34]I have indeed seen the oppression of my people in Egypt. I have heard their groaning and have come down to set them free. Now come, I will send you back to Egypt.' [35]"This is the same Moses whom they had rejected with the words, 'Who made you ruler and judge?' He was sent to be their ruler and deliverer by God himself, through the angel who appeared to him in the bush.

[26]That is, the angel of the Lord, a manifestation of God himself (see Exod. 3:2–22 where God speaks), or rather of the preincarnate Son. Note that He is distinguished as a separate person, and yet is identified with God. Jesus is and has always been the one Mediator between God the Father and humankind. See P. C. H. Lenski, *The Interpretation of the Acts of the Apostles* (Columbus, Ohio: Wartburg Press, 1940), 280–81.

[27]Exod. 3:1 mentions Horeb, the range of which Mt. Sinai is a part.

[28]Stephen is recounting this from memory and is not primarily concerned about the exact order of events. He is preparing to reemphasize Israel's rejection of Moses.

God had "indeed seen"[29] the ill treatment of His people in Egypt and heard their groaning. He had "come down to set them free." To do this He would send Moses with a commission to Egypt.

Stephen then emphasizes his main point in this part of the history: This Moses whom "they had rejected" (denied, repudiated, refused), God himself had sent, through the angel who had appeared to him in the bush, to be "their ruler and deliverer" (ransomer, liberator; originally used of those who paid a ransom to liberate slaves or prisoners).

36He led them out of Egypt and did wonders and miraculous signs in Egypt, at the Red Sea and for forty years in the desert. 37"This is that Moses who told the Israelites, 'God will send you a prophet like me from your own people.'

After showing the people of Israel wonders and miraculous signs in Egypt and in the wilderness, Moses "led them out." Then, as a climax to this section, Stephen reminds his audience that this same Moses, the Moses whom the people of Israel rejected and God used to save them out of Egypt, told them, "God will send you a prophet like me." To him they must listen (see Deut. 18:15).

The Jewish leaders knew how the apostles applied this passage about the prophet like Moses (3:22): All the believing Jews applied it to Jesus. Stephen was saying that by not listening to Jesus the Sandhedrin was disobeying God and treating Moses with contempt.[30]

c. God Rejected 7:38–43

38He was in the assembly in the desert, with the angel who spoke to him on Mount Sinai, and with our fathers; and he received living words to pass on to us. 39"But our fathers refused to obey him. Instead, they rejected him and in their hearts turned back to Egypt.

[29]Lit. "I have seen, I have seen" (KJV); the repetition is an idiomatic way of expressing emphasis in Heb. Here it draws attention to the faithfulness of God.

[30]Cf. H. B. Hackett, *A Commentary on the Acts of the Apostles* (Philadelphia: American Baptist Publication Society, 1882), 100.

Stephen in this section identifies a second rejection of Moses—
and an even worse rejection, a rejection of God. Moses was in the
"assembly" (Gk. *ekklēsia*, "assembly of citizens")[31] in the desert
with "the angel who spoke to him on Mount Sinai"[32] and with
all the fathers.[33] He welcomed the "living words" (divine utter-
ances; i.e., the Torah, the Pentateuch) given to Israel. But the
fathers, refusing to become obedient to him, rejected him "and
in their hearts turned back to [pagan] Egypt."

**[40]They told Aaron, 'Make us gods who will go before us.
As for this fellow Moses who led us out of Egypt—we
don't know what has happened to him!' [41]That was the
time they made an idol in the form of a calf. They
brought sacrifices to it and held a celebration in honor of
what their hands had made.**

They showed their rejection of Moses and God by asking
Aaron to make gods to "go before" them—to lead and direct
them. They despised Moses by saying in a derogatory way: "As
for *this fellow* Moses[34] who led us out of Egypt—we don't know
what has happened to him" (v. 40; see Exod. 32:1). Then they
made an image of a calf[35] and sacrificed to the idol and "held a
celebration in honor of" (Gk. *euphrainonto*, "rejoiced, reveled
in") the works of their own hands.

**[42]But God turned away and gave them over to the worship
of the heavenly bodies. This agrees with what is written in
the book of the prophets: "'Did you bring me sacrifices
and offerings forty years in the desert, O house of Israel?
[43]You have lifted up the shrine of Molech and the star of
your god Rephan, the idols you made to worship.
Therefore I will send you into exile' beyond Babylon.**

[31]The same word is translated "church" when applied to Christians.

[32]Jewish traditions and the LXX interpreted Deut. 33:2–3 to mean that the
"holy ones" were angels who were active in the giving or expounding of the Law.
See Gal. 3:19; Heb. 2:2.

[33]The repeated mention of the fathers of Israel (in this case, the tribes in the
wilderness) prepares for the conclusion in v. 51.

[34]Compare with "this Jesus" said by false witnesses in 6:14.

[35]Many believe it was not the actual image of a calf but of a small golden bull,
which was called a calf because of its small size.

Because this was a rejection not merely of Moses but of God, God turned and "gave them over to the worship of [to serve] the heavenly bodies [Gk. *stratia,* "army" of heaven]," that is, heavenly bodies considered gods by the pagans. Consequently, they were taken into exile. Stephen saw this confirmed in Amos 5:25–27. His quotation shows that the Israelites in the wilderness did not really offer their sacrifices to the Lord during the remainder of the forty years in the wilderness. They apparently did go through the proper form of worship, but also began to practice idolatry, which became an ongoing temptation (ultimately taking them into exile in Babylonia). Thus, even after seeing God's glory in the wilderness, they "'carried the tent where the god Molech is worshiped'" (v. 43, CEV) (a form of Venus worshiped by the Ammonites and several other Semitic peoples).[36] What a contrast to the "tabernacle of the Testimony" mentioned in verse 44! They also worshiped the star of the god Rephan (probably the Assyrian name for the planet Saturn, called Chiun in Amos 5:26, KJV). Both were idols the Israelites made for themselves to worship (probably small images carried by them secretly). As a result, God told Israel He would send them into exile "beyond Babylon."[37]

From this also we see that Stephen is saying that it was "our fathers" who rejected Moses and the Law, thereby rebelling against the God who gave the Law. The Fathers of Israel, not Jesus, had been the ones who wanted to change the laws, customs, and teachings given by Moses.

d. The Temple Insufficient 7:44–50

44"Our forefathers had the tabernacle of the Testimony with them in the desert. It had been made as God directed Moses, according to the pattern he had seen. 45Having received the tabernacle, our fathers under Joshua brought it with them when they took the land from the nations God drove out before them. It remained in the land until the time of David,

[36]See Andrew K. Helmbold, "Gods, False," in *Wycliffe Bible Encyclopedia* (Chicago: Moody Press, 1975) 1:705–6.

[37]Stephen here is condensing the account. Amos (5:27) said "beyond Damascus." Stephen is thinking of the later deportation to the east of Babylon, which was also prophesied (cf. 2 Chron. 36:15–21; Isa. 39:6–7).

Now Stephen answers their accusation concerning what he had said about the temple. He does not try to explain what Jesus really meant by "'destroy this temple'" (John 2:19). Instead, he reminds them that the fathers "had the tabernacle [tent] of the testimony," so-called because it contained the ark of the covenant with the two tablets of stone, a testimony (or witness) to the covenant between God and His people. This tent "had been made as God directed," Moses making it according to the pattern he had seen (Exod. 25:9,40; 26:30; 27:8).

The next generation of the Fathers received it in their turn, and with Joshua[38] brought it into the land, possessed by the nations whom God drove out before them, "until the time of David." That is, the tabernacle lasted until the days of David;[39] it had been a blessing, but its time came to an end.

46who enjoyed God's favor and asked that he might provide a dwelling place for the God of Jacob. 47But it was Solomon who built the house for him.

David found favor before God and personally desired to provide a permanent "dwelling place for the God of Jacob"[40] (cf. Ps.132:4–5). But God did not allow him to do this. God had used David to win victories and establish the kingdom. Now God wanted a man of peace to build the temple. So He chose Solomon (Heb. *Shlomoh*, "peaceful") instead (2 Sam. 7:13).

48"However, the Most High does not live in houses made by men. As the prophet says: 49"'Heaven is my throne, and the earth is my footstool. What kind of house will you build for me? says the Lord. Or where will my resting place be? 50Has not my hand made all these things?'

Then Stephen declared that the Most High God does not live (permanently) in what is made by human hands. To prove this, Stephen quoted Isaiah 66:1 and part of verse 2. There, God told

---

[38]"Jesus" (KJV) is the Gk. form of Joshua, as in Heb. 4:8.

[39]The ark was captured by Philistines in the days of Eli. After its return the tabernacle was set up at Nob (possibly Mount Scopus; see 1 Sam. 21:1). Later the ark was taken to Gibeon (see 1 Chron. 16:39).

[40]Several ancient manuscripts have "the *house* of Jacob" (see, for example, v. 46, NASB, alternate reading). This seems to be the best-attested reading.

Isaiah that heaven is His throne and the earth His footstool. What kind of house could they build Him, or what was the place of His rest? Or, in what place could God settle down and make it His permanent abode?[41] Had He not made all these things?

Stephen was not denying that God had manifested His presence in the temple. Rather, he was saying that they must not trust the temple more than they trust God. Like the prophets, Stephen saw that the God who created the heavens and the earth cannot be limited to any earthly building. Actually, Solomon agreed with this (see 1 Kings 8:27; 2 Chron. 6:1–2,18; cf. Isa. 57:15).

This verse brings Stephen's speech to a climax. He has indicated again and again that God's presence and power operated in many places and under many circumstances. They should realize that God is not limited to the temple. The fact that God does not live permanently in what is made by hands also implied that the temple would pass away just as the tabernacle did. (Now believers individually and as a body are temples of the Holy Spirit; see 1 Cor. 3:16; 6:19; cf. Eph. 2:19–22; 1 Pet. 2:5.) Therefore, prophesying the destruction of the temple was not a betrayal of true Judaism nor was it apostasy.

e. The Holy Spirit Rejected 7:51–53

51"You stiff-necked people, with uncircumcised hearts and ears! You are just like your fathers: You always resist the Holy Spirit!

Stephen apparently saw that his message was not being accepted. Possibly there was angry whispering among his hearers. He therefore rebuked them. They were "stiff-necked [stubborn] people, with uncircumcised hearts and ears." (See Exod. 32:9; 33:3; Lev. 26:41; Deut. 10:16; 30:6; 2 Chron. 30:7–8; 36:14–16; Jer. 6:10; 9:26; Ezek. 44:7.) Circumcision was the sign of acceptance of God's covenant and submission to His Word, will, and plan. The attitude of these Jews and their refusal to listen to the gospel put them in the same class as the Gentiles who were outside God's covenant and were rejecting Him. They were hearing, thinking, and planning in the way unbelieving,

---

[41]"Rest" in the Heb. also suggests the ceasing of activity. Where would God do this? As Isa. 40:28 shows, God is never weary.

uncircumcised Gentiles did. In fact, these Jewish leaders were actively resisting the Holy Spirit just as their fathers had.

52Was there ever a prophet your fathers did not persecute? They even killed those who predicted the coming of the Righteous One. And now you have betrayed and murdered him—

None of the prophets escaped persecution by the Fathers. (See Matt. 5:11–12; 23:30–31; Heb. 11:32–38.) They killed "those who predicted the coming of the Righteous One" (Acts 3:14; 22:14; 1 John 2:1). And now, as a climax to the father's rejection of the prophets, it was He, the Righteous One,[42] their children had "betrayed and murdered." (As with the apostles, Stephen focuses on the Cross.)

53you who have received the law that was put into effect through angels but have not obeyed it."

In fact, their guilt was greater than those who killed the prophets. These Jewish leaders who rejected Jesus had "received the Law that was put into effect [ordered, appointed] through angels."[43] But they did not keep it. That is, the Jewish leaders, not Jesus, not Stephen, nor the Christians, had disregarded the Law in killing Jesus.[44]

4. STEPHEN STONED 7:54–60

54When they heard this, they were furious and gnashed their teeth at him.

This rebuke infuriated the Sanhedrin (cut, sawed through, to their hearts), and these dignified Sanhedrin members "gnashed [ground] their teeth" at Stephen (cf. Pss. 35:16; 37:12; 112:10; Lam. 2:16). By this expression of rage and frenzied exasperation

---

[42]See Joel 2:23, "He will give you the teacher for righteousness" (my translation; cf. NIV footnote; Heb. *nathan lakhem 'eth hammoreh litsdaqah,* where *hammoreh* means "the teacher." See the translation in Job 36:22; Prov. 5:13; Isa. 30:20; Hab. 2:18). The Dead Sea Scrolls also refer to "the teacher of righteousness."

[43]See p. 151, n. 32.

[44]Note that Stephen did not call for repentance. These Jewish leaders had already rejected Peter's calls to repentance. Stephen's words recognized them as hardened in their rejection of Jesus.

they only proved they were truly resisting the Holy Spirit.

> 55But Stephen, full of the Holy Spirit, looked up to heaven and saw the glory of God, and Jesus standing at the right hand of God. 56"Look," he said, "I see heaven open and the Son of Man standing at the right hand of God."

In contrast to those who were resisting the Spirit, Stephen, being still "full of the Holy Spirit," "gazed intently into heaven and saw the glory of God" (NASB)[45] and Jesus standing at the right hand of God (in the place of authority).[46] Other passages speak of Jesus seated at the right hand of God (Matt. 26:64; Mark 14:62; 16:19; Luke 22:69; Eph. 1:20; Heb. 1:3,13; 8:1; 10:12). Stephen's description seems to indicate that Jesus rose to welcome the first martyr to give a witness at the cost of his life (see Matt. 20:22). Note, too, that Stephen used the term the Sanhedrin had heard Jesus use so often of himself, "the Son of Man." They must have remembered how Jesus identified himself with the Son of Man in Daniel 7:13–14, something they considered blasphemy (Mark 14:62–63).

> 57At this they covered their ears and, yelling at the top of their voices, they all rushed at him, 58dragged him out of the city and began to stone him. Meanwhile, the witnesses laid their clothes at the feet of a young man named Saul.

Hearing this, the Sanhedrin yelled (shrieked) and put their hands over their ears; thus they closed not only their ears but also their minds to Stephen's words and vision, proving their hearts were indeed uncircumcised (see v. 51 and commentary). Then, with one spontaneous impulse and purpose, they "rushed[47] at him," threw him out of the city (as the law of Moses required; Num. 15:35), and "began to stone him."

Roman law did not allow the Jews to carry out the death penalty (John 18:31). However, this was probably near the close of Pilate's governorship when he had fallen into disfavor with the Roman government, and these Jews took advantage of his weakness. There is also evidence that the imperial legate Vitellus (A.D.

[45]Cf. Exod. 33:18,22; Deut. 5:24; Ezek. 1:28; 8:4.
[46]Note the revelation of the Trinity here.
[47]The same word is used of the swine rushing down into the sea (Mark 5:13).

35–37) was at this time trying to win Jewish favor and would have been inclined to overlook whatever they did.

The Sanhedrin did follow legal procedure, however, with the witnesses casting the first stone (Lev. 24:13–23; Deut. 17:7). But they forgot justice and "'the more important matters of the law'" (Matt. 23:23). Then they took off their outer garments to allow them more freedom (and force) in throwing the large stones and laid the garments at the feet of a "young man"[48] named Saul. By this we see that Saul was an eyewitness to Stephen's death and probably to his preaching. This is the first mention of Saul and prepares us for what is said later.

> [59]While they were stoning him, Stephen prayed, "Lord Jesus, receive my spirit." [60]Then he fell on his knees and cried out, "Lord, do not hold this sin against them." When he had said this, he fell asleep.

Though they were stoning him Stephen did not pray for deliverance. Instead he prayed, "Lord Jesus, receive [welcome] my spirit." By addressing this prayer to Jesus he was recognizing that Jesus is divine, truly God. This must have enraged the Sadducees even further. Then he knelt and cried out with a loud voice, "Lord, do not hold this sin against them."[49] How like Jesus this was! (See Luke 23:34.)

Having said this, Stephen "fell asleep";[50] that is, he died (cf. 2 Cor. 5:8; Phil 1:23; 1 Thess. 4:15).[51] There was something peaceful about his death in spite of its violent nature. Thus Stephen went to be with Jesus and became the first martyr of the

---

[48]Gk. *neaniou,* referring to a man in his prime, up to the age of forty. Saul (Paul) was old enough to be a member of the Sanhedrin, probably about thirty-five. (In Acts 26:10, "'cast my vote'" is lit. "cast my pebble.") To vote, he had to be a member of the Sanhedrin. It is important to note that Saul was present at the death of Stephen and probably heard Stephen in the synagogue.

[49]"Lay not this sin to their charge" (v. 60, KJV) is a paraphrase that does give the meaning.

[50]Kistemaker points out, "The use of this verb indirectly points to the resurrection of the body." *Acts,* 282.

[51]I note that liberals who deny the historicity of much of Acts accept Stephen's criticism of law and cult as well as his death as historical. Gerd Lüdemann, *Early Christianity According to the Traditions in Acts* (Minneapolis: Fortress Press, 1984), 93.

Early Church, the first of a long line of believers who would give their lives for Jesus and the gospel, people who loved God and determined to "obey God rather than men" (Acts 5:29).[52]

5. Resulting Persecution Spreads The Gospel
    8:1–4

¹And Saul was there, giving approval to his death. On that day a great persecution broke out against the church at Jerusalem, and all except the apostles were scattered throughout Judea and Samaria.

Verses 1 and 3 of this chapter mention Saul. Then he is not mentioned again until chapter 9.[53] It says here that Saul was "giving approval to [Stephen's] death." The Greek is a little stronger: Saul wholly and completely approved of ("Saul was in hearty agreement with," NASB) Stephen's "death" (Gk. *anairesei*, "murder," cf. NEB et al.), and continued to act accordingly. He did not share the feelings of his former teacher, Gamaliel (Acts 5:38). Instead, Paul considered Stephen's ideas dangerous and felt that they should be rooted out. But neither he nor the rest of the Sanhedrin could root out the work of the Spirit.

Saul was undoubtedly one of the chief instigators of the persecution against the Church in Jerusalem that began "on that day," the very day Stephen was murdered. So intense was this persecution that the Christians were all "scattered throughout Judea and Samaria."[54] Only the apostles remained in Jerusalem. Verse 2 may indicate why.

²Godly men buried Stephen and mourned deeply for him.

[52]The word "martyr" originally meant simply "witness." As the Church was persecuted the word eventually came to mean one who was killed because of his or her testimony, or witness, to Christ.

[53]The first sentence of Acts 8:1 really belongs with the end of chap. 7. See, for example, Phillips.

[54]Some commentators believe the persecution was primarily, or even entirely, against the Hellenistic, or Greek-speaking, Jewish Christians and that only they fled. But the Bible says "all the believers except the apostles fled" (NLT). Some modern writers also suppose that the Jerusalem church contained no Hellenists after this. But the presence of Barnabas, a Hellenist, in Acts 11:22 and his being sent as a representative of the Jerusalem church refutes this idea. See Harrison, *Acts,* 130.

Devout men carried Stephen out, buried him, and "mourned deeply" (publicly beating their breasts) over him. This was unusual, for Jewish tradition was against showing this kind of respect or sorrow for an executed person, especially one executed for blasphemy. "Godly [devout] men" refers to men like those of Acts 2:5 where the same word is used. They were sincere, godly Jews who had not yet accepted Christ as their Messiah and Savior, but who respected Stephen and courageously rejected the decision of the Sanhedrin as wrong and unjust.[55] Through them the church in Jerusalem would grow again. In fact, by the time Paul returned to Jerusalem after his conversion, a strong church was there; and it continued to grow (9:31; 21:20).

3But Saul began to destroy the church. Going from house to house, he dragged off men and women and put them in prison.

In contrast to the devout men who lamented over Stephen, Saul became more and more furious, more violent in his persecution. In fact, he "made havoc of the church" (KJV). Literally, he kept on ravaging and devastating it.[56] Entering house after house, he dragged out men and women and handed them over to be put into prison. Then, as we learn later, when they were brought to trial he cast his vote to have them killed (Acts 22:4; 26:10).[57]

4Those who had been scattered preached the word wherever they went.

The persecution did not stop the spread of the gospel, however. It had exactly the opposite effect. Prior to this persecution the believers were receiving teaching and training from the apostles; now they were ready to move out. It took the persecution to make them do it, but move out they did (cf. Rom. 8:28).

---

55 See Hackett, *Commentary,* 107; Earle, *Acts of the Apostles,* 349.

56 The Gk. tense indicates continuous action. The LXX uses this word of a wild boar tearing up vineyards (Ps. 80:13). Cf. what 1 Pet. 5:8 says about the devil as our adversary.

57 Some suggest that Saul was repressing what he feared was the truth and had "a passionate desire to stamp out a conviction that the Christians were right." E. M. Blaiklock, *Acts: The Birth of the Church* (Old Tappan, N.J.: Fleming H. Revell, 1980), 72.

Those who were scattered did not settle down. Instead, hundreds of them kept traveling from place to place, spreading the good news, the gospel. Acts 11:19 says some traveled as far as Cyprus, Phoenicia, and Antioch. We can be sure they traveled equally far in other directions as well. Luke gives us hints of this from time to time, letting us know there were Christians in Galilee, Tyre, and Sidon, and even in Rome before Paul arrived there.

This does not mean the believers were all preachers in the modern sense. They were simply joyous and free in their witness to Jesus. Though just ordinary people, they were full of the Spirit, knew the Word, and became channels of the love and power of Jesus. Apparently none complained because of the persecution. They seized it as another opportunity to see what God would do.

STUDY QUESTIONS

1. What effect did the miracles Stephen performed have on the enemies of the gospel?
2. Why did Stephen's opponents not accept the truth when they found they had no arguments that would stand against it? See 1 Corinthians 2:14.
3. What grounds did the Sanhedrin think they had for the charges they made against Stephen?
4. How did Stephen respond to these unfair charges?
5. What effect did Stephen's martyrdom have on the Church?

III. MINISTRY IN SAMARIA AND JUDEA 8:5–11:18

A. Philip's Ministry 8:5–40

1. PHILIP'S PREACHING AND MIRACLES IN SAMARIA 8:5–13

⁵Philip went down to a city in Samaria and proclaimed the Christ there.

Many of those who were scattered did preach or proclaim the gospel publicly, however. After the general statement in verse 4, Luke gives us an example of what must have happened wherever the believers went. Philip the deacon (6:5; 21:8) is chosen as this example, not because what happened in Samaria was greater than what happened elsewhere, but because of the lessons learned there and because Samaria was next in line in the commission given in Acts 1:8.

Samaria was important, too, because the Spirit broke down another barrier there. Samaritans were descended from those of the ten northern tribes who had intermarried with people the Assyrians brought in after they captured Samaria in 722 B.C. At first, they had worshiped the Lord plus other gods (2 Kings 17:24–41). Later they also built a temple on Mount Gerizim. But about 128 B.C. the Jews under King John Hyrcanus went up and destroyed that temple and forced the Samaritans to give up their idolatry. In New Testament times the Samaritans followed the law of Moses much as the Jews did, but said sacrifices must be made on Mount Gerizim instead of at the Jerusalem temple (John 4:20).

Samaria was somewhat familiar territory to the Jews. Jewish travel through Samaria was constant and normal except for occasional periods of violence, as Josephus, the New Testament, and rabbinic literature confirm. At established stops Jews could obtain kosher food. So it was not unusual for Philip to go to Samaria. However, like the others who were scattered, he went there because the Spirit (see Acts 6:3,5) led him.

The city of Samaria, about ten miles north of where Jesus talked to the woman at the well, was rebuilt by Herod the Great and renamed Sebaste (Gk. for Augustus, thus honoring the emperor Caesar Augustus). But the Jews still called it Samaria. When Philip came to the city (the NIV follows a few ancient manuscripts that have "*a* city" rather than "*the* city"), he "proclaimed the Christ there" (and continued to proclaim the truth about Him as the Messiah and Savior, probably for several weeks or even months). We can be sure the ministry of Jesus in Samaria (John 4) was not forgotten. These things were "'not done in a corner'" (Acts 26:26). The Samaritans, like the Jews, looked for a Messiah in fulfillment of Deuteronomy 18:15,18–19 (see John 4:25–26,29).

⁶When the crowds heard Philip and saw the miraculous signs he did, they all paid close attention to what he said. ⁷With shrieks, evil spirits came out of many, and many paralytics and cripples were healed. ⁸So there was great joy in that city.

The crowds, all classes of people, with one accord "paid close attention" to Philip's message, listening to him, both hearing and seeing the miracles (signs) he kept doing. Here we see that the Lord's promise to confirm the Word "with signs following" (Mark 16:20, KJV) was not limited to the apostles. The people heard the loud shrieking of unclean spirits as they were cast out. They saw those who were paralyzed[1] and who were deaf healed. The result was "great joy in that city"—new and overflowing, the joy of health and salvation, real joy that is the fruit of the Spirit (Gal. 5:22). They were truly born again.

⁹Now for some time a man named Simon had practiced sorcery in the city and amazed all the people of Samaria. He boasted that he was someone great, ¹⁰and all the people, both high and low, gave him their attention and exclaimed, "This man is the divine power known as the Great Power." ¹¹They followed him because he had amazed them for a long time with his magic.

This success of the gospel was an even greater miracle than it first appeared. For these people previously had been "amazed"[2] by a man named Simon who "practiced sorcery" ("magic," NASB), saying he was "someone great" (or some great being).[3] Everyone, from the least to the greatest, paid attention to Simon and exclaimed, "This man is the divine power known as the Great Power." Or, as many ancient manuscripts have it, "This man is the great power of God."[4] They had given him their attention for

[1]"Palsy" (see v. 7, KJV) is from the Middle English word for paralysis. It does not refer to "shaking" palsy. These people were in a helpless condition, paralyzed.

[2]The same verb is translated "astonished" in v. 13. But here it does not imply any supernatural powers on the part of Simon. He deceived the Samaritans.

[3]"Great" in Latin is *magus,* so he is often called Simon Magus. It is also possible that the Gk. *megalē* may be "the transliteration of a Samaritan expression meaning 'revealing.' Simon may have given himself out to be 'the Revealing Power.'" David John Williams, *Acts* (Peabody, Mass.: Hendrickson Publishers, 1990), 159.

[4]Like some modern cult leaders, he did not exactly say he was a manifestation

a considerable time because he amazed them with his magic arts—not only magic tricks, but occult powers that had their origin in Satan and were forbidden by God (Deut. 18:10–12).

> **12But when they believed Philip as he preached the good news of the kingdom of God and the name of Jesus Christ, they were baptized, both men and women. 13Simon himself believed and was baptized. And he followed Philip everywhere, astonished by the great signs and miracles he saw.**

The Samaritans saw something far more wonderful in the miracles of Philip than in the works of Simon, accepting in effect the rule and power of God's kingdom and the name of Jesus Christ. Philip emphasized this rule and power as being manifested through the character and nature of the Messiah and Savior. Certainly Philip presented everything that Peter had presented on the Day of Pentecost (and later). This included Christ's work as the crucified and risen Savior and Lord. Then they were baptized,5 "both men and women."

Finally, even "Simon himself believed" exactly as the others did and "was baptized." Then he "attached himself closely" (Phillips) to Philip. Simon was used to deceiving people by his magic arts; he also knew astonishing things could be done by trickery. He had watched Philip with the professional eye of a magician and had concluded that these miracles were real. Clearly, these "great[6] signs and miracles," deeds of power, were supernatural. So Simon too was "astonished" (filled with wonder and amazement). These miracles were quite unlike the magic arts he used.

Some have questioned whether Simon truly believed.7 But the Bible says he did and does not qualify the statement in any way.

---

of God or that he was the Messiah, but he tried to leave that impression. The people probably thought he was a "manifestation or embodiment of 'the Great Power'." James D. G. Dunn, *The Acts of the Apostles* (Valley Forge, Pa.: Trinity Press International, 1996), 109.

5Not a mass baptism but numerous baptisms over a period of time.

6Gk. *megalas;* cf. 6:8.

7French L. Arrington, "The Acts of the Apostles," in *Full Life Bible Commentary to the New Testament,* ed. French L. Arrington and Roger Stronstad (Grand Rapids: Zondervan Publishing House, 1999), 576.

Moreover, Philip, a man led by the Spirit, surely would not have baptized him if he had not given evidence of being a true believer.

2. Peter And John Minister In Samaria 8:14–25

a. Samaritans Receive The Holy Spirit 8:14–17

14When the apostles in Jerusalem heard that Samaria had accepted the word of God, they sent Peter and John to them.

The news that Samaria had "accepted [welcomed and was continuing to welcome] the word of God [the gospel]"[8] soon reached the apostles in Jerusalem. The gospel had gotten beyond its first ethnic and geographic hurdle. So the apostles sent Peter and John to Samaria (with a message and a purpose) to find out the facts and encourage the new believers. There is no indication in this, however, that the apostles thought Philip's ministry was in any way inferior or lacking. They just wanted to see if the Holy Spirit had sanctioned this, and they wanted to help.

15When they arrived, they prayed for them that they might receive the Holy Spirit, 16because the Holy Spirit had not yet come upon any of them; they had simply been baptized into the name of the Lord Jesus.

When the two apostles arrived, in line with the teaching of Jesus (Luke 11:13) the first thing they did was to pray for the Samaritan believers to "receive the Holy Spirit." Clearly, the apostles believed the baptism in the Holy Spirit to be important for everyone. Though the Samaritans had been baptized in water and "into the name [into the worship and service] of the Lord Jesus," none had received the gift of the Spirit with the evidence of speaking in other tongues. That is, the Spirit had not fallen on any of them in the way He had fallen on the believers on the Day of Pentecost.[9]

Some suppose the faith of the Samaritans was not truly in Jesus until Peter and John came and prayed. But Philip was a

---

[8]"Accepting (receiving, welcoming) the word of God" is one of the ways the NT refers to the "born again" experience.

[9]See J. W. Packer, *Acts of the Apostles* (Cambridge, England: Cambridge University Press, 1975), 65.

man "full of the Spirit and wisdom" (Acts 6:3). He would not have baptized any of them if their faith had not been real.[10]

Others suppose Philip did not teach the Samaritans about the baptism in the Holy Spirit. But the very fact that Philip came and preached Christ to them shows he believed the promise was for them. It is clear also that the believers were not able to withhold any part of the message (see Acts 4:20). "There is nothing in Luke's account which would suggest that Philip's message was either deficient or misunderstood."[11]

As we have seen, the Samaritans believed what Philip preached concerning the rule of God and the authority of Jesus. The preaching in Acts associates these things with the promise of the Holy Spirit. We can be sure Philip, like the other preachers in the Book of Acts, included the message of Jesus' exaltation to the right hand of the Father and the giving of the promise of the Father, the baptism in the Holy Spirit.

> The problem seems to be on the side of the Samaritans. Now they realized they had been wrong, not only about the deceptions of Simon the sorcerer, but also about their Samaritan doctrines. Perhaps, humbled, they found it difficult to express the next step of faith necessary to receive the baptism in the Spirit. When Jesus found faith expressed in a simple way based solely on His Word, He called it great faith, and things happened (Matt. 8:10,13). When faith rose above hindrances and testing, Jesus called it great faith, and things happened (Matt. 15:28). But when faith was weak, He did not destroy what there was. He helped it, sometimes by laying on His hands.[12]

Whether or not Peter and John gave further teaching first, Luke does not record. But when we compare what was done at other

[10]Turner rightly challenges James D. G. Dunn's view that the Samaritans' faith was inadequate before Peter and John came. Max Turner, *Power From on High: The Spirit in Israel's Restoration and Witness in Luke-Acts* (Sheffield, England: Sheffield Academic Press, 1996), 362–67. See also Anthony D. Palma, *Baptism in the Holy Spirit* (Springfield, Mo.: Gospel Publishing House, 1999), 23–24.

[11]William W. Menzies and Robert P. Menzies, *Spirit and Power: Foundations of Pentecostal Experience* (Grand Rapids: Zondervan Publishing House, 2000), 53–54.

[12]Stanley M. Horton, *What the Bible Says About the Holy Spirit* (Springfield, Mo.: Gospel Publishing House, 1976), 154.

times, it seems very probable that they did.

17Then Peter and John placed their hands on them, and they received the Holy Spirit.

Then, after the two apostles prayed for the Samaritans, they laid their hands on them, recognizing them as fellow members of the body of Christ. God confirmed the faith of the believers, and they received the Spirit (publicly, probably one after the other as the apostles laid their hands on them). Since God's gifts are all by grace through faith (Eph. 2:8; see also Acts 3:16; 6:8; 14:9–10; Rom. 12:6) and distributed as the Spirit determines (1 Cor. 12:11), it is evident that the touch of the apostles' hands was simply a means of encouraging faith and expectation.

b. Simon Offers To Buy The Gift 8:18–24

18When Simon saw that the Spirit was given at the laying on of the apostles' hands, he offered them money 19and said, "Give me also this ability so that everyone on whom I lay my hands may receive the Holy Spirit."

Something that happened caught Simon's attention. Luke does not describe what it was, but, as we have seen, Luke often does not explain everything when it is clear elsewhere. For example, he does not mention water baptism every time he tells about people believing or being added to the Church; however, it is clear that the failure to mention water baptism is not significant. Other places show that all believers were baptized in water. For this reason we can say that the fact Luke does not mention speaking in tongues here is not significant.

It is clear, however, that Simon had already seen Philip's miracles. Prophecy would not have attracted his attention, because it would have been in a known language and not obviously supernatural. There is actually only one thing that fits: On the Day of Pentecost, they spoke in tongues as the Spirit gave utterance; this attracted the attention of the crowd.[13] Speaking in tongues by the Samaritan believers obviously did the same for Simon.[14] But

---

[13]"Luke knows of no silent comings of the Spirit!" Dunn, *Acts of the Apostles,* 111.

[14]Johannes Munck, *The Acts of the Apostles,* rev. William F. Albright and C. S. Mann, vol. 31 of *Anchor Bible Series* (Garden City, N.Y.: Doubleday & Co., 1979), 75.

speaking in other tongues is not the point at issue in this passage. Nor did it have the same effect as on the Day of Pentecost, for there were no others present who knew foreign languages. Luke says nothing about the tongues, therefore, in order to focus attention on Simon's wrong attitude.

Simon, "when [he] saw that the Spirit was given at the laying on of the apostles' hands," did not come himself to receive. Instead, he fell back into his old greed and desire for self-exaltation: He brought to them riches as an offering if they would give him the authority to lay his hands on people with the same result.[15]

Verses 17 and 18 do not mean, however, that the apostles had any such authority. They prayed first that the believers might receive the Spirit. They certainly recognized that it was the promise of the Father and that it must come from heaven. The word "at" (Gk. *dia*) in verse 18 indicates secondary agency. That is, Jesus is the Baptizer in the Holy Spirit (Acts 2:33). The apostles were merely His agents, praying for and encouraging the faith of these believers to receive.

Nor is there any implication here that the laying on of hands was necessary to receive the Spirit, though Simon jumped to that conclusion, just as many modern teachers have.[16] Many other passages show Simon was wrong. There was no laying on of hands on the Day of Pentecost or at the house of Cornelius (2:4; 10:44). Nor was the laying on of hands limited to the apostles, since Ananias, a layman of Damascus, laid his hands on Paul for both healing and the receiving of the Holy Spirit (9:17). The Galatians received the Spirit not by the laying on of hands but by believing what they heard (Gal. 3:2).[17] The laying on of hands here was a means of welcoming them as fellow believers as well as a means of encouraging their faith to receive the gift of the Spirit in answer to their prayers.[18]

[15]Turner says, "It is an interesting and sobering question whether Simon Magus would be tempted in the same way by what he saw (or did not see) in many of our churches today." *Power from on High,* 440.

[16]Rudolf Bultmann, *Theology of the New Testament,* 2 vols. (New York: Charles Scribner's Sons, 1951), 1:139.

[17]This refutes the Roman Catholic doctrine of apostolic succession and shows that their sacrament of confirmation is not biblical.

[18]See J. A. Alexander, *A Commentary on the Acts of the Apostles,* 3d ed. (1875; reprint, London: Banner of Truth Trust, 1956), 1:332; F. F. Bruce, *Commentary*

20Peter answered: "May your money perish with you, because you thought you could buy the gift of God with money! 21You have no part or share[19] in this ministry, because your heart is not right before God.

Peter rebuked Simon severely. Literally, he said, "Let your money (silver) together with you go into destruction [probably the destruction of the lake of fire] because you thought the free gift of God [that is, God's gift of the Holy Spirit, as in 2:38; 10:45] could be purchased with [earthly] riches. You have neither part nor share in this matter, for your heart is not right [straight] before God." Though he had believed and been baptized, he allowed his heart to turn away from God to self.

Some suppose that Simon's desire to purchase God's gift (free and freely given) for money means that he wanted to offer it for sale. But this would have made no sense: The apostles were offering it freely, as the free gift of God. Anyone could receive it. More probably, Simon saw an opportunity to restore his prestige and leadership among the people by becoming an authoritative giver of the gift of the Spirit (which is what he incorrectly concluded about the apostles).

Actually, Peter's rebuke of Simon for his thinking that God's gift could be bought suggests also that Simon *could* have had a share in the matter—if he had come in faith for the gift instead of offering money. In other words, anyone who has received the free gift of the Spirit can pray for others to receive the same gift.

22Repent of this wickedness and pray to the Lord. Perhaps he will forgive you for having such a thought in your heart. 23For I see that you are full of bitterness and captive to sin."

Peter then showed that Simon's case was not entirely hopeless by exhorting him to "repent of this wickedness and pray to [request of] the Lord" that the "thought" (including the wicked purpose) might be forgiven. There is no question here about

---

on the Book of Acts (Grand Rapids: Wm. B. Eerdmans, 1954), 182–83. See also Robert L. Brandt and Zenas J. Bicket, *The Spirit Helps Us Pray: A Biblical Theology of Prayer* (Springfield, Mo.: Logion Press, 1993), 249.

19"Part" and "share" are synonyms here. The repetition is for emphasis.

God's willingness to forgive. God always freely forgives those who come to Him confessing their sin (1 John 1:9). Peter added the "perhaps" because of the condition of Simon's heart: His pride and greed had caused him to fall into this sin. Peter realized Simon was "full of bitterness," having an embittered, resentful spirit, because the people ceased to give him prominence (cf. Deut. 29:18; 1 Sam. 30:6; Jer. 2:19 for OT use of these expressions). Such a spirit often refuses reconciliation and certainly grieves the Holy Spirit (Eph. 4:30–31). Simon was also "captive to sin," in the grip of iniquity, injustice, and unrighteousness; he was unjust in wanting to receive this power for himself, and also his wrong attitude had such a grip on him that it would be difficult for him to break loose. It is possible, however, that the Greek means Simon was headed for such bitterness and captivity. This would mean they did not yet bind him and there was greater hope for him if he would repent immediately.

[24]Then Simon answered, "Pray to the Lord for me so that nothing you have said may happen to me."

Simon responded by begging Peter and John to pray in his behalf (emphatic, "you add your prayers to mine") so that none of these things Peter had spoken would come upon him.[20]

There is considerable controversy about what happened to Simon. Some suggest that he wanted prayer only because he was afraid of judgment. But the Greek indicates he wanted the apostles to pray along with him. This does indicate a change of attitude and therefore repentance.[21] The Bible says nothing more about him. The traditions that arose about him in later times have no biblical basis.[22] However, he is a warning to those who

[20]Codex Bezae (D) adds that Simon did not stop weeping much tears.

[21]John Calvin thought Simon repented. *Commentary on the Acts of the Apostles* (Grand Rapids: Wm. B. Eerdmans, 1966), 1:241.

[22]Some say he introduced a Gnostic sect. Others try to connect him with an Italian deity and say he went to Rome and declared himself a god there. But there is not a shred of real evidence for any of this. Because of what he attempted, "simony" has become a term for buying a place of authority or an office in the church. Actually, as Lenski points out, we should be thankful to God for his repentance. See P. C. H. Lenski, *The Interpretation of the Acts of the Apostles* (Columbus, Ohio: Wartburg Press, 1940), 332–33.

project themselves as "someone great" (v. 9) and equate "the gift of the Spirit with worldly standards of power and success."[23]

c. Peter And John Preach In Samaria 8:25

25When they had testified and proclaimed the word of the Lord, Peter and John returned to Jerusalem, preaching the gospel in many Samaritan villages.

Peter and John continued in Samaria for a time, presenting strong biblical evidence in their witness for the Lord. Probably they included more of the life, ministry, and teachings of Jesus. Then on the way back to Jerusalem they preached the good news "in many Samaritan villages" (cf. Acts 1:8) (the last time Luke records any of John's activities). Luke mentions no Samaritan opposition to the gospel. However, the fact that Peter and John did not preach to the Samaritans on the way into Samaria may suggest that the outpouring of the Spirit in Samaria made them realize that the gospel's relevance went beyond the Jews.

3. THE ETHIOPIAN EUNUCH 8:26-40

26Now an angel of the Lord said to Philip, "Go south to the road—the desert road—that goes down from Jerusalem to Gaza."

Now that Judea and Samaria had received the gospel it was time for the gospel to begin to move out toward "'the ends of the earth'" (Acts 1:8). At this point "an angel of the Lord"[24] spoke to Philip telling him to rise up[25] and go toward the south[26] to the desert road going down from Jerusalem to Gaza. "Desert" also means "deserted, abandoned, desolate." Here, the emphasis is that the area was largely uninhabited.

The Bible tells of angels appearing to people comparatively

[23]William H. Willimon, *Acts* (Atlanta: John Knox Press, 1988), 70.

[24]"Angel" means "messenger." This was an angelic messenger the Lord sent from heaven.

[25]The Gk. *anastethi*, left untranslated by the NIV, calls for immediate action; the timing here was important. (Cf. NLT, CEVs footnote.)

[26]Gk. *kata mesēmbrian* more often means "about noon," when few travelers would be on the road. Some commentators believe the angel was directing Philip to be on the road when few travelers would be there—another step of faith.

few times. Yet they are often present and function as "ministering spirits, sent to serve those who will inherit salvation" (Heb. 1:14).[27] However, since they are spirits, God has to give them a physical form temporarily in order for them to appear and speak to people.

There may have been a special reason for sending an angel. Philip was in the midst of a great revival in Samaria. It probably took something unusual to get him to leave the crowds and go down to a seldom-used back road. Some take "desert" to refer to Old Testament Gaza, the most southern of the five cities of the Philistines. About sixty miles southwest of Jerusalem, it was destroyed in 93 B.C. In 57 B.C. a new city was built nearer the Mediterranean Sea. The road to old Gaza might be called the road to desert (deserted) Gaza. To go there must have seemed unreasonable, but the desert road may have reminded Philip of Isaiah's cry, "'In the desert prepare the way for the Lord'" (Isa. 40:3).

> [27]So he started out, and on his way[28] he met an Ethiopian eunuch, an important official in charge of all the treasury of Candace, queen of the Ethiopians. This man had gone to Jerusalem to worship, [28]and on his way home was sitting in his chariot reading the book of Isaiah the prophet.

The angel revealed nothing about God's purpose, but when the angel spoke, that was enough: Philip did not hesitate; he arose and went in obedience and, we can be sure, with faith and expectation. His faith was like the faith of Abraham "who obeyed and went, even though he did not know where he was going" (Heb. 11:8).

God was leading him, for at the very time he reached the Gaza road,[29] the chariot of an Ethiopian eunuch was approaching. In ancient times, most officers in palaces were eunuchs. He was a highly placed officer (a potentate), a member of the court of the Ethiopian queen Candace and "in charge of all [her] treasury."

---

[27]Heb. chap. 1 shows Christ's superiority to angels; Jesus himself at the cross could have had ten legions of angels if He had desired them. Heb. 12:22 speaks of an innumerable company of angels. Rev. 5:11 also speaks of great numbers.

[28]The Gk. has *idou*, "behold" (indicating something unexpected or surprising), at this point (cf. NEB).

[29]Philip was surprised, but God's timing was just right.

We might say he was a member of the cabinet and would compare to the secretary of the treasury, but with full responsibility for the care and disbursement of funds.

"Candace" was not a personal name but the hereditary title of the queens of Ethiopia, whose seat of government was on the island of Meroë in the Nile River. Ethiopia itself corresponds to what is today called the Sudan,[30] though it may have included part of modern Ethiopia. The eunuch probably attended a Jewish synagogue on Meroë.

This eunuch had come a long distance "to Jerusalem to worship." Though he was a God-fearing Gentile or a convert to Judaism (or, possibly a Diaspora Jew), because of his being a eunuch he could go only as far as the Court of the Gentiles.[31] Even so, he purchased the scrolls of Isaiah (and probably of other OT books) to take back with him.[32] These were hand-copied and extremely expensive in those days. Usually a whole synagogue would join together to buy one set, which they would keep locked up except for use in the worship and in the synagogue school.

[29]The Spirit told Philip, "Go to that chariot and stay near it."

Now the eunuch was returning home, sitting in his chariot "reading the book of Isaiah."

At this point the Spirit spoke to Philip, possibly by an inner voice.[33] (Guidance by the Spirit is prominent in Acts.) Philip did not need an angel to speak to him this time. He was undoubt-

[30]Its people may have been dark skinned, but they were members of the Caucasoid race.

[31]See Deut. 23:1; some writers believe that because of Isa. 56:3–5, this rule was relaxed in NT times. On the other hand, the fact that he was a eunuch may have kept him from being a full proselyte, so that he would be classed as a God-fearing Gentile who worshiped the true God but could not go beyond the Court of the Gentiles in the temple.

[32]Since Greek was the language of higher education and of trade and government communications, he would have known Greek; the scrolls would have been of the LXX.

[33]Shepherd points out that the Spirit speaks here independently. He qualifies as a "character" who "acts explicitly and extraordinarily . . . (8:39–40)." William H. Shepherd, Jr., *The Narrative Function of the Holy Spirit as a Character in Luke-Acts* (Atlanta: Scholars Press, 1994), 90–91.

edly looking to the Lord to know what to do. The Spirit's command was to "go . . . and stay near" this chariot.[34]

> **30Then Philip ran up to the chariot and heard the man reading Isaiah the prophet. "Do you understand what you are reading?" Philip asked. 31"How can I," he said, "unless someone explains it to me?" So he invited Philip to come up and sit with him.**

In obedience Philip ran to the chariot. As he ran alongside the chariot he "heard the man reading Isaiah the prophet." (Reading in those days was almost always done aloud.) Philip interrupted him and asked if he understood what he was reading. His reply was a question that let Philip know he felt he was incapable of understanding it and needed someone to explain[35] it to him. Then he "invited"[36] Philip "to come up and sit with him" in the chariot.

> **32The eunuch was reading this passage of Scripture: "He was led like a sheep to the slaughter, and as a lamb before the shearer is silent, so he did not open his mouth. 33In his humiliation he was deprived of justice. Who can speak of his descendants? For his life was taken from the earth."**

Philip did not need a second invitation. In the providence of God the eunuch was reading Isaiah 53:7–8 (from the LXX). This must have been exciting to Philip as he saw how wonderful and how exact God's timing was! It must have made him realize how God himself focused on the message of the suffering, death, and resurrection of Jesus as the crux of the gospel.

> **34The eunuch asked Philip, "Tell me, please, who is the prophet talking about, himself or someone else?" 35Then Philip began with that very passage of Scripture and told him the good news about Jesus.**

The eunuch then asked Philip, "Who is the prophet talking about?" His question shows he had been considering Isaiah 53 earnestly but was not satisfied with any of the interpretations he

---

34The Gk. uses a figure of speech: He was to "glue" himself to the chariot.

35Gk. *hodēgēsai*, "lead along a road, guide," cf. Luke 6:39.

36The Gk. *parekalesen* followed by the accusative indicates urgency ("he begged Philip," NLT).

had heard. Jews at this time did not apply it to a suffering Messiah. Some applied the passage to Isaiah. Isaiah became a martyr and Jewish tradition says Manasseh had him sawn in half (see Heb. 11:37). But Isaiah had position and wealth and had free access to the king's palace. He was not the humble sufferer of Isaiah 53. Others applied the passage to Jeremiah, who suffered more than any other Old Testament prophet. Jeremiah, however, did open his mouth often to complain (Jer. 12:3; 20:14–18).[37]

Isaiah 53 speaks of the One who suffers wholly for the sins of others and not for any of his own. The eunuch knew no one who could do that and he was puzzled.

This was Philip's great opportunity. Isaiah 53 is a high point in God's revelation of His will and plan. Someone has called it "the Mount Everest of Messianic Prophecy." Beginning at that very Scripture passage, this Spirit-filled, Spirit-led evangelist "told him the good news about Jesus." Jesus alone never sinned and never did anything to deserve suffering or death. For those who will see it, no passage in the prophets more clearly pictures the vicarious suffering, death, resurrection, and triumph of Jesus. He alone is the sacrificial Lamb of God.[38] Though His life was taken, He arose, and His spiritual descendants are "heirs of God and co-heirs with Christ" (Rom. 8:17). But Philip only began at Isaiah 53. He went on to explain the gospel further, with its commands, promises, and call to repentance, as Peter did (Acts 2:38). He made it clear that without Jesus no one can properly understand the Old Testament Scriptures.[39]

36As they traveled along the road, they came to some water and the eunuch said, "Look, here is water. Why

[37]In a class I took at Harvard Divinity School, a Jewish rabbi said, "Our rabbis teach that the suffering servant in Isaiah is Israel and that now that we have no temple and cannot offer sacrifices, we are made acceptable to God by our own sufferings." The professor pointed out that the suffering in Isa. 53 is vicarious—totally for others. None of us can say we have never sinned or that we have never brought any of our sufferings on ourselves. Jesus alone fits Isa. 53. Cf. Mark 10:45 and Isa. 53:11–12.

[38]Because this passage so clearly applies to Christ, this chap. is seldom read in Jewish synagogues and I have found that some Jews are not familiar with it.

[39]Clare Amos, "Acts," in *Sowers and Reapers,* ed. John Parr (Nashville: Abingdon Press, 1994), 413.

shouldn't I be baptized?" [37][Philip said, "If you believe with all your heart, you may." The eunuch answered, "I believe that Jesus Christ is the son of God."]

The Holy Spirit must have helped the eunuch to understand the gospel and accept the way of salvation. As Philip and the eunuch went down the road they came to some water. The eunuch called attention to it. "Look" is the same word translated "behold" in verse 27 (KJV) and indicates something unexpected. Most of southern Palestine is rather dry. The eunuch did not want to pass by the water without being baptized. He put his request in the form of a question, "Why shouldn't I be baptized?" (Gk. *ti kōluei me baptisthēnai,* "'What prevents[40] me from being baptized?'" NASB). Probably he was afraid that his being a Gentile and a eunuch might bar him from this, just as it barred him from most of the Jewish worship. Philip then asked for and received a confession of faith.[41]

[38]**And he gave orders to stop the chariot. Then both Philip and the eunuch went down into the water and Philip baptized him.**

Then, after commanding the driver of the chariot to stop, they both left the chariot and "went down into the water." In fact, Luke draws attention to the fact that both went "down into" the water. Then Philip baptized him and they came "up out of" the water (v. 39). The language here makes it clear that the word "baptize" has its usual meaning of immerse, submerge, dip

[40]This verb is translated "keep from" in 10:47 and "oppose" in 11:17. In both cases it is "linked with the Spirit and baptism." Howard Clark Kee, *To Every Nation Under Heaven: The Acts of the Apostles* (Harrisburg, Pa.: Trinity Press International, 1997), 111. This indicates that when the eunuch was baptized in water he was also baptized in the Holy Spirit. See comment on v. 39.

[41]Some ancient manuscripts omit v. 37, but it fits the context and reflects the practice of the Early Church. It is found in the Western Text and is also quoted by early church fathers such as Cyprian and Irenaeus (*Against Heresies* 3.22.8). Some say the v. has a different style and must be an insertion; see Simon J. Kistemaker, *Exposition of the Acts of the Apostles* (Grand Rapids: Baker Book House, 1990), 320. However, for reasons that the v. cannot "be dismissed as an obvious example of pious expansion in the text," see W. A. Strange, *The Problem of the Text of Acts* (Cambridge, England: Cambridge University Press, 1992), 69–75.

under. Many other passages make it clear that immersion was the practice of the Early Church.[42]

> [39]When they came up out of the water, the Spirit of the Lord suddenly took Philip away, and the eunuch did not see him again, but went on his way rejoicing.

After they came up out of the water the Spirit took charge and with power snatched away Philip.[43] Luke does not explain how the Spirit "took Philip away."[44] The verb used usually means "to snatch away." In 1 Thessalonians 4:17 it is used of the rapture of the Church. In 2 Corinthians 12:2,4 it is used of Paul's being caught up to heaven. In any case, the eunuch saw Philip no more, but as a child of God he "went on his way rejoicing." A few ancient manuscripts and versions add that the Holy Spirit fell on the eunuch.[45] We can be sure that he was indeed baptized in the Spirit and that this added to his rejoicing (cf. Acts 13:52). Undoubtedly, he then spread the gospel in his own country.

> [40]Philip, however, appeared at Azotus and traveled about, preaching the gospel in all the towns until he reached Caesarea.

Apparently the Spirit gave Philip a supersonic ride over to the coast at Azotus (near the site of the ancient Ashdod, about eighteen miles north of Gaza and fifty-five miles south of Caesarea), where he "appeared" (Gk. *eurethē,* "was found" or "found

[42]Archaeologists have discovered baptisteries for immersion in the ruins of second-century church buildings, indicating that for at least two centuries baptism was practiced by immersion.

[43]Roger Stronstad points out that "Philip's witness to the Ethiopian is both introduced and concluded by references to the Holy Spirit, on the narrative strategy of inclusio (Acts 8.29,39). Thus, . . . Philip is another example of the many disciples who were prophets powerful in works and word." *The Prophethood of All Believers: A Study in Luke's Charismatic Theology* (Sheffield, England: Sheffield Academic Press, 1999), 93.

[44]Cf. Elijah (2 Kings 2:11), Ezekiel (Ezek. 8:3), Jesus and His disciples in a boat (John 6:21).

[45]The longer reading that says the Spirit fell on the eunuch after his baptism in water fits Luke's deliberate pairing of the account of the eunuch and that of Simon Magus. It also fits the account in 19:5–6. "The longer text of Acts 8:39 is the original reading, the text in most witnesses having been accidentally shortened by scribal error." Strange, *Problem of the Text,* 76.

himself"—also indicating suddenness or "unexpectedness"[46]).

From there Philip proceeded northward along the Mediterranean coast preaching the gospel (evangelizing) in all the towns until he came to Caesarea.[47] Built by Herod the Great, it was the capital of the province of Judea. Philip was still there years later. Evidently he made it his home and headquarters from this point on. But he still traveled around and became known as Philip the evangelist (Acts 21:8).[48]

STUDY QUESTIONS

1. What were Philip's qualifications for ministry?
2. What was the result of Philip's powerful preaching in Samaria?
3. Was Simon the sorcerer really saved? Explain.
4. In what ways did the Lord guide Philip?
5. What qualifications of a successful soul winner did Philip have?
6. What indicates that God's Word had truly satisfied the heart and mind of the Ethiopian eunuch?

B. Saul's Conversion 9:1–31

1. SAUL THREATENS THE DISCIPLES 9:1–2

[1]Meanwhile, Saul was still breathing out murderous threats against the Lord's disciples. He went to the high priest [2]and asked him for letters to the synagogues in Damascus, so that if he found any there who belonged to the Way, whether men or women, he might take them as prisoners to Jerusalem.

What happened at Samaria apparently did not concern Saul

---

[46]Dunn, *Acts of the Apostles*, 115.

[47]The itinerary from Gaza to Ashdod to Caesarea makes sense and is true to the geography of Palestine—another indication of the reliability and antiquity of Acts.

[48]Papias and others reported that Philip and his prophet daughters later went to Hierapolis in Phrygia (Eusebius HE 3.39.9).

since the participants were not Jewish. But other believers who were scattered went north, probably through Galilee and on to Damascus. Damascus was the oldest and most important city in Syria.[1] It seems to have had a large Jewish population at this time, for verse 2 speaks of "synagogues," in the plural. Saul must have at least heard rumors that the scattered believers were having success in preaching the gospel there. This leads to a most important event, one so important that it is recorded three times in the Book of Acts (9:1–19; 22:3–21; 26:4–23).[2]

Some of the others who joined in the persecution of Acts 8:1 may have lost their zeal against the Christians—but not Saul. He was "still breathing out murderous threats" ("threatening," the Gk. is singular, and "slaughter" [KJV], or "murder" [NASB]). Later (Acts 26:10) he told about how he voted for their deaths.

"Breathing out" here is literally "breathing in." It is a Greek participle *(empneōn)* indicating it had become characteristic and continuous. In other words, Saul created an atmosphere around him of threats and murder so that he was constantly breathing it in. As oxygen enables an athlete to keep going, so this atmosphere kept Saul going. He put many in prison and voted to put them to death (26:10; see also Gal. 1:13).

Now, however, most of the believers had left Jerusalem. So Saul went of his own accord to the high priest, probably Caiaphas, and asked for official letters to the synagogues at Damascus,[3] giving him authority to arrest any of "the Way," men or women, and to bring them bound as prisoners to Jerusalem (Acts 26:11–12). This would mean a trial before the Sanhedrin and probably the death sentence (like that of Stephen).

"The Way" was an interesting title for the believers, one they

---

[1]At this time Damascus was probably outside the Roman Empire and was under King Aretas, who made it part of Arabia. Aretas was anti-Roman; so were the Jews. Thus, it seems Aretas allowed Jews freedom and gave the Jerusalem leaders authority over the Jews in Damascus. See Everett F. Harrison, *Acts: The Expanding Church* (Chicago: Moody Press, 1975), 146.

[2]Paul indicates that he was converted fourteen to seventeen years before the Jerusalem Council of A.D. 49 (Gal. 1:18; 2:1). This is another indication that Jesus was crucified in A.D. 29 or 30.

[3]One of the oldest cities in the world, having an almost continuous history to the present.

could accept: Jesus is the way of salvation, the way of life. (See many OT passages that speak of the ways of the Lord. In addition, in John 14:6 Jesus identifies *himself* as the Way; and in Acts 19:9,23; 22:4; 24:14,22 the Way designates those who have accepted the full gospel message of Jesus and the Holy Spirit. See also 18:25–26.)[4]

That Paul wanted to make arrests regardless of gender, "whether men or women," shows he noticed that the believing women were as active as the men, and he considered them just as dangerous. The law of Moses placed women on a high level, but Pharisees tended to ignore and degrade them. In the Church, women from the beginning were outstanding in prayer, in Christian love and service, and in the gifts of the Spirit. In Christ and in the ministry of the Spirit there is "neither . . . male nor female" (Gal. 3:28).

2. Jesus Appears To Saul In Blinding Light
9:3–9

³As he neared Damascus on his journey, suddenly a light from heaven flashed around him. ⁴He fell to the ground and heard a voice say to him, "Saul, Saul, why do you persecute me?"

Damascus was about 140 miles northeast of Jerusalem, and nearly 200 miles by road in those days. Near the end of the journey a light from heaven unexpectedly flashed like lightning around Saul. As he told King Agrippa, it continued to shine around him with a light brighter than the noonday sun (26:13).

Light in the Bible is often associated with manifestations of the presence of the Lord or the manifestation of His glory. Rabbis called it the Shekinah. On the Mount of Transfiguration, Peter, James, and John saw Jesus' face shining "like the sun" (Matt. 17:2). In John 17:5, Jesus prayed to His Father, saying, "'Glorify me in your presence with the glory I had with you before the world began.'" When Jesus rose from the dead, His resurrection body was transformed—it was immortal and incorruptible, as ours will be (1 Cor. 15:52–53). But the glory was not restored

---

[4]The Dead Sea sectarian scrolls also use the term repeatedly of those who chose to follow the Qumran community's way of life.

until after He ascended. Probably the disciples could not have stood the glory during the forty days Jesus remained on earth with them. But now He came to Saul as the risen and glorified Christ. Later on, Saul spoke of this in writing to the believers at Corinth: "Last of all [after Jesus' other resurrection appearances] he appeared to me also, as to one abnormally born" (1 Cor. 15:8).[5]

Saul, who was probably walking, recognized the light as beyond the ordinary, or supernatural, so fell facedown to the ground, prostrating himself (as Orientals did to show humility, respect, and, sometimes, worship). Then he heard a voice, "Saul, Saul, why do you persecute me?" Luke, in referring to Saul, always uses the Greek form of his name (as in v. 1, *Saulos*). Jesus used the Hebrew form *(Saoul),* which the Book of Acts is careful to preserve here. Saul later confirms that Jesus was speaking in Hebrew (Acts 26:14).[6] Jesus repeated the name twice. Compare this with how God sometimes addressed men in the Old Testament: "'Abraham! Abraham!'" (Gen.22:11), "'Jacob, Jacob'" (Gen. 46:2), "'Moses, Moses!'" (Exod. 3:4). This would make Saul realize that the voice was not that of an ordinary man.

[5]"Who are you, Lord?" Saul asked. "I am Jesus, whom you are persecuting," he replied.

Saul knew the Hebrew Bible very well and recognized this had to be a divine manifestation. But the question he heard confused him. Who was he persecuting other than the Christians? So he asked, "Who are you, Lord?" Some take this to mean, "Who are you, sir?" using the word "lord" merely as a term of polite address. But in response to this obviously supernatural manifestation, the word can only mean divine Lord.

The answer came at once, "I [emphatic] am Jesus, whom you [emphatic] are persecuting." In persecuting the Church, Saul was persecuting the body of Christ whose individual members are in Christ (see Matt. 25:40,45; Eph. 1:22–23; 2:6). Then Jesus

---

[5]"Abnormally born" usually means a premature birth, but it is used by Saul to mean that this appearance of the risen Christ was something special, something extraordinary, beyond the normal. Jesus made no other such appearances on earth after His ascension.

[6]Some take this to mean Aramaic, a related language spoken by the Jews after their return from Babylon.

added, "'It is hard [rough, dangerous] for you to kick against the [ox] goads'"7 (NKJV).

By this Jesus recognized that much of Saul's persecution of the Christians was because he knew he had no answer for their arguments. In his ignorance and unbelief (see 1 Tim. 1:13) it was a reaction by which he was trying to resist the conviction of the Holy Spirit. Like a man driving an ox, the Holy Spirit had been driving Saul toward the truth of the gospel, but he was resisting violently, kicking against the goads. The arguments of Stephen were just such a goad; his final speech and the way he died were goads; the spread of the gospel and the response of the believers were goads; the miracles that confirmed the Word were all goads. In resistings this, Saul was dangerously hurting himself.

This does not mean that he was conscious of these being goads, or that he even realized he had no good arguments against the believers. He was so full of fury that he could think of nothing but how He could stop them. But now that he was faced with the truth—and with Christ, not just as the man Jesus but as the divine Lord—he answered simply, "'Lord, what do You want me to do?'"(Acts 9:6, NKJV).8 This shows a complete change in Saul's attitude, which is the evidence of genuine repentance on his part.

6Now get up and go into the city, and you will be told what you must do."

The Lord then told him to "get up and go into the city" of Damascus. There he would be told what would be necessary for him to do. Jesus actually told Saul more here, but Luke leaves the rest for Saul to tell in his defense before Agrippa (Acts 26:16–18). In Galatians 1:1,11–12,16 Saul also makes it clear that he was commissioned directly by Jesus, not by man. In other words, he was a genuine apostle, or "sent one," sent by Jesus himself.

7The men traveling with Saul stood there speechless; they heard the sound but did not see anyone.

7Many ancient manuscripts leave out this phrase (see Acts 26:14). Goads were sharp-pointed rods about eight feet long used to get balky animals to move.

8Saul's response in the first part of v. 6 for some reason is not found in any of the Gk. manuscripts we now have (it was probably omitted in copying). It is in the Latin Vulgate version here, and it is found in the Gk. manuscripts of Acts 22:10.

Meanwhile, the men who were traveling with Saul "stood . . . speechless," in our idiom, "almost scared to death." They heard the sound of Jesus' (or, Paul's) voice but saw no one.[9] They, as Acts 26:14 says, "all fell to the ground" but apparently got up before Saul did (and "led him by the hand," v. 8).

[8]Saul got up from the ground, but when he opened his eyes he could see nothing. So they led him by the hand into Damascus. [9]For three days he was blind, and did not eat or drink anything.

Saul, it seems, shut his eyes because of the continuing brightness, but He did see Jesus (1 Cor. 9:1; 15:8). Then, when he got up off the ground, "he could see nothing."[10] His traveling companions took him by the forearm[11] and led him into Damascus. He was there three days—no longer self-confident but as dependent on others as a little child—unable to see and he neither ate nor drank anything. The Jewish way of counting made the first day the day he entered Damascus and the third day the day Ananias came. This gave Saul a day in between to think things over and to pray. Some relate these three days to Jesus' three days in the tomb.[12] That he "did not eat or drink" implies he was holding himself "in disciplined readiness for further revelation (e.g. Ex. 34:28; Dan. 10:2–3)."[13]

3. Jesus Sends Ananias To Saul 9:10–19

[10]In Damascus there was a disciple named Ananias. The Lord called to him in a vision, "Ananias!" "Yes, Lord," he

[9]Here, some see a contradiction between Acts 9:7 and 22:9, which reads literally, "They heard not the voice." The Gk. construction is different in 22:9, however. Here in 9:7 it simply says they heard the sound. F. F. Bruce, *Commentary on the Book of Acts* (Grand Rapids: Wm. B. Eerdmans, 1954), 197, suggests it was the sound of Saul's voice they heard here, and that they did not hear the voice of Jesus at all. One Old Latin manuscript (h) confirms this.

[10]It is also possible for the Gk. to mean that his eyes had remained open and he couldn't shut them because of the "something like scales" that fell off when he was healed (Acts 9:18). See Simon J. Kistemaker, *Exposition of the Acts of the Apostles* (Grand Rapids: Baker Book House, 1990), 337.

[11]The Heb. word for "hand," *yad,* includes the forearm. Greek pottery shows the blind being led by the forearm.

[12]See Harrison, *Acts,* 150.

[13]James D. G. Dunn, *The Acts of the Apostles* (Valley Forge, Pa.: Trinity Press International, 1996), 122.

answered. ¹¹The Lord told him, "Go to the house of Judas on Straight Street and ask for a man from Tarsus named Saul, for he is praying. ¹²In a vision he has seen a man named Ananias come and place his hands on him to restore his sight."

On the third day the Lord (Jesus) appeared to an ordinary disciple, not an apostle or officer of the church, named Ananias. He was a devout Jew converted to the Lord and still respected by his fellow Jews (Acts 22:12). Now the Lord was going to use this otherwise unknown disciple to minister to the highly educated Saul who would become the apostle Paul and be mightily used of God.

Jesus appeared to Ananias "in a vision," telling him to go to the street called Straight, the main street of the city. In ancient times it was about fifty feet wide, lined with Corinthian columns, and went straight from the west end of the city to the east end; it is still an important street in Damascus today. There he was to "ask" (Gk. *zēteson,* "seek, search") in the house of Judas for Saul of Tarsus— for, "behold," surprisingly and unexpectedly, while Saul was praying he had seen, also "in a vision," a man named Ananias coming in and laying hands on him, so that he should recover his sight.

¹³"Lord," Ananias answered, "I have heard many reports about this man and all the harm he has done to your saints in Jerusalem. ¹⁴And he has come here with authority from the chief priests to arrest all who call on your name."

Ananias objected at first. He had heard "many reports" about "all the harm" Saul had done to the Lord's "saints"[14] in Jerusalem. Ananias was apparently a Jew who was born in Damascus or who had lived there for a long time. Obviously, many of the believers who fled from the persecution had come there and brought news of Saul's fury. The news had already come also that Saul had authority from the chief priests to arrest all who called on the

---

[14]Holy (separated) dedicated ones, consecrated to the Lord and to His service. The Bible uses this term for believers because they turned their backs on the world to follow Jesus. The word "saint" does not imply ultimate perfection. Rather, it simply means they were headed in the right direction. Saul later calls believers "saints" about forty times in his preaching and writings. See Ralph Earle, *The Acts of the Apostles* (Kansas City, Mo.: Beacon Hill Press, 1965), 365.

name of Jesus. The church in Damascus may have been getting ready to face the same sort of scattering that had occurred in Jerusalem because of persecution.[15]

> [15]But the Lord said to Ananias, "Go! This man is my chosen instrument to carry my name before the Gentiles and their kings and before the people of Israel. [16]I will show him how much he must suffer for my name."

The Lord again commanded Ananias to go and reassured him that Saul was His own "chosen instrument"[16] to carry His name before the Gentiles (the nations) and also before both kings and "the people of Israel." (Note that Paul's mission was never to be against the Jews.) Moreover, Jesus himself would "show" (warn, point out to) Saul how much it would be necessary for him to suffer for the sake of His name—that is, as an ambassador personally representing Him and letting people know who He is and what His will is.

> [17]Then Ananias went to the house and entered it. Placing his hands on Saul, he said, "Brother Saul, the Lord— Jesus, who appeared to you on the road as you were coming here—has sent me so that you may see again and be filled with the Holy Spirit."

Then Ananias obeyed, entered the house, and laid his hands on Saul, calling him "brother." By this he recognized that Saul was now a believer. Then he explained that the Lord had sent him, and identified the Lord as "Jesus, who appeared[17] to you on the road" to Damascus. This explanation probably seemed necessary to Ananias, for the Jews normally used the term "Lord" to mean Jehovah (Yahweh), the one true God. But it really was not necessary, as Saul had already recognized Jesus as Lord.

Ananias added that the Lord sent him for two reasons. First, that Saul might "see again"; second, that he might be "filled with the Holy Spirit."[18] Because some writers identify filling with the

[15]See Donald Guthrie, *The Apostles* (Grand Rapids: Zondervan Publishing House, 1975), 73.

[16]Gk. *skeuos*, "vessel"; the idea is "chosen agent." Cf. 1 Thess. 2:4.

[17]The word "appeared" confirms that before Paul was blinded he did indeed see Jesus. See also 9:27.

[18]Again we see that, since Ananias was a "layman," God did not limit this ministry of the Spirit to the apostles or to officers of the Church. Also, since Ananias

Spirit with conversion, they suppose that Paul was not converted until this point. But Ananias did not ask Saul to repent and
believe. When he placed his hands on Saul to encourage his
faith, it was in order for Saul to be healed and filled with the
Spirit. In fact, "[n]owhere in Scripture is the laying on of hands
presented as a means of imparting salvation."[19]

**18Immediately, something like scales fell from Saul's eyes,
and he could see again. He got up and was baptized,
19and after taking some food, he regained his strength.
Saul spent several days with the disciples in Damascus.**

The healing was immediate.[20] The physical blindness was
gone. So was the spiritual blindness. Luke records additional
details later (Acts 22:14–16). By being baptized in water, Paul
declared his death to his old life and his rising to new life. Then
he ended his fast, took food, and "regained his strength." After
that he stayed some days with the disciples in Damascus.

Verse 12 does not tell the command of Jesus to lay hands on Saul
that he might be filled with the Spirit. Neither does verse 18 tell
how Saul did receive the Spirit. Once again, we see that Luke does
not repeat everything in every place. In effect, he indicates that
Saul's experience in being filled with the Holy Spirit was no different from that experienced on the Day of Pentecost. We can be sure
he spoke in other tongues at that time as they did in Acts 2:4.

Titus 3:5–7 confirms this by showing that the Holy Spirit was
poured out on both Saul and Titus abundantly. Each had his
own personal Pentecost.[21] Actually, there is no question about
whether Saul spoke in tongues or not. He told the Corinthians
years later that he spoke in tongues more than they all did

---

was a native of Damascus and the apostles had not left Jerusalem, no apostle had
laid hands on him. He was simply being obedient to the command of Jesus.

[19]Anthony D. Palma, *Baptism in the Holy Spirit* (Springfield, Mo.: Gospel
Publishing House, 1999), 25.

[20]The description of "something like scales" seems to be a common idiom. Cf.
Tob. 3:17; 11:13.

[21]Bruce, *Commentary,* 201, suggests that Saul may have been filled with the
Spirit immediately before he was baptized in water, as was the case with Cornelius
(Acts 10:44–47). Certainly there are parallels between the way God sent Ananias
to Saul and the way He sent Peter to Cornelius. See Earle, *Acts of the Apostles,* 366.

(1 Cor. 14:18).[22] Acts 13:9 also shows he was a man of the Spirit.

Nothing more is said of Ananias. He undoubtedly continued living in humble obedience to the Lord and to His Word. But Saul never forgot this godly man who was the first believer to call him brother.

4. Saul Preaches In Damascus 9:20–25

20At once he began to preach in the synagogues that Jesus is the Son of God. 21All those who heard him were astonished and asked, "Isn't he the man who raised havoc in Jerusalem among those who call on this name? And hasn't he come here to take them as prisoners to the chief priests?"

Saul at once became part of the body of disciples in Damascus. Because he accepted the Lord's commission, he did not wait to start preaching Christ. He did not go to the Gentiles immediately (cf. Rom. 1:16). Instead, as he would continue to do, he went to "the people of Israel" (v. 15) first. Here he went to the synagogues where he had intended to search out the believers and send them bound to Jerusalem. But to everyone's astonishment, almost knocking them out of their senses, Saul, filled with the Spirit, repeatedly proclaimed Christ Jesus as the "Son of God."[23] The people could hardly believe that this was the same person who "raised havoc" among (laid waste, ravaged, brought destruction on) those in Jerusalem who called on this Name.

22Yet Saul grew more and more powerful and baffled the Jews living in Damascus by proving that Jesus is the Christ.

[22]The fact he preferred to limit his speaking in tongues in the public meeting shows he spoke in tongues primarily in his private devotions, speaking unto God (1 Cor. 14:2, KJV; cf. v. 19). This coupled with 1 Cor. 14:5 "indicates that Paul considered the private manifestation of tongues to be edifying, desirable, and available to every Christian." William W. Menzies and Robert P. Menzies, *Spirit and Power: Foundations of Pentecostal Experience* (Grand Rapids: Zondervan Publishing House, 2000), 127.

[23]This is the first time in Acts that the title "Son of God" is used of Jesus. Jesus drew attention to the fact that God is His own Father (John 5:17–18), and Paul emphasized again and again that Jesus is the Son of God (Rom. 1:4,9; 8:3, for example).

Saul, however, was "more and more" filled with the mighty power of the Holy Spirit. He later said, "I can do everything through him who gives me strength" (Phil. 4:13). By divine enablement he "baffled the Jews" living in Damascus, confounding and throwing them into consternation and confusion. He did this by deducing from the Scriptures that this "Jesus is the Christ," the Messiah (God's anointed Prophet, Priest, and King). In other words, he used Old Testament prophecies and showed how they were fulfilled in Jesus. The fact they knew the Scriptures was the reason he went to the Jew first even though his call was to the Gentiles. We know, too, that he never lost his love for his fellow Jews (see Rom. 9:1–5; 11:23–26).

Galatians adds here that Saul received the gospel he preached (including the sayings of Jesus) "by revelation" directly from Jesus himself (Gal. 1:12,16). He also says he left Damascus for a time during this period and went into Arabia, returning again to Damascus. Since, as most scholars believe, the kingdom of the Nabatean Arabs included Damascus at this time, Saul did not need to go very far out of the city. (He probably went east.) Jesus may have given Saul some of this revelation during the time that he was blind, but probably most of it was given during the time he was in Arabia.

²³After many days had gone by, the Jews conspired to kill him, ²⁴but Saul learned of their plan. Day and night they kept close watch on the city gates in order to kill him. ²⁵But his followers took him by night and lowered him in a basket through an opening in the wall.

After a considerable time ("three years," probably counting parts of the first and third years; Gal. 1:18), "the Jews [that is, the unbelieving Jews] conspired to kill" Saul, keeping "a close watch on the city gates" in order to carry out their plot. Second Corinthians 11:32 indicates that the governor under King Aretas IV of Arabia (who reigned from 9 B.C. to A.D. 40) cooperated with, or perhaps was paid by, the Jews to help them seize Saul. It is also probable that during Saul's time in Arabia he preached the gospel to the Nabatean Arabs[24] (cf. 1 Cor. 9:16, "Woe to me if I

[24]Wagner suggests that this was the beginning of Paul's cross-cultural ministry. C. Peter Wagner, *Lighting the World: Book 2, Acts 9–15* (Ventura, Calif.: Gospel Light, Regal Books, 1995).

do not preach the gospel," and Gal. 1:16). This may have antago-
nized King Aretas. In any case, Saul somehow learned of the plot.

Saul's "followers" (Gk. *mathētai,* "disciples," that is, converts
whom he was teaching) foiled the plot, lowering[25] him from the
wall in a large flexible basket woven of rushes, or something similar. In 2 Corinthians 11:33 Saul adds that he was let down
through a window.[26] (Houses with a section built over the city
wall were common in the ancient Near East and can still be seen
in Damascus. Cf. Josh. 2:15.)

5. Barnabas Befriends Saul 9:26–31

**[26]When he came to Jerusalem, he tried to join the disci-
ples, but they were all afraid of him, not believing that he
really was a disciple. [27]But Barnabas took him and
brought him to the apostles. He told them how Saul on
his journey had seen the Lord and that the Lord had spoken to him, and how in Damascus he had preached fearlessly in the name of Jesus.**

Arriving at Jerusalem,[27] Saul "tried to join the disciples" (in
the worship and service of the Church). But they were "all afraid
of him." They knew what he had done to the Church; their first
thought was that surely this was some sort of trick or deception
to identify members of the Church and then destroy them.

Barnabas, however, was sympathetic, living up to his name as
the "Son of Encouragement" (see Acts 4:36). Apparently he did
some investigation and then "brought him to the apostles,"[28]
explaining how he had "seen the Lord" and "preached fearlessly"
in Damascus. This implies Barnabas gave them all the details.

[28]So Saul stayed with them and moved about freely in

[25]The Gk. indicates they paid out ropes.

[26]Which probably took place in A.D. 38. See J. W. Packer, *Acts of the Apostles*
(Cambridge, England: Cambridge University Press, 1975), 74.

[27]For evidence that this visit must be identified with the visit mentioned in
Gal. 1:18–24 see Joe Morgado, Jr., "Paul in Jerusalem: A Comparison of His
Visits in Acts and Galatians," *Journal of the Evangelical Theological Society* 37, no.
1 (March 1994): 59–60.

[28]Some of the apostles. Gal. 1:18–24 shows that Saul (Paul) met only Peter
and James the brother of Jesus at this time. James was considered an apostle
because of Jesus' special appearance to him (1 Cor. 15:7).

Jerusalem, speaking boldly in the name of the Lord. 29He talked and debated with the Grecian Jews, but they tried to kill him.

For a time Saul was associated with the believers coming in and going out of Jerusalem. He continued to speak boldly and freely in the name of the Lord (cf. Rom. 15:19), but he spent most of his time talking to and discussing or debating with the "Grecian Jews," that is, with the Hellenistic, or Greek-speaking, Jews who had migrated to Jerusalem. He went to the Hellenistic synagogues, including the same ones that had debated with Stephen (Acts 6:9). He did not visit the churches of Judea (outside Jerusalem), however, for he says later that he was "personally unknown" to them at this time (Gal. 1:22).

As with Stephen's message of the gospel, so it was with Saul's—rousing the anger of the Hellenistic Jews until they "tried to kill him." Probably they considered him a traitor who did not need a trial. (See 1 Thess. 2:15 where Paul speaks of Jews driving him out.)

30When the brothers learned of this, they took him down to Caesarea and sent him off to Tarsus.

As soon as the "brothers"29 (the Jerusalem believers) heard about this, they took Saul to Caesarea and put him on a ship to Tarsus. (Jesus had also appeared to him and told him to leave Jerusalem [22:17–21].) The believers did not send him away simply to save him from being a martyr, however: He was sent out as their representative and as a person qualified to take the gospel to the Jews at Tarsus, his birthplace (21:39; 22:3).30 Tarsus, about three hundred miles to the north, was the capital and most important city of Cilicia. It was located on the coastal plain, ten miles from the Mediterranean Sea. It was a free city and a well-known university city, exceeded in educational opportunities only by Athens and Alexandria. Saul was needed there. Later, he and Silas31 would go "through Syria and Cilicia, strengthening

---

29"Brothers" in Acts most often designates groups of Jewish believers, including both men and women, until the Jerusalem Council in Acts 15.

30Note that in Jerusalem, Paul had debated only with Jews (v. 29).

31Possibly the Gk. form of the Aramaic equivalent of Saul, *Sh'ila'* ("asked for" [from God]).

the churches" (15:41), some of which may have been founded during these years of Paul's at Tarsus.

³¹Then the church throughout Judea, Galilee and Samaria enjoyed a time of peace. It was strengthened; and encouraged by the Holy Spirit, it grew in numbers, living in the fear of the Lord.

With Saul gone, everything quieted down again. Luke, in another brief summary, shows that the church[32] throughout the whole of Judea, Galilee, and Samaria "enjoyed a time of peace": "Strengthened" (continually edified, being built up spiritually and in numbers) and "living [going on, progressing] in the fear of the Lord," it experienced the encouragement of the Holy Spirit,[33] and continued to grow (though limited still to Jews and Samaritans in "biblical Israel").

We see from this that both Galilee and Samaria had been well evangelized by this time, even though Luke gives no details about how it was done—though it must have been done by those believers scattered after the death of Stephen (8:1). Notice also that the word "church" is singular. The various assemblies in these regions were in fellowship with each other and constituted one body under the headship of Christ (Eph. 1:22–23).

"Living in the fear of the Lord" does not mean a cowardly fear (2 Tim. 1:7; 1 John 4:18). It means a way of life full of reverence for Him, recognizing His awesome presence. It means living in loving obedience to His Word, worshiping and serving Him in the freedom, and with the help, of the Holy Spirit (Rom. 8:13–15; Phil. 2:12–13).

STUDY QUESTIONS

1. What atmosphere did Saul create around himself and with what results?
2. What must have happened in Damascus before Saul came?

[32]"Church" is singular, including all the local churches in one body as in Eph. 2:19–22.

[33]Including the Spirit's exhortation to come to Christ (as the Gk. *paraklēsei* indicates).

3. What made Saul want to go to Damascus?
4. How did Saul respond to the Lord?
5. How did Ananias respond to the Lord?
6. What shows Saul was truly converted?
7. Why did Barnabas risk his reputation to befriend Saul?

C. Peter's Ministry In Judea 9:32-11:18

1. PETER MINISTERS IN LYDDA 9:32-35

32As Peter traveled about the country, he went to visit the saints in Lydda.

Luke now returns to Peter's activities. It is important for us to know that Luke "shows that Peter, the great apostle to the Jews, and Paul, the great apostle to the Gentiles, were not teaching or doing two different things but were actually one in their doctrine and work."[1]

After the summary statement in verse 31, Luke begins a sequence that leads to Peter's taking the gospel to the Gentiles in Caesarea.[2] Since the conditions in Jerusalem had become peaceful, Peter could leave the city. So he began to travel throughout "Judea, Galilee and Samaria" (v. 31). As he journeyed "he went to visit the saints [dedicated believers] in Lydda" (at the base of the Shephelah, the foothills on the west of the central highlands, about twenty-four miles northwest of Jerusalem on the road to Joppa).

Luke selected Philip as an example of those who were scattered and spread the gospel (Acts 8:4). Now we see that others must have scattered through the towns of Judea so that groups of "saints" were already the beginnings of local churches there.

33There he found a man named Aeneas, a paralytic who had been bedridden for eight years. 34"Aeneas," Peter said to him, "Jesus Christ heals you. Get up and take care of your mat." Immediately Aeneas got up. 35All those who lived in Lydda and Sharon saw him and turned to the Lord.

[1]James M. Boice, *Acts* (Grand Rapids: Baker Book House, 1997), 164.

[2]Dunn calls this "a deliberate attempt at evenhandedness between Paul and Peter." James D. G. Dunn, *The Acts of the Apostles* (Valley Forge, Pa.: Trinity Press International, 1996), 128.

Finding a Jewish paralytic there named Aeneas[3] who "had been bedridden for eight years," he said, "Aeneas, . . . Jesus Christ heals you. Get up and take care of your mat [now, at this moment, while I am speaking]."[4] Jesus (not Peter) healed him instantaneously and completely. All the inhabitants of Lydda and Sharon (Gk. *ton Sarōnan,* "the Sharon," the coastal plain west and northwest of Lydda toward Caesarea) "saw him and turned to the Lord," accepting Christ as Savior and Lord.

2. PETER BROUGHT TO JOPPA 9:36–43

36In Joppa there was a disciple named Tabitha (which, when translated, is Dorcas), who was always doing good and helping the poor.

At Joppa,[5] a seaport on the Mediterranean coast about eleven miles northwest of Lydda and thirty-five miles from Jerusalem (that is, by air), lived a woman "disciple,"[6] Tabitha (her Aramaic name). She was also known by the corresponding Greek name, Dorcas ("gazelle," an antelope that was considered a symbol of gracefulness; also used as a metaphor for the beloved in Song of Sol. 2:9; 8:14). She was "always doing good," especially deeds for the poor. Some commentators believe her ministry is an example of the gift of helps (1 Cor. 12:28).

37About that time she became sick and died, and her body was washed and placed in an upstairs room. 38Lydda was near Joppa; so when the disciples heard that Peter was in Lydda, they sent two men to him and urged him, "Please come at once!" 39Peter went with them, and when he arrived he was taken upstairs to the room. All the widows stood around him, crying and showing him the robes and other clothing that Dorcas had made while she was still with them.

---

[3]A Gk. name; a Trojan hero also had this name.

[4]"'Make your bed'" (v. 34, NASB) is a phrase that in Gk. can be used of making a bed but is also used of preparing a meal (as in Mark 14:15 and Luke 22:12). Thus, another possible meaning is that Aeneas should make his dining couch ready and take food.

[5]Modern Jaffa, now a suburb of Tel Aviv.

[6]The Gk. *mathētria* is fem.

While Peter was at Lydda, Dorcas fell sick and died. They washed her body—something usually done in preparation for burial—but they did not anoint it and were not expecting to bury her. Instead, they "placed [her] in an upstairs room"[7] and sent two men to ask Peter to "come at once."[8] In probably about three hours Peter arrived. In the upper room, all the widows were standing around weeping and "showing him the robes" (Gk. *chitōnas,* "tunics," undergarments) and the long, flowing outer garments Dorcas was (always) making "while she was still with them."[9] By this they showed their desire to see Dorcas restored to life. Nevertheless, they were in tears.

The Bible encourages us to weep with those who weep (Rom. 12:15). But these weeping women who had expressed such faith and expectation in sending for Peter were still overwhelmed by the fact that Dorcas was really dead. Perhaps also they had a little self-pity because they thought no one else would care for them as Dorcas had. Some may have been feeling guilty for not showing more appreciation to her while she was alive. So, in spite of their initial faith, their grief was probably giving way to hopeless sorrow. (They didn't have the assurance yet of 1 Thess. 4:1–18.)

> [40]Peter sent them all out of the room; then he got down on his knees and prayed. Turning toward the dead woman, he said, "Tabitha, get up." She opened her eyes, and seeing Peter she sat up. [41]He took her by the hand and helped her to her feet. Then he called the believers and the widows and presented her to them alive.

Probably because of the example of Jesus in Mark 5:40,[10] Peter "sent them all out of the room"; then after going to his knees and praying, he turned to the body and in faith said, "Tabitha, get up!" (Many observe a parallel between *"Tabitha cumi"* here and

---

[7]That her home had a second floor indicates she was wealthy. Most of the houses I helped excavate in Dothan had only one or two rooms and a small courtyard about three by seven feet. Even in Rome only about three percent of the houses had large rooms opening off a courtyard or had a second floor.

[8]The custom was to bury a person on the day of death (Deut. 21:23).

[9]Again, Luke emphasizes that the new covenant community included women, just as Jesus did, especially widows.

[10]See C. Peter Wagner, *Lighting the World: Book 2, Acts 9–15* (Ventura, Calif.: Gospel Light, Regal Books, 1995), 64–65.

"Talitha cumi" in Mark 5:41.) Putting the mourners out paralleled what Jesus did when He raised the daughter of Jairus (Luke 8:54). Peter was with Him then and learned that an atmosphere of unbelief is not conducive to the faith that sees miracles. Peter did something Jesus did not do at that time, however. He spent time in prayer, possibly remembering how Jesus sent out the twelve apostles to "'Heal the sick, raise the dead, cleanse those who have leprosy, drive out demons'" (Matt. 10:8).

In answer to his prayer, Dorcas was restored to life; opening her eyes, she looked at Peter, and then sat up. Giving her his hand, he "helped her to her feet." Then, calling all the believers, he presented her to them.

> **42This became known all over Joppa, and many people believed in the Lord. 43Peter stayed in Joppa for some time with a tanner named Simon.**

This miracle became known throughout the whole of Joppa and became a means of spreading the gospel. "Many . . . believed in the Lord" (Jesus), but Peter took no credit for this. However, he stayed in Joppa for a considerable time with a certain Simon, a tanner who lived by the seashore, where there was plenty of water for skinning the animals and soaking their hides. Many Jews considered tanning an unclean occupation, but the Christians accepted Simon.[11]

3. Cornelius Sends For Peter 10:1–8

Chapters 10 and 11 bring us to a turning point in the Book of Acts. Though Jesus commissioned the apostles to "'make disciples of all nations'" (Matt. 28:19), they were not eager to do this. Believers who were scattered by the persecution after Stephen's death preached the gospel at first to Jews only (Acts 11:19). Apparently they interpreted "all nations" to mean the Jews scattered among all nations.

It was obvious from the beginning of the Church that being converted to Christ and even being baptized in the Holy Spirit

---

[11]The coast was the most Hellenized area of Israel. (Waverly Nunnally suggests that God was placing Peter in "boot camp," breaking down his prejudice against the "unclean," step-by-step.)

did not automatically remove the prejudices people had grown up with.[12] Peter had made some progress: He had accepted the Lord's work in saving the Samaritans. But they were circumcised and kept the Law about as well as many of the Jews did. He was also willing to stay in the home of an "unclean" tanner who was a believer. He had not faced the biggest barrier, however. Many laws and customs separated Jews from Gentiles, especially the dietary laws.[13] Nor would any Jew eat food prepared by a Gentile, for he believed this too would make him unclean. For the Jerusalem church Jesus' words recorded in John 3:16 did not apply to Gentiles; consequently they made no provision for fellowship with Gentiles who did not first come under the Law and consent to circumcision. So the Holy Spirit had to deal with Peter to remove his prejudice and then to enable him to use the keys (Matt. 16:19) to open "the door to Rome and the Gentiles."[14] God's working through Peter in the healing of Aeneas and the raising of Dorcas to life would help the Jewish believers to accept what God was about to do in the house of Cornelius.

That God took the initiative in what follows "does not deny personal decisions or make Peter and Cornelius robots. As occurs throughout Acts, the divine initiative calls for human response. It is a matter of divine direction and human obedience, as Peter's response to the words of the Holy Spirit in 10:19–20 illustrates."[15]

¹At Caesarea there was a man named Cornelius, a centurion in what was known as the Italian Regiment. ²He and all his family were devout and God-fearing; he gave generously to those in need and prayed to God regularly.

[12]Prejudice is usually an opinion we have received from our parents, teachers, or society as a whole, but which we have not sufficiently examined for ourselves. When we do examine prejudices, some prove to be valid—coming out of long experience of the past and still true. Others may be based on false or insufficient grounds—or circumstances may have changed so they are no longer valid.

[13]The laws against unclean food had good reason behind them. Much of the ceremonially unclean food was likely to spread diseases such as trichinosis and tapeworm.

[14]E. M. Blaiklock, *Acts: The Birth of the Church* (Old Tappan, N.J.: Fleming H. Revell, 1980), 87.

[15]French L. Arrington, "The Acts of the Apostles," in *Full Life Bible Commentary to the New Testament*, ed. French L. Arrington and Roger Stronstad (Grand Rapids: Zondervan Publishing House, 1999), 585.

Caesarea, a beautiful harbor city about thirty miles north of Joppa, was built by Herod the Great from 12 to 2 B.C. From A.D. 6 on, it was the capital of Judea under the Roman procurators.[16] There Rome stationed a special regiment (Gk. *speirēs,* "cohort," the tenth part of a Roman legion)[17] of volunteer soldiers, Roman citizens, known as the Italian Regiment.[18] One of the soldiers, Cornelius, was a centurion commanding one hundred infantry.[19] He would compare to a modern army captain in authority and responsibility. Like all the centurions mentioned in the New Testament, he was a good man, and, like the one Jesus commended in Matthew 8:10–11, he was also a man of faith.

Some Gentiles in those days were tired of the foolishness, idolatry, and immorality of the religions of Rome and Greece. Many, including Cornelius, found something better in the teaching of the synagogues and accepted the truth of the one true God. Luke calls Cornelius "devout." In other words, he was right in his attitudes toward both God and people and by grace was living a godly life. He was also "God-fearing," having reverence for God, as did his entire household, both family and servants. Through his influence they all attended the synagogue (sitting in the back), listened to the teaching, and believed God. However, they had not become full proselytes, or converts, to Judaism. Consequently, they had not accepted circumcision and did not keep the dietary laws. Cornelius, however, "gave generously to those in need" (among the Jews; see NASB, NEB, TEV) and "prayed to God regularly" (that is, daily, and in every circumstance). In other words, he looked to the Lord to guide him in all things.

From later statements by Peter (i.e., v. 37) it is also evident that Cornelius knew the historical aspects of the gospel. Many

[16]It was designated as "Maritima" to distinguish it from Caesarea Philippi. Howard Clark Kee, *To Every Nation Under Heaven: The Acts of the Apostles* (Harrisburg, Pa.: Trinity Press International, 1997), 130–32.

[17]An ordinary cohort had six hundred foot soldiers under a tribune. But evidence has been found that this was an auxiliary cohort of one thousand men. See F. F. Bruce, *Commentary on the Book of Acts* (Grand Rapids: Wm. B. Eerdmans, 1954), 215.

[18]Rome recruited soldiers from many parts of its empire. Identifying them as Italian indicated they were a favored group.

[19]Some suggest he may have been retired at this time. Kee, *To Every Nation,* 130. His distinguished Roman name means "of a horn."

Bible scholars believe that Cornelius was already a believer in Christ[20] and wanted to be filled with the Holy Spirit but was told that he would have to become a Jew first. It is quite possible that at this very time he was considering taking that step.[21]

> **3One day at about three in the afternoon he had a vision. He distinctly saw an angel of God, who came to him and said, "Cornelius!"**

We can be sure, however, that God saw Cornelius's desire. "About three in the afternoon," the Jewish hour of evening prayer,[22] he was fasting and praying (see v. 30). Suddenly an angel appeared to him in a vision ("something seen"), that is, in an actual appearance or revelation, openly in full daylight. This was no dream or dream type of vision: "He distinctly saw an angel." Notice verse 7: "When the angel . . . had gone." This confirms that the visitation was an actual occurrence, not merely a dream type of vision.

> **4Cornelius stared at him in fear. "What is it, Lord?" he asked. The angel answered, "Your prayers and gifts to the poor have come up as a memorial offering before God. 5Now send men to Joppa to bring back a man named Simon who is called Peter. 6He is staying with Simon the tanner, whose house is by the sea."**

As Cornelius "stared at" the angel, he became afraid (full of awe, fear, even terror). This was a natural, even a normal, reaction to the supernatural in the Bible. But, in spite of his fear, he asked, "What is it, Lord?" thus taking the angel to be a divine manifestation. The angel, however, directed his attention to God. Cornelius's prayers and charitable giving had gone up (ascended) as a "memorial offering"[23] before God. Then the angel directed

---

[20]This indicates that the outpouring of the Spirit at the house of Cornelius was an empowering experience, "not a delayed salvation experience." James B. Shelton, review of *Power from on High: The Spirit in Israel's Restoration and Witness in Luke-Acts,* by Max Turner, *Pneuma* 21, no. 1 (spring 1999): 167.

[21]This was first suggested to me in 1943 in a New Testament Introduction class by one of my professors at Gordon Divinity School, Dr. Merrill C. Tenney.

[22]This was also the hour of the evening sacrifice (Exod. 29:39; Num. 28:8). God spoke to him while he was observing his regular devotions.

[23]The OT offerings included memorials. See Lev. 2:2; Num. 5:26.

him to "send men" (of his own choice) to Joppa for "Simon who is called Peter,"[24] who was being entertained by Simon the tanner. Many ancient manuscripts add that Peter would then tell him what would be necessary for him to do (see KJV).[25]

> **7When the angel who spoke to him had gone, Cornelius called two of his servants and a devout soldier who was one of his attendants. 8He told them everything that had happened and sent them to Joppa.**

As soon as the angel left, Cornelius called "two of his servants" (household slaves); as verse 2 indicates, they were God-fearers or maybe even Jews. He also called "one of his attendants," a soldier who was, like himself, "devout" (godly, a true worshiper of God). After detailing to the three of them what the angel had said, he sent them on the thirty-mile trip to Joppa to get Peter.

4. PETER'S VISIONS 10:9-22

> **9About noon the following day as they were on their journey and approaching the city, Peter went up on the roof to pray. 10He became hungry and wanted something to eat, and while the meal was being prepared, he fell into a trance.**

The next day "about noon" the three men sent by Cornelius were nearing Joppa. God is always faithful to work on both ends of the line, and it was time to continue Peter's preparation (which was begun by directing him to the Hellenized coast to stay with a tanner).

Peter went up to the flat roof of the house by an outside stairway. Most Jews considered noon one of the hours of prayer (Ps. 55:17; Dan. 6:10). But, even though he intended to pray, he "became hungry and wanted something to eat." He let his hosts know this; while he remained on the roof waiting for them to prepare the food, he "fell into a trance." This does not mean a trance in the modern sense of the word, however; nor does it

---

[24]Jesus had wanted Peter to strengthen his "brothers" (Luke 22:31–32). Now he was about to find along with those Jewish "brothers" new believers in Jesus— Gentiles.

[25]Some ancient manuscripts omit the last part of v. 6, but it fits the context.

imply a hypnotic state. It simply means his mind was distracted from whatever he was thinking about as he sensed something important was about to happen.

> **11He saw heaven opened and something like a large sheet being let down to earth by its four corners. 12It contained all kinds of four-footed animals, as well as reptiles of the earth and birds of the air. 13Then a voice told him, "Get up, Peter. Kill and eat." 14"Surely not, Lord!" Peter replied. "I have never eaten anything impure or unclean."**

Then Peter saw heaven opened and something descending, "something like a large sheet."[26] It was tied at the corners and filled with "all kinds of four-footed animals, as well as reptiles . . . and birds." A voice commanded, "Get up, Peter. Kill and eat." Peter was sensitive enough spiritually to know that this was the voice of the Lord (that is, the Lord Jesus)—but his prejudices overcame his normal desire to obey Him. So he replied, "Surely not [not at all, never], Lord." For at no time had he ever eaten anything "impure" (profane, dirty) or "unclean" (that is, ritually unclean—nonkosher).[27]

> **15The voice spoke to him a second time, "Do not call anything impure that God has made clean." 16This happened three times, and immediately the sheet was taken back to heaven.**

The voice replied with a strong rebuke. The negative here is very emphatic. From now on Peter must not ever treat anything as impure when God has cleansed it (and declared it clean; cf. Mark 7:18–19). Then, for further emphasis, this was repeated "three times." Peter's prejudice was so strong it took this extreme emphasis to fix this truth in his mind.

---

[26]Or "sailcloth" (see NEB)—which seems reasonable, since Joppa was the main port for the Judean hill country. See J. W. Packer, *Acts of the Apostles* (Cambridge, England: Cambridge University Press, 1975), 82.

[27]See Lev. 11:3,4,43,47; cf. Ezek. 4:14. Clean animals were those that both chewed the cud and had split hooves. Jesus had prepared His disciples for the abolishing of these food laws (Mark 7:15–19), but so far they failed to understand. They had long been demonstrating their loyalty to their Jewishness by observing them.

> ¹⁷While Peter was wondering about the meaning of the vision, the men sent by Cornelius found out where Simon's house was and stopped at the gate. ¹⁸They called out, asking if Simon who was known as Peter was staying there. ¹⁹While Peter was still thinking about the vision, the Spirit said to him, "Simon, three men are looking for you. ²⁰So get up and go downstairs. Do not hesitate to go with them, for I have sent them."

Peter had enough spiritual discernment to know that this vision had a meaning beyond that of eating nonkosher food. The fact that he "was wondering about the meaning" does not indicate that he doubted that it had a meaning. Rather, he was having difficulty figuring out what it meant. He was totally perplexed, at a loss to explain it.

God did not let him speculate for long, however. The men sent by Cornelius were already "at the gate," shouting to get attention and inquiring for Peter. So the Holy Spirit interrupted him "while [he] was still thinking [pondering, weighing this and that possibility] about the vision" and told him three men were looking for him. He must "get up and go downstairs" (by the outside stairway)²⁸ from the rooftop, and "not hesitate[²⁹] to go with them." The Holy Spirit had sent them by telling Cornelius to send them.³⁰

> ²¹Peter went down and said to the men, "I'm the one you're looking for. Why have you come?" ²²The men replied, "We have come from Cornelius the centurion. He is a righteous and God-fearing man, who is respected by all the Jewish people. A holy angel told him to have you come to his house so that he could hear what you have to say."

Peter obeyed, told the men he was the one they were looking for, and politely asked the reason they had come. They explained that they had come from Cornelius, who, they added emphatically (Gk. *te*), was a man "respected [Gk. *marturoumenos*, "borne

---

²⁸I have seen such outside stairways made of stone in the ruins of biblical cities excavated in Palestine.

²⁹The KJV has "doubting nothing." The "doubting" of this verse, however, translates a different Gk. word *(diakrinomenos)* than does the "doubted" in v. 17 *(diēporei)* (KJV). Here it means Peter is not to have any misgivings.

³⁰Wagner calls attention to "the power of the vision" and "the incredible divine synchronization of the timing of these interlocked events." *Lighting the World*, 78.

witness to"] by all the Jewish people." Then they relayed the message of the angel.

5. PETER MEETS CORNELIUS 10:23–33

23Then Peter invited the men into the house to be his guests. The next day Peter started out with them, and some of the brothers from Joppa went along. 24The following day he arrived in Caesarea. Cornelius was expecting them and had called together his relatives and close friends.

Ordinarily a Jew would not invite a Gentile into his home. Peter must have done some explaining of his vision to his host Simon to be allowed to show the three men hospitality for the night.[31] Then, in the morning, Peter went with them. But he was careful to take six "of the brothers from Joppa" with him (see Acts 11:12). He knew other believers would call him into question for going into a Gentile house, so he wanted some reliable witnesses. Just to be sure, he took double the two or three required by the Law (see Matt. 18:16; Deut. 19:15).

The next day when they arrived at Caesarea, they found Cornelius waiting for them with a house full of people. He had believed the Lord's promise: Expecting Peter to come at once, he had judged the time of his arrival and took it upon himself to call together all "his relatives and close friends." They came together with prepared hearts and minds.

25As Peter entered the house, Cornelius met him and fell at his feet in reverence. 26But Peter made him get up. "Stand up," he said, "I am only a man myself."

When Peter arrived, Cornelius was so conscious that God had sent him that he "fell at his feet in reverence," showing submission to Peter's authority. This probably shocked Peter and the six Jewish believers who were with him. Quickly he took hold of Cornelius and raised him up, telling him to "stand up" and saying emphatically that he too was "only a man," a human being.[32] Peter did not want anyone to give any human personality pre-

[31]Or, the slaves were Jews and the "devout" soldier was considered a proselyte.
[32]Cf. the way Paul and Barnabas responded to the Lycaonians (14:14–17), as well as how the angel of Rev. responded to John (Rev. 22:8–9). This is in strong contrast to Jesus, who accepted worship (Matt. 14:33; John 9:38).

eminence in the Church. His response certainly offers no precedent for considering him a pope.

> 27Talking with him, Peter went inside and found a large
> gathering of people. 28He said to them: "You are well
> aware that it is against our law for a Jew to associate with
> a Gentile or visit him. But God has shown me that I should
> not call any man impure or unclean. 29So when I was
> sent for, I came without raising any objection. May I ask
> why you sent for me?"

The text implies that when Peter went into the house he was
surprised to see so many people. He began his sermon by
reminding them that it was "against [Jewish] law" (Gk. *athemi-
ton*, "illegal, forbidden, taboo") for a Jew to "associate with"33 or
"visit" (implying agreement with) a foreigner. But he had
responded to their invitation because God had shown him not
to say any human being is unacceptable to God or beyond His
saving grace. And although Cornelius's messengers had given
Peter the reason for the invitation (v. 22), he asked again so the
six witnesses could hear for themselves. (Jewish law and custom
did not accept hearsay evidence.)

> 30Cornelius answered: "Four days ago I was in my house
> praying at this hour, at three in the afternoon. Suddenly
> a man in shining clothes stood before me 31and said,
> 'Cornelius, God has heard your prayer and remembered
> your gifts to the poor. 32Send to Joppa for Simon who is
> called Peter. He is a guest in the home of Simon the tan-
> ner, who lives by the sea.' 33So I sent for you immediate-
> ly, and it was good of you to come. Now we are all here
> in the presence of God to listen to everything the Lord
> has commanded you to tell us."

In answer, Cornelius recounted how four days before (counting that day as the fourth day) "a man in shining clothes" told
him to send for Peter, which he did. Now Peter was courteous
enough to respond to the request.34 All of them were there, rec-

---

33Translates the same Gk. word used of Paul attempting "to join" the disciples
in Jerusalem (Acts 9:26).

34This is an idiomatic phrase: It does not mean Peter had done a good thing,
but rather, they were simply pleased that he had come. Cf. NEB, JB.

ognizing God's sacred presence with them and wanting to hear everything that God had instructed Peter to tell them.

6. PETER ANNOUNCES GOOD NEWS FOR GENTILES 10:34–43

34Then Peter began to speak: "I now realize how true it is that God does not show favoritism 35but accepts men from every nation who fear him and do what is right.

Peter's sermon at the house of Cornelius is a landmark in the history of the Early Church.[35] From its beginning, he indicates that now he is fully aware of the meaning of his repeated vision given on the rooftop. He saw that "God [truly] does not show favoritism." In every nation, those who worship and reverence God and do what is right (give operation to righteousness as evidence of the divine grace they have received by faith) are acceptable to Him[36] (cf. Rom. 2:10–11).

God's impartiality is not a new idea here. The Old Testament teaches it in such passages as Deuteronomy 10:17; 2 Samuel 14:14; 2 Chronicles 19:7. (See also Amos 9:7; Rom. 2:11; 1 Pet. 1:17). This does not mean that God cannot make a choice, but that He does not base His choice on, or limit it to, national or external differences. So, these Gentiles, if they fulfilled these qualifications of worship, faith, and faithfulness, were just as acceptable to God as any Jew (cf. Mal. 4:2; Matt. 3:8–9).

36You know the message God sent to the people of Israel, telling the good news of peace through Jesus Christ, who is Lord of all.

[35]The phrase "opened his mouth" (v. 34, KJV) was used to introduce an important discourse. C. H. Dodd draws attention to the similarity between Peter's preaching here and the Gospel of Mark. *The Apostolic Preaching and Its Developments* (London: Hodder & Stoughton, 1936), cited by Everett F. Harrison, *Interpreting Acts: The Expanding Church* (Grand Rapids: Zondervan Publishing House, Academie Books, 1986), 173. Ancient tradition says Mark reported Peter's preaching in his Gospel.

[36]Or, "is accepted by Him." See F. F. Bruce, *Acts: Greek Text,* 261. Bruce adds, "While divine salvation is according to grace (cf. 15:11), the undeviating principle in divine judgment is to every one according to his works (cf. Rom. 2:6; Rev. 20:12f.)."

Peter then reminds Cornelius and his friends of the message ("the word," NASB; see Ps. 107:20) God sent to Israel, proclaiming "the good news [the gospel] of peace through Jesus Christ." Peace with God comes only through Jesus.

At this point, Peter cannot help interjecting that Jesus is "Lord of all," that is, of all people everywhere—Gentiles as well as Jews. He removed the barriers between Jews and Gentiles and those between humanity and God.

> [37]You know what has happened throughout Judea, beginning in Galilee after the baptism that John preached— [38]how God anointed Jesus of Nazareth with the Holy Spirit and power, and how he went around doing good and healing all who were under the power of the devil, because God was with him.

Then he goes on, reminding them of the message[37] that they knew. "You know" is emphatic in the Greek here (*humeis oidate,* "you, you know"); although it is not at the beginning of v. 36, it applies there as well. This means they knew the facts about Jesus, including the promise of the Holy Spirit. Possibly they had heard Philip preach (8:40). In any case, Peter recognized that someone had given them the message, for it was preached through all Judea beginning from Galilee after the baptism John had preached. No one who attended the synagogues could have escaped hearing about it.

The message was Jesus himself, Jesus of Nazareth. After John had baptized Him, God anointed[38] Him with the Holy Spirit and mighty power (see Isa. 11:2; 61:1–2; Luke 4:18–19,31–37).[39] This Jesus "went around doing good" (kind) deeds and "healing all who were under the power of the devil": overpowered, oppressed, or treated harshly by the devil ("the slanderer," the chief slanderer of all). God had not only identified Jesus as His

---

[37]"Message" (v. 36) or "word" (vv. 36, 37, KJV) is *logon* in verse 36 and *rhēma* in v. 37. Clearly *logos* and *rhēma* are used interchangeably.

[38]Gk. *echrisen,* from the same root as *Christos,* "Anointed One."

[39]"This same anointing with the Spirit for witness and service is given to the church in Acts." Douglas A. Oss, "A Pentecostal/Charismatic View," in *Are Miraculous Gifts for Today?* ed. Wayne A. Grudem (Grand Rapids: Zondervan Publishing House, 1996), 253.

Son when John baptized Him (as all four Gospels remind us), "God was with Him."

39"We are witnesses of everything he did in the country of the Jews and in Jerusalem. They killed him by hanging him on a tree, 40but God raised him from the dead on the third day and caused him to be seen. 41He was not seen by all the people, but by witnesses whom God had already chosen—by us who ate and drank with him after he rose from the dead.

Peter then adds, "We [meaning the apostles rather than the believers from Joppa] are witnesses of everything He did in the country of the Jews [including Judea and Galilee] and in Jerusalem." Then Peter goes on with the message: This One who did nothing but good, they killed and hung on a "tree."[40] In contrast to what men did to Jesus, God "raised" (resurrected) Him on the third day (see Hos. 6:2; 1 Cor. 15:4,20,23). Then God (lit.) "granted Him to be plainly seen"—not to "all the people" but to witnesses chosen by God beforehand, namely, to Peter and the others who "ate and drank with him after he rose from [out from among] the dead." This was concrete proof of the reality of Christ's resurrection body. He was not a bodiless spirit, not a ghost, not a figment of their imagination, but a very real Person with whom they had fellowship (Acts 1:3–4).

42He commanded us to preach to the people and to testify that he is the one whom God appointed as judge of the living and the dead. 43All the prophets testify about him that everyone who believes in him receives forgiveness of sins through his name."

Because of Christ's command these witnesses were proclaiming this good news to the people and solemnly testifying that Jesus was "appointed [designated] as judge of the living and the dead." By this Peter did not mean the spiritually living and the spiritually dead. Rather, Jesus is and will be judge of all who have ever or will ever live on earth.[41] This bears out what Jesus said in

[40]Gk. *xulou,* "tree" can also mean anything made from the wood of a tree, such as the rough-hewn cross Jesus died on. Cf. Gal. 3:13–14 and Deut. 21:23.

[41] J. A. Alexander, *A Commentary on the Acts of the Apostles,* 3d ed. (1875; reprint, London: Banner of Truth Trust, 1956), 1:414.

John 5:22, "'The Father judges no one, but has entrusted all judgment to the Son.'" Therefore, just as Jesus is the Mediator between God and humankind in redemption, so He will be in judgment.

Then, as he usually did, Peter brought in the witness of the prophets. Their witness as a whole gives further proof that whoever believes in Jesus receives "forgiveness of sins through his name"—by His authority and because of who He is (the crucified and risen Savior).

7. Gentiles Baptized In The Holy Spirit
10:44–48

44While Peter was still speaking these words, the Holy Spirit came on all who heard the message.

While Peter was still speaking "these words" (Gk. *rhēmata*), there came an unexpected interruption from heaven. The Holy Spirit fell suddenly and powerfully on all who heard "the message" (Gk. *ton logon*).[42] They received the promise that Jesus gave to His disciples. This identified them as true believers.

45The circumcised believers who had come with Peter were astonished that the gift of the Holy Spirit had been poured out even on the Gentiles. 46For they heard them speaking in tongues and praising God.

This amazed the Jewish believers who had come with Peter. In fact, it almost put them in a state of shock to see the Holy Spirit poured out on the Gentiles.[43] In identifying them as "circumcised believers" (in contrast to the uncircumcised Gentiles), Luke is emphasizing their devotion to the Jewish ideas about circumcision being the mark of the covenant—which disposed them to being dismayed. It was hard for them to believe that Gentiles could be accepted by God without first becoming Jews.

Three elements relate this occurrence to what happened on

---

[42]What Peter spoke was *rhēma*, but what they heard was *logos*. Again, the two words are used interchangeably.

[43]The Targum Pseudo-Jonathan on Exod. 33:16 has Moses saying that God's speaking by the Holy Spirit to him and to Israel was "that we may be distinguished from all the peoples upon the face of the earth." This indicates Jews expected God to withhold the Holy Spirit from Gentiles.

the Day of Pentecost (Acts 2:17,33): (1) the verb describing the manifestation of the Spirit, "poured out" (Gk. *ekcheō*), (2) their speaking with tongues (languages), and (3) those tongues magnifying God. This evidence clearly convinced these Jewish believers. It also shows that the Pentecostal experience can be repeated.

Menzies and Menzies draw attention to Luke's "sign value of speaking in tongues" that is "rooted in Luke's prophetic pneumatology."[44] They add, "Whether from the lips of a Jew in Jerusalem [2:4–5,17–20] or a Gentile in Caesarea, the manifestation of tongues-speech marks the speaker as a member of the end-time prophetic community."[45]

Then Peter said, [47]"Can anyone keep these people from being baptized with water? They have received the Holy Spirit just as we have." [48]So he ordered that they be baptized in the name of Jesus Christ. Then they asked Peter to stay with them for a few days.

Peter recognized this as further confirmation that these Gentile believers were not only accepted by God but were made part of the Church. The Holy Spirit at Pentecost was poured out on believers who were already identified as the Church and as the temple of the Holy Spirit.[46] With this kind of evidence, who could "keep [them] from being baptized with [in] water?" Their experience in receiving the Spirit was exactly the same as that of the Jewish believers.

From this we can see that these Gentiles, whose hearts were prepared by the angel's message, believed and were saved while Peter was preaching.[47] They then were ready for the outpouring of the Holy Spirit. Acts 11:15–17 describes this baptism in the

[44]William W. Menzies and Robert P. Menzies, *Spirit and Power: Foundations of Pentecostal Experience* (Grand Rapids: Zondervan Publishing House, 2000), 129.

[45]Ibid. Menzies and Menzies argue further that the doctrine of "tongues as initial evidence" is "an appropriate inference."

[46]See Stanley M. Horton, *What the Bible Says About the Holy Spirit* (Springfield, Mo.: Gospel Publishing House, 1976), 141–42.

[47]Because they responded in faith, they were saved and then almost immediately baptized in the Spirit. Some Pentecostals believe that since they already knew the gospel (vv. 37–38) and because Peter did not ask them to repent, they were already saved before Peter came. See French Arrington, *The Acts of the Apostles* (Peabody, Mass.: Hendrickson Publishers, 1988), 112–13.

Holy Spirit as just like what happened on the Day of Pentecost and that it came "'after believing'" (v. 17, NASB). Later, in Acts 15:8, Peter says, "'God, who knows the heart, showed that he accepted them by giving the Holy Spirit to them, just as He did to us.'" This surely means that the baptism in the Holy Spirit bore witness to the faith they already had before they were filled with the Spirit.[48]

At Peter's instructions, the six Jewish believers baptized the whole crowd "in the name [by the authority] of Jesus Christ."[49] This was a public declaration of their faith, a witness to the faith they already had, a witness to the faith that had already brought cleansing to their hearts (Acts 15:9).[50]

Then the people "asked Peter to stay with them for a few days." Undoubtedly they wanted more instruction and desired to share both table fellowship and spiritual fellowship with him. Peter could now have fellowship with them as believers and as members of the body of Christ.

8. PETER EXPLAINS TO THE APOSTLES AND THE CHURCH IN JERUSALEM 11:1–18

[1]The apostles and the brothers throughout Judea heard that the Gentiles also had received the word of God. [2]So when Peter went up to Jerusalem, the circumcised believers criticized him [3]and said, "You went into the house of uncircumcised men and ate with them."

Peter was right in believing he would need witnesses with him when he went to the house of Cornelius. He found it necessary to explain everything that happened there. The fact that Luke records this, repeating much of what was said in chapter 10, shows how important these events in Caesarea were. From them they learned that God would accept the Gentiles without cir-

---

[48]Compare Titus 3:5–6, which shows that the pouring out of the Spirit in Pentecostal fullness is something that happens after regeneration. See Horton, *What the Bible Says,* 250.

[49]See comments on Acts 2:38.

[50]See 1 Pet. 3:20–21, noting it was the faith Noah had before the Flood that was witnessed to by the fact he came through the Flood. So water baptism testifies to the faith which has already purified the heart. The water is a symbol and has no power or grace in itself, nor does it convey any. Cf. Rom. 10:9–10.

cumcision, that is, without their becoming Jews. The repetition thus emphasizess that Christianity was not something just to add on to Judaism. Gentiles could come directly under the new covenant without coming first under the old covenant. They could have the promise to Abraham without the outward sign of the Abrahamic covenant.

The Gentiles at the house of Cornelius "received the word of God."[51] This means they welcomed it, acknowledging its truth and accepting its message of repentance, forgiveness, and salvation. This was striking news, and to some of the Jews was probably not good news. Such news travels fast and reached the apostles and the rest of the believers in Jerusalem before Peter returned!

When he arrived, "the circumcised believers"[52] were ready for him. Immediately they "criticized him"[53] severely (and passed judgment on him) for entering the "house of uncircumcised men" (which they considered defiling) and, even worse, eating their nonkosher food. Just how upset these Jewish believers were is shown by their use of a very derogatory slang word for Gentile, (lit.) "foreskinned" (Gk. *akrobustian*). It is quite probable they were also upset because they feared that Peter's action might turn the unconverted Jews against them and bring to an end the period of peace they had been enjoying (see 9:31). Besides rejecting Peter, they were more concerned about themselves than about the spread of the gospel. They forgot also that God's call to repentance was "'Come, *all you* who are thirsty'" (Isa. 55:1), not only "every *Jew* who is thirsty."

4Peter began and explained everything to them precisely as it had happened: 5"I was in the city of Joppa praying, and in a trance I saw a vision. I saw something like a large sheet being let down from heaven by its four corners, and it came down to where I was. 6I looked into it and saw four-footed animals of the earth, wild beasts, reptiles, and birds of the air. 7Then I heard a voice telling

[51]The same phrase used with the Samaritans (Acts 8:14).

[52]These would include the whole church, for all were either Jews or proselytes.

[53]This implies that all the Jewish believers up to this point believed Gentiles had to become Jews before becoming Christians. See H. B. Hackett, *A Commentary on the Acts of the Apostles* (Philadelphia: American Baptist Publication Society, 1882), 138. Harrison, *Acts,* 177, disagrees, but without sufficient reason.

me, 'Get up, Peter. Kill and eat.' ⁸"I replied, 'Surely not,
Lord! Nothing impure or unclean has ever entered my
mouth' ⁹"The voice spoke from heaven a second time,
'Do not call anything impure that God has made clean.'
¹⁰This happened three times, and then it was all pulled
up to heaven again. ¹¹"Right then three men who had
been sent to me from Caesarea stopped at the house
where I was staying. ¹²The Spirit told me to have no hesitation about going with them. These six brothers also
went with me, and we entered the man's house.

Peter then proceeded to defend himself by explaining everything to them "as it had happened," that is, from the time he saw
the vision in Joppa. He does add that the sheet (sailcloth) "came
down to where [he] was" so that he was able to look closely and
inspect the contents without any possibility of being mistaken.
If they still wanted to require circumcision, they would have to
blame God, not him. He emphasized that the Spirit said "to have
no hesitation about going" (implying no disputing or criticiz-
ing). He was also careful to point to the "six brothers" as witnesses who were with him at Caesarea and whom he had
brought with him to Jerusalem (v. 12).

¹³He told us how he had seen an angel appear in his
house and say, 'Send to Joppa for Simon who is called
Peter. ¹⁴He will bring you a message through which
you and all your household will be saved.' ¹⁵"As I began to
speak, the Holy Spirit came on them as he had come on
us at the beginning.

As further proof of God's leading, he adds that the angel told
Cornelius that Peter would "bring . . . a message through which
[he] and all [his] household [would] be saved."

Then, without repeating the sermon he gave at Caesarea,
Peter told them that as he "began to speak,[54] the Holy Spirit
came *on them* as he had come *on us*": that is, just as supernaturally and as evidently on the Gentiles at Cornelius's house as on
the 120 and the 3000 on the Day of Pentecost.[55] Some writers

---

[54]Evidently Peter considered what he said in Caesarea to be just the introduction to the sermon he could have preached.
[55]The Gk. is emphatic.

try to avoid mentioning the Day of Pentecost here.[56] But this can only mean as on the Day of Pentecost (Acts 2:4), since there was no falling upon or pouring out of the Spirit in fulfillment of Joel's prophecy until then.

> **16Then I remembered what the Lord had said: 'John baptized with water, but you will be baptized with the Holy Spirit.' 17So if God gave them the same gift as he gave us, who believed in the Lord Jesus Christ, who was I to think that I could oppose God?"**

Peter next added something that had gone on in his own mind. He "remembered what the Lord had said" (in Acts 1:5)—that John baptized in water but that they would be baptized in the Holy Spirit. This remembering was brought about by the Holy Spirit (John 14:26). Consequently, Peter clearly saw that this outpouring was also a baptism in the Spirit.

Peter then went on to say emphatically that God gave these Gentile believers "the same gift" He had given the Jewish believers; God was doing the work. "Same" in the Greek means "equal" or "identical."[57] This is significant because the convincing evidence was not wind or fire (which preceded only the Pentecostal outpouring of the Spirit and was not actually a part of it). The Jewish believers needed a convincing evidence, and the one convincing evidence given was the fact they spoke in other tongues and praised God (Acts 10:46).

The Gentiles did not have to ask if they had really received this mighty outpouring. They knew. Peter and the six witnesses did not say "I think" or "I suppose," or even "I trust" or "I believe,s" these Gentiles were baptized in the Spirit. They knew. Surely, in the midst of all the questioning and discussion about the Holy Spirit today, we need the same convincing evidence. We too can know that when we speak in tongues we have received an experience identical to the one described in Acts 2:4.

Peter was no longer perplexed (see Acts 10:17). He had come to a new understanding. Since God gave the Gentiles this gift of

[56]Dunn, however, says "at Pentecost." *Acts of the Apostles,* 150.

[57]The masculine form of the same word is *isos,* which is found in our word "isosceles" when describing a triangle having two of its three sides equal, or identical.

the Spirit, for Peter to refuse to accept them would be to "oppose God," and who was he—and by implication who was his audience (who is any person)—to do that?

> **18When they heard this, they had no further objections and praised God, saying, "So then, God has granted even the Gentiles repentance unto life."**

The Jewish believers in Jerusalem would not oppose God either. After learning the facts of the case, "they had no further objections." The Holy Spirit was guiding them into a new understanding of truth (John 16:13). They were responsive enough to the Spirit and the Word to glorify God and to recognize that He had given "even the Gentiles repentance unto life." More specifically, God had accepted their repentance and given them spiritual life without their being circumcised; their baptism in the Holy Spirit with the evidence of speaking in other tongues bore witness to that. It is still important that we accept people whom God has accepted, no matter how different they are from us.

STUDY QUESTIONS

1. How did the Lord remove Peter's prejudice against Gentiles?
2. How did the Lord deal with Cornelius and with what results?
3. How did Peter know that the experience of the Gentiles in the house of Cornelius was identical to the experience of the 120 at Pentecost?

IV. ANTIOCH: A NEW CENTER 11:19-18:22
A. The Gospel Reaches Antioch 11:19-30
1. GENTILES BELIEVE IN ANTIOCH 11:19-21

19Now those who had been scattered by the persecution in connection with Stephen traveled as far as Phoenicia, Cyprus and Antioch, telling the message only to Jews.

Though the Jerusalem apostles and believers accepted the fact that Gentiles in Caesarea were saved and had become part of the

Church, this did not excite them very much. There was no rush to go out and win more Gentiles to the Lord. In fact, even Peter continued to consider his ministry as primarily to the Jews (Gal. 2:7–9). Thus Luke turns our attention to an ethnically mixed congregation in a new center for the spread of the gospel, the capital of the Roman province of Syria, Antioch, located on the Orontes River, over three hundred miles north of Jerusalem. It was a great trade center, the largest city in Asia Minor, having a population of half a million. Founded about 300 B.C. by Seleucus I Nicator, its importance was recognized by the Romans, who made it a free city in 64 B.C. But it was full of evil.

Verse 19 makes a connection with Acts 8:1,4 (see also 9:31). Up to this point the examples of what happened had been taken from Judea and Samaria. Now we see that the wave of itinerant evangelism did not stop there. But, as always, Luke does not try to cover everything. Instead, following the inspiration of the Holy Spirit, he selects one direction this evangelism took and presents it as an example of what went on as the believers were scattered in many directions. There was a special reason for choosing the direction toward Antioch, however. It forms a link with the apostle Paul and prepares for the account of his journeys, which takes up the major portion of the rest of the Book of Acts.

Even outside of Palestine, however, those who spread the gospel preached the Word only to Jews. This may not have been entirely due to prejudice. The Jews had the Old Testament Scriptures and knew the prophecies (see Rom. 3:2). These evangelists based their message on the fact that God, through Jesus, had fulfilled prophecy. Most Gentiles had no background for understanding this. But these evangelists were missing the fact that many Gentiles had lost confidence in their idols and were seeking something better.

The evangelizers traveled up the coast of Asia Minor as far as Phoenicia, where churches were established in Ptolemais, Tyre, and Sidon (Acts 21:3–4,7; 27:3). From there some went to the island of Cyprus, the third largest island of the Mediterranean. Others kept going north, to Antioch, the capital of Syria, in a fertile valley on the north bank of the Orontes River. Its population of five hundred thousand included about sixty-five thousand Jews.

20Some of them, however, men from Cyprus and Cyrene, went to Antioch and began to speak to Greeks also, telling them the good news about the Lord Jesus. 21The Lord's hand was with them, and a great number of people believed and turned to the Lord.

Some of these were "men from Cyprus and Cyrene"[1] and may have been among the three thousand who were saved and filled with the Spirit on the Day of Pentecost. They were probably from among the Greek-speaking believers (Acts 6:1). They began (undoubtedly led and prompted by the Holy Spirit) at Antioch "to speak to Greeks" (Gk. *Hellēnas*, "Greek-speaking Gentiles"),[2] telling them the gospel of the Lord Jesus.

The men are not named, but "the Lord's hand was with them." This expression is often used in the Bible to mean the power of the Lord or even the Spirit of the Lord (as in Ezek. 1:3; 3:14,22,24; 8:1; 11:1).[3] Certainly, the miracle-working power of the Lord was triumphantly manifest, confirming the Word as in Samaria (Acts 8:5–8); "a great number . . . believed and turned to the Lord." This means they turned away from their pagan customs and worldly ways to follow Jesus. We can be sure also that like the household of Cornelius, they were all baptized in the Holy Spirit with the evidence of speaking in other tongues. As Peter said, "'God does not show favoritism'" (10:34).

We see again also that the Holy Spirit delights in breaking down barriers of language, culture, race, or whatever else may separate believers from each other. As the Bible says, Gentiles were once far off from God but now are brought near by the blood of Jesus (Eph. 2:13–18). Thus, the Cross reconciles both Jews and Gentiles to God in one Body. Both have access to God's throne by the one Holy Spirit. Then, when both are in right relationship with the Lord, the result is a community of believers where every believer is recognized and loved by every other believer as a part of the family of God.

[1]A district east of Libya. It was about 725 miles west of Jerusalem.

[2]Many ancient manuscripts have the word *Hellēnistas*, "Greek-speakers," here, which is sometimes used of Greek-speaking Jews. But in this context it clearly means Greek-speaking Gentiles. All educated Gentiles in this area spoke Greek.

[3]See Stanley M. Horton, *What the Bible Says About the Holy Spirit* (Springfield, Mo.: Gospel Publishing House, 1976), 66.

2. Barnabas Sent To Antioch 11:22–26

²²News of this reached the ears of the church at Jerusalem, and they sent Barnabas to Antioch. ²³When he arrived and saw the evidence of the grace of God, he was glad and encouraged them all to remain true to the Lord with all their hearts.

When news of the conversion of these Gentiles in Antioch reached the Jerusalem church, they recognized that this great spread of the gospel among Gentiles was an important new development. Antioch itself was significant, since it was the third most important city in the entire Roman Empire, exceeded only by Rome and Alexandria. So they "sent Barnabas to Antioch."

The choice of Barnabas is important. It shows that the Jerusalem church (not just the apostles) were concerned about this new assembly in Antioch and sent out their best encourager to help them. He was sent literally "to go through as far as Antioch" (Gk. *dielthein heōs Antiocheias*), which means also that he was to preach the gospel and encourage assemblies of believers all along the way.

Some writers have assumed that sending Barnabas meant the church at Jerusalem wanted to maintain control over this new development or, at least, to investigate it. However, there is no evidence of this. It was just brotherly love and concern. They were happy that God was working. The same loving Spirit that sent Peter and John to Samaria to help the people there moved the church here also. Barnabas did not have to report back to Jerusalem, nor did he have to seek their advice about further steps in ministry that might be necessary.

At Antioch Barnabas "saw the evidence of the grace of God." These outwardly observable expressions of the Spirit's gifts made him rejoice. He accepted these Gentiles just as Peter accepted the believers at the house of Cornelius. Barnabas then lived up to his name by continually encouraging[4] them all to purpose openly from their hearts "to remain true to" (or, "continue loyally with") the Lord Jesus. Barnabas knew that difficulties, persecutions, and

---

[4]Gk. *parakalei*. Barnabas was a "son of *paraklēseos*," and Jesus called the Holy Spirit "another *paraklētos*," both from the same Gk. root (see Acts 4:36 and John 14:16).

temptations lay ahead. Persistence in a close walk with the Lord would be needed.

> **24He was a good man, full of the Holy Spirit and faith, and a great number of people were brought to the Lord.**

Barnabas's life, not simply his preaching and teaching, made him a most effective witness: "a great number" (Gk. *ochlos hikanos*, "a considerable crowd") of believers were "brought" (Gk. *prosetethē*, "added") to the Lord (Jesus). That is, they became part of the body of Christ, the Church. A "great number" *(polus arithmos)* had already been added (v. 21). Now a large crowd is added. "The *rate* of growth had evidently increased as a result of Barnabas's ministry."[5]

> **25Then Barnabas went to Tarsus to look for Saul, 26and when he found him, he brought him to Antioch. So for a whole year Barnabas and Saul met with the church and taught great numbers of people. The disciples were called Christians first at Antioch.**

This growth in numbers made Barnabas see that he needed help to teach and train the new converts. He did not, however, send back to Jerusalem to ask them to send someone.[6] Led by the Spirit we can be sure, he went about one hundred miles up the coast to Tarsus to search for Saul. Since Barnabas was the one who had earlier taken the time and effort to find out about Saul and introduce him to the apostles in Jerusalem (Acts 9:27), he obviously knew what God had said about sending Paul to the Gentiles (Acts 22:21). Now it was God's time for Saul to begin this ministry.[7]

This search for Saul probably took some time. When Barnabas found him, "he brought him back to Antioch" (v. 26, NLT). The two of them then became the chief teachers of the church, gath-

---

[5]C. Peter Wagner, *Lighting the World: Book 2, Acts 9–15* (Ventura, Calif.: Gospel Light, Regal Books, 1995), 105, Wagner's emphasis.

[6]It is evident that the local churches became sovereign assemblies and yet cooperated in voluntary fellowship.

[7]F. F. Bruce, *Commentary on the Book of Acts* (Grand Rapids: Wm. B. Eerdmans, 1954), 240–41, suggests that Saul had been disinherited (pointing to Phil. 3:8), and that he had begun his work evangelizing Gentiles in his native province of Cilicia. See Acts 22:21.

ering the believers together[8] and teaching "great numbers."

At Antioch, the disciples, also called the saints, first received the name (and were publicly called by their fellow citizens) "Christians." Up to this time the believers were practically all Jews. The Gentiles, and even the Jews, considered the believers simply as another sect of Judaism. In fact, their lifestyle was hardly more different from the Pharisees' lifestyle than the Pharisees' was from the Sadducees'. But now there was a large, well-established, growing assembly of believers composed chiefly of uncircumcised Gentiles.

Obviously, these Gentile believers could not be identified by a Jewish name, nor could they any longer be considered a sect of Judaism. They needed a new name. Soldiers in the Roman army often took the name of their general and added "ian" (Lat. *iani*, Gk. *ianos*) to indicate they were a soldier and follower of that general. For example, Caesar's soldiers were called *Caesariani*, and Pompey's soldiers were called *Pompeiani*. Political parties, such as the Herodians (Mark 12:13), were also designated in the same sort of way.

So the people of Antioch began to call the believers *Christiani* or "Christians": soldiers, followers, partisans, of Christ. Some believe the name was first given in derision,[9] but there is no great evidence of this. The believers did not reject the name. They were indeed in the Lord's army, clothed with the full armor of God (see Eph. 6:11–18). It should be noted, however, that the term "Christian" is used elsewhere in the New Testament only in Acts 26:28 and 1 Peter 4:16.[10] For the most part the believers continued to refer to themselves as disciples, brothers, saints, those of the Way, or servants (slaves) of Jesus.

3. Agabus Prophesies a Famine 11:27–30

[27]During this time some prophets came down from Jerusalem to Antioch. [28]One of them, named Agabus,

[8]The Gk. implies they met, and were entertained, in the homes of believers.

[9]Simon J. Kistemaker, *Exposition of the Acts of the Apostles* (Grand Rapids: Baker Book House, 1990), 423. Wagner agrees with him. *Lighting the World,* 108.

[10]Some in those days called them *chrestians,* "followers of kindness and goodness."

stood up and through the Spirit predicted that a severe
famine would spread over the entire Roman world. (This
happened during the reign of Claudius.)

The various assemblies of believers continued to keep in
touch with each other. After Barnabas, others came from
Jerusalem to encourage the believers at Antioch. In fact, about
the time Saul's first year in Antioch was up, several prophets
"came down from Jerusalem."[11] The Holy Spirit regularly used
men and women in the ministry of the gift of prophecy: for edi-
fication, strengthening spiritually and confirming faith; for
exhortation, awakening, encouraging, and challenging believers
to move ahead in faithfulness and love; and for comfort, cheer-
ing, reviving, and encouraging hope and expectation.[12] Their
ministry in this way dealt with the needs of the believers to
whom they ministered.[13]

Sometimes they reinforced their exhortations by foretelling
the future. But this was the exception rather than the rule.
Prophecy in the Bible is always primarily "forthtelling," speaking
for God whatever His message may be, rather than foretelling
the future. However, on this occasion[14] Agabus ("Grasshopper"),
one of the prophets, "stood up and through the Spirit predicted
[a manifestation of the gift of prophecy given directly by the
Spirit in their own language] that a severe famine would spread
over the entire Roman world."[15] And as Luke indicates, the
famine took place "during the reign of Claudius" Caesar (A.D.
41–54). It was especially severe in Judea in A.D. 45–48.

**29The disciples, each according to his ability, decided to
provide help for the brothers living in Judea. 30This they
did, sending their gift to the elders by Barnabas and Saul.**

[11]Jews both "went up to" and "came down from" Jerusalem. This was not a
matter of map direction but spiritual ascendancy.

[12]See 1 Cor. 14:3; Horton, *What the Bible Says,* 225.

[13]Cf. Acts 13:1; 15:32; Eph. 4:11.

[14]The Western Text inserts at the beginning of v. 28 "There was much rejoicing; and when we were gathered together . . . " If this is original it would mean
Luke was present in Antioch at this time (see 16:10 and comments).

[15]"World" is the Gk. *oikoumenēn,* "inhabited earth." But this word was used
in those days to mean the Roman world (hence NIV, NLT), for the Romans did
not think anything outside the empire was worth noticing.

Because the disciples (both Jewish and Gentile believers) in Antioch felt gratitude for the blessings and teaching brought them from "the brothers . . . in Judea" (i.e., Jewish believers), they decided that each one would contribute "according to his [financial] ability" (lit. "as he was prospered") and send relief (cf. 2 Cor. 9:7). This they did, sending it not to the apostles but to the Jerusalem "elders,"[16] by Barnabas and Saul. This was done probably about A.D. 46, when Judea especially was hard hit by famine.[17]

STUDY QUESTIONS

1. What may have prompted the first preaching to Gentiles at Antioch?
2. Why was Barnabas sent to Antioch and what did he accomplish there?
3. Why did the people of Antioch begin to call the disciples Christians?

B. Peter's Deliverance 12:1–24

The conversion of Cornelius and the spread of the gospel to Gentiles in Antioch gave a new direction to the Church. As we have seen in chapter 11, Jewish believers in Jerusalem lent their support and gave encouragement to this new development. Though the Jerusalem believers themselves were careful to observe the laws and customs of the Jews, the Jewish rulers and leaders must have been aware of what was happening outside of Jerusalem.

---

[16]Gk. *presbuterous,* having leadership similar to the synagogue rulers (Mark 5:22).

[17]Bruce, *Commentary,* 244, also suggests that Saul's (Paul's) visit described in Gal. 2:1–10 fits here. The facts seem to favor this, as is pointed out by Joe Morgado, Jr., "Paul in Jerusalem: A Comparison of His Visits in Acts and Galatians," *Journal of the Evangelical Theological Society* 37, no. 1 (March 1994): 65–68. Thus, at this time Peter, John, James, and other Jerusalem leaders recognized that the gospel Paul preached was the same one they preached.

For some time there had been no persecution of the believers in Jerusalem. In fact, persecution was never steady or continuous in the times of the Early Church, even under the Romans of the second and third centuries A.D. But the Jewish religious leaders in Jerusalem always saw the Church as a threat. They were also aware of the ministry of the apostles and saw how many thousands were following them and turning to the Lord (see 21:20).

It should be noted that "12:1–24 constitutes a kind of flashback. . . . Luke . . . does not mean that the events of 12:1–24 happened while Barnabas and Saul were in Jerusalem."[1]

1. HEROD KILLS THE APOSTLE JAMES 12:1–2

[1]It was about this time that King Herod arrested some who belonged to the church, intending to persecute them. [2]He had James, the brother of John, put to death with the sword.

From A.D. 6 to 41, procurators sent by the Roman emperor governed Judea. These men were never popular. Pilate, especially, had angered the Jewish leaders in many ways. He had even taken money from the temple treasury to build an aqueduct into Jerusalem.

In A.D. 41 the emperor added Judea to the realm of King Herod Agrippa I, the King Herod of this chapter. This Herod (born in 10 B.C.) was the son of Aristobulus and grandson of the Idumaean (Edomite converted to Judaism) Herod the Great and his wife Mariamne, a Jewish princess of the Hasmonean (Maccabean) family. Because Herod Agrippa I was educated in Rome and became a friend of the Roman emperors, Gaius (Caligula) made him king of part of Syria in A.D. 37. Then, two years later, after exiling Herod Antipas, who killed John the Baptist, Gaius added Galilee and Perea to Agrippa's rule. (Antipas was an uncle of Agrippa I). In A.D. 41 the emperor Claudius gave Agrippa Judea and Samaria, uniting practically the whole territory, once ruled by Herod the Great, under him.

[1]Richard Bauckham, "James and the Jerusalem Church," in *The Book of Acts in its Palestinian Setting*, ed. Richard Bauckham, vol. 4 of *The Book of Acts in Its First Century Setting*, ed. Bruce W. Winter (Grand Rapids: Wm. B. Eerdmans, 1995), 433.

When Herod Agrippa I became king over Judea and Jerusalem he did everything he could to gain and hold the favor of the Jews. Unlike most of the other Herods, he practiced the forms of the Jewish religion faithfully, offered sacrifices daily in the temple, and on occasion read the law of Moses publicly.[2] Apparently, he also saw and heard enough from the Jewish leaders to know of their fears and frustrations with respect to the apostles and the Church. He undoubtedly heard how the Sanhedrin had threatened the apostles, who simply continued to preach about Jesus.

Somewhere in the early part of his reign over Jerusalem, then, he decided to take steps to show he was a king who could do more than threaten. So he arrested some from the Church "intending to persecute them."[3] Among them was the apostle James, brother of John (together, the sons of Zebedee). With Peter, James and John constituted the inner circle of Jesus' disciples while He ministered on earth. Luke does not give any details, but there does not seem to have been a trial. James was given no opportunity even to witness to his faith. Herod simply had him "put to death with the sword."[4] To the Jews this would mean Herod considered James no longer a true Jew but an apostate.[5]

2. HEROD ARRESTS PETER 12:3-6

[3]When he saw that this pleased the Jews, he proceeded to seize Peter also. This happened during the Feast of Unleavened Bread. [4]After arresting him, he put him in

[2]He was educated with the children of the emperor in Rome, lived an immoral life in his youth, got into debt and begged help from Herod Antipas, and even thought of suicide. But when he became king, he amended his ways.

[3]Gk. *kakōsai*, "to harm, mistreat." Cf. Jesus' warnings in Matt. 20:23; 24:9.

[4]In the Roman style this would mean he was beheaded. Some modern critics suppose John was killed at this time too, since Jesus said they would both drink of the cup of suffering (Mark 10:39). But Jesus did not say they would die at the same time. John actually lived until about A.D. 100 and died in Ephesus, according to strong early tradition, including that of Clement (A.D. 150–215). Papias of Hierapolis (about A.D. 100), according to the early church historian Eusebius, supposedly spoke of another John in Ephesus, an elder John. But Papias has been proved wrong about other things. John the apostle did suffer much (see Rev. 1:9; cf. John 21:20–22).

[5]Luke T. Johnson, *The Acts of the Apostles* (Collegeville, Minn.: Liturgical Press, 1992), 211.

prison, handing him over to be guarded by four squads
of four soldiers each. Herod intended to bring him out
for public trial after the Passover.

The execution of James "pleased" (was acceptable to) the
Jewish leaders and their friends. They had not forgotten how the
apostles defied them. Moreover, since most of these leaders were
Sadducees, they did not like the teachings of the Christians; they
wanted them stopped. They were probably aware also of the
spread of the gospel among the Gentiles.

When Herod saw how pleased they were, "he proceeded to
seize Peter," the most outspoken of the apostles, intending "to
bring him out for public trial after the Passover." The King
James Version in verse 4 translates the word *Pascha*, which is the
Aramaic name for the Passover, as "Easter," but the Passover and
Unleavened Bread combined is what is meant. That is, this arrest
took place during the seven days of the Feast of Unleavened
Bread, which at this time was combined with the day of the
Passover Feast. All eight days were called Passover (beginning on
Nisan 14, which in the Gregorian calendar varies between
March and April). This feast celebrated Israel's deliverance from
Egyptian slavery. Ironically, Peter was "languishing in bondage,
not celebrating liberation."[6]

Why Herod decided to wait until "after the Passover" season
before bringing Peter out[7] to the people we are not told. Perhaps
Herod wanted to show them how strict he was in keeping the
Passover.[8] Or, he may have wanted to wait until most of the
crowd went home lest there be a riot he could not control.
Others suggest he wanted the people's whole attention for the
display he intended to put on.

Whatever the reason, Herod put Peter in prison (probably in
the Antonia Fortress)[9] under a heavy guard. He had surely heard
how the apostles had escaped from prison before (5:18–19), so

[6]William H. Willimon, *Acts* (Atlanta: John Knox Press, 1988), 111.

[7]Gk. *anagagein,* "to bring [him] out" of the prison; that is, either for the people's amusement, or so they could witness his execution.

[8]Herod was an observant Jew, and Pharisaic oral law forbade trials during these
holy days.

[9]Or in the dungeon of Herod the Great's palace on the west side of Jerusalem.

he was taking no chances, using four squads of four soldiers each. This meant one squad for each of the four three-hour "watches" of the night. Two chains bound Peter to the two soldiers on each side of him; two guards in front of the door were on watch over the prison (v. 6). In the natural Peter's situation did look hopeless.

> 5So Peter was kept in prison, but the church was earnestly praying to God for him. 6The night before Herod was to bring him to trial, Peter was sleeping between two soldiers, bound with two chains, and sentries stood guard at the entrance.

In the meantime, the Church "was earnestly [Gk. *ektenōs*, "fervently,"10 NASB] praying to God for him." We can be sure they prayed that he would be sustained and be able to give a witness as well as be delivered.

The night before Herod intended to bring him out for trial, sentencing, and execution,11 Peter was sleeping soundly.12 He must have committed his case to the Lord (cf. Ps. 3:5; 1 Pet. 5:7); even though he expected to face execution the next day he could sleep peacefully. He had Christ with him. It would only be more of Christ if he died (cf. Phil. 1:21). The early believers were so full of the Lord they did not fear death.

3. An Angel Rescues Peter 12:7–19

> 7Suddenly an angel of the Lord appeared and a light shone in the cell. He struck Peter on the side and woke him up. "Quick, get up!" he said, and the chains fell off Peter's wrists. 8Then the angel said to him, "Put on your clothes and sandals." And Peter did so. "Wrap your cloak around you and follow me," the angel told him. 9Peter followed him out of the prison, but he had no idea that what the angel was doing was really happening; he thought he was seeing a vision.

The days of the Passover season came and went without any

10Used of Jesus' prayer, Luke 22:44.

11The Gk. here is like that used of the apostle Paul being brought to trial before King Agrippa (Acts 25:26).

12The Gk. present middle participle *koimōmenos* indicates continuous sound sleep.

hint of deliverance. Then, "suddenly an angel of the Lord appeared" and stood by Peter. A light[13] "shone in the cell" (possibly from the angel, or possibly as a separate manifestation) so Peter could see what to do. The angel then "struck Peter [sharply] on the side," roused him, and told him to get up quickly. (The Gk. verb does not necessarily mean that the angel raised or lifted him, but simply that he woke him up.) At the same time, "the chains fell off Peter's wrists" (the Heb. word *yad* includes hand, wrist, and forearm).

After obeying the angelic command to put on his cloak as well as his tunic and sandals[14] and to follow him, Peter went out. But during all this time he did not realize that what was happening was really true. "He thought he was seeing a vision." The guards also were not conscious of what was happening, nor did they see the angel.[15]

10They passed the first and second guards and came to the iron gate leading to the city. It opened for them by itself, and they went through it. When they had walked the length of one street, suddenly the angel left him.

After passing through two gates with their guards (which shows Peter was in the innermost prison; cf. Paul and Silas, 16:24), the heavy iron gate allowing entrance into the city (street) "opened . . . by itself."[16] Then, after the angel led him "the length of one street,"[17] the angel "suddenly . . . left him" (and disappeared).[18]

11Then Peter came to himself and said, "Now I know without a doubt that the Lord sent his angel and rescued me from Herod's clutches and from everything the Jewish people were anticipating."

Not until the angel left and Peter found himself alone out in the street did he "come to himself" and realize this was not a dream or vision. The Lord had actually sent His angel to rescue

[13]A supernatural light, like the Shekinah.

[14]Nights were still cold in the Judean hill country during Passover (March–April).

[15]Guards on a night shift would not be asleep.

[16]Gk. *automatē*, "automatically, spontaneously." Codex Bezae (D) adds that they "went down seven steps [to the street]."

[17]Or, possibly to the next cross street.

[18]All these details make it probable that Luke got them from Peter himself.

him from Herod's power and from the expectation of the Jewish people, that is, from the expectation that Herod would do to him what he had done to the apostle James.

12When this had dawned on him, he went to the house of Mary the mother of John, also called Mark, where many people had gathered and were praying. 13Peter knocked at the outer entrance, and a servant girl named Rhoda came to answer the door.

"When this had dawned on him," Peter went to the house of Mary, John Mark's mother. (Mark or Marcus was an added Lat. name.)[19] There a considerable number of believers had assembled and were praying. Notice that after several days, people were still praying day and night for Peter. Faithful prayer marked the Early Church and kept them in touch with God.

Mark's mother's house was a large one, with a passageway from the street into the inner part of the house where the believers were gathered. The fact that a slave girl, Rhoda (Gk. *Rhodē*, "rose bush"),[20] answered the door when Peter knocked shows that it was a wealthy home as well. It was obviously the regular meeting place for a large group of believers. Peter knew he would find people there. Undoubtedly, he also felt a special kinship with this group because Mark was his convert and one to whom he had given special training. (See 1 Pet. 5:13 where Peter refers to Mark as "my son," used metaphorically in the sense of "my student," a usage common among both Jews and Greeks.)

14When she recognized Peter's voice, she was so overjoyed she ran back without opening it and exclaimed, "Peter is at the door!" 15"You're out of your mind," they told her. When she kept insisting that it was so, they said, "It must be his angel."

When Rhoda answered, the sound of Peter's familiar voice so filled her with joy that in her excitement she did not open the door. Instead, she ran in and announced Peter's presence to the assembled believers.

They told her she was "out of [her] mind" (Gk. *mainē*, "rav-

---

[19]Mark was a cousin of Barnabas (Col. 4:10).
[20]Details that show the authenticity and accuracy of the material.

ing mad, absolutely crazy"). But she "kept insisting that it was so." Then they began to say it was "his angel." Some of the Jews had a tradition that a guardian angel could take a person's form. There is absolutely no biblical ground for such a teaching, but Luke records their opinion here to show they thought Peter was already dead. Though they were praying day and night for his deliverance, they could not believe it had really taken place.

It had been several years since the apostles had been delivered from prison (Acts 5:18,19). But it was not the passage of time alone that dulled their faith. The shock of James's death made them wonder if perhaps the Lord might let Peter be killed too. Jesus had indicated to Peter that he would die a martyr's death when he was old (John 21:18–19). However, Jesus did not say how old, and Peter was probably older than the other apostles.

Actually, the Bible makes no explanation of why God allowed James to be killed at this time and rescued Peter. We can be sure that in His divine wisdom he knew James's work was done and Peter was still needed on earth. God does all things well!

16But Peter kept on knocking, and when they opened the door and saw him, they were astonished.

While all this discussion was going on in the prayer group, Peter was still standing out front knocking. Probably he did not knock too loudly lest he wake the neighborhood and someone sound an alarm. But finally they opened the door, and the sight of him nearly made them all fall over with astonishment and amazement. He was no ghost. He was really there.

17Peter motioned with his hand for them to be quiet and described how the Lord had brought him out of prison. "Tell James and the brothers about this," he said, and then he left for another place.

Apparently they started to cry out excitedly. But Peter waved his hand to silence them and "described how the Lord had brought him out of prison." Then he asked them to report this to James (the brother of Jesus)[21] and to "the brothers," that is,

---

[21]Some writers take this to mean James the son of Alphaeus. They also conjecture that he was the only apostle left in Jerusalem and was therefore in charge. See J. A. Alexander, *A Commentary on the Acts of the Apostles*, 3d ed. (1875;

leading believers associated with James, possibly elders of other local house groups. No doubt others were meeting for prayer under the leadership of James and other elders of the Church. James would get word to the rest about Peter's deliverance.

Then Peter, knowing that by dawn Herod's men would be searching for him, left and went to another place (probably a house in Jerusalem that was not so well known as a Christian meeting place). He did not tell anyone where he was going so that they could say honestly that they did not know where he was. Luke does not resume Peter's story. But Peter was still in Jerusalem several years later for the council of Acts 15[22] in A.D. 49.

From this also we can see the increasing place of leadership given to James. This may be partly due to the fact he was Jesus' brother.[23] But Jesus had other brothers; there is no evidence that any of them drew attention to their relationship to Jesus or that they tried to capitalize on it in any way. Both James and Jude in their epistles refer to themselves simply as servants (slaves) of the Lord Jesus. James continued to be a leading elder in the church at Jerusalem until he was stoned to death in A.D. 61 just after Festus died. James's death shocked the majority of the Jews in Jerusalem, for even those who did not accept Christ held James in high honor and appreciated his many prayers for the people.

It does seem that after Jesus appeared to James (1 Cor. 15:7) he won his other brothers to the Lord and then they all were taught by the apostles and baptized in the Holy Spirit on the Day

---

reprint, London: Banner of Truth Trust, 1956), 1:454. But what is said later on in Acts and in Paul's epistles makes it clear that James the brother of Jesus is meant. (See Gal. 1:19; 2:9,12; cf. Mark 6:3.)

[22]See Bauckham, "James and the Jerusalem Church," 434–36. Some writers speculate that Peter went to Rome at this time. There is no evidence for this. In fact, there is no real evidence that Peter ever visited Rome before his martyrdom. See H. B. Hackett, *A Commentary on the Acts of the Apostles* (Philadelphia: American Baptist Publication Society, 1882), 146. He did visit Babylon later, for Babylon was the greatest center of orthodox Judaism outside Palestine (see 1 Pet. 5:13, noting that there is every reason to take this as actual Babylon at the time Peter wrote). There was no reason to disguise Rome by calling it Babylon at that time.

[23]In the Gospel lists of Jesus' half brothers, James is always mentioned first. He may have been the oldest.

of Pentecost (Acts 1:14). From that point they gave themselves to prayer and the service of others. James especially seems to have grown spiritually at a very rapid pace. Later tradition says he had calluses like those of a camel on his knees and that he wore holes in a stone floor by kneeling repeatedly in the same place. All agree that prayer and the gifts of the Spirit made him a spiritual leader.

18In the morning, there was no small commotion among the soldiers as to what had become of Peter. 19After Herod had a thorough search made for him and did not find him, he cross-examined the guards and ordered that they be executed. Then Herod went from Judea to Caesarea and stayed there a while.

At dawn there was more than a little disturbance among the soldiers as they tried to find out what had become of Peter. Though Herod had "a thorough search" made for him, he was not to be found. Then Herod brought the guards in for a preliminary examination. However, he did not give them a formal trial; instead, he had them summarily executed. (Roman law punished a guard with the same punishment the escaped prisoner would have received; cf. 16:27; 27:42–43; also 1 Kings 20:39–40; Matt. 28:14.) What a contrast between the power of prayer that brought deliverance to Peter and the power of Herod that brought death!

After that, probably in anger, disgust, and disappointment, Herod left Judea (that is, Jerusalem) and went to coastal Caesarea, the other provincial capital, and stayed there. Perhaps feeling he had been disgraced in Jerusalem, he never returned in the three or four years before his death.

4. Herod's Death 12:20–24

20He had been quarreling with the people of Tyre and Sidon; they now joined together and sought an audience with him. Having secured the support of Blastus, a trusted personal servant of the king, they asked for peace, because they depended on the king's country for their food supply.

At this time and probably for some time previously, Herod "had been quarreling" (Gk. *thumomachōn*, "being in bitter hostility," "furiously angry") with Tyre and Sidon, practically to the point of war (though war would not have been allowed between two Roman provinces or dependencies). In an attempt to smooth over the disagreement, the leaders of Tyre and Sidon "joined together [Gk. *homothumadon*, "in one accord"] and sought an audience with him." But first they made a friend of Blastus, "a trusted personal servant of the king,"[24] one of Herod's confidential advisers. Using his influence, they asked for peace for themselves. They had good reason: Tyre and Sidon are on a narrow strip of land between the mountains and the sea and they had very little area suitable for agriculture; thus they "depended on the king's country [i.e., Palestine] for their food supply" (see 1 Kings 5:11; Ezra 3:7; Ezek. 27:17). It is indicated also that Barnabas and Saul were in Jerusalem bringing an offering for famine relief at this time. This famine would have been affecting Tyre and Sidon too, so they must have been near desperation.

21On the appointed day Herod, wearing his royal robes, sat on his throne and delivered a public address to the people.

Herod responded, and the leaders along with (undoubtedly) many of the people of Tyre and Sidon gathered in Caesarea on an appointed day. Among the ruins of ancient Caesarea is a Greek-style amphitheater beside the Mediterranean Sea—still a marvel of good acoustics. The crowd probably gathered there. Then Herod appeared on the stage "wearing his royal robes." According to the Jewish historian Josephus, the outer robe was of silver (either adorned with silver or actually woven of silver threads). Josephus also adds that the sun's rays were reflected from Herod's silver robe.

22They shouted, "This is the voice of a god, not of a man." 23Immediately, because Herod did not give praise to God, an angel of the Lord struck him down, and he was eaten by worms and died.

After taking his seat on an elevated throne, Herod "delivered a public address" (v. 21) to the multitude from Tyre and Sidon. They were Greek speaking, and they had adopted Greek culture

---

[24]Gk. *ton epi tou koitōnos*, "the one in charge of the bedroom." He was a personal servant who had power because of his access to the king.

and Greek idolatry. In response to Herod's speech, they shouted out, "The voice of a god, not of a man." Herod made no objection to this, nor did he "give praise to [the true] God." Immediately "an angel of the Lord struck him down." He was "eaten by worms,"[25] dying at the age of fifty-four. Josephus adds that Herod lingered five days with agonizing stomach pains.[26] This agrees with the text, which says only that he was struck down immediately, not that he died on the spot. This took place in A.D. 44. After that the Roman emperors again appointed a series of rather weak procurators, not just over Judea and Samaria but over the whole of Palestine.

[24]But the word of God continued to increase and spread.

In spite of the death of James, the arrest of Peter, the attitude and death of Herod, "the word of God continued to increase and spread." None of this hindered the continued growth of the Church or the spread of the gospel in Palestine. As Jesus said, "'Heaven and earth will pass away [Gk. *pareleusetai,* "will come to an end, disappear," cf. Rev. 21:1], but my words will never pass away'" (Matt. 24:35).

The new Roman governor maintained peace in the land, and the Church grew rapidly and was free from persecution for some time. As John R. W. Stott points out, chapter 12 "opens with James dead, Peter in prison, and Herod triumphing; it closes with Herod dead, Peter free, and the word of God triumphing."[27]

STUDY QUESTIONS

1. Why did Herod decide to persecute the Church?
2. How was Peter rescued from prison and with what results?

[25]"Eaten by worms" is one word in the Gk. *(skōlēkobrōtos).* It produced violent agony.

[26]Josephus *Jewish Antiquities* 19.346.377–81.

[27]John R. W. Stott, *The Spirit, the Church, and the World: The Message of Acts* (Downers Grove, Ill.: InterVarsity Press, 1990), 213.

C. Paul's First Missionary Journey 12:25–14:28

1. Barnabas And Saul Return To Antioch 12:25

25When Barnabas and Saul had finished their mission, they returned from Jerusalem, taking with them John, also called Mark.

It seems possible that Barnabas and Saul were in Jerusalem at least during the Passover season when these events took place. Others, because Josephus indicates the famine took place in A.D. 46, two years after Herod's death, suggest that the visit of Saul and Barnabas did not take place until then.[1]

Though the date is not certain, it is clear that Saul and Barnabas fulfilled their ministry and delivered the famine relief to the Jerusalem elders (see 11:28–30). Then they returned to their home base, Antioch, taking with them John Mark to assist them in the ministry of the church there. Colossians 4:10 tells us that Mark was the cousin of Barnabas. The return to Antioch with Mark introduces the events of chapter 13.

2. Sent Out By The Spirit And The Church 13:1–3

1In the church at Antioch there were prophets and teachers: Barnabas, Simeon called Niger, Lucius of Cyrene, Manaen (who had been brought up with Herod the tetrarch) and Saul.

This chapter takes another important step in the progress of the gospel. Up to this point those who were scattered carried the gospel to new places. But there were none who deliberately went to new places to start and organize new assemblies of believers.

By this time in the growing church at Antioch, God had raised up others besides Barnabas and Saul to aid in ministering to the church. They are identified here as "prophets and teachers." The Spirit used those who were prophets to bring supernatural

---

[1]See F. F. Bruce, *Commentary on the Book of Acts* (Grand Rapids: Wm. B. Eerdmans, 1954), 257–58; Richard P. Rackham, *The Acts of the Apostles* (1901; reprint, Grand Rapids: Baker Book House, 1964), 183. Others say the famine extended from A.D. 44 to 46.

strengthening, encouragement, and comfort (1 Cor. 14:3). Those who were teachers received gifts from the Holy Spirit that would enable them to teach the Word of God effectively.[2]

These included people from a variety of backgrounds, beginning with "Simeon called Niger." Simeon was a common Hebrew name; Niger (his Roman name) means "black." Some writers believe he was the child of a Jew who had married an African. Others speculate that he may have been Simon the Cyrenian who carried the cross (Matt. 27:32; Mark 15:21; Luke 23:26). It is not said here that he was from Cyrene, but since the first witnesses in Antioch included men from Cyrene, it is possible.

The next prophet or teacher, Lucius (a Lat. name), is definitely said to be "of Cyrene" (in North Africa west of Egypt). Possibly he was one of those who first brought the gospel to Antioch, having left Jerusalem after the death of Stephen (Acts 8:4; 11:20).[3]

Manaen (a Gk. form of the Heb. *Menahem*, "[God is my] Comforter or Consoler"), the other prophet or teacher, was "brought up with Herod the tetrarch" (Herod Antipas, who killed John the Baptist). He is called literally a foster brother (Gk. *suntrophos*) and was probably about the same age as Herod. He grew up in the palace, and some believe he also became a courtier or officer of this Herod (cf. RSV). John the Baptist must have influenced him; later he was saved. It is also possible that he was among those present on the Day of Pentecost when the Holy Spirit was first outpoured.

Luke wants us to see that the gospel was reaching into all classes of society. The church at Antioch was integrated, united in its worship and service, well taught in the Word, and responsive to the Holy Spirit.

[2]While they were worshiping the Lord and fasting, the Holy Spirit said, "Set apart for me Barnabas and Saul for the work to which I have called them." [3]So after they had

---

[2]Some believe all those listed were both prophets and teachers. See H. B. Hackett, *A Commentary on the Acts of the Apostles* (Philadelphia: American Baptist Publication Society, 1882), 148. However, Sir William Ramsay suggested that the first three were prophets and the last two teachers. This has some support from the Gk., and Luke repeatedly says that Paul taught (20:20; 28:31).

[3]He is not to be confused with Luke, though some believe Luke was present in Antioch and witnessed this scene.

fasted and prayed, they placed their hands on them and sent them off.

These prophets and teachers, along with the whole congregation, were worshiping the Lord in a public service (as the Gk. indicates here).[4] They were also fasting. Jesus did not emphasize fasting; as long as He was with His disciples they could not be expected to fast because they were like friends or attendants of a bridegroom at a feast (Luke 5:34). Many passages, however, indicate there is a place for fasting. It enabled believers to give themselves to prayer, served notice to their own flesh that they had matters of the spirit to attend to, and encouraged soul-searching and renewed dedication to holiness and love. Evidently the leaders, and probably the whole congregation, regularly put other things aside for a time of worship, prayer, and praise. "Add to that fasting, and you confront an intense and united devotion to the Lord. In such a setting, vision is born and people find divine direction for their lives."[5]

During the service, the Holy Spirit took the initiative: He spoke, commanding the whole church to "set apart" for Him Barnabas and Saul for the work to which He had (already) called them. The Greek is imperative here and includes a particle expressing a strong command or demand. Jesus had already called Saul as an apostle to the Gentiles (9:15; cf. Rom. 1:1; 1 Cor. 1:1; Gal. 1:15; 2:8). He had commissioned Barnabas as an apostle ("sent one") also (see Acts 14:14; 1 Cor. 9:1–6).

Just how the Holy Spirit gave this message we are not told.[6] Perhaps it was by tongues and interpretation. More likely it was a message in prophecy for the assembly, probably a message given by one of the three other prophets and teachers named in verse 1. This does not give grounds for so-called directive prophecy, or personal prophecy, however. It was not meant to

---

[4]Believers met in house churches, likely scattered through the city. It is probable that they also found some place where they could all meet together. Jerusalem believers had an advantage. They could meet in Solomon's Colonnade in the temple. Luke does not tell us where these believers were meeting.

[5]Robert L. Brandt and Zenas J. Bicket, *The Spirit Helps Us Pray: A Biblical Theology of Prayer* (Springfield, Mo.: Logion Press, 1993), 258.

[6]Note that the Spirit speaks directly using the first person, "I."

give direction for Barnabas and Saul. The Greek perfect tense ("have called") means an action in the past with present results. This shows that the Holy Spirit had already dealt with both Barnabas and Saul personally. However, they were serving not only the Lord but also the Church. They had responsibilities in the ministry to the church at Antioch. Thus the whole assembly had to become willing to let them go. The Spirit's message was therefore directed to the believers as a whole, not to any one individual.

Then they all "fasted and prayed" further. Paul taught the Corinthians that prophecies should be judged by other members of the Body (1 Cor. 14:29). It is always wise to hold steady until we are sure that the message is from the Lord.

The assembly also must have prayed for God's blessing on this new ministry. Then they "sent them off" (Gk. *apelusan,* "set them free, released them," that is, from their obligations at Antioch, and thus they permitted them to depart). It is clear that the entire assembly was involved in this new phase of the Great Commission and concurred with their leaders.

3. Evangelizing In Cyprus 13:4–13

⁴The two of them, sent on their way by the Holy Spirit, went down to Seleucia and sailed from there to Cyprus. ⁵When they arrived at Salamis, they proclaimed the word of God in the Jewish synagogues. John was with them as their helper.

Because the Spirit directed the assembly at Antioch to send out Barnabas and Saul, Luke emphasizes that they were "sent on their way by the Holy Spirit."[7] The Holy Spirit is a Person. They did not treat him as a power "to seize and use,"[8] as Simon had wanted to do (Acts 8:19). Paul and Barnabas were willing to let the Holy Spirit use them. He sent them. He continued to be with them.

They began their journey, taking John (Mark) along as their "helper"[9] (Gk. *hupēretēn,* "servant, attendant, assistant"), by

---

[7]Gk. *ekpemphthentes hupo to pneumatos tou hagiou,* "having been sent out by the Holy Spirit." The term *hupo* indicates personal agency.

[8]James M. Boice, *Acts* (Grand Rapids: Baker Book House, 1997), 229.

[9]Some believe that like Elisha who waited on Elijah, Mark helped them as a personal servant while he trained for the ministry. Luke uses the same word in

going down the mountain from Antioch to its harbor, Seleucia, about sixteen miles to the west, on the Mediterranean coast. There they took a sailing ship to the island of Cyprus. The Bible does not say why they took this direction. But since the Holy Spirit sent them out, we can be sure He continued to guide them. We can see wisdom also in the fact that the Holy Spirit took them first to Cyprus, where Barnabas grew up (Acts 4:36) and therefore knew the people and the customs. It was a good place to start.

At the most important town, Salamis, on the eastern end of the island, there were many Jews, and the apostles took advantage of the opportunity given visiting rabbis to preach in the synagogues (see v. 15). It was always Saul's practice to go to the Jews first, for they had the Scriptures, the promises, and the background to understand the gospel (Rom. 1:16; 3:2; 9:4–5).

> **⁶They traveled through the whole island until they came to Paphos. There they met a Jewish sorcerer and false prophet named Bar-Jesus, ⁷who was an attendant of the proconsul, Sergius Paulus. The proconsul, an intelligent man, sent for Barnabas and Saul because he wanted to hear the word of God.**

After proclaiming the gospel at Salamis, they went "through the whole island," covering it rather thoroughly without any opposition until they came to Paphos on the western end. This was a sensible itinerary for a small island like Cyprus, but Saul changed his method after they left. Instead of trying to cover the whole territory, they went to key cities to establish churches. These assemblies then became centers where the local body could spread the gospel into the surrounding area.

At Paphos they came in contact with a Jew named Bar-Jesus[10]

Luke 1:2 for "*servants* of the word," however. Other writers say they took Mark along because he was an eyewitness of the arrest, death, and resurrection of Jesus, probably being the young man mentioned in Mark 14:51,52. However, Paul did not depend on others for the facts of the gospel (see Gal. 1:11–12,15–16).

[10]"Son of Joshua" or "son of Jesus." He may have claimed to be a new Joshua sent to lead people into a new "promised land" of spiritual power. Or he may have claimed to be a follower of Jesus, but only as a pretense for getting a following for himself. The phrase "son of" often means a follower of, as in the case of the "sons of the prophets" in the times of Samuel and Elijah (see 2 Kings 4:1,38, KJV).

who was a "sorcerer [Gk. *magos,* "magician"] and false prophet." This means he falsely claimed to be a prophet. Like Simon, the sorcerer of Samaria, Bar-Jesus used the occult and practiced magic to fool the people and gain power over them.

Saul and Barnabas found this man with the proconsul, that is, the governor appointed by the Roman Senate.[11] The proconsul was a man of intelligence, both sensible and well educated, and he called in Barnabas and Saul "because he wanted to hear the word of God."

8But Elymas the sorcerer (for that is what his name means) opposed them and tried to turn the proconsul from the faith.

Then the sorcerer—now called by a Semitic name meaning "sorcerer" (v. 6), Elymas—took a stand against them; apparently to retain his influence, he sought to turn away (pervert, twist away) the proconsul from "the faith." This implies that Barnabas and Saul had presented the faith, the full content of the gospel, to the proconsul, and he was accepting it. Then Elymas tried to retain his influence over the proconsul by distorting and perverting what Barnabas and Saul were teaching.

9Then Saul, who was also called Paul, filled with the Holy Spirit, looked straight at Elymas and said 10"You are a child of the devil and an enemy of everything that is right! You are full of all kinds of deceit and trickery. Will you never stop perverting the right ways of the Lord?

But Saul received a new, special filling of the Holy Spirit (just as Peter had when he faced the Sanhedrin in Acts 4:8).

Luke notes at this point also that Saul had another name, a Roman name, Paul ("the little one"). Gentiles probably preferred it to his Hebrew name. This is significant because in the rest of the Book of Acts he is always called Paul. In his epistles also, he always calls himself Paul. The use of his Roman name draws attention to his Roman citizenship and, of course, fits in with his divine call to minister to the Gentiles.

---

[11]Cyprus had been under the control of the Roman Senate since 22 B.C. Luke was careful to give the governor his correct title, that is, "proconsul" (Gk. *anthupato,* the head of a Roman senatorial province).

By this new, special filling of the Spirit also, the Lord gave Paul the leadership in the missionary journey. In verse 13, instead of Barnabas and Saul, we read "Paul and his companions." This is in line also with the prophecy given through Ananias after Paul was converted (see Acts 9:15).

What Paul did next was not his own idea but was a prompting given directly by the Spirit. As a true prophet he fixed his eyes on the false prophet, Elymas, and addressed him as one "full of all kinds of deceit [guile, treachery] and trickery [wickedness, unscrupulousness, reckless facility for doing evil, fraud]," and as a son of the devil,[12] "an enemy of everything that is right [or, righteous]."

Then Paul asked a rhetorical question, which was really an affirmation that Elymas was determined to "never stop perverting" (twisting, distorting) "the right [upright, straight] ways of the Lord" (including the way of salvation and God's purposes for the believer).

11Now the hand of the Lord is against you. You are going to be blind, and for a time you will be unable to see the light of the sun." Immediately mist and darkness came over him, and he groped about, seeking someone to lead him by the hand.

Because of this, Paul declared that "the hand [power] of the Lord" would be in judgment (at last) "against" him. He would be blind "for a time" (Gk. *achri chairou,* "until an appointed time"), that is, until God saw fit to let him see again. (Probably this was intended as an opportunity for Elymas to repent.)

"Mist and darkness" immediately fell on Elymas and he "groped about," searching for someone to lead him by the hand. Apparently everyone withdrew from him in fear and he had difficulty finding help.

12When the proconsul saw what had happened, he believed, for he was amazed at the teaching about the Lord.

---

[12]See Gen. 3:15, referring to the seed of the serpent, and John 8:44. "Devil" means "slanderer" and, thus, the false accuser (as the plural form is translated in 2 Tim. 3:3, KJV). Note the contrast with the name Bar-Jesus, "son of Jesus" (v. 6).

The proconsul, "when [he] saw what had happened," believed. But he was not amazed so much by the judgment on Elymas as by "the teaching about the Lord." God's judgment drove home the truth about Jesus, the Cross, and the Resurrection, as well as the rest of the gospel that had been presented to him.

As we have seen, Luke often condenses his account and does not tell us everything every time. But we can be sure that as a believer Sergius Paulus would obey the gospel and be baptized both in water[13] and in the Holy Spirit with the evidence of speaking in other tongues. It is important to note also that the truth of the gospel preached in the power of the Spirit, and this alone, is effective against astrology, pagan magic, and the occult (see also Acts 19:11–20; cf. Luke 10:19).

13From Paphos, Paul and his companions sailed to Perga in Pamphylia, where John left them to return to Jerusalem.

From Paphos, Paul and his companions set sail for Perga, a chief city of Pamphylia, a district on the south coast of Asia Minor. Barnabas was still with Paul, of course, but "son of encouragement" that he was, he willingly dropped into the background (i.e., now identified as being among "his companions") and upheld Paul as the new leader of the group. He recognized, we can be sure, that this was the Holy Spirit's choice and that the Spirit was leading Paul in a special way.

At Perga, John Mark left (Gk. *apochōrēsas,* "deserted") them and returned to Jerusalem. Later (Acts 15:38) it is indicated that he had left (Gk. *apostanta,* used of religious falling away and apostasy) when they really needed him. It may be that the work became more difficult as they encountered unfamiliar territory on the mainland. Some have suggested that since Mark was from a wealthy home where there were servants, he decided to go home where life would be easier. Others suggest he left because he resented the fact that his cousin Barnabas was no longer the

---

[13]Sir William Ramsay disputed this and without any evidence did not believe it likely that the proconsul was baptized. However, Ramsay did find evidence that the proconsul's daughter and her son were Christians. See Bruce, *Commentary,* 265. This should have been taken as confirmation that the proconsul also was a true believer as Acts tells us he was. The gospel was reaching into every stratum of society.

leader or that he resented preaching to the Gentiles.[14] Still others suggest that the lowlands on the coast were full of malaria and that Paul had contracted it (cf. Gal. 4:13). In any case, Paul looked at this as an almost inexcusable failure on the part of Mark.

4. MINISTERING IN PISIDIAN ANTIOCH 13:14–52

a. Preaching Effectively 13:14–41

[14]From Perga they went on to Pisidian Antioch. On the Sabbath they entered the synagogue and sat down. [15]After the reading from the Law and the Prophets, the synagogue rulers sent word to them, saying, "Brothers, if you have a message of encouragement for the people, please speak."

From Perga they traveled 160 miles on a dangerous mountain road to an elevation of 3,600 feet at Antioch[15] near Pisidia on the right bank of the River Anthios. As usual, they went first to the synagogue. Someone else was appointed to read the selections from the Law (i.e., the Pentateuch) and from one of the Prophets. Then the "synagogue rulers," or elders, "sent word to them" (for they were sitting in the back of the synagogue) and courteously asked them to give a word of "encouragement" (or, challenge, exhortation; Gk. *paraklēseōs*).

[16]Standing up, Paul motioned with his hand and said: "Men of Israel and you Gentiles who worship God, listen to me!

Paul then stood, waved his hand for silence, and asked the Israelites and the God-fearing Gentiles to listen. By this we see that there were interested Gentiles in the synagogue audience. As mentioned previously, many Gentiles were tired of the immorality and idolatry of heathen religion. They were hungry for something better and were attracted to the synagogues and to the

[14]Simon J. Kistemaker, *Exposition of the Acts of the Apostles* (Grand Rapids: Baker Book House, 1990), 466.

[15]Called "of Pisidia" or "Pisidian" to distinguish it from other cities named Antioch and also because it was near the border of Pisidia (not actually in Pisidia but in the Phrygian southern part of the Roman province of Galatia). Pisidia was the southwestern part of this province of Galatia. Many distinguished Romans lived in the city.

worship of the one true God, who—unlike their pagan gods—identified himself as holy. Yet many of them did not become full proselytes by accepting circumcision and self-baptism and other rites. Even though, as Jesus said, the Pharisees traveled "'over land and sea to win a single convert'" (Matt. 23:15), some rabbis did not give them much encouragement after winning them, even calling proselytes "as hard for Israel as a scab."[16] But these Gentiles still came to hear the Word and to learn more about the God of Israel. Thus, they had a background in Old Testament teachings that prepared them for the gospel Paul preached.

Paul's sermon at Pisidian Antioch is given in considerable detail. Luke records it here as an example of the kind of missionary preaching Paul did in the Jewish synagogues.[17] His sermon shows he usually surveyed Israel's history, proclaimed the life, death, and resurrection of Jesus, and applied the message to his audience. Luke does not, however, give such detail in the record of later sermons, but it seems clear that Paul followed the same pattern the first time he preached in any synagogue.

As Paul began he courteously addressed both the Jews and Gentiles in the audience and recognized them both as "brothers" (see v. 26),[18] keeping both in mind throughout the sermon.[19]

[17]The God of the people of Israel chose our fathers; he made the people prosper during their stay in Egypt, with mighty power he led them out of that country, [18]he endured their conduct for about forty years in the desert, [19]he overthrew seven nations in Canaan and gave their land to his people as their inheritance. [20]All this took about 450 years. "After this, God gave them judges until the time of Samuel the prophet. [21]Then the people

[16] Jacob Neusner, trans., *The Talmud of Babylonia: An American Translation, Volume 29.B: Qiddushin: Chapters 2–4* (Atlanta: Scholars Press, 1992), 126.

[17]"A summary in writing was no doubt kept; . . . from Abraham and Moses onward, . . . the documents came from literary ages. . . . [A]ll the imperial peoples had a passion for recording." E. M. Blaiklock, *Acts: The Birth of the Church* (Old Tappan, N.J.: Fleming H. Revell, 1980), 110.

[18]The Talmud states, "Among proselytes, there is not conception of brotherhood, since there is no valid paternity." Neusner, *Talmud of Babylonia: Volume 13.A: Tractate Yebamot: Chapters 1–3*, 102.

[19]See William M. Ramsay, *The Cities of Saint Paul* (1907; reprint, Grand Rapids: Baker Book House, 1979), 300–303.

asked for a king, and he gave them Saul son of Kish, of
the tribe of Benjamin, who ruled forty years.

The first part of the sermon (13:17–25) reviews the history of
Israel, recognizing it as salvation history, starting from God's
choice of Israel and the deliverance from Egypt and leading up
to God's choice of David. Both the content and literary form[20]
were very familiar to his audience and showed them Paul knew
the Scriptures.

Unlike Stephen, Paul did not emphasize Israel's failures.
Rather, he spoke of God's choosing (for His own purpose and
service) and exalting the Israelites during their time as foreigners
in Egypt. God confirmed this choice by leading them out of
Egypt "with mighty power" (Gk. *brachionos hupsēlou*, "a high
arm," KJV; see Exod. 6:1,6; Deut. 4:34,37; Ps. 136:11–12).
That is, God increased their number during the time of persecution and protected them from the plagues.

Then Paul only mentioned that God "endured their conduct"
(ways, disposition)[21] during forty years in the wilderness. Then
Joshua's conquest and the time of the judges are quickly summarized, as is the reign of Saul.

The "seven nations" of verse 19 are the tribes of Canaanites and
others that were in Palestine (see Deut. 7:1; Josh. 3:10; 24:11).
The "about 450 years" of verse 20 refers not merely to the time of
the Book of Judges, but to the whole time after the people of
Israel entered the land up to the beginning of David's reign.[22]

[20]As used by Joshua, Nehemiah, the Psalmists, Isaiah, Peter, Stephen, and others.

[21]Several ancient manuscripts read a word with only one letter different. It
means "carried them" (as a nurse would). Deut. 1:31 in the LXX has the same
variant.

[22]Some manuscripts apply the 450 years to the 400 years in Egypt plus the
time of the conquest up to the dividing of the land in Josh. 14. It should be noted
that the terms of the judges overlapped in many cases. Note also that the 40 years
of Saul's reign are not given in the OT. In fact 1 Sam. 13:1 reads literally, "Saul
was a son of year in his reigning [when he began to reign], and he reigned two
years over Israel." This follows the usual formula for giving a king's reign, like that
found in 2 Kings 14:2; 16:2; 18:2. It probably means that early in the process of
copying 1 and 2 Sam. the actual age of Saul was accidentally left out and so was
the length of his reign. Many Bible scholars conjecture that Saul was 40 years old
when he began to reign and that he reigned 32 years. Paul, however, was including in Saul's reign the 7 1/2 years when David reigned in Hebron and Saul's son

22After removing Saul, he made David their king. He testified concerning him: 'I have found David son of Jesse a man after my own heart; he will do everything I want him to do.' 23"From this man's descendants God has brought to Israel the Savior Jesus, as he promised.

The climax of this historical account is reached when Paul says God bore witness to David as a man after His own heart, who would do "everything I want him to do" (see 1 Sam. 13:14; Ps. 89:20). The purpose and desire to do all God's will is, of course, the thing that made David a man after God's own heart.

Now the people in Paul's audience knew God's promise to David (2 Sam. 7:12; Ps. 89:29-34).23 They also knew the prophecies that God would raise up a greater seed to David (Isa. 9:6-7; 11:1-5), as well as the prophecy that He would give David's throne to the One it rightfully belonged to (Ezek. 21:27). In this way Paul declares that God had fulfilled His promise and "from this man's descendants"24 raised up to Israel a Savior, Jesus (Matt. 1:21; Luke 1:32; 2:11; Acts 5:31).

24Before the coming of Jesus, John preached repentance and baptism[25] to all the people of Israel. 25As John was completing his work, he said: 'Who do you think I am? I am not that one. No, but he is coming after me, whose sandals I am not worthy to untie.'

Paul further identified Jesus as having been recognized by John the Baptist as the One to come. John the Baptist's ministry was well known to Jews everywhere, as well as his denial of being the one to come, the promised Messiah and Savior (Luke

---

continued Saul's reign and kingdom. Jews in those days usually rounded off the last 1/2 year or part year of a reign and added it as a year to the total, thus giving 40 years here. However, some writers follow Josephus, who says Saul reigned 20 years and Samuel judged 20 years, together making the 40. Still other writers conjecture that Saul reigned 42 years and that Paul rounded it off here to 40 years.

23For a chart comparing 2 Sam. 7:6–16 and Acts 13:16–38 see Mark L. Strauss, *The Davidic Messiah in Luke-Acts* (Sheffield, England: Sheffield Academic Press, 1995), 154–55, 157. He points out that "the fulfillment of the promises to David is the focal point of the sermon."

24"This" is emphatic in the Gk.

25"The baptism of [because of] repentance" (v. 24, KJV) declared and symbolized a repentance that had already taken place (see Matt. 3:8).

3:15–16). John's testimony to Jesus was therefore important. For John to say that he was not worthy to take off the sandals of the one to come, a most menial service, indicates how far above him John considered Jesus (John 1:27).

> 26"**Brothers, children of Abraham, and you God-fearing Gentiles, it is to us that this message of salvation has been sent.**

After dealing with Israel's history in the second part of the sermon (13:26–37), Paul deals with the death and resurrection of Jesus and with the witness of the apostles as well as that of the Scriptures.

In verse 26 Paul emphasizes that this message of salvation was sent out to them personally (through those commissioned by the Lord Jesus), and not only to the Jews present, but to the Gentile God-fearers[26] among them as well.

> 27**The people of Jerusalem and their rulers did not recognize Jesus, yet in condemning him they fulfilled the words of the prophets that are read every Sabbath. 28Though they found no proper ground for a death sentence, they asked Pilate to have him executed.**

Then Paul shows that the death of Jesus was the fulfillment of God's prophetic Word. God ordained it and Jerusalem dwellers and their rulers carried it out.

It is important to notice here that Paul didn't blame Jesus' death on the Jews in general, but only on those in Jerusalem who were actually involved. He also recognizes that they did it because they were ignorant of Him and of the voices of the prophets read every Sabbath (in their synagogues). Although translated "did not recognize," the Greek used here (*agnoēsantes*) sometimes implies willful ignorance or a deliberate ignoring of the truth. Since they did know these prophecies, willful ignorance is indeed meant here.[27]

---

[26]These were not proselytes, but Gentiles who sat in the back of the synagogue and worshiped God. Some writers call them "proselytes of the gate," but this phrase was first used by eleventh-century Judaism.

[27]Cf. v. 27, Phillips: "'For the people of Jerusalem and their rulers refused to recognise him or to understand the voice of the prophets which are read every Sabbath day—even though in condemning him they fulfilled these very prophecies!'"

Paul also says they found "no proper ground" for a death sentence on Jesus,[28] yet "they asked Pilate to have him executed."

29When they had carried out all that was written about him, they took him down from the tree and laid him in a tomb. 30But God raised him from the dead, 31and for many days he was seen by those who had traveled with him from Galilee to Jerusalem. They are now his witnesses to our people.

But after the prophecies of Christ's death were fulfilled, they (i.e., the people of Jerusalem) took him from the "tree" (the cross; cf. Deut. 21:23 and Gal. 3:13)[29] and "laid Him in a tomb." (Nicodemus and Joseph of Arimathea were the ones who actually did this, John 19:38–39.) Then God raised Jesus from the dead. His disciples, Galileans "who had traveled with him to Jerusalem," were witnesses of this and were with Him "for many days" ("forty days," Acts 1:3).

32"We tell you the good news: What God promised our fathers 33he has fulfilled for us, their children, by raising up Jesus. As it is written in the second Psalm: "'You are my Son; today I have become your Father.'

This was the good news which Paul and Barnabas were bringing: God's promise to the Old Testament fathers was now fulfilled for "their children" (descendants) "by [God's] raising up Jesus" from the dead. Paul confirmed this by quoting Psalm 2:7 where "today I have become your Father" means "I am declaring this day that I am your Father." This was a formulaic phrase used of one who was already a king's son. Most commentators today believe it was a formula by which a king made a public declaration that he was raising his son to the throne—to share it as an associate and an equal. Consequently, in the psalm it refers to Jesus being declared by God to be His divine Son. God did this first when Jesus began His ministry and God sent His Spirit upon Him (Luke 3:22). Then He did it even more unmistakably when He raised Jesus from the dead. As Romans 1:3–4 says, Jesus, "who as to his human nature was a descendant of David,"

---

[28]Neither did Pilate (Luke 23:4,14,22).

[29]See Acts 5:30 and commentary.

was "through the Spirit of holiness [or, by means of the Holy Spirit] . . . declared with power to be the Son of God by his resurrection from the dead." Since Luke is even here condensing a sermon that took a long time to preach, it is probable that Paul explained these things more fully to his audience.

> ³⁴The fact that God raised him from the dead, never to decay, is stated in these words: "'I will give you the holy and sure blessings promised to David.' ³⁵So it is stated elsewhere: "'You will not let your Holy One see decay.' ³⁶"For when David had served God's purpose in his own generation, he fell asleep; he was buried with his fathers and his body decayed. ³⁷But the one whom God raised from the dead did not see decay.

Next Paul pointed out further Scripture, mentioning first the "sure blessings" of David and an everlasting covenant (Isa. 55:3), from a passage that speaks of pardon and salvation. He then showed those mercies to include the promise of Psalm 16:10b, saying that "you [God] will not let your Holy One see decay." Furthermore, David, after he had "served God's purpose [Gk. *boulē*, "plan"] in his own generation," died, and his body did decay. In contrast to David, the One whom God raised up (Jesus) did not see decay. He was raised with an incorruptible, imperishable body (as we will be; see 1 Cor. 15:52). Paul saw the same truth as Peter did, but presented it in a little different way (cf. Acts 2:29). Clearly, Paul preached the same gospel the other apostles did (see Gal. 1:8–9; 2:2,9; see 1 Cor. 15:11). Paul was not preaching his own ideas. All believers have a responsibility to proclaim the facts of God's saving acts.

> ³⁸"Therefore, my brothers, I want you to know that through Jesus the forgiveness of sins is proclaimed to you. ³⁹Through him everyone who believes is justified from everything you could not be justified from by the law of Moses.

The final part of this sermon (13:38–41) gives a challenge. "Through Jesus the forgiveness of sins is proclaimed [preached, announced] to you." By this One also all believers are "justified"—made righteous, acquitted, treated as if they had never sinned, and therefore freed from the guilt and punishment of their sin. The believers are even forgiven and delivered from the guilt of all those things for which one "could not be justified from by the law of Moses" (or could not be treated as righteous).[30] Jesus is indeed the Savior everyone needs.

⁴⁰Take care that what the prophets have said does not happen to you: ⁴¹"'Look, you scoffers, wonder and perish, for I am going to do something in your days that you would never believe, even if someone told you.'"

Paul then concluded the sermon with a warning using language taken from Habakkuk 1:5 (in the LXX). "Perish" (v. 41) means to be removed or disappear.[31] Paul wanted his audience to be on their guard, for fear that if they rejected the fulfillments of prophecy in Jesus' death and resurrection, an even greater judgment would come on them than came on the rebels addressed by Habakkuk.[32]

b. Turning To The Gentiles 13:42–49

⁴²As Paul and Barnabas were leaving the synagogue, the people invited them to speak further about these things on the next Sabbath.

Some ancient manuscripts say the Gentiles were urging the apostles to continue (see NKJV). But a number of ancient manuscripts leave out the word "Gentiles" and indicate that as Paul and Barnabas were going out the people as a whole (as the NIV translates) asked them this.[33]

⁴³When the congregation was dismissed, many of the Jews and devout converts to Judaism followed Paul and

---

[30]The Gk. word order is, "even from all which you were not able to be justified by the law of Moses, in this One every one believing is justified." Some take this to mean that the Law provided justification for some things and the gospel provides justification for the rest. But the meaning is rather that the Law could not really provide justification at all, and the gospel provides justification for everything. See Bruce, *Commentary,* 278–79.

[31]The same word was used of cities destroyed by an earthquake.

[32]The prophet Habakkuk warned of the Babylonian invasions that began in 605 B.C.

[33]Sir William Ramsay gives good reasons for seeing this as the correct picture. See Ramsay, *Cities of Saint Paul,* 307–8.

Barnabas, who talked with them and urged them to continue in the grace of God.

Afterward, many of both Jews and "devout" (worshiping, God-fearing) converts to Judaism "followed Paul and Barnabas." Not wanting to wait until the next Sabbath, they spent some time talking to them and were "urged . . . to continue in the grace of God." This means they believed the gospel and accepted the grace of God that brings salvation; they were saved. Then they must have been baptized, even though Luke does not mention it here. He makes it clear elsewhere that believers were always baptized in water and also in the Holy Spirit (see v. 52).

44On the next Sabbath almost the whole city gathered to hear the word of the Lord. 45When the Jews saw the crowds, they were filled with jealousy and talked abusively against what Paul was saying.

The God-fearing Gentiles who believed the gospel spread the word so effectively that on the next Sabbath "almost the whole city" assembled to hear God's Word. The sight of the crowd filled the unconverted Jews with jealousy (quite a contrast to the believers who were filled with the Spirit and joy), and they "talked abusively [blasphemously] against what Paul was saying." This implies they were afraid of losing their influence over those Gentiles who had been looking to them for teaching. It may also imply that they had a zeal for a Judaism that had no room for blessing Gentiles who did not first become Jews.

46Then Paul and Barnabas answered them boldly: "We had to speak the word of God to you first. Since you reject it and do not consider yourselves worthy of eternal life[34] we now turn to the Gentiles. 47For this is what the Lord has commanded us: "'I have made you a light for the Gentiles, that you may bring salvation to the ends of the earth.'"

Paul and Barnabas "answered them boldly" that "it was necessary" (KJV et al.; Gk. *en anagkaion*), in order to fulfill God's plan, to speak God's Word first to "'you Jews'" (NLT). But since

[34]The Gk. has *idou,* "behold," at this point. KJV translates it as "lo," the NIV "now."

they had scorned it and thus judged themselves unworthy of eternal life (by their unbelief and abusive language), "now" (Gk. *idou*, "'behold,'" NKJV, NASB) the two apostles were turning to the Gentiles. "Behold" indicates that this turning to the Gentiles was something unexpected and surprising to the Jews.

This development should not have been surprising, however. Turning to the Gentiles was not really the apostles' own idea. Rather it was part of God's plan, in obedience to the prophetic word given in Isaiah 49:6 concerning the Messiah, God's Servant (see also Isa. 42:6; Luke 2:30–32). Christ and His body (the Church, the believers) share in bringing the light of the gospel to the world. They too are God's servants and must act accordingly.

Some writers suppose that Paul's turning to the Gentiles meant that he had turned against the Jews and that salvation was transferred to the Gentiles, leaving no hope for the Jews. However, this turning to the Gentiles was a localized situation, not a turning point for "replacement theology." Salvation was still available to all—Paul continued to go to the synagogues—and the number of Jews who became Christians continued to increase (cf. 14:1; 17:12; 18:8). God had not rejected Israel and replaced her with the Gentiles or with the Church. It was through the ministry of the Jews that the Gentiles share in the blessings of the gospel. But Luke does appear "to stress the division that the gospel brings to the Jews of the Diaspora and to contrast the refusal of salvation by some Jews with the potential for salvation among the Gentiles."[35] (See Acts 18:6; 19:9; 26:20–21; 28:28; cf. Rom. 11:25–32.)

> [48]When the Gentiles heard this, they were glad and honored the word of the Lord; and all who were appointed for eternal life believed. [49]The word of the Lord spread through the whole region.

Hearing this, the Gentiles were kept rejoicing and glorifying the Word of the Lord. "And all who were appointed for eternal life believed." This may sound as if the Bible is teaching arbitrary predestination here. However, it is not said that God "appointed" them. The word "appointed" here can mean "fixed on." That is, in contrast to the Jews who didn't consider themselves worthy of eternal life (v. 46), these Gentiles (by the Holy Spirit's work) accepted the truth of eternal life through Jesus and did not let the Jews' contradiction move them from it.[36] The result was that "the word of the Lord spread" (Gk. *diephereto*, "was being carried"): The Gentiles responded to the apostles' witness by becoming witnesses who evangelized the whole region. (Paul continued this pattern of going to major centers and training believers to go out and establish churches in the surrounding area.)

c. Paul And Barnabas Expelled 13:50–52

50But the Jews incited the God-fearing women of high standing and the leading men of the city. They stirred up persecution against Paul and Barnabas, and expelled them from their region.

The unbelieving Jews then proceeded to incite "God-fearing [devout, worshiping] women of high standing" in society[37] and the chief men of the city government. By these means they "stirred up persecution" of Paul and Barnabas to the point that they were thrown out of the district (see 1 Thess. 2:15–16).

51So they shook the dust from their feet in protest against them and went to Iconium. 52And the disciples were filled with joy and with the Holy Spirit.

In response, Paul and Barnabas simply shook off the dust of their feet as a testimony against them. (Jews did this to symbolize separating themselves from uncleanness, leaving behind even its [unclean] dust; cf. Matt. 10:14; Mark 6:11; Luke 9:5; 10:11). Then they went on to Iconium, a Phrygian city in the southern part of the Roman province of Galatia.[38]

---

[36]NEB (v. 48) suggests that because they accepted the truth of the gospel they were "marked out" for eternal (resurrection) life. See J. W. Packer, *Acts of the Apostles* (Cambridge, England: Cambridge University Press, 1975), 112. Others "take the verb to be in the middle voice, not the passive, and render, 'As many as had set themselves [by the Spirit's prompting] for eternal life became believers.'" David John Williams, *Acts* (Peabody, Mass.: Hendrickson Publishers, 1990), 239.

[37]These may have been the wives of the city government leaders. In Pisidian Antioch women also held important positions, however. The Gk. indicates they were wealthy. Blaiklock, *Acts*, 113.

[38]Now called Konya or Konia, a city in southwest Turkey.

The persecution did not destroy the church in Pisidian Antioch, however. They were true "disciples" (Gk. *mathētai,* "learners, students") of the Lord, constantly studying His Word, and "were filled [Gk. *eplērounto,* "continually filled"] with joy and with the Holy Spirit." Joy is a common experience when believers are filled with or full of the Holy Spirit (cf. Luke 10:21; Rom. 14:17; 15:13; 1 Thess. 1:6).[39] Once again we see that Acts does not tell everything every time. Though Luke does not mention it here, we can be sure that these believers were also baptized in water as well as in the Holy Spirit. Then they continued in the Spirit and the Word and that brought the joy—as it will for us. Note that joy was also part of their response to the persecution, as Jesus said it should be (Matt. 5:11–12; cf. Acts 5:41).

5. Ministering In Iconium, Lystra, And Derbe 14:1–25

a. Preaching, Miracles, And Opposition 14:1–7

[1]At Iconium Paul and Barnabas went as usual into the Jewish synagogue. There they spoke so effectively that a great number of Jews and Gentiles believed.

The preaching (at Pisidian Antioch), the greater response of the Gentiles, and the persecution that followed set a pattern. Much or all of this was repeated at practically all of the cities Paul visited on his missionary journeys.

Paul now followed a major Roman highway, the Via Sebaste, to another important city, Iconium, about sixty miles east and a little south of Pisidian Antioch, on a fertile plateau that rises to 3,370 feet. Arriving there, Paul and Barnabas followed their practice and went to the synagogue. As guests, they were accorded the Jewish custom of being given the opportunity to speak. Luke does not record their sermon. He simply indicates that they "spoke so" (thus), in their usual manner, that is, just as they did in Pisidian Antioch.[40]

The results were similar. A large number of both Jews and Greeks (Greek-speaking Gentiles who sat in the back seats of the

---

[39]Max Turner, *Power From on High: The Spirit in Israel's Restoration and Witness in Luke-Acts* (Sheffield, England: Sheffield Academic Press, 1996), 411.

[40]See Packer, *Acts of the Apostles,* 115.

synagogue) believed (and, of course, were baptized in water and in the Holy Spirit).

2But the Jews who refused to believe stirred up the Gentiles and poisoned their minds against the brothers. 3So Paul and Barnabas spent considerable time there, speaking boldly for the Lord, who confirmed the message of his grace by enabling them to do miraculous signs and wonders.

Then, as before, unbelieving (disobedient,[41] rebellious) Jews in their zeal and jealousy "stirred up the Gentiles" and "poisoned their minds [Gk. *psuchas,* "souls, self, desire"] against the brothers" —the new believers who were now disciples of Jesus and fellow members of His body. There was persecution as well (2 Tim. 3:11).

The Jews in this case, however, were not able initially to get much support from the Gentiles. Therefore Paul and Barnabas stayed in Iconium a "considerable time," probably all winter. With bold freedom they spoke "for" (or, "in") the Lord Jesus (relying on Him). As they did so, the Lord bore witness to the "message of his grace"[42] by giving miraculous signs and wonders to be done by them. Consequently many recognized them as Christ's agents doing His work by His authority.[43]

4The people of the city were divided; some sided with the Jews, others with the apostles. 5There was a plot afoot among the Gentiles and Jews, together with their leaders, to mistreat them and stone them.

In time, however, the city crowd became sharply divided. "Some sided with the [unbelieving] Jews, others with the apostles."[44] Then both Gentiles and Jews with their synagogue rulers joined with a hostile intention: They proposed to treat the apos-

[41]As translated in 1 Pet. 2:8, KJV. Note that belief in the gospel was not optional, but was a matter of obedience to God's word and will.

[42]That is, the whole gospel—with all the provisions of God's grace in salvation, healing, the baptism and gifts of the Holy Spirit, our future inheritance, including new bodies, which will be ours when Jesus comes again—was witnessed to.

[43]Bruce, *Commentary,* 287, points out that Paul in Gal. 3:5 shows that these miracles were evidence of the gospel of grace, not of the works of the Law.

[44]Note that Paul and Barnabas are both called apostles here. Barnabas was thus a witness of the resurrection of Jesus and was commissioned by Jesus. Possibly he

tles outrageously and stone them. The Greek, however, does not mean an assault occurred, but only the intent.

> **6But they found out about it and fled to the Lycaonian cities of Lystra and Derbe and to the surrounding country, 7where they continued to preach the good news.**

The apostles became aware of the plot, however, and fled. This was not because they were afraid, but because the local assembly was well established and there were other places that needed their ministry. Thus, they went on to Lystra[45] and Derbe, Lycaonian[46] cities on a high plateau in the southern part of the Roman province of Galatia. Lystra, like Iconium, had the status of a Roman military colony[47] and was responsible for protecting the interests of Rome and guarding the Roman roads. Probably at several places in the region, the apostles "continued to preach the good news." What follows is an example of how Paul preached to Gentiles who had no knowledge of the Scriptures.

b. A Cripple Healed 14:8–18

> **8In Lystra there sat a man crippled in his feet, who was lame from birth and had never walked. 9He listened to Paul as he was speaking. Paul looked directly at him, saw that he had faith to be healed 10and called out, "Stand up on your feet!" At that, the man jumped up and began to walk.**

At Lystra Paul did not go to a synagogue as usual. Perhaps there was none. Instead, it seems he went to the marketplace or to an open square just inside the city gates (as v. 13 indicates); there he began to preach. Among those nearby was "a man crippled in his feet." To draw attention to the hopelessness of this unusual case the Bible uses repetition: "crippled in his feet," "lame

---

was part of the 120 in the Upper Room. (See also 1 Cor. 9:6; Gal. 2:9–10.) Two relatives of Paul, Andronicus and Junia (possibly the sister of Andronicus), are also "among the apostles" (Rom. 16:7).

[45]About twenty-five miles south of Iconium.

[46]Lycaonia included both Lystra and Derbe from A.D. 37 to 72. See William M. Ramsay, *St. Paul the Traveler and the Roman Citizen* (London: Hodder & Stoughton, 1895), 110–13.

[47]That is, Rome had settled Roman citizens there (usually veterans of the Roman army) to make the city a center for the defense of the empire.

from birth," "had never walked." Paul fixed his eyes on the man as he kept listening and "saw that he had faith to be healed."[48] Paul encouraged the activation of the man's faith by commanding him in a very loud voice to stand (erect) on his feet. Not only did the man jump up, he also "began to walk." He was totally healed.[49]

[11]When the crowd saw what Paul had done, they shouted in the Lycaonian language, "The gods have come down to us in human form!" [12]Barnabas they called Zeus, and Paul they called Hermes because he was the chief speaker.

Paul's command caught the attention of the crowd. When they saw the man leap up and walk, they began shouting. However, though they knew the Greek Paul was using, in their excitement they reverted to their native Lycaonian language,[50] which Paul and Barnabas did not understand.

The miracle made the people (who were pagan Gentiles) believe that the Greek gods had "come down . . . in human form." Thus they began to call Barnabas Zeus (Gk. *Dia* or *Dios*), who was identified by the Lycaonians with their chief god.[51] Then, since Paul was "the chief speaker" ("the leader of the word"), they called him Hermes (Gk. *Hermēn,* the messenger and herald of the gods, especially of Zeus).[52]

[48]Gk. *sōthēnai,* from the verb *sōzō,* which is ordinarily translated "saved" but also means to rescue from danger or from severe situations and thus to be restored or made whole. It does imply that the man accepted the gospel Paul was preaching and believed in Jesus as well.

[49]Cf. the healing of the lame man in Acts 3 where Luke says nothing about the faith of the lame man. See C. Peter Wagner, *Lighting the World: Book 2, Acts 9–15* (Ventura, Calif.: Gospel Light, Regal Books, 1995), 180–81.

[50]The language was a Celtic dialect. The crowd did not include the Roman colonists, who spoke Latin. This sort of thing is a common occurrence. Usually when a person is educated to use a second language, he will fall back into his native language, the language of his childhood, when excited.

[51]The Romans called Zeus "Jupiter" and Hermes "Mercury." This kind of syncretistic identification of deities was common in the ancient Roman Empire. Marion L. Soards, "The Historical and Cultural Setting of Luke-Acts," in *New Views on Luke and Acts,* ed. Earl Richard (Collegeville, Minn.: Liturgical Press, 1990), 43–44.

[52]It is possible that they used the Lycaonian names of these gods, which Luke identifies with the Gk. names.

¹³The priest of Zeus, whose temple was just outside the city, brought bulls and wreaths to the city gates because he and the crowd wanted to offer sacrifices to them.

Accordingly, the people took what they thought was appropriate action: They contacted the priest of Zeus whose temple was in front of the city (at the main gate), for they considered him the guardian of the city. The priest brought bulls (the most costly sacrifices they could offer). These were decorated with wreaths and brought to the gates where the crowds gathered, wanting to sacrifice.

¹⁴But when the apostles Barnabas and Paul heard of this, they tore their clothes and rushed out into the crowd, shouting: ¹⁵"Men, why are you doing this? We too are only men, human like you. We are bringing you good news, telling you to turn from these worthless things to the living God, who made heaven and earth and sea and everything in them. ¹⁶In the past, he let all nations go their own way. ¹⁷Yet he has not left himself without testimony: He has shown kindness by giving you rain from heaven and crops in their seasons; he provides you with plenty of food and fills your hearts with joy."

In verses 12 and 14 Barnabas is again named before Paul because as *Dios* (Zeus, Jupiter) he was the leading one for whom the sacrifice was to be made. Finally someone probably explained to them in Greek what was going on. When the apostles heard and understood this, "they tore their clothes" (taking hold of them at the neck and ripping them down as a sign of horror, dismay, and disapproval of blasphemy; cf. Num. 14:6; Jer. 36:24; Joel 2:13). As they did so, they "rushed out into the crowd, shouting," trying to stop them by declaring they were "only men," with feelings like theirs (implying a nature like theirs: "human like you"). They had come to preach "good news" to turn them from such "worthless [unreal, useless, unfruitful] things to the living God."

Since these Gentiles had no knowledge of the Scriptures, Paul did not identify God as the God of Israel, nor did he appeal to the Old Testament prophecies of the Messiah. He did use scriptural language, however,[53] and took them back to the time of the creation: God is the God who made all things, "heaven and earth

---

[53]Cf. Exod. 20:11; Ps. 146:6.

and sea," who in past generations permitted all nations (all the Gentiles) "to go their own way" (in contrast to God's ways). Yet He did not leave himself "without testimony" (witness). He calls us "to pay heed to the order of the world and to observe the wisdom displayed in the structure of things. God speaks even where Christ is not yet named."[54] He did good deeds, giving us "rain from heaven and crops in their seasons," filling our hearts with gladness.

18Even with these words, they had difficulty keeping the crowd from sacrificing to them.

Even with this message about the true God, the apostles had a hard time restraining the crowd from carrying out their intention to sacrifice to them. (See comments on 10:25.)

c. Paul Stoned 14:19–20

19Then some Jews came from Antioch and Iconium and won the crowd over. They stoned Paul and dragged him outside the city, thinking he was dead. 20But after the disciples had gathered around him, he got up and went back into the city. The next day he and Barnabas left for Derbe.

Paul and Barnabas stayed in Lystra long enough (as v. 20 indicates) for a number to believe and become disciples (and, as always, to be baptized in water and in the Holy Spirit according to Acts 2:4). Then some (unbelieving) Jews from Pisidian Antioch (about one hundred miles away) who had thrown Paul out of their city and some from Iconium (about thirty miles away) who had wanted to stone him heard of Paul's success at Lystra. They came and persuaded the pagan crowds to help them, or at least to permit them, to carry out their plot. (Some of the pagans may have felt they were disgraced when Paul and Barnabas did not let them sacrifice to them. They did not forget this, so they listened to Paul's enemies.)

This time they did stone Paul and "dragged him outside the city, thinking he was dead" (cf. 2 Cor. 11:23,25). Clearly he was not dead; however, he was probably unconscious and no doubt

[54]Clark H. Pinnock, *Flame of Love: A Theology of the Holy Spirit* (Downers Grove, Ill.: InterVarsity Press, 1996), 193.

severely bruised and bloody—as well as having broken bones.[55]
Paul never blamed God for such sufferings. He spoke of them as
"light and momentary troubles" that "are achieving for us an eternal weight of glory that far outweighs them all" (2 Cor. 4:17).

As soon as the crowd left, the disciples formed a circle around
Paul. Undoubtedly they were looking to God, who did not dis-
appoint them. Suddenly, in what must have seemed like a resurrection, Paul stood up, obviously completely healed, "and went
back into the city" with them. But, knowing the mood of the
crowds, he and Barnabas left the next day for Derbe (now identified as a ruin called Kerti Hüyük, about sixty miles southeast
of Lystra, near the border of the Roman province of Galatia).

d. Confirming Believers 14:21–25

**[21]They preached the good news in that city and won a
large number of disciples. Then they returned to Lystra,
Iconium and Antioch, [22]strengthening the disciples and
encouraging them to remain true to the faith. "We must
go through many hardships to enter the kingdom of
God," they said.**

At Derbe also there was apparently no synagogue. Consequently Paul and Barnabas must have preached the gospel much
as they did at Lystra, but without the Jewish opposition since
Paul's enemies now thought he was dead. He was probably
thankful for a time of peace.

After they had made "a large number of disciples,"[56] thus
establishing a growing church, they courageously returned to
Lystra, Iconium, and Pisidian Antioch. This time, however, they
did not stir up the Jews. Apparently leaving evangelistic work to
local believers, their ministry was pastoral, to the local church.
In each place, they strengthened and established the disciples,
challenging and encouraging them "to remain true to the faith."
The Greek is very strong here. They told the people they must
maintain the faith, standing by it, that is, living by its principles.

[55]See 2 Cor. 11:25, where Paul includes this stoning along with beatings and
shipwrecks as calamities he endured. There is no suggestion here that he died. He
refers to his scars also in Gal. 6:17, calling them "the marks of Jesus."

[56]Gaius, who became a companion of Paul, was from Derbe (20:4; cf. 19:29).

They also challenged them to share the suffering of the apostles and to accept the fact that "through many hardships" (persecutions, afflictions, distresses) they would "enter the kingdom of God" (come under His rule and authority).

23Paul and Barnabas appointed elders for them in each church and, with prayer and fasting, committed them to the Lord, in whom they had put their trust.

Because the believers needed organization to be able to work together and carry on the work of the Lord, the apostles then "appointed elders" (Gk. *presbuterous,* "elders," used interchangeably in the NT with *episkopoi,* "overseers, superintendents, presidents of the congregation or assembly," cf. 20:17,28; Titus 1:5,7[57]) in each place, that is, in each of the local house churches. This, however, was not an ordination in the modern sense. The Greek for "appointed" ("ordained," KJV) is *cheiratonēsantes,* where *cheir* is the Greek word for "hand"; the whole word means they conducted an election by a show of hands.[58]

When the seven deacons were chosen (in chapter 6), the apostles laid down the qualifications and the people did the choosing. We can be sure the same thing happened here. Paul must have given the qualifications, which he recorded later in 1 Timothy 3:1–7 and Titus 1:6–9. Then the people of the local assembly made the choice by an election (undoubtedly after prayer for the Spirit's help in deciding who best met these qualifications).[59]

At the beginning, elders were Spirit-filled men chosen from among the members of the local congregation.[60] Not until many years later did churches begin to feel that they needed to bring in pastor-teachers who could also be the administrative head of the assembly, men who would combine the office of elder (also called bishop and presbyter) with the God-called ministry of

[57]George E. Ladd, *A Theology of the New Testament* (Grand Rapids: Wm. B. Eerdmans, 1983), 352.

[58]Plato *Laws* 763E.

[59]Some commentators who believe in the episcopal system of appointments being made by the leadership deny that these elder-presbyters were chosen by the congregation. However, the Gk. and the context support the fact that they were.

[60]See P. C. H. Lenski, *The Interpretation of the Acts of the Apostles* (Columbus, Ohio: Wartburg Press, 1940), 585–86.

pastor-teacher. Elders in the first century were expected to be "able to teach" (1 Tim. 3:2), and they were responsible to see that the teaching was done. But they could bring in others who had the pastor-teacher ministry from the Lord, with gifts from the Spirit to accompany it. They did not have to do the teaching themselves. Paul's statement, "The elders who direct the affairs of the church well are worthy of double honor [Gk. *times,* "honorarium"; "double pay," TEV], especially those whose work is preaching and teaching" (1 Tim. 5:17), shows that not all preached and taught. But as time went on, leadership became more and more aware of the need for consistent teaching ministry in the local church, and it was natural for them to look to these teachers for leadership. In this way, the modern idea of a pastor who is also an administrator gradually developed.

Before Paul and Barnabas went on to the next city, they always spent time in "prayer and fasting" with the believers. Then they entrusted them (as something precious and valuable) to the care and keeping of the Lord (Jesus) "in whom they had put their trust" (and continued to believe in). The initial believing, of course, had taken place on Paul's previous visit.

24After going through Pisidia, they came into Pamphylia, 25and when they had preached the word in Perga, they went down to Attalia.

From Pisidian Antioch they went on through Pisidia back to Pamphylia and Perga, evangelizing wherever possible. At Perga they preached the Word apparently without opposition or mistreatment. Evidently, they had not preached there when they first landed and Mark deserted them. After establishing the church there, they went to Attalia, Pamphylia's chief seaport.

6. Reporting Back To Syrian Antioch 14:26–28

26From Attalia they sailed back to Antioch, where they had been committed to the grace of God for the work they had now completed. 27On arriving there, they gathered the church together and reported all that God had done through them and how he had opened the door of faith to the Gentiles. 28And they stayed there a long time with the disciples.

From Attalia they sailed away to Syrian Antioch. This was the home base they had started from. The church there had sent them out, entrusting them to the gracious favor of God. With this visit, Paul and Barnabas felt they had fulfilled the ministry the Spirit sent them out to do (Acts 13:2–4).

Therefore, they gathered the church together and "reported all that God had done through them." That is, they told of the great things God had done as they worked as fellow laborers with Him. To the Gentiles also He had "opened the door of faith." (The Gk. has "*a* door" [NASB], not "*the* door," here.) That is, He brought about circumstances and opportunities that enabled many Gentiles to come to faith in Jesus. Then the two apostles remained "a long time" with the disciples. That is, they resumed a ministry of teaching and help in the assembly of believers for several months, probably as much as a year.

STUDY QUESTIONS

1. Who were the prophets and teachers at Antioch and how did they minister to the Lord?
2. After the Spirit confirmed the ministry of Saul and Barnabas, why was it necessary for the local church to take further action?
3. Why did Saul and Barnabas go to Cyprus first, and with what results?
4. For what reasons did Paul go to the Jew first?
5. What caused Paul to turn to the Gentiles?
6. What happened at Lystra and why?
7. How were elders chosen and what was to be their ministry?

D. The Jerusalem Council 15:1–35

The Jerusalem Council of A.D. 49, dealt with in this chapter, is another turning point in the history of the Church. The Jerusalem church leaders were satisfied by Peter's account of the Lord's accepting uncircumcised Gentiles in Caesarea and baptizing them in the Holy Spirit. Then, according to Galatians

2:1–10, when Paul visited Jerusalem and presented the gospel he preached among the Gentiles, the leaders gave their approval to his message and did not require Titus, Paul's Gentile fellow worker, to be circumcised.

A little later (Gal. 2:11–16), when Peter came to Syrian Antioch, he enjoyed table fellowship and ate nonkosher food with the Gentiles as he had in the house of Cornelius.[1] But then some Jewish believers came up from James (not sent officially, but sent to help and encourage the believers). However, they were probably converted Pharisees who were still strict about Jewish believers keeping tradition. In fear of them, Peter quit eating with the Gentiles and withdrew from their fellowship; his example affected the other Jewish believers in Antioch. Even Barnabas was carried away with this hypocrisy. Paul therefore took a strong stand against Peter and faced him with the hypocrisy of what he was doing (Gal. 2:14).

1. BELIEVING PHARISEES DEMAND CIRCUMCISION
15:1–5

a. Opposition Comes From Judea 15:1

[1]Some men came down from Judea to Antioch and were teaching the brothers: "Unless you are circumcised, according to the custom taught by Moses, you cannot be saved."

Later, after Peter's visit, other unnamed Jewish believers "came down from Judea" to Antioch and went a step further.[2] They

---

[1]See F. F. Bruce, *Commentary on the Book of Acts* (Grand Rapids: Wm. B. Eerdmans, 1954), 298–300, for an excellent presentation of conclusive reasons showing that Galatians was written to the churches in South Galatia visited by Paul on his first missionary journey. This makes Galatians the earliest of Paul's epistles. Its whole attitude shows that the controversy was heated, just as it was immediately before the Jerusalem Council. This view of its authorship and of a date of A.D. 49 for the Book of Galatians was developed by Sir William Ramsay in *A Historical Commentary on St. Paul's Epistle to the Galatians* (1900; reprint, Minneapolis: Klock & Klock Christian Publishers, 1978), 180ff. I heard Dr. Merrill C. Tenney in Gordon Divinity School (now Gordon-Conwell Theological Seminary) make statements in his lectures in favor of this dating.

[2]Bruce, *Commentary,* 303, suggests that these were the same ones who "came from James" in Gal. 2:12, and they took things into their own hands when they saw so many Gentile believers.

began teaching the Gentile brothers that their salvation was conditioned on circumcision "according to the custom taught by Moses."[3]

These teachers, called "Judaizers" by modern commentators, did not deny that these Gentiles were believers baptized in the Holy Spirit. But the salvation they had in mind was the ultimate salvation whereby we shall receive our new bodies (at the Rapture) and be changed (cf. Rom. 13:11, "Our salvation is nearer now than when we first believed"). As Romans 8:17,23–24; 1 Corinthians 15:57; and 1 John 3:2 show, we are already sons of God, but we do not yet have all God has promised. Not until Jesus comes again and we see Him as He is will our bodies be changed and become like His glorified body. God's promise also includes our reigning with Christ and making our ultimate home in the New Jerusalem and the new heaven and the new earth (2 Pet. 3:13; Rev. 21:1–2).

What these Judaizers were really saying was that the Gentile believers must be circumcised and come under the old covenant of Moses' law;[4] otherwise, they could not be heirs of the promises that are yet to come. By this they also implied that Gentile believers would lose the salvation they had already received if they did not become Jews and undergo circumcision.

This has often been the cry of false teachers: You will lose your salvation if you do not accept our special teaching. Some still say that a person is not really or fully saved unless they go through certain prescribed rites or ceremonies. All these fail to recognize that salvation is by grace through faith alone, as is clearly taught in Romans 10:9–10 and Ephesians 2:8–9.

b. Paul And Barnabas Sent To Jerusalem 15:2–4

2This brought Paul and Barnabas into sharp dispute and debate with them. So Paul and Barnabas were appointed, along with some other believers, to go up to Jerusalem to see the apostles and elders about this question.

[3]They obviously represented themselves to be gifted teachers of the Church. This teaching was later carried to an extreme by the Ebionite heresy, mentioned by Irenaeus, Origen, and others. At least some Ebionites eventually denied the divine nature of Jesus and His virgin birth.

[4]See Gen. 17:10–14; Lev. 12:3.

This Judaizing teaching brought "sharp dispute" (Gk. *staseōs,* "commotion, disturbance, discord, upheaval") and "debate" (Gk. *zētēseōs,* "questioning, controversy") between the Judaizers—or, more probably, between the brothers—and Paul and Barnabas. The brothers then assigned Paul, Barnabas, and some others "to go up to Jerusalem to see the apostles and elders about this question" of circumcision.

It is probable that the Judaizers had already gone on to try to spread their teaching in the other churches Paul had established in South Galatia. Since Paul had to go to Jerusalem, he could not go to these churches and correct matters. It seems evident that at this time (A.D. 48, 49)[5] the Spirit directed and inspired Paul to write the epistle to the Galatians.[6]

3The church sent them on their way, and as they traveled through Phoenicia and Samaria, they told how the Gentiles had been converted. This news made all the brothers very glad.

The whole church turned out to escort Paul and Barnabas and the others (probably including Titus; Gal. 2:1) for a little distance on the way. By this the believers showed they still loved them, respected them, and had confidence in them in spite of the questions these Judaizing teachers had raised.

Paul took the road south through Phoenicia and the province of Samaria, stopping to visit churches all along the way.[7] In each place he gave a complete account (Gk. *ekdiēgoumenoi,* "declaring fully, telling in detail"; cf. NASB) of the Gentiles turning to the

[5]Most scholars date the Jerusalem Council with some certainty at A.D. 49. Harold H. Rowden, "The Historical and Political Background and Chronology of the New Testament," in *A New Testament Commentary,* ed. G. C. D. Howley (Grand Rapids: Zondervan Publishing House, 1969), 64. For arguments to date it at A.D. 51 see Charles B. Puskas, *An Introduction to the New Testament* (Peabody, Mass.: Hendrickson Publishers, 1989), 197–99.

[6]Note that the "so quickly" of Gal. 1:6 indicates that Paul wrote the book just before the Jerusalem Council. This fits the view that Gal. was addressed to the churches in South Galatia, a view held by most interpreters today. See Ronald Y. K. Fung, *The Epistle to the Galatians* (Grand Rapids: Wm. B. Eerdmans, 1988), 2.

[7]Phoenicia at this time extended south to Mount Carmel on the Mediterranean coast, so it was not necessary to go through Galilee. From Mount Carmel they took the inland route through Samaria to Jerusalem.

Lord. Though made up of circumcised Jewish believers in Phoenicia and circumcised Samaritan believers in Samaria who still followed the customs prescribed by the law of Moses, the churches all accepted the spread and effectiveness of the Word of God among the Gentiles without question. More than that, the "news made all the brothers very glad."

⁴When they came to Jerusalem, they were welcomed by the church and the apostles and elders, to whom they reported everything God had done through them.

In Jerusalem, also, the church welcomed them, and the apostles and elders gave them a favorable reception. They all listened to the report of how much "God had done through them" (with them as His fellow laborers). They gave God all the glory; He had been with them; He had really done the work (cf. 1 Cor. 3:5-7).

In giving a full report, Paul undoubtedly included an account of the persecution as well as the miracles. We can be sure also that he told of the baptism in the Holy Spirit and the confirmation of the faith of the Gentile believers.

c. Believing Pharisees Rise Up 15:5

⁵Then some of the believers who belonged to the party of the Pharisees stood up and said, "The Gentiles must be circumcised and required to obey the law of Moses."

It was not long, however, before some converted Pharisees rose up out of the assembly in Jerusalem. They forcefully expressed the view that it was (and continued to be) necessary both to circumcise the Gentiles and to command them to obey the law of Moses. The majority of the Jerusalem believers probably agreed that circumcision was necessary for Gentile converts (possibly on the basis of Gen. 17:27). But those who were Pharisees made it an issue.

2. THE QUESTION OF CIRCUMCISION CONSIDERED 15:6-12

⁶The apostles and elders met to consider this question.

The "apostles and elders" (leaders of the house churches) then assembled to consider the matter. It was not a closed meeting, however. Verse 12 indicates a crowd was present. No one tried to

dominate the meeting. Free, open discussion probably continued for several days.

> [7]After much discussion, Peter got up and addressed
> them: "Brothers, you know that some time ago God
> made a choice among you that the Gentiles might hear
> from my lips the message of the gospel and believe.
> [8]God, who knows the heart, showed that he accepted
> them by giving the Holy Spirit to them, just as he did to
> us. [9]He made no distinction between us and them, for he
> purified their hearts by faith.

At first there was "much discussion" and questioning as they
probed the subject. (See v. 2. The Pharisees who were believers in
Jesus were convinced they had tradition on their side.) Wisely, the
leaders allowed the people to present various points of view.

Finally, "Peter got up"[8] and reminded them that by God's
choice he had taken the gospel to the Gentiles (in Caesarea) and
they had believed.[9] Then God, who saw the faith in their hearts,
bore witness to the fact they were believers by giving them the
Holy Spirit (with the evidence of speaking in tongues, 10:46), just
as He had to all the Jewish believers. God thus "made no distinction," no separation, between the Gentile and Jewish believers in
any way, "for He purified [cleansed] their hearts by faith." That is,
God had already cleansed their hearts by faith when He showed
there was no distinction by baptizing them in the Holy Spirit.[10] In
other words, not circumcision, not keeping the Law of Moses, but
a heart cleansed by faith was all that was necessary for God to bear
witness to that faith by pouring out His Spirit. Therefore, the
acceptance of uncircumcised Gentiles was God's doing.

---

[8]Some ancient manuscripts read "Peter rose up in the Holy Spirit."

[9]See chaps. 10 and 11.

[10]Some commentators point out that both the giving (v. 8) and the cleansing
(v. 9) are Gk. aorists, which they claim are simultaneous here. But the cleansing
is clearly prior to the giving and is definitely not simultaneous with it. See Stanley
M. Horton, *What the Bible Says About the Holy Spirit* (Springfield, Mo.: Gospel
Publishing House, 1976), 159–61, for the use of the aorist participle in relation
to the main verb of a Gk. sentence. Roger Stronstad also sees that Luke is teaching a pattern of Spirit baptism as Peter connects "the latter gift of the Spirit to
the former." *The Prophethood of All Believers: A Study in Luke's Charismatic
Theology* (Sheffield, England: Sheffield Academic Press, 1999), 25.

¹⁰Now then, why do you try to test God by putting on the necks of the disciples a yoke that neither we nor our fathers have been able to bear?

Peter then asked why, in contrast to what God had done, they would "try to test God," showing a spirit of disobedience by disregarding what He had made plain at Caesarea, thus stirring His anger. Even worse, by refusing to admit uncircumcised believers into the Church they were really suggesting that God did wrong to baptize the Gentile Cornelius and his household in the Holy Spirit.[11]

Further, to put a yoke on the necks of these Gentile disciples that neither the Jewish Christians nor their Jewish ancestors "[had] been able to bear" would indeed "test God" after His gracious revelation at Caesarea.[12]

¹¹No! We believe it is through the grace of our Lord Jesus that we are saved, just as they are."

Then Peter concluded by declaring that "through the grace of [the] Lord Jesus . . . we" Jewish disciples keep believing in order to keep on being saved, in exactly the same way "as they [those Gentiles] are." That is, by grace, apart from the heavy yoke of the Law and the legalistic bondage encouraged by the Pharisees (who were very severe at this time), they all continued in their relation to Christ.[13]

¹²The whole assembly became silent as they listened to Barnabas and Paul telling about the miraculous signs and wonders God had done among the Gentiles through them.

These words of Peter quieted the crowd. They had no answer for his "message of wisdom" (see 1 Cor. 12:8). So they listened

---

[11]Peter received an earlier lesson about this when he visited Antioch and Paul had had to rebuke him for withdrawing from fellowship with Gentiles (Gal. 2:11–16). Peter's response here shows he had indeed learned his lesson.

[12]How different the "yoke" of the Law was from the yoke Jesus invites us to take upon ourselves (Matt. 11:28–30).

[13]Peter does not mention the lesson he had learned at Antioch (Gal. 2:11–21), but what he says reflects what Paul had told him. F. F. Bruce suggests that "Peter may have gone straight back to Jerusalem from Antioch to play a leading part in arranging the consultation [i.e., the Jerusalem Council]." *Acts: Greek Text*, 335. This is another indication of the early date of the Book of Galatians.

in silence as Barnabas and Paul explained the many miracles, signs, and wonders God had done through them "among the Gentiles."[14] By this they implied that the miracles showed God's concern for winning these Gentiles to Christ and establishing them in the faith. As Paul later wrote to the Corinthians, he preached to them "with a demonstration of the Spirit's [mighty, miracle-working] power" so their faith might not stand on men's wisdom "but on God's power" (1 Cor. 2:4–5).

3. James Gives A Word Of Wisdom 15:13–21

[13]When they finished, James spoke up: "Brothers, listen to me. [14]Simon has described to us how God at first showed his concern by taking from the Gentiles a people for himself.

After Barnabas and Paul finished, the crowd waited until James broke the silence by asking them to listen. But in this request he speaks as a brother, not as one who had superior authority. First, he drew attention to what Peter said, calling Peter by his Hebrew name, Simon (Gk. *Sumeōn,* a transliteration of the Heb. form of his name). He summarized Peter's words by saying that God "first showed his concern" for the Gentiles (that is, before any of them were saved) at the house of Cornelius—intervening to bring them blessing, taking from among them a people for himself (lit. "for His name"), a people who would honor His Name and be His people. God took the initiative: Accepting the Gentiles was His idea, not Peter's.

[15]The words of the prophets are in agreement with this, as it is written: [16]'After this I will return and rebuild David's fallen tent. Its ruins I will rebuild, and I will restore it, [17]that the remnant of men may seek the Lord, and all the Gentiles who bear my name, says the Lord, who does these things' [18]that have been known for ages.

For a firm decision to settle the issue, Scripture was necessary.[15] So James then turned to the prophets, quoting Amos 9:11–12

---

[14]Note that Barnabas is mentioned first again, for he was known and respected by the Jerusalem leaders and believers. This time he was the spokesman.

[15]Richard Bauckham, "James and the Jerusalem Church," in *The Book of Acts in Its Palestinian Setting,* ed. Richard Bauckham, vol. 4 of *The Book of Acts in Its First Century Setting,* ed. Bruce W. Winter (Grand Rapids: Wm. B. Eerdmans, 1995), 452–58.

from the LXX.[16] However, it differs from the present Hebrew text, substituting "the remnant of men [Heb. *adam,* "humankind, human beings"]" for "'the remnant of Edom.'" Actually, the Hebrew, written originally without vowels and capitals, could be read either *adam* or *edom.*[17] Thus, reading from another version of the Old Testament helped the Holy Spirit to make the point "much more forcefully."[18]

"After this" probably means after the fulfillment of the judgments on Israel prophesied by Amos. Then God would return and do a work of restoration. Also James apparently took the Lord's promise to "rebuild David's fallen tent" (tabernacle) as parallel to Isaiah's prophecy that the Messiah would come as a new shoot or branch out of the stump of Jesse and the root of David. Though David's glory would be gone and his kingdom fallen, God would raise up the Messiah from among David's descendants and restore the hope of not only Israel but also the Gentiles, who would accept the Messiah and become part of God's people.[19] This was, as the prophets said, the work of the Lord, "'who does these things' that have been known for ages," who has known all these things from the beginning of time: It was always God's plan to include Gentiles in the Church. As Paul points out, the Church was also in God's plan from eternity (Eph. 3:10–11).[20]

[16]In the LXX it begins with "in that day" instead of "after this," and does not have "I will return."

[17]This difference involves only a slight change in the vowels, which the ancient Heb. did not write anyway. In fact, Heb. was written only in consonants until several hundred years after Christ. Note also that "'Edom'" in Amos is parallel to "'all the nations'" (the Gentiles). At least, Edom is representative of the Gentiles. But some Bible scholars believe the vowels for "Edom" were added by later Jews to change the meaning because they knew the Book of Acts used this verse to uphold the acceptance of uncircumcised Gentiles.

[18]C. Peter Wagner, *Lighting the World: Book 2, Acts 9–15* (Ventura, Calif.: Gospel Light, Regal Books, 1995), 242.

[19]James is not equating David's tent with the Church. Rebuilding the tent refers to the restoring of the Davidic dynasty. The "tent" of David is reminiscent of the "'house'" God promised to establish for David (2 Sam. 7:11). For other views see Mark L. Strauss, *The Davidic Messiah in Luke-Acts* (Sheffield, England: Sheffield Academic Press, 1995), 185–92.

[20]Robert Wall suggests that Acts 15:13 to 28:28 "is a (travel-)narrative commentary on the Amos prophecy . . . of a rebuilt 'tent of David,'" telling "the story

¹⁹"It is my judgment, therefore, that we should not make it difficult for the Gentiles who are turning to God. ²⁰Instead we should write to them, telling them to abstain from food polluted by idols, from sexual immorality, from the meat of strangled animals and from blood. ²¹For Moses has been preached in every city from the earliest times and is read in the synagogues on every Sabbath."

"My judgment" (v. 19) is better translated "I think it good" or "I propose" (cf. TEV). Wycliffe's translation, the first major translation of the Bible in English, reads, "I deem." James was not acting as a judge here, nor as a leading elder of the Church. In verse 28 we read, "It seemed good to the Holy Spirit and to us," not, "to James and to us." In this situation James was simply a Christian brother, a member of the Body, who gave a message of wisdom as the Spirit determined (see 1 Cor. 12:8,11).

Gentile believers were turning to God, and the Spirit's message of wisdom was that the Jewish believers should not "make it difficult" for them by adding a further requirement to their faith and practice. Let the assembly instead write a letter directing the Gentile believers "to abstain [keep away] from food polluted by idols [Gk. *alisgēmatōn tōn eidōlōn*, "pollutions of the idols," that is, everything connected with idol worship, which would include meat offered to idols], from sexual immorality [the various types of heterosexual and homosexual immorality habitually practiced by so many Gentile pagans], from the meat of strangled animals [killed without draining the blood, Lev. 17:13; cf. Gen. 9:4] and from blood [i.e., from drinking blood]," recognizing that "the life of a creature is in the blood" (Lev. 17:10,11).²¹

Observing these things was to be expected of the Gentiles, not to put them under a burden or list of rules but for the sake of promoting fellowship with the Jewish believers and for the sake of the testimony of the synagogues where "Moses [had] been preached in every city from the earliest times."

---

of that 'tentmaker' (so 18:3) Paul." "'Purity and Power' According to the Acts of the Apostles," *Pneuma* 21, no. 2 (fall 1999): 216.

²¹Some ancient manuscripts leave out "things strangled" (Acts 15:20, KJV) and interpret "blood" as bloodshed or murder. But the evidence is in favor of the usual text given above.

Jewish colonies date from the time of Solomon.

The first two requests—to keep away from the pollutions, or polluted things, of idolatry and from all forms of sexual immorality—were for the sake of the Jewish witness to the one true God and to the high moral standards a holy God requires. Gentiles should not retain anything of their former idol worship, not even as family heirlooms, even though they now knew these things were meaningless and harmless. Their idolatrous neighbors would misinterpret this and suppose the worship of God could be mixed with pagan worship or pagan ideas.

The Gentile believers also had to be reminded of the high moral standards God requires. They came from a background where immorality was accepted, even encouraged, in the name of religion. It took considerable teaching to make them realize that the things everyone else was doing were wrong. In several of Paul's epistles he had to deal very sternly with the problems of immorality.[22] (See Rom. 6:12–13,19–23; 1 Cor. 5:1,9–12; 6:13,15–20; 10:8; Gal. 5:19–21; Eph. 5:3,5; Col. 3:5–6; 1 Tim. 1:9–10.)

The second two requests, to abstain from the meat of strangled animals and from blood, were for the sake of promoting fellowship between Jewish and Gentile believers. Table fellowship was very important in the Early Church. If there was anything that would nauseate a Jewish believer, it was the thought of eating meat that had not been bled or to eat blood itself. If the Jewish believers were going to accept nonkosher foods in Gentile believers' homes, then the least Gentile believers could do was avoid serving and eating those things which no Jew, no matter how long he had been a Christian, could tolerate.

There was precedent for these last two requests because long before Moses' time, long before the Law was given, God told

[22]See Bruce, *Commentary,* 315. Some writers take "sexual immorality" (Gk. *porneias*) here to mean the prohibited degrees of marriage in Lev. 18:8–18. First Cor. 5:1 might be an example of *porneia* used in that sense, but it seems rather to be just an example of one kind of sexual immorality. Paul goes on to use *porneia* to mean immorality in a more general sense in 1 Cor. 5:9–11. It seems clear also that here in Acts the word is used in the more general sense, including all forms of sexual immorality both before and after marriage. Certainly the kind of sexual immorality mentioned in 1 Cor. 5:1 was not common among the Gentiles, as that v. itself indicates.

Noah not to eat blood because it represented a creature's life (Gen. 9:4). Therefore, as descendants of Noah, Gentiles could be asked to keep these strictures without bringing them under the law of Moses. The same restriction in Moses' law treated blood as a type that pointed ahead to the blood of Christ and showed its importance. James, however, did not bring out this typology. Primarily he was concerned about fellowship between Jews and Gentiles. This was the kind of wisdom James speaks of in his epistle (James 3:17–18); it was pure, peace loving, and considerate.[23]

4. A Letter Sent 15:22–29

22Then the apostles and elders, with the whole church, decided to choose some of their own men and send them to Antioch with Paul and Barnabas. They chose Judas (called Barsabbas) and Silas, two men who were leaders among the brothers.

The Holy Spirit was again breaking down barriers. The response to the Spirit's message of wisdom given by James was unanimous. The apostles and elders together "with the whole church" thought it good to send men they chose from among themselves to go with Paul and Barnabas to Antioch to present the decision and the letter. Those chosen were Judas Barsabbas[24] and Silas (the Semitic equivalent of the Lat. *Silvanus;* found in the Gk. of 2 Cor. 1:19; 1 Thess. 1:1; 2 Thess. 1:1; 1 Pet. 5:12), "leaders among the brothers" of the Jerusalem church. They would confirm that the decision was truly from the Holy Spirit and that the letter was genuine.

23With them they sent the following letter: The apostles and elders, your brothers, To the Gentile believers in Antioch, Syria and Cilicia: Greetings. 24We have heard that some went out from us without our authorization and disturbed you, troubling your minds by what they

---

[23]Sanders suggests that table fellowship was not the main issue. The point rather was that "Gentiles being converted to Christianity come under no obligation to obey any additional laws in the Torah that were not already obligatory for them in their preChristian state." Jack T. Sanders, *The Jews in Luke-Acts* (Philadelphia: Fortress Press, 1987), 123.

[24]Possibly related to Joseph Barsabbas; see Acts 1:23.

said. 25So we all agreed to choose some men and send them to you with our dear friends Barnabas and Paul— 26men who have risked their lives for the name of our Lord Jesus Christ. 27Therefore we are sending Judas and Silas to confirm by word of mouth what we are writing.

The greeting that opens the letter is similar in form to that of the Book of James. "The style of the decree has that touch of frank forthrightness so evident in James' Epistle."25

The letter stated clearly that the Jerusalem church had not sent out the men who "disturbed"26 the church at Antioch, "troubling"27 their minds. Nor had the church given a command that the Gentile believers be circumcised and keep the Law. Their decision to send chosen men with their "dear friends Barnabas and Paul" was unanimous. Moreover, they loved both Barnabas and Paul (Gk. *agapētois hēmōn,* lit. "our beloved," is plural in the Gk.; hence, "dear friends"). Thus they recommended them to the Gentile believers in Antioch as men who had "risked [and devoted] their lives for the name of our Lord Jesus Christ" (that is, for all that His name expresses: His love, His salvation, His grace, His Person, etc.). Judas and Silas would personally confirm that the letter was genuine and unanimous.

28It seemed good to the Holy Spirit and to us not to burden you with anything beyond the following requirements: 29You are to abstain from food sacrificed to idols, from blood, from the meat of strangled animals and from sexual immorality. You will do well to avoid these things. Farewell.

Only the necessary things that "seemed good to the Holy Spirit" and to the Jerusalem believers would be asked of them.28

25E. M. Blaiklock, *Acts: The Birth of the Church* (Old Tappan, N.J.: Fleming H. Revell, 1980), 130.

26Gk. *etaraxan,* "agitated," "stirred up."

27Gk. *anaskeuazontes,* "upsetting," a term used in classical Gk. of tearing down or plundering a town.

28Note that the Holy Spirit was not rubber-stamping a "merely human or ecclesial" decision. The Spirit took the initiative, as we should expect. The Church should follow the Spirit's leading. Max Turner, *Power From on High: The Spirit in Israel's Restoration and Witness in Luke-Acts* (Sheffield, England: Sheffield Academic Press, 1996), 440.

If they would keep themselves safe from these things, they would do well. "Farewell" is literally, "Make yourselves strong," but had become a common phrase used at the end of a letter to mean farewell or goodbye.

5. THE LETTER CAUSES REJOICING AT ANTIOCH
15:30–35

30The men were sent off and went down to Antioch, where they gathered the church together and delivered the letter. 31The people read it and were glad for its encouraging message.

When Paul and his companions arrived and read the letter to the believers in Antioch, the whole Body rejoiced greatly for its encouragement (challenge, exhortation). Clearly, Paul also accepted and rejoiced in the decision of the Jerusalem Council.[29]

32Judas and Silas, who themselves were prophets, said much to encourage and strengthen the brothers.

Judas and Silas[30] then did more than confirm the facts of the letter. As prophets, they were speakers for God, used by the Holy Spirit in the gift of prophecy for the strengthening, encouragement, and comfort of the believers (cf. 1 Cor. 14:3). Through their words they supported and established the church at Antioch. That is, they gave them solid encouragement to forget the arguments of the Judaizers and to maintain their faith in Christ and in the gospel they had received, the gospel of salvation by grace through faith alone—apart from the works of the Law— as Paul emphasizes in his epistles to the Romans and Galatians.

33After spending some time there, they were sent off by the brothers with the blessing of peace to return to those who had sent them. 34[but Silas decided to remain there.]

After a time, the "brothers" (the believers at Antioch) released Judas and Silas with the farewell "blessing of peace" (and well-being) to go back "to those who had sent them," that is, to the

---

[29]See R. N. Longenecker, *Paul, Apostle of Liberty* (1964; reprint, Grand Rapids: Baker Book House, 1976), 254–60.

[30]"Silas" is a contraction of the Roman name Silvanus; he was a Roman citizen.

whole church in Jerusalem, as shown by the Greek. Judas Barsabbas did return, but Silas chose to remain.[31]

35But Paul and Barnabas remained in Antioch, where they and many others taught and preached the word of the Lord.

Paul and Barnabas also "remained in Antioch," to teach and preach the gospel along with "many others," for the Lord had raised up many other teachers and bearers of the gospel in the still growing church. These may have included some from Jerusalem and elsewhere, but undoubtedly the majority were from the local assembly. They too were entering the work of ministry for building up the body of Christ; Paul later wrote that all believers should receive from Christ and do the same (Eph. 4:12,15–16).

STUDY QUESTIONS

1. What in Galatians indicates it was written before the Jerusalem Council of Acts 15?
2. What points did Peter emphasize at the Jerusalem Council?
3. What recommendation did James make and why?
4. What else did the Jerusalem church do besides repudiate the teachings of the Judaizers?
5. What sort of prophecies did Silas and Judas give?

E. Paul's Second Missionary Journey 15:36–18:22

1. PAUL AND BARNABAS SEPARATE 15:36–39

36Some time later Paul said to Barnabas, "Let us go back and visit the brothers in all the towns where we preached

---

[31]Some writers take this to be a contradiction to v. 33. However, the church only released them to go. The Bible does not say they went. Many modern versions do omit v. 34 (thus NIV brackets) and suppose Silas went back to Jerusalem and returned later. It is more likely that v. 33 "only stated that they were given permission to leave, and v. 34 in its original form added that Silas did not avail himself of the permission." W. A. Strange, *The Problem of the Text of Acts* (Cambridge, England: Cambridge University Press, 1992), 142.

the word of the Lord and see how they are doing."

After a considerable time of preaching and teaching in Antioch, Paul suggested to Barnabas that they "visit the brothers" in the assemblies established "in all the towns" throughout Cyprus and South Galatia during their first missionary journey, to "see how they are doing." All through his ministry Paul maintained a love and concern that kept him praying for the churches and believers to whom he had ministered. His epistles are evidence of this (see Phil. 1:3–6; Col. 1:3; 1 Thess. 1:2–3; and especially 2 Cor. 11:28). He may have been concerned also to see if his letter to the Galatians had counteracted the false teachings of the Judaizers.

[37]Barnabas wanted to take John, also called Mark, with them, [38]but Paul did not think it wise to take him, because he had deserted them in Pamphylia and had not continued with them in the work.

When Barnabas "wanted to" (willed to, purposed to) take along John Mark, "Paul did not think it wise." Mark had left them abruptly at a critical juncture, when they needed him for the work. Paul evidently did not believe that it would be good to bring into these young churches a person who might not set a good example of faith and diligence. Barnabas, however, was determined to give his cousin another chance.

[39]They had such a sharp disagreement that they parted company. Barnabas took Mark and sailed for Cyprus,

Both Paul and Barnabas felt so strongly about this—the Greek indicates heated feelings between them, even anger—"that they parted company." But they did not let this hinder the work of the Lord; they came up with a productive resolution: They would divide up the responsibility of visiting and encouraging the believers. Barnabas therefore took his cousin Mark and went to Cyprus to visit the assemblies founded on the first part of the first journey. This was wise, for Cyprus was familiar territory to Mark. He had been faithful there. It was better to take him back to the area where he had been a success.

That Barnabas was right in wanting to give Mark a second chance is shown by the fact that Mark later joined Paul (Col. 4:10; Philem. 24), and that Paul asked Timothy to bring Mark with him because Mark was helpful to Paul for ministry (2 Tim. 4:11). Mark was also with Peter on his visit to Babylon (1 Pet. 5:13).[1] Early tradition says also that Mark recorded the preaching of Peter in his Gospel. So we have both Barnabas and Peter to thank that Mark was in a position where the Holy Spirit could direct and inspire him to write the second Gospel.

2. PAUL CHOOSES SILAS 15:40–41

40but Paul chose Silas and left, commended by the brothers to the grace of the Lord. 41He went through Syria and Cilicia, strengthening the churches.

Paul then chose Silas, who was a mature believer, a prophet already used by the Spirit to challenge and encourage the churches. He would be an excellent helper for Paul in his effort to encourage the churches in South Galatia, which were in a most difficult environment.

Since Silas was an outstanding member of the Jerusalem church, this would also help to show the Galatian churches the unity between Paul and the Jerusalem leaders and thus further weaken the arguments of the Judaizers.[2] It was also helpful that Silas was, like Paul, a Roman citizen (see Acts 16:37–38).

The brothers at Antioch then released them and committed them anew to the grace of God. And so they went on their way through Syria and Cilicia, "strengthening [and spiritually building up] the churches." These would include assemblies in cities north of Antioch in Syria as well as Paul's home city of Tarsus in Cilicia.[3]

---

[1]Some writers take "Babylon" here to mean Rome. But Babylon had one of the largest orthodox Jewish communities outside of Palestine. (The Jewish community at Alexandria was probably larger, but they were Hellenistic rather than strictly orthodox.) It would be strange if Peter, the apostle to the circumcision (Gal. 2:7), did not visit this large Jewish community. Peter's visit to Babylon probably took place before Paul went to Rome.

[2]See Richard N. Longenecker, *Paul, Apostle of Liberty* (1964; reprint, Grand Rapids: Baker Book House, 1976), 226.

[3]Codex Bezae (D) and other ancient manuscripts add that they delivered the injunctions of the elders, that is, the instructions given in the letter of Acts 15 from the Jerusalem church.

3. Paul Takes Timothy With Him 16:1–5

¹He came to Derbe and then to Lystra, where a disciple named Timothy lived, whose mother was a Jewess and a believer, but whose father was a Greek. ²The brothers at Lystra and Iconium spoke well of him.

From Cilicia Paul and Silas went through the Taurus Mountains by way of a famous pass called the Cilician Gates.[4] Coming from this direction they would arrive at Derbe first and then, about twenty miles further, Lystra.

At Lystra, Paul came across a young disciple named Timothy (short for Timotheus). His mother was a believing Jewess named Eunice. His grandmother Lois was also a very godly believer (see 2 Tim. 1:5; 3:14–15). His father, however, was a Greek, probably a member of a prominent and wealthy family, but apparently never converted. (The Greek tense implies he was dead.)

Fortunately, the faith and training given by his mother and grandmother had more effect on young Timothy than the unbelief of his father. They had trained him in the Scriptures from his earliest childhood (2 Tim. 1:5; 3:15). Then, when he accepted Christ, he made great progress in the Christian life. Verse 2 indicates clearly that God had given Timothy a spiritual ministry in the cities of Lysytra and Iconium and that both his life and ministry were a blessing to the assemblies there.

It is probable also that he was converted under Paul's ministry during one of Paul's previous visits to Lystra. However, when Paul calls him "my son" later, he was probably using the term "son" to mean "student" as well as younger fellow worker that he loved. (See 1 Cor. 4:17; 1 Tim. 1:2,18; 2 Tim. 1:2. See also Phil. 2:19–24 for the confidence Paul had in him and for his unique qualifications for ministry.)

³Paul wanted to take him along on the journey, so he circumcised him because of the Jews who lived in that area, for they all knew that his father was a Greek.

---

[4]Sir William Ramsay describes this pass in *Pauline and Other Studies* (London: Hodder & Stoughton, 1906), 273–75, cited by F. F. Bruce, *Commentary on the Book of Acts* (Grand Rapids: Wm. B. Eerdmans, 1954), 321.

Paul wanted to take Timothy out of the church at Lystra for further training as well as for help in the ministry on these missionary journeys. But when he decided to do this, he did something very unusual: He circumcised Timothy. Paul makes quite a point in Galatians 2:3–5 that the Jerusalem leaders did not require Titus to be circumcised. Why, then, did he circumcise Timothy?

Titus was a Gentile. To circumcise him would have been to yield to the Judaizers, who said Gentiles must become Jews to keep their salvation. Timothy, however, had been brought up in the Jewish traditions by his mother and grandmother. Even today Jews accept a person as a Jew if only the mother is Jewish. They rightly understand that the mother has the greatest influence on the values and religious attitudes of a young child. We can be sure that the Jews in Paul's day also considered Timothy a Jew.

Further, Paul still went to the Jew first in every new city that he visited. For him to take an uncircumcised Jew into a synagogue would be like taking a traitor into an army camp. It would have been intolerable to the Jews; none of them would have listened to his message. Therefore, Paul took Timothy and circumcised him for the sake of his witness to his own people,[5] and to preempt the accusation of teaching against the law of Moses that would ultimately come (18:13; 21:28).

Perhaps 1 Corinthians 9:20–23 gives further insight into Paul's reasoning. Unless the cultural norms of the people he ministered to were immoral or idolatrous, Paul did not go against them. In other words, he removed anything that would hinder the promotion of the gospel and the salvation of souls. "They all knew that [Timothy's] father was a Greek,"[6] so Paul had to confirm Timothy's Jewish heritage before they could go on. First Timothy 4:14 indicates that the elders of the local assembly accepted this, prayed for Timothy, and sent him out with their blessing.

[5]See H. B. Hackett, *A Commentary on the Acts of the Apostles* (Philadelphia: American Baptist Publication Society, 1882), 181–82. Note also that Paul in 1 Cor. 7:19; Gal. 5:6; and 6:15 shows that circumcision and uncircumcision in themselves mean nothing. See also Irena Levinskaya, *The Book of Acts in Its Diaspora Setting*, vol. 5 of *The Book of Acts in Its First Century Setting*, ed. Bruce W. Winter (Grand Rapids: Wm. B. Eerdmans, 1996), 15–16.

[6]The Gk. tense of "was," *hupērken*, indicates his father was dead.

⁴As they traveled from town to town, they delivered the decisions reached by the apostles and elders in Jerusalem for the people to obey. ⁵So the churches were strengthened in the faith and grew daily in numbers.

As Paul, Silas, and Timothy went on their way through South Galatia, they presented copies of the decisions, or regulations, in the letter of Acts 15 for the Gentile believers to obey. These regulations they recognized as decided by "the apostles and elders in Jerusalem." But we can be sure that Paul and Silas also pointed out that "it seemed good to the Holy Spirit" (Acts 15:28) as well.

The result was that the upsetting teachings of the Judaizers were checked. What had been a critical issue was now no longer a threat or a cause of division; everyone accepted the decision of the Jerusalem Council. Undoubtedly, Paul's having written to the Galatians had helped prepare the way for this acceptance.

Then all the assemblies in the various cities "were strengthened," not only in faith but also in "*the* faith"; that is, they grew in their understanding of the truth of the gospel and their obedience to its teachings and precepts. Because of this, the assemblies continued to grow, increasing in number day by day.

4. THE MACEDONIAN CALL 16:6–10

⁶Paul and his companions traveled throughout the region of Phrygia and Galatia, having been kept by the Holy Spirit from preaching the word in the province of Asia.

After Paul and his company went through the region of Phrygia and Galatia,[7] logic suggested the Roman province of Asia just to the north and west. Its great city of Ephesus represented

---

[7]This refers to the southern half of the Roman province of Galatia. Some commentators suppose Paul went through North Galatia, but as Simon J. Kistemaker points out, "Evidence for the southern Galatian theory is decisive." *Exposition of the Acts of the Apostles* (Grand Rapids: Baker Book House, 1990), 583–84. See also E. M. Blaiklock, *Acts: The Birth of the Church* (Old Tappan, N.J.: Fleming H. Revell, 1980), 139. G. Walter Hansen says, "Paul did not visit north Galatia. A detour of 1083 kilometers is indeed hardly conceivable." "Galatia," in *The Book of Acts in Its Graeco-Roman Setting,* ed. David W. J. Gill and Conrad Gempf, vol. 2 of *Acts in Its First Century Setting,* ed. Winter (Grand Rapids: Wm. B. Eerdmans, 1994), 379.

a challenge. But it was not God's time. They had already "been kept by the Holy Spirit from preaching the word in the province of Asia." The Bible does not say how the Spirit did this. He may have done it by a message of wisdom given through one of Paul's company, or perhaps given by a Spirit-filled believer in one of the churches.[8]

> [7]When they came to the border of Mysia, they tried to enter Bithynia, but the Spirit of Jesus would not allow them to. [8]So they passed by Mysia and went down to Troas.

Since they were forbidden to enter Asia, they moved north along the eastern border of Mysia and made an attempt "to enter Bithynia," a senatorial province to the northeast along the Black Sea.[9] Paul was never one to sit around and do nothing when he did not know where God wanted him to go or what God wanted him to do next. He was always conscious of the missionary burden laid upon him. So when the Spirit checked him from going in one direction, he would take a step in another, trusting that the Holy Spirit would either confirm or deny the new direction.

Again "the Spirit of Jesus"[10] would not let them go, this time into Bithynia. Only one direction was left, so they took it, turning west and going to Troas. To do this they had to go through Mysia. But the Greek says literally that they "passed by," or skirted, Mysia. That is, they were not given permission to minister in Mysia either, and they bypassed it as far as preaching the gospel was concerned.

Think of what this must have meant to the apostle Paul, who said, "Woe to me if I do not preach the gospel" (1 Cor. 9:16). How he must have been burdened as he passed city after city, still forbidden to preach the Word. But because he was obedient, God brought him to Troas when He wanted him there.

[8]Bruce, *Commentary,* 326, suggests that this may have come through a prophet in Lystra.

[9]Bithynia had important Jewish settlements, especially in the Greek-speaking cities of Nicaea and Nicomedia. First Peter 1:1 shows that Bithynia was later evangelized by others.

[10]Some ancient manuscripts do not contain the phrase "of Jesus" (cf. v. 7, KJV). Whatever the case, it is of course another title of the Holy Spirit, the Spirit of God. It may mean simply that Jesus checked him by the Holy Spirit.

⁹During the night Paul had a vision of a man of Macedonia standing and begging him, "Come over to Macedonia and help us." ¹⁰After Paul had seen the vision, we got ready at once to leave for Macedonia, concluding that God had called us to preach the gospel to them.

At Troas,¹¹ a harbor city of Mysia across the Aegean Sea from Macedonia, came another important turning point in Paul's ministry and missionary travels. Had he gone into Bithynia, he might have continued eastward and never gone to Greece or Rome.¹² But God had new centers He wanted to establish in Europe. It was left for other apostles and believers to go eastward.¹³

God made the call westward clear in a night vision given to Paul in which a (pagan) Macedonian stood "begging him" to cross over to Macedonia and help them. Immediately Paul and his companions (now including Luke)¹⁴ sought to go over to Macedonia, concluding that God had called them "to preach the gospel to them." Note that Luke switches from the third to the first person in this, the first of the "we passages" (16:10–17; 20:5–15; 21:1–18; 27:1 through 28:16). Luke hereby lets us know he was with Paul and was an eyewitness of certain events.

5. MINISTRY IN PHILIPPI 16:11–40

a. An Open Door 16:11–15

¹¹From Troas we put out to sea and sailed straight for Samothrace, and the next day on to Neapolis. ¹²From there we traveled to Philippi, a Roman colony and the leading city of that district of Macedonia. And we stayed there several days.

---

¹¹About ten miles south of ancient Troy.

¹²He also might never have met Luke and we would not have the Gospel of Luke or the Book of Acts.

¹³There is strong tradition in South India that the apostle Thomas went there. Some believe it was another Thomas, but it is not impossible that the apostle himself went.

¹⁴Blaiklock suggests that Luke was from Philippi at this point, though he may have been originally from Syrian Antioch and may have known Paul there. So now at Troas, he sought out Paul. Blaiklock, *Acts,* 141.

A ship took them about 125 miles in two days to Neapolis,[15] the harbor town of Philippi, by way of the mountainous island of Samothrace.[16] (The wind must have been very favorable. Later, the journey in the other direction would take five days [Acts 20:6].) Then they traveled 12 miles on the Via Egnatia to Philippi.

Philippi, named for the father of Alexander the Great, was "the leading city" of the first division[17] of the Roman province of Macedonia, north of Greece.[18] The city also was a Roman "colony." That is, in 31 B.C. Octavian, who became the Emperor Augustus, had settled there a garrison of Roman soldiers who were citizens of Rome and followed Roman laws and customs.[19] It was an important city also because it was located at the eastern end of a famous Roman road, the Via Egnatia. As before, Paul went to a chief city to establish a gospel center. Then his converts would take the gospel to the surrounding cities and towns.

13On the Sabbath we went outside the city gate to the river, where we expected to find a place of prayer. We sat down and began to speak to the women who had gathered there.

There was no Jewish synagogue in the city, which means it lacked the ten Jewish men necessary to have one. Probably by making inquiries, Paul and his company heard that there was "a place of prayer"[20] about a mile outside the city gate on the bank of the Gangites River.[21] There they sat down and proceeded to talk to "the women who had gathered there."

14One of those listening was a woman named Lydia, a dealer in purple cloth from the city of Thyatira, who was

[15]The modern Kavalla.

[16]One of its peaks, Mount Fengari, over a mile high, helped guide ships across the northern Aegean Sea.

[17]Aemilius Paulus in 167 B.C. divided Macedonia into four districts for administrative purposes.

[18]Thessalonica was the capital of the Roman province of Macedonia.

[19]See Richard B. Rackham, *The Acts of the Apostles* (1901; reprint, Grand Rapids: Baker Book House, 1964), lvii; Blaiklock, *Acts,* 143.

[20]Gk. *proseuchē.* Philo used this term to mean a synagogue. However, v. 13 speaks only of women.

[21]See Bruce, *Commentary,* 329. Rabbinical tradition decreed that locations near rivers were ritually pure even in pagan countries.

a worshiper of God. The Lord opened her heart to respond to Paul's message. [15]When she and the members of her household were baptized, she invited us to her home. "If you consider me a believer in the Lord," she said, "come and stay at my house." And she persuaded us.

One of them, Lydia, was a wealthy businesswoman, an independent seller of purple-dyed cloth used by people of power and prestige (cf. Dan. 5:7; Luke 16:19).[22] She was a God-fearing Gentile originally from Thyatira in the Roman province of Asia, a city famous for its dyes. She probably first learned about the things of God by attending a synagogue in her home city, for there was a large Jewish colony in Thyatira. At Philippi, she continued to pray and seek God. Now she kept listening to Paul. Soon "the Lord opened her heart" to give full attention to the things Paul was saying. The result was "she and the members of her household," that is, her staff and servants, believed the gospel and were baptized in water. No doubt it was by her influence that they believed, so together they became the first body of believers in Europe.

This took place over a period of time. (The Gk. present tenses in v. 14 indicate she kept paying attention to what Paul kept speaking about.) By winning her household to the Lord, Lydia demonstrated her own faithfulness to the Lord. On this basis she besought Paul and his entire company to make her large home their home and headquarters. Then she kept urging them until they finally did so. This became an opportunity to teach and establish a growing assembly. Other women (including Euodia and Syntyche) worked with Paul "in the cause of the gospel" (Phil. 4:2–3).

b. A Demon Cast Out 16:16–18

[16]Once when we were going to the place of prayer, we were met by a slave girl who had a spirit by which she predicted the future. She earned a great deal of money

---

[22]The ancient "royal" purple referred to here was actually a deep shade of red, later called "Turkey red." The product of the shellfish murex, it was very expensive because eight thousand of the shellfish produced only one gram of the dye. (Some think the cloth Lydia sold was dyed with a cheaper dye, from the juice of the madder root.)

for her owners by fortune-telling. ¹⁷This girl followed Paul and the rest of us, shouting, "These men are servants of the Most High God, who are telling you the way to be saved."

Paul, Silas, Timothy, and Luke continued going to "the place of prayer" regularly. One day a demon-possessed slave girl met them on the way there. The Greek says she had a spirit of ventriloquism; that is, a demon spirit controlled her, speaking through her and practicing fortune-telling. The Greek also calls her a "pythoness." The python was the symbol of the Greek god Apollo: Her masters claimed that her fortune-telling was the voice of Apollo. This kind of fortune-telling (Gk. *manteuomenē*, "giving of oracles") brought much money to her masters. It may be implied also that they used her to attract people to other businesses they carried on.

This slave girl kept following Paul and his company shouting, practically shrieking, over and over: "These men are servants of the Most High God,[23] who are telling you the way to be saved."24

¹⁸She kept this up for many days. Finally Paul became so troubled that he turned around and said to the spirit, "In the name of Jesus Christ I command you to come out of her!" At that moment the spirit left her.

This she kept doing "for many days." That is, she did not do it continuously, but during part of every day she would follow them, shouting out the same thing.

Her shrieks and cries must have attracted a great deal of attention. It surely let the city know Paul and his companions were there. However, it was not the kind of witness that brings real glory to God, nor did it proclaim the whole truth. Paul was greatly troubled by her unpleasant shrieking, and he undoubtedly felt it was hindering the work of the Lord. Finally he turned and spoke "to the [evil] spirit" (not to the woman), commanding it "in the name [authority] of Jesus Christ" to come out of her. In this he was following the example of Jesus, who also spoke

23Cf. Gen. 14:18; Isa. 14:14.

24"*The* way" is better translated "*a* way," in that the Gk. has no article. Satan still does not mind calling the gospel "*a* way" of salvation as long as we do not say it is the *only* way.

directly to the demons who possessed people. It came out of her "at that moment." She probably then accepted the gospel.

c. Paul And Barnabas In Prison 16:19–26

19When the owners of the slave girl realized that their hope of making money was gone, they seized Paul and Silas and dragged them into the marketplace to face the authorities.

The slave girl's masters were quite upset when they saw "that their hope of making money was gone." So they seized Paul and Silas and dragged them "into the marketplace [Gk. *agora*] to face the authorities,"[25] that is, before the two praetors, or chief Roman magistrates, of the city.

20They brought them before the magistrates and said, "These men are Jews, and are throwing our city into an uproar 21by advocating customs unlawful for us Romans to accept or practice."

In their accusation they did not mention the real reason they brought Paul and Silas there. Instead, they contemptuously called them big Jewish troublemakers[26] who were proclaiming things "unlawful for . . . Romans to accept [welcome] or practice." Though Judaism was a legal religion in the Roman Empire, it was only tolerated by the majority of the people and was not looked on with any real favor by the government. It did not encourage Jews to convert Romans.

22The crowd joined in the attack against Paul and Silas, and the magistrates ordered them to be stripped and beaten.

The people of Philippi were proud of their status as citizens of a Roman colony and were sensitive to anything that might threaten their privileges. They were ready to believe that Jews could be troublemakers. The accusation of the owners of the slave girl stirred up the crowd in the marketplace. So they "joined in the attack." The chief magistrates then, to satisfy the

---

[25]The marketplace was also a public square and place of assembly.
[26]Gk. *ektarrasousin*, "they exceedingly trouble" our city.

mob, tore the clothes off Paul and Silas (or ordered soldiers to do it)[27] and ordered them to be beaten (flogged) with rods—a common Roman punishment (see 2 Cor. 11:25). All the noise and confusion gave Paul and Silas no opportunity to say a word in their own defense, nor were they able to say a word for the Lord. Instead they suffered as "Jews."

It may be also that Paul at this point deliberately emphasized his Jewishness rather than his Roman citizenship. Otherwise people "might wonder whether only those suitably protected by Roman citizenship should become believers in Christ and they might think it disingenuous for Paul and Silas to ask others to suffer what they themselves were able to avoid."[28]

[23]After they had been severely flogged, they were thrown into prison, and the jailer was commanded to guard them carefully. [24]Upon receiving such orders, he put them in the inner cell and fastened their feet in the stocks.

After many blows, the magistrates had them thrown into prison and ordered the jailer to "guard them carefully" (securely). To make sure they could not escape, the jailer then "put them in the inner cell," "a place reserved for dangerous, low class felons,"[29] and fastened their feet securely in wooden stocks, with their legs painfully forced apart so they could not move them.

[25]About midnight Paul and Silas were praying and singing hymns to God, and the other prisoners were listening to them. [26]Suddenly there was such a violent earthquake that the foundations of the prison were shaken. At once all the prison doors flew open, and everybody's chains came loose.

After all this rough treatment, to be put into such an uncomfortable position must have indeed been most painful. The inner

---

[27]The Gk. reads lit.: "The magistrates, having torn off them, were commanding to beat with rods." This probably means that the magistrates themselves were so worked up that they tore the clothes off of Paul and Silas while calling the soldiers to come with the rods.

[28]Brian M. Rapske, *The Book of Acts and Paul in Roman Custody*, vol. 3 of *Acts in Its First Century Setting*, ed. Winter (Grand Rapids: Wm. B. Eerdmans, 1994), 134.

[29]Ibid., 126–27.

prison was probably damp, cold, and insect infested. Yet Paul and Silas did not complain. We can be sure they did not feel like singing at this point either. They could not move because of the chains and stocks, but they could turn their hearts heavenward. The Greek indicates they prayed for some time. Then they sang praises to God in spite of their circumstances.[30] Undoubtedly as they did so, God brought them a sense of peace and victory.

About midnight Paul and Silas were still "praying and singing hymns" and the "other prisoners were listening." Suddenly a great earthquake shook the prison to its foundations. As the walls swayed back and forth "all the prison doors flew open, and everybody's chains came loose" (they were probably fastened into the wall). As God often does, He used natural forces in a supernatural way with supernatural timing and purpose.

d. The Jailer Converted 16:27–34

[27]The jailer woke up, and when he saw the prison doors open, he drew his sword and was about to kill himself because he thought the prisoners had escaped. [28]But Paul shouted, "Don't harm yourself! We are all here!"

The earthquake woke up the jailer. It seems he immediately rushed to the prison, saw all the doors were open, and jumped to the conclusion that all "the prisoners had escaped." He knew the penalty that would be his if this was so (cf. 12:19; 27:42). Rather than face the trial, shame, and disgraceful death that he expected to come, "he drew his sword," intending to commit suicide.

From the deep darkness of the prison, Paul could see what the jailer was doing even though the jailer could not see into the prison. Immediately he shouted out, telling the jailer not to harm himself, for all the prisoners were still there. The singing of Paul and Silas and the unexpected earthquake must have made them willing to stay. Or, they may have been paralyzed with fright.

[29]The jailer called for lights, rushed in and fell trembling before Paul and Silas. [30]He then brought them out and asked, "Sirs, what must I do to be saved?"

After asking for lights (lamps or torches), the jailer rushed

[30]Cf. 2 Cor. 6:10, "sorrowful, yet always rejoicing."

into the prison. Completely overcome by fear and awe because of what had happened, he "fell trembling before Paul and Silas."

Then, recovering his composure,[31] he brought Paul and Silas out of the prison and asked them, "What must I do to be saved?" This might seem a strange question from a pagan Roman. But he must have remembered the words of the demon spirit that possessed the slave girl: "These men are servants of the Most High God, who are telling . . . the way to be saved" (v. 17).

31They replied, "Believe in the Lord Jesus, and you will be saved—you and your household."

Paul's answer was simple: "Believe in the Lord Jesus, and you will be saved" (cf. John 6:28–29); then he quickly added, "you and your household." By this Paul did not mean that the jailer's household would be saved simply because the jailer was. Paul wanted the jailer to know that the offer was not limited to him, that the same kind of faith would bring salvation to all who believed (cf. Rom. 10:9–10). He probably could see that the earthquake and its results had affected them all. He wanted to conceive of them all being saved, not just one.[32]

32Then they spoke the word of the Lord to him and to all the others in his house.

Paul and Silas then presented the gospel to all who were in the household. Thus they explained to them all what it meant to believe in Jesus and what it meant to be saved.

33At that hour of the night the jailer took them and washed their wounds; then immediately he and all his family were baptized. 34The jailer brought them into his house and set a meal before them; he was filled with joy because he had come to believe in God—he and his whole family.

Converted, the jailer took the apostles and lovingly "washed their wounds" from the beating, and immediately he and all his family and servants were baptized in water. This was probably

---

[31]Codex Bezae (D) adds that he first secured the other prisoners. This was undoubtedly true.

[32]See Hackett, *Commentary on the Acts,* 191.

done in a pool in the courtyard of his house. After this he took the apostles back inside the house and set before them a table loaded with food. The whole household was then full of joy[33] because they believed in God with a faith that was strong and continuing.

Some writers try to use this passage to argue for infant baptism since the entire household was baptized in water. But when we examine the passage more carefully it is easy to see that everyone in the household heard the Word of God, everyone believed, and everyone was full of joy. Clearly, no infants were included. It is possible that the jailer had no small children. He was actually the "governor" of the prison and was probably an older man, to have been appointed to this position. It is probable too that Roman custom would not consider babies or small children as part of the household until they reached a certain age.

Their joy was so great (cf. NASB, "rejoiced greatly," and Phillips, "overjoyed") that it might translate they "jumped for joy." Again, Luke does not tell everything every time. We can be sure that part of the reason for that great joy was the fact they were also baptized in the Holy Spirit and spoke in other tongues as the early believers did on the Day of Pentecost (Acts 2:4) and at the house of Cornelius (10:46). After all, would God do any less for these Gentile believers than He did for Cornelius?

e. Paul And Silas Released 16:35-40

35When it was daylight, the magistrates sent their officers to the jailer with the order: "Release those men." 36The jailer told Paul, "The magistrates have ordered that you and Silas be released. Now you can leave. Go in peace."

The rejoicing probably continued the rest of the night. It would be hard to sleep after such experiences. In the morning the chief magistrates sent "officers," orderlies or law-enforcement agents called "lictors,"[34] to tell the jailer to let Paul and Silas go.

---

[33]The Gk. is lit. "He rejoiced with all his household, having believed in God" (cf. NEB, RSV, JB, TEV et al.).

[34]They carried an ax projecting from a bundle of sticks, symbolizing their authority to carry out the magistrates' judgments.

The jailer passed the word to them that they could leave the prison area and "go in peace."

37But Paul said to the officers: "They beat us publicly without a trial, even though we are Roman citizens, and threw us into prison. And now do they want to get rid of us quietly? No! Let them come themselves and escort us out."

Paul knew, however, that the crowds still had the wrong idea about them and about both Jews and Christians. Paul therefore refused to sneak away like a guilty criminal. The magistrates had beaten them publicly, without any semblance of a trial, "even though [they were] Roman citizens,"[35] and then just as publicly thrown them into prison. Paul refers to this as an insult (1 Thess. 2:2). Were they now going to dismiss them secretly? "No! Let them come themselves and escort us out." In this way the city would know that the charges were false and that Paul and Silas were restored to good standing in the community. This would bring advantage to the new body of believers as well.

38The officers reported this to the magistrates, and when they heard that Paul and Silas were Roman citizens, they were alarmed. 39They came to appease them and escorted them from the prison, requesting them to leave the city.

When this was reported to the chief magistrates, they realized they had been wrong in yielding to the mob and not questioning Paul and Silas. "They were alarmed" (Gk. *ephobēthēsan*, "they became frightened"), too, because Roman citizens had rights to trial before punishment, rights that could not be ignored with impunity. They knew also that if Paul and Silas were to lodge a complaint with the government in Rome, severe punishment would result. So they came very humbly and begged[36] Paul and Silas not to bring charges against them. Then they led them out of the prison compound publicly. (Paul and Silas by this time had been taken from the jailer's house back to the prison itself.)

---

[35]See Howard Clark Kee, *To Every Nation Under Heaven: The Acts of the Apostles* (Harrisburg, Pa.: Trinity Press International, 1997), 200, 201, for his excursus on Roman citizenship.

[36]Implied by the Gk. *parakalesan*, "implore, appeal to." (See NASB, NLT.)

The magistrates then asked them to leave the city. This was not because they were unwilling to have the gospel preached in Philippi. But they were afraid that Paul and Silas might change their minds. Or, perhaps they were afraid that the sympathies of the people would now swing to Paul and Silas and against them. So they asked the apostles to leave for the sake of peace in the city. We can be sure also that there was no more persecution of the believers as long as these magistrates were in power.

⁴⁰After Paul and Silas came out of the prison, they went to Lydia's house, where they met with the brothers and encouraged them. Then they left.

Before leaving the city, Paul and Silas went to Lydia's house where a large courtyard (or upper room)³⁷ was full of believers who were gathered, undoubtedly praying for Paul and Silas. How Paul and Silas encouraged them is reflected in Philippians 1:25–29. After the meeting, the apostles left town.³⁸

Evidently Luke did not accompany them. The next chapter (Acts 17:14) shows that Timothy did leave with them, but Luke no longer says "we." He obviously stayed in Philippi to give further encouragement and teaching to the assembly there. He was still in Philippi in Acts 20:6.

6. MINISTRY IN THESSALONICA 17:1–9

¹When they had passed through Amphipolis and Apollonia, they came to Thessalonica, where there was a Jewish synagogue.

After Paul, Silas, and Timothy left Philippi, they proceeded westward on the Via Egnatia. The next two towns of any size, each about a day's journey apart, apparently had no Jewish synagogue; and so they pushed on to Thessalonica (one hundred miles from Philippi), "where there was a Jewish synagogue." Still important today, Thessalonica was the most important city of

---

³⁷See 193, n. 7.

³⁸Note that the believers were no longer limited to a few women. Brothers took the leadership, though in Heb. usage "brothers" included the sisters (just as the "children of Israel" in Heb. is literally the "sons of Israel" but included both men and women).

ancient Macedonia. It was founded in 315 B.C. and named by Cassander, its founder, for his wife, who was a stepsister of Alexander the Great. Made a free city in 42 B.C., it became the capital of the second district of Macedonia. The Roman proconsul resided there. Paul, directed by the Spirit, stopped at this strategic center and proceeded to establish a church.

²As his custom was, Paul went into the synagogue, and on three Sabbath days he reasoned with them from the Scriptures, ³explaining and proving that the Christ had to suffer and rise from the dead. "This Jesus I am proclaiming to you is the Christ," he said.

Again Luke draws attention to Paul's "custom" of going to the Jew first and taking advantage of their background and of the opportunity given by the synagogue to teach. For three successive Sabbaths, Paul "reasoned with them," undoubtedly following the same pattern as in Pisidian Antioch (Acts 13:16–41). As always he opened with Scriptures that prophesied the Messiah, explaining them fully. That is, he set them out in such a way that they clearly showed it was God's divine purpose for the Messiah to "suffer and rise from the dead."[39] As in Antioch also, he showed that none of these prophecies could apply to anyone but Jesus. Therefore, "this Jesus" truly is "the Christ," the Messiah, God's anointed Prophet, Priest, and King.

⁴Some of the Jews were persuaded and joined Paul and Silas, as did a large number of God-fearing Greeks and not a few prominent women.

Paul's reasoning with them was effective. Some of the Jews were "persuaded" (believed in Jesus and obeyed the gospel; thus they were baptized in water and in the Holy Spirit) and decided to join Paul and Silas. So did a large crowd of God-fearing Greeks, including a number of "prominent women," some filling high positions in the city, others the wives of the chief men of the city. Thus the

---

[39]F. F. Bruce notes that other NT writers insist that "these two facts" are "the foundation of the gospel (cf. 1 Th. 4:14; 1 Cor. 15:3f.; 1 Pet. 1:11). The necessity *(edei)* [Gk. "had to," v. 3] lay in their being the subject of OT prophecy, which had to be fulfilled since it expressed 'the definite plan and foreknowledge of God' (2:23)." *Acts: Greek Text*, 369.

Gentile converts far outnumbered the Jewish believers.

First Thessalonians 2:1–13 gives a further description of the ministry of Paul and Silas at this time. Their preaching and ministry were very effective. Even though they were treated outrageously at Philippi, this did not cause them to be timid or fearful. At Thessalonica they preached openly and boldly with pure motives as servants of Jesus Christ. They were gentle to the new converts also, giving them all kinds of loving, tender care. Yet they were firm in their stand for righteousness and encouraged every one of them to live in a manner worthy of the God who called them to His own kingdom and glory. It is obvious that after the three weeks preaching in the synagogue, Paul and Silas continued to preach and teach in the city, probably in Jason's house (v. 5).[40] First and 2 Thessalonians show that Paul covered all the great truths of the gospel. However, both letters show the Thessalonians were loving, self-sacrificing people who suffered persecution and stood true, but the death of some believers brought questions about the Rapture and about the Second Coming.

> **5But the Jews were jealous; so they rounded up some bad characters from the marketplace, formed a mob and started a riot in the city. They rushed to Jason's house in search of Paul and Silas in order to bring them out to the crowd.**

After some time the Jews (probably the leaders) who rejected Paul's message became "jealous" of the increasing numbers of Gentiles who were accepting the gospel. These Jews rebelled against what God was doing and even went so far as to forbid Paul and his companions to talk to Gentiles about their salvation (1 Thess. 2:14–16).

When they saw that the Gentiles continued to respond to the gospel and paid no attention to them, these unbelieving Jews proceeded to stir up a riot. First, they "rounded up some bad characters," marketplace loungers who were always ready to join any agitators who came along. Then, with their help, they "formed

---

[40]In the Book of Acts all churches were established in large houses of wealthy converts. They would often meet in an upper room; cf. 20:9. See Kee, *To Every Nation,* 205–6. Philippian believers sent Paul aid several times while he was in Thessalonica (Phil. 4:16).

a mob" and set up a disturbance that threw the whole city into a panic. "In search of Paul and Silas," they then "rushed to [Gk. *epistantes*, "assaulted"] Jason's house."[41] But evidently the word had already gotten to the apostles and they had left for another part of the city.

> 6But when they did not find them, they dragged Jason and some other brothers before the city officials, shouting: "These men who have caused trouble all over the world have now come here, 7and Jason has welcomed them into his house. They are all defying Caesar's decrees, saying that there is another king, one called Jesus."

Because Paul and Silas were not there, the mob "dragged Jason and some other brothers before the city officials."[42] There were five or six of them, and they were the chief magistrates of the city.

As usual, the accusation did not reveal the real reason for wanting to get rid of Paul and Silas. The unbelieving Jews and their coconspirators accused them of having "caused trouble all over the world." This was a phrase used of political agitators or revolutionaries who had caused trouble elsewhere and who upset not only the status quo, but everything. They also accused Jason of welcoming these "troublemakers" to his house and joining with them to practice things contrary to the decrees of Caesar, speaking of "another king" (really, a rival emperor), Jesus. (Cf. John 19:15.)

> 8When they heard this, the crowd and the city officials were thrown into turmoil.

These things disturbed both "the crowd and the city officials." Part of their problem may have been that they knew Jason and many of the other converts and had not seen any evidence of political activity. It is probable, also, that the believers who were "prominent women" (v. 4) included wives of some of these city officials.

> 9Then they made Jason and the others post bond and let them go.

Apparently the city officials did not take the charges seriously,

---

[41]Implies a house church was already established there.

[42]Gk. *politarchas*. Archaeologists have found sixteen inscriptions referring to these politarchs. They were Macedonians, not Romans.

but to satisfy the crowd they "made Jason and the others post bond" (Gk. *hikanon,* "security"). This probably means Jason and his friends provided bail as a guarantee that Paul and Silas would leave the city and not come back lest there be further disturbance.[43] This was later used by Satan to hinder Paul's return (see 1 Thess. 2:17–18).

Paul probably refers to this also when he says the Thessalonians "in spite of severe suffering . . . welcomed the message with the joy given by the Holy Spirit" (1 Thess. 1:6). The unbelieving Jews had apparently begun causing trouble some time before the incident with Jason. In fact, Paul indicates that from the beginning he spoke the gospel of God to them "in spite of strong opposition" (1 Thess. 2:2). Then, when Paul wanted to return, Satan hindered him, probably by bringing up the question of the posted bond. Thus Paul was not able to return when he wanted to do so.

The Thessalonian church remained strong, however. They became imitators of Paul and his company and "became a model to all the believers in Macedonia and Achaia," ringing out the Lord's message, so that their faith became "known everywhere" (1 Thess. 1:6–8). They became missionaries themselves.

7. NOBLE BEREANS 17:10–15

[10]As soon as it was night, the brothers sent Paul and Silas away to Berea. On arriving there, they went to the Jewish synagogue. [11]Now the Bereans were of more noble character than the Thessalonians, for they received the message with great eagerness and examined the Scriptures every day to see if what Paul said was true.

The Christian brothers saw how bitter and determined the unbelieving Jews were, so they took no chances: By night they "sent Paul and Silas away to Berea,"[44] about fifty miles to the southwest on the road to Greece. Although the second most important city in Macedonia, it was off the main road, the Via Egnatia, which Paul and his company had been following; the local believers may have thought they would be safer there.

---

[43]See Hackett, *Commentary on the Acts,* 196.

[44]Gk. *Beroian.* Timothy may have been left at Philippi; v. 14 shows he later joined them at Berea.

The Bereans did respond quite differently than the Thessalonians. Instead of reacting against Paul's message, they "received the message" with all kinds of eagerness, zeal, and enthusiasm. Even more important, they "examined the Scriptures" daily, searching it out like lawyers investigating a case, "to see if what Paul said was true."

Because of their attitude and their searching of the Scriptures, which obviously they loved, the Bible says they were "of more noble character" than the Jews in Thessalonica. Because they searched the Scriptures these Bereans not only set an example for us all, but Paul did not have to correct them later, as he did so many other churches.[45]

12Many of the Jews believed, as did also a number of prominent Greek women and many Greek men.

In Thessalonica some of the Jews believed; others just let their old prejudices guide them, and they reacted against the gospel. In Berea, however, "many of the Jews believed," probably the majority of them. There was no opposition stirred up among them. Many Gentiles also believed, both women who had an honorable position in society (as in Thessalonica), and men as well.[46] Thus a strong church developed with both men and women giving leadership.

13When the Jews in Thessalonica learned that Paul was preaching the word of God at Berea, they went there too, agitating the crowds and stirring them up.

Though the synagogue at Berea caused no trouble, the news of Paul's effective proclamation of the gospel there reached the Jews of Thessalonica. They came to Berea then and did the same thing they had done in their home city, "agitating the crowds and stirring them up," trying to rouse mob violence against Paul.

14The brothers immediately sent Paul to the coast, but Silas and Timothy stayed at Berea. 15The men who escorted Paul brought him to Athens and then left with instructions for Silas and Timothy to join him as soon as possible.

---

[45]They searched the Scriptures, not looking for proof texts to uphold their own preconceived ideas but seeking to find the meaning intended by the Holy Spirit, who had inspired the Scriptures.

[46]These included Sopater the son of Pyrrhus; see 20:4.

Before the Thessalonian Jews could do any harm, the Berean brothers hurried Paul off in the direction of the coast (of the Aegean Sea), probably intending to send him away by ship. Silas and Timothy stayed behind to teach and encourage the new believers further.

Those who were conducting Paul then changed directions, possibly because they got word of the Thessalonian Jews plotting something else. So they (or a part of the group) took Paul overland to Athens.[47] He then sent them back "with instructions for Silas and Timothy to join him as soon as possible."

8. Ministry In Athens 17:16–34

a. Encountered By Philosophers 17:16–21

16While Paul was waiting for them in Athens, he was greatly distressed to see that the city was full of idols. 17So he reasoned in the synagogue with the Jews and the God-fearing Greeks, as well as in the marketplace day by day with those who happened to be there.

Athens was famous for its Acropolis and all its temples. About six hundred years before Paul's time it was a world leader in art and philosophy. By this time, however, it had lost its glory. No longer politically or commercially important, its leadership in culture and education had been overtaken by Alexandria in Egypt. Nevertheless, Athens still nurtured the memory of its past, and its temples were still beautiful examples of the best in Greek architecture. Even so, everywhere Paul looked he saw a city that was "full of idols,"[48] and this caused his own spirit to be "greatly distressed" (almost "angered" or "outraged") within him.

As always, Paul first went to the synagogue on the Sabbath and preached to the Jews and the godly Gentiles there. But he was concerned about the rest of the Gentiles too. Every day he talked to whoever "happened to be" in the "marketplace" (Gk. *agora,* not only a marketplace but also a center of public political and cultural life).

---

[47]Codex D specifies that they went by road.

[48]One ancient writer said there were three thousand in the city. Many were out in public view.

¹⁸A group of Epicurean and Stoic philosophers began to dispute with him. Some of them asked, "What is this babbler trying to say?" Others remarked, "He seems to be advocating foreign gods." They said this because Paul was preaching the good news about Jesus and the resurrection.

In the marketplace some Epicurean and Stoic philosophers "began to dispute with him" (Gk. *suneballon auto,* "kept encountering" Paul with hostile intent). Epicureans were followers of Epicurus (342–270 B.C.), who said that Nature is the supreme teacher and provides sensations, feelings, and anticipations for testing truth. By "feelings" Epicurus meant pleasure and pain. These he said could be used to distinguish between the good and the evil around us. He also taught that the world was formed by a chance clustering of atoms and that the gods were incapable of wrath and indifferent to human weakness, neither intervening nor participating in human affairs. Thus he denied the possibility of miracles, prophecy, and divine providence, and considered death to be endless sleep.[49] In the beginning what Epicurus meant by "pleasure" was real happiness. At first his followers merely sought a quiet life free from fear, pain, and anger. Later, some made sensual pleasures the goal of life.

Stoics were followers of Zeno, a Semite of Citium (336–264 B.C.) who came to Athens in 320 B.C. and taught for about twenty years in the Painted Colonnade, or *stoa,* which gave them their name. He believed in a creative power and made duty, reason (or accordance with divine reason), and self-sufficiency the goal of life. He encouraged his followers to accept and submit to the laws of nature and conscience and to try to be indifferent to pleasure, pain, joy, and grief. His followers included Cicero (106–43 B.C.), the Roman statesman Seneca (4 B.C.–A.D. 65), and Marcus Aurelius Antoninus (A.D. 121–180), the adopted son of the emperor Antoninus Pius (A.D. 138–161).

Some of these philosophers were quite contemptuous of Paul's gospel and called him a "babbler" (Gk. *spermologos,* "a seed-picker"). This term was also used as slang for parasites and ignorant pla-

---

[49]See Norman W. DeWitt, *St. Paul and Epicurus* (Minneapolis: University of Minnesota Press, 1954), 9–10, 20.

giarists who picked up scraps of information from others and presented them as their own. Then, because Paul preached "the good news about Jesus and the resurrection," they said he seemed to be proclaiming "foreign gods" (Gk. *daimoniōn,* a term used in the NT most often of demons).[50] The philosophers were primarily concerned about their being "foreign" and therefore illegal.

> [19]Then they took him and brought him to a meeting of the Areopagus, where they said to him, "May we know what this new teaching is that you are presenting? [20]You are bringing some strange ideas to our ears, and we want to know what they mean." [21](All the Athenians and the foreigners who lived there spent their time doing nothing but talking about and listening to the latest ideas.)

Apparently, they felt Paul's teaching was dangerous to their own ideas and philosophies, so they "took him" (the Gk. *epilabomenoi* means they seized him against his will) and brought him before the Council of the Areopagus, the supreme court of Athens. This court formerly met on the Hill of Ares,[51] a rocky ridge facing the foot of the Acropolis. There is some evidence the court met in a colonnade in the public marketplace in New Testament times, but it retained its original name.

The Council politely asked Paul the meaning of his "new teaching," which was bewildering them. It was not an unusual request. The Athenians as a whole, as well as "the foreigners who lived there," were full of curiosity and "spent their [leisure] time" telling and listening to "the latest ideas" ("the latest novelty").[52]

b. Message To The Council Of Mars' Hill 17:22–34

> [22]Paul then stood up in the meeting of the Areopagus and said: "Men of Athens! I see that in every way you are very religious. [23]For as I walked around and looked carefully at your objects of worship, I even found an altar

[50]Some commentators say that the plural means they took "Jesus" (the Gk. is masculine) and "Resurrection" (the Gk. word is feminine) to be a pair of deities.

[51]Mars' hill (cf. KJV, v. 22). The Greek Ares was identified with the Roman Mars, the god of war.

[52]Johannes Munck, *The Acts of the Apostles,* rev. William F. Albright and C. S. Mann, vol. 31 of *Anchor Bible Series* (Garden City, N.Y.: Doubleday & Co.), 168.

with this inscription: TO AN UNKNOWN GOD. Now what you worship as something unknown I am going to proclaim to you. 24"The God who made the world and everything in it is the Lord of heaven and earth and does not live in temples built by hands.

Standing in the midst of the Council, Paul wisely began in a positive way. The translation that says they were "too supersti-tious" (v. 22, KJV) sounds as if he was intending to insult them. Though the Greek can bear that meaning, here it is better to translate it with the meaning of "very religious" (see also v. 22, NKJV), in the sense of very respectful to their gods.[53]

Then Paul used an inscription on an altar in Athens to give him an opportunity to speak about the one true God in contrast to their many gods. The "unknown god" of one of their altars, whom they worshiped without knowing Him (and who was therefore not a foreign god), is the Creator and Lord of heaven and earth. Thus, He is too great to "live in temples built by hands." Here Paul is echoing a truth of the Old Testament, stat-ed by Solomon (1 Kings 8:27) and then by the prophets (Isa. 57:15; 66:1). What a contrast to the little gods of Athens whose idols they washed and pretended to feed!

25And he is not served by human hands, as if he needed anything, because he himself gives all men life and breath and everything else.

The true God does not need to be "served [cared for, attended, treated, as a physician would tend a patient] by human hands, as if he needed anything." How could He need anything or any care? He is the true Source of and Giver of "all . . . life and breath and everything else." As James 1:17 points out, "Every good and perfect gift is from above"—from Him.

26From one man he made every nation of men, that they should inhabit the whole earth; and he determined the times set for them and the exact places where they should live.

God also has made "from one man" (Gk. *ex henos*, "out of

[53]This is the way the Greek philosopher Aristotle used it.

one"),[54] that is, from Adam, "every nation" of humankind to dwell on the whole face of the earth. We are all part of Adam's race and no one has room for any special pride of ancestry or of race. (Athenians believed they were a separate race specially created from the soil of Greece.) God also "determined," or fixed, both "the times" (appointed seasons, occasions, opportunities) and "exact places" (boundaries of habitation) of humankind, that is, by separating the dry land from the waters (Gen. 1:9–10). This also implies He regulates the rise and fall of nations (Dan. 4:34–35; 5:18–21).

> **[27]God did this so that men would seek him and perhaps reach out for him and find him, though he is not far from each one of us.**

By this Paul does not mean people could not or should not move from one place to another. All peoples have done that to a greater or lesser extent. Rather, Paul meant that God brought people to the places and times where they would have opportunities to seek God and find Him (cf. Rom. 1:20–21).

> **[28]'For in him we live and move and have our being.' As some of your own poets have said, 'We are his offspring.'**

Actually, it should not be hard to find Him, for, as Paul went on to say, He is not far from each one of us. "For in him we live and move and have our being." This statement is a quotation from one of the ancient poets, possibly Minos or Epimenides (ca. 600 B.C.) of Crete.[55] As one of their own poets, Aratus (315–240 B.C.) of Cilicia, had said, "We are his offspring."

> **[29]"Therefore since we are God's offspring, we should not think that the divine being is like gold or silver or stone—an image made by man's design and skill. [30]In the past God overlooked such ignorance, but now he commands all people everywhere to repent.**

Being the offspring of the true God (in the sense of being cre-

---

[54]Some ancient manuscripts add the word "blood," i.e., from one blood line—which does not change the meaning.

[55]See Charles W. Carter and Ralph Earle, *The Acts of the Apostles* (Grand Rapids: Zondervan Publishing House, 1959), 261.

ated in His image), humans would be totally unreasonable to think of the divine nature as "gold or silver or stone," an engraved work of the art and meditations or thoughts of a human being. Old Testament teaching is strong and clear in what it says about idols and their makers. (See Pss. 115:4–8; 135:15–18; Isa. 40:18–22; 41:24; 44:9–17.)

All of this idolatry showed humankind's "ignorance" of what God is really like. This ignorance, God in mercy and long-suffering overlooked "in the past." "But now" He (through the gospel) was commanding "all people everywhere to repent," that is, change their minds and attitudes toward God by turning to Him through Christ and the gospel.

31For he has set a day when he will judge the world with justice by the man he has appointed. He has given proof of this to all men by raising him from the dead."

Though God has been patient, this repentance is imperative. God has "set a day" in which He is about to judge the inhabited earth with justice (in righteousness) "by the man he has appointed," whom He has designated. That is, there is a judgment day coming and God has revealed who the judge will be (cf. Dan. 7:13–14; John 5:22,27). That this day is actually coming and that there will be no escape from it, God guaranteed to everyone by His raising that Man (Jesus) "out from among the dead ones" (lit. trans.).

32When they heard about the resurrection of the dead, some of them sneered, but others said, "We want to hear you again on this subject."

The mention of "the resurrection of the dead" brought immediate mockery from some. The Epicureans, especially, refused to believe that any god would show wrath or perform miracles. Many other Greeks believed in an immortal soul that existed in a shadowy Hades after death, but they considered the body a prison and had little regard for its being resurrected.[56] Many therefore scoffed and sneered at Paul. "But others," who seemed to have a desire for the truth, said they wanted "to hear [him] again on this subject."

---

[56]See Stanley M. Horton, *Our Destiny: Biblical Teachings on the Last Things* (Springfield, Mo.: Logion Press, 1996), 70–71.

> ³³At that, Paul left the Council. ³⁴A few men became followers of Paul and believed. Among them was Dionysius, a member of the Areopagus, also a woman named Damaris, and a number of others.

These sessions of the Council of the Areopagus were open to the public. Some men did respond and joined Paul, believing the gospel. "Among them was Dionysius, a member of the Areopagus" and thus a very important person in Athens, "part of the intellectual aristocracy."[57] A prominent woman named Damaris along with others also joined them and believed.

This is the second recorded sermon of Paul given to Gentiles who had no background in, or knowledge of, the Old Testament Scriptures. In Lystra Paul had used a similar approach, drawing attention to God as the Creator (Acts 14:15–17). But here more details of his approach are given.

With the Jews who claimed to believe the Scriptures, Paul always based his reasoning on the Old Testament. But with Gentiles like these, he was guided by the Holy Spirit to use a different approach. His reasoning was still based on Scripture, but he started where the people were and led them to the point where he could introduce the gospel. Missionaries in recent times have sometimes had to do the same sort of thing. One missionary to Amazon jungle Indians found he could not start with John 3:16, for his listeners had no word for love and the only world they knew was the valley and tributary river where they lived. So he started with creation and gradually led them to the point where they could understand about Jesus.

Some writers suppose that Paul was disappointed in the results of this approach.[58] They say that his disappointment caused him to say to the Corinthians, "I resolved to know nothing while I was with you except Jesus Christ and him crucified"

---

[57]William Barclay, *The Acts of the Apostles,* 2d ed. (Philadelphia: Westminster Press, 1955), 144.

[58]See Rackham, *Acts of the Apostles,* 320. But N. B. Stonehouse, *The Areopagus Address* (Grand Rapids: Wm. B. Eerdmans, 1957), 39ff., has a good answer to this opinion (cited by Bruce, *Acts: Greek Text,* 365). See also Marion L. Soards, "The Historical and Cultural Setting of Luke-Acts," in *New Views on Luke and Acts,* ed. Earl Richard (Collegeville, Minn.: Liturgical Press, 1990), 46.

(1 Cor. 2:2). But such a statement does not mean Paul said nothing more about other truths. Rather, he meant he would see, experience, and live out the crucified Christ.

It seems probable also that some of the Jews and God-fearing Gentiles in the synagogue at Athens believed and that they joined with these pagan Gentiles who had no biblical background. Together they must have formed a thriving assembly that did not have the problems faced by some of the other assemblies, so they did not need any corrective letters from Paul. Later, in his first letter to the Corinthians, Paul referred to the household of Stephanas as being the "first converts in Achaia," or Greece[59] (1 Cor. 16:15). However, this may stem from Athens having been considered a free, independent city, and not a part of Greece.[60]

Luke does not give any more details, but it is clear that Paul left a body of believers, an assembly, behind in Athens. Tradition says Dionysius the Areopagite was its first pastor (elder, bishop). Nothing more is said of Damaris, but as a woman of prominence she must have influenced many to accept the gospel.

9. MINISTRY IN CORINTH 18:1–17

a. Working With Priscilla And Aquila 18:1–4

[1]After this, Paul left Athens and went to Corinth.

Why did Paul leave Athens when he had intended to wait for Silas and Timothy (Acts 17:16)? Luke does not tell us.[61] But Paul did leave a number of believers behind, and the Greek indicates he separated himself from them with regret.

He may have left Athens because of personal need: He found no opportunity to carry on his trade of tentmaking. Athens was not a commercial center. Paul included among his sufferings for

---

[59]In NT times Achaia included the southern part of what is modern Greece; Macedonia included the northern part.

[60]See Carter and Earle, *Acts of the Apostles,* 263.

[61]There must have been some communication with them, since they knew to join Paul in Corinth (v. 5). Bruce suggests on the basis of 1 Thess. 3:1–2,6 that they did meet Paul in Athens earlier and Paul sent Timothy back to Thessalonica and Silas to somewhere in Macedonia (18:5). F. F. Bruce, *The Book of Acts,* rev. ed. (Grand Rapids: Wm. B. Eerdmans, 1988), 328.

the Lord's sake times when he did not have enough to eat, that is, enforced fasting for financial reasons (2 Cor. 11:27).

On the other hand, he may have left Athens because of the great need in Corinth. Originally a city-state competitive with Athens, Corinth had a history as a prosperous commercial center. Involved in rebellion against Rome, it was destroyed in 146 B.C. and was not rebuilt until Julius Caesar took an interest in it a century later. He made it a Roman colony, and it again became prosperous. The Romans in 46 B.C. probably resettled Jews there. Then Augustus made it the capital of the province of Achaia in 27 B.C. But it became a center of idolatry and licentiousness (as it had been before its destruction by the Romans). The Greeks even coined a new word to express extreme sexual immorality and profligacy—"to Corinthianize." The Corinthians were encouraged in this immorality by their worship of the so-called goddess of love, Aphrodite.

> ²There he met a Jew named Aquila, a native of Pontus, who had recently come from Italy with his wife Priscilla, because Claudius had ordered all the Jews to leave Rome. Paul went to see them, ³and because he was a tentmaker as they were, he stayed and worked with them.

At Corinth Paul met a husband and wife who were to become some of his most faithful friends and fellow laborers in the gospel. The husband, Aquila, was a Jew, "a native of Pontus," a Roman province located in northern Asia Minor, east of Bithynia, on the Black Sea. Since Aquila ("eagle") was a common slave name in Rome, there is speculation that when the Romans conquered Pontus, Aquila's family was captured and sold or given away as slaves in Rome. Later many of the Jewish slaves were set free. There was a large class of freedmen in Rome who were set up in business by their former masters or who carried on trades.

The name Priscilla, a diminutive of Prisca (see 2 Tim. 4:19, KJV), indicates that she was an upper-class Roman. It is at least possible that her father had been the owner of Aquila, who may have helped her to believe in the one true God, the God of Israel. Then, when her father set Aquila free he married Priscilla.

They had recently come to Corinth from Italy, the fourth

Roman emperor, Claudius,[62] having "ordered all the Jews to leave Rome."[63] Paul came to them and found in their home a place to live and to carry on his trade, for they also were tentmakers and had been able to establish their business in Corinth successfully.[64] Paul worked with them "in order not to be a burden to anyone while [he] preached the gospel of God" (1 Thess. 2:9).

⁴Every Sabbath he reasoned in the synagogue, trying to persuade Jews and Greeks.

Luke's reference to the emperor's edict may imply that Priscilla and Aquila were Christians before Paul met them; further, Paul identifies his first converts in Achaia as "the household of Stephanas" (1 Cor. 16:15). In any case if Priscilla and Aquila were not believers when Paul met them, he soon won them to the Lord. They became faithful followers of Christ. We can be sure they accompanied him to the synagogue every Sabbath and encouraged him as he sought to persuade both Jews and Greeks.

b. Turning To The Gentiles 18:5–11

⁵When Silas and Timothy came from Macedonia, Paul devoted himself exclusively to preaching, testifying to the Jews that Jesus was the Christ.

---

[62]Tiberius Claudius Caesar Augustus Germanicus ruled A.D. 41–54. Bruce, *Commentary,* 368, prefers the date of A.D. 49–50 for this expulsion. Paul probably arrived in Corinth in the fall of A.D. 50.

[63]The Roman historian Suetonius said this expulsion was due to Jews who rioted because of "Chrestus." It is reasonable to suppose that those who brought the gospel to Rome encountered Jewish opposition like Paul did in Asia Minor and Greece.

[64]Some writers believe they were also leather workers and makers of felted cloth for tents. See J. W. Packer, *Acts of the Apostles* (Cambridge, England: Cambridge University Press, 1975), 152. Paul's native province of Cilicia was, however, famous for its goats' hair cloth, most of which was used for tentmaking, and tentmaking would be an obvious trade for him, as a future rabbi, to learn. Jewish rabbis were expected to learn a trade; most did not believe in taking money for their teaching. Many also believed that hard work would help to keep them from sin. See Bruce, *Commentary,* 367. See also Brian M. Rapske, "Acts Travel and Shipwreck," in *Book of Acts in Its Graeco-Roman Setting,* ed. Gill and Gempf, 7. He suggests the tents were made of leather and that Paul carried a bag of cutting tools, awls, and a sharpening stone.

When Silas and Timothy came to Corinth from Macedonia, they brought an offering for Paul (2 Cor. 11:9; Phil. 4:14–15). So Paul was able to give himself "exclusively to preaching" (cf. Acts 6:4). That is, the Spirit put unusual pressure on him to preach the Word. Jeremiah had a similar experience when he felt the Word of God "like a fire shut up in [his] bones" (Jer. 20:9).

Paul wrote 1 Thessalonians shortly after they came, for they brought good news of the faith and love of the believers there (1 Thess. 3:6–10). The enemies of the gospel had not been able to turn them away from the Lord or from Paul. During his painful circumstances and crushing pressure or persecution, their faith and continuance in the gospel cheered him and relieved the pressure of his passionate concern for them, giving him new courage to go on (3:7).

Apparently, up to this point there had been no great response to the gospel in Corinth. Now he felt such pressure from the Word that he gave witness with greater and greater intensity and zeal. Everywhere, he declared the fact "that Jesus was the Christ" (Messiah), God's anointed Prophet, Priest, and King. The word "testifying" indicates an emphasis on his personal experience as well (cf. 1 Cor. 2:1–4).[65]

6But when the Jews opposed Paul and became abusive, he shook out his clothes in protest and said to them, "Your blood be on your own heads! I am clear of my responsibility. From now on I will go to the Gentiles."

Paul's increased intensity in the synagogue caused most of the unbelieving Jews to cease their indifference and line up against the gospel. In opposing Paul, they even became "abusive" (Gk. *blasphēmountōn,* "blaspheming"—not God, but Paul), speaking against him and the gospel.

This was too much for Paul. So he "shook out his clothes" (outer garments, or robes; cf. Neh. 5:13; Acts 13:51) against them as a sign that he was rejecting their blasphemy. Then he declared that their "blood be on [their] own heads," that is, that they would be responsible for the judgment God would send on them. He had warned them, and he was clear of his responsibil-

[65]Blaiklock, *Acts,* 177.

ity. They would understand, of course, that he was referring to the responsibility God put on Ezekiel to warn the people (Ezek. 3:16-21). Paul had done his part with respect to warning the Jews. From now on (in Corinth)[66] he would "go to the Gentiles."

> **[7]Then Paul left the synagogue and went next door to the house of Titius Justus, a worshiper of God. [8]Crispus, the synagogue ruler, and his entire household believed in the Lord; and many of the Corinthians who heard him believed and were baptized.**

Paul then "left the synagogue and went next door" to the house of a God-fearing Gentile named Titius Justus.[67] There he began to preach the gospel.

Paul, Silas, and Timothy were not the only ones to leave the synagogue. Even the ruler of the synagogue, Crispus, made a decision to believe in the Lord, and his "entire household" (including close relatives and servants) followed his example and made the same decision (see 1 Cor. 1:14). "Many of the [Gentile] Corinthians" also "believed and were baptized."

> **[9]One night the Lord spoke to Paul in a vision: "Do not be afraid; keep on speaking, do not be silent. [10]For I am with you, and no one is going to attack and harm you, because I have many people in this city."**

The Lord confirmed to Paul that he had done the right thing: In a night vision Jesus told Paul not to be afraid. The form of the Greek used here indicates Paul was beginning to fear that he would have to leave Corinth as he had so many other cities when persecution began. But Jesus told him that he should "keep on speaking" the Word in Corinth and "not be silent." The Lord was with him, as He had promised His disciples He would be (Matt. 28:20). He promised further that He would not allow anyone to attack him or harm him in Corinth, for He had "many people in this city." That is, many would yet come to Jesus and become part of the true people of God (cf. Acts 13:48).

---

[66]As in Acts 13:46, this was a local shift in emphasis, not a general one.

[67]His Roman name indicates he was a Roman citizen. Sir William Ramsay and others have suggested that his full name was Gaius Titius Justus and that he was the Gaius mentioned in Rom. 16:23 and 1 Cor. 1:14. See Bruce, *Commentary*, 371; Rapske, "Acts Travel," 174-75.

11So Paul stayed for a year and a half, teaching them the word of God.

With this encouragement Paul remained in Corinth eighteen months, "teaching them the word of God."[68] During all this time there was no violence and no one harmed Paul, just as the Lord promised. Paul's letters to the Corinthians show that they were filled with the Holy Spirit, spoke in tongues, and exercised many spiritual gifts. Their growth brought problems, however, as 1 and 2 Corinthians show.[69] However, "There is no hint that the miraculous gifts *themselves* at Corinth were abnormal. Indeed they appear from Acts and Paul's own testimony ([1Cor.] 14:18) to be an accepted and normal feature of new covenant life."[70]

c. Brought Before Gallio 18:12–17

12While Gallio was proconsul of Achaia, the Jews made a united attack on Paul and brought him into court.

In the summer of A.D. 51 a new proconsul, named Gallio, was appointed by the Roman Senate to govern the province of Achaia (Greece).[71] The unbelieving Jews apparently thought they could take advantage of his lack of knowledge of the situation. So they "made a united attack on Paul and brought him into court," or before the governor's judgment seat (tribunal). Archaeologists have discovered this seat (Gk. *bēma*, "throne"), built of blue and white marble.

13"This man," they charged, "is persuading the people to worship God in ways contrary to the law."

[68]While his party was there the gospel spread to the rest of Achaia (2 Cor. 1:1).

[69]See Stanley M. Horton, *I and II Corinthians* (Springfield, Mo.: Logion Press, 1999).

[70]Douglas A. Oss, "A Pentecostal/Charismatic View," in *Are Miraculous Gifts for Today?* ed. Wayne A. Grudem (Grand Rapids: Zondervan Publishing House, 1996), 275.

[71]Lucius Iunus Gallio became proconsul in the spring of A.D. 52, according to some scholars. Others say he began a little earlier, in July of A.D. 51. See Packer, *Acts of the Apostles*, 53; Bruce, *Commentary*, 374. He was given his name by adoption; he was born Lucius Annaeus Novatus and was the brother of the famous Stoic philosopher Seneca. A man of great personal charm or great graciousness, Gallio remained in office until the spring of A.D. 53. An inscription found at Delphi confirms these dates.

To Gallio they accused Paul of "persuading"[72] men to worship God "in ways contrary to the law." Since they were before a Roman court, they probably meant worship contrary to Roman law. Since Roman law allowed Judaism as a legal religion, these unbelieving Jews were now saying that Christianity was different from Judaism and therefore illegal.

> **14Just as Paul was about to speak, Gallio said to the Jews, "If you Jews were making a complaint about some misdemeanor or serious crime, it would be reasonable for me to listen to you. 15But since it involves questions about words and names and your own law—settle the matter yourselves. I will not be a judge of such things." 16So he had them ejected from the court.**

Paul did not get a chance to open his mouth before Gallio answered the Jews. Gallio had sufficient insight to realize that no crime or wicked act of immorality was involved. Because it seemed to him that the case against Paul involved nothing but questions "about words and names and [their] own [Jewish] law," he told them they could see to that for themselves. He did not want to be a judge of such matters. Then he had them "ejected from the court," which was probably set up in an open public square.

> **17Then they all turned on Sosthenes the synagogue ruler and beat him in front of the court. But Gallio showed no concern whatever.**

This pleased the crowd, for the Jews were not popular with them. They then took advantage of Gallio's attitude and seized Sosthenes,[73] the new ruler of the synagogue, striking him down and beating him before he could leave the tribunal. Gallio, as the people expected, "showed no concern whatever." He considered the whole matter outside his jurisdiction.[74] Thus, the Jews who had hoped to turn the governor against Paul found only indifference. It had looked at first as if the promise Jesus gave Paul that he would not be harmed in Corinth could not be fulfilled. But it was Paul's enemies who had their plans frustrated.

[72]Gk. *anapeithei* implies inciting, seducing, misleading.

[73]"Of sound strength."

[74]See Everett F. Harrison, *Introduction to the New Testament* (Grand Rapids: Wm. B. Eerdmans), 280.

The whole incident must have had a deep effect on Sosthenes. After this Paul remained in Corinth "for some time" (v. 18). Finally Sosthenes must have yielded to the truth of the gospel. In 1 Corinthians 1:1 "our brother Sosthenes" joins Paul in greeting the Corinthians. Though we cannot prove it with certainty, this must be the same Sosthenes. It would be unlikely that there would be another prominent Sosthenes who was well known to the Corinthian church. Truly the grace of God is marvelous: The leader of the opposition, a man who must himself have blasphemed Paul and the gospel, became a brother in the Lord. With this victory before Gallio and the conversion of Sosthenes, there must have been more freedom than ever for the Christians to witness for Christ in Corinth.

10. Returning to Antioch 18:18–22

18Paul stayed on in Corinth for some time. Then he left the brothers and sailed for Syria, accompanied by Priscilla and Aquila. Before he sailed, he had his hair cut off at Cenchrea because of a vow he had taken.

After "some time" (probably several months) Paul sailed for Syria, in the final part of his second missionary journey.[75]

He took Priscilla and Aquila with him. As is usually the case, Priscilla is named first. She seems to have been gifted by the Spirit for ministry, but we always find Aquila working with her. They must have been a wonderful team!

At Cenchrea,[76] Corinth's eastern harbor[77] (six or seven miles from Corinth), Paul had his hair cut,[78] for he had taken a vow.[79] This is not explained but it was probably a modified Nazirite vow, which expressed total dedication to God and to His will.

[75]Note that Luke was not with him on this sea voyage (i.e., no "we" passage).

[76]There was a church at Cenchrea. Rom. 16:1 mentions "our sister Phoebe" as one of its deacons ("deacon" is masculine, referring to the office; she was a deacon, not deaconess; see NLT).

[77]Lechaeum was the harbor on the western side of the isthmus.

[78]The Gk. may mean Paul cut his own hair.

[79]A few scholars take the Gk. to mean that Aquila rather than Paul had taken the vow. See P. C. H. Lenski, *The Interpretation of the Acts of the Apostles* (Columbus, Ohio: Wartburg Press, 1940), 762–63. Paul is the one, however, who continued to keep Jewish customs; cf. Acts 21:23–26.

It probably also expressed thanksgiving for all God had done in Corinth.[80] The hair was always cut at the conclusion of the period of the vow (see Num. 6:1–21).

[19]They arrived at Ephesus, where Paul left Priscilla and Aquila. He himself went into the synagogue and reasoned with the Jews. [20]When they asked him to spend more time with them, he declined. [21]But as he left, he promised, "I will come back if it is God's will." Then he set sail from Ephesus.

When they came to the great city of Ephesus, Paul left Priscilla and Aquila.[81] This time the Holy Spirit did not check him from preaching there. So he "went into the synagogue" and found Jews willing to listen to his reasoned presentation of the gospel. In fact, they wanted him to stay longer, but he did not consent. However, in his farewell he promised to return, "'God willing'" (v. 21, NKJV).

[22]When he landed at Caesarea, he went up and greeted the church and then went down to Antioch.

After landing at Caesarea, he paid his respects to the Jerusalem church. He probably let them know he had carried out the instructions of the Council of Acts 15. He also wanted to maintain a good relationship with them.

From Jerusalem he "went down"[82] to Antioch of Syria, thus ending the second missionary journey.

STUDY QUESTIONS

1. What caused Paul and Barnabas to separate?
2. How did Paul respond when the Spirit did not let him preach in Asia?

---

[80]F. F. Bruce points out, "A Nazirite vow was a purely voluntary undertaking, with a long tradition of Jewish piety behind it; there was nothing in it that would compromise the gospel as Paul understood it." *Acts: Greek Text*, 57.

[81]They stayed several years in Ephesus, the capital of the Roman province of Asia. A flourishing center of culture, education, trade, and commerce, it had a population of over three hundred thousand.

[82]Note the "up" and "down" in relation to Jerusalem—giving it spiritual priority. Was this Paul's Jewish influence on the Gentile Luke?

3. What difficulties did Paul meet at Philippi?
4. What does the New Testament teach about suffering for Christ?
5. What did Paul mean when he told the Philippian jailer to believe in Christ?
6. What would enable the jailer's household to be saved?
7. What was noble about the Bereans?
8. What two schools of philosophers engaged in a discussion with Paul, and why did they react to his teachings as they did?
9. How did Paul try to bring the philosophers to a decision?
10. What sort of persons were Priscilla and Aquila, and how did they get along with Paul?
11. What problems and successes did Paul have in Corinth?

V. EPHESUS: A NEW CENTER 18:23-20:38

A. Paul's Third Missionary Journey Begins 18:23

²³After spending some time in Antioch, Paul set out from there and traveled from place to place throughout the region of Galatia and Phrygia, strengthening all the disciples.

Paul spent some time, probably about six months, in Antioch encouraging and teaching the church. Then he went north by land on a fifteen-hundred-mile journey "throughout the region of Galatia and Phrygia." One after another he visited the churches founded on his first and second journeys. Paul never started churches and forgot them. Always he sought to go back to give further teaching and to establish and strengthen new believers. That is, he was always as much concerned with follow-up as he was with evangelism.

STUDY QUESTIONS

1. What do you suppose Paul did in Antioch at this time?
2. Why did Paul go first through Galatia and Phrygia?

B. A Better Baptism 18:24–19:7

1. Apollos Helped By Aquila And Priscilla 18:24–28

24Meanwhile a Jew named Apollos, a native of Alexandria, came to Ephesus. He was a learned man, with a thorough knowledge of the Scriptures. 25He had been instructed in the way of the Lord, and he spoke with great fervor and taught about Jesus accurately, though he knew only the baptism of John.

Alexandria, founded by Alexander the Great in 323 B.C., was located on the north coast of Egypt west of the mouth of the Nile River. By the first century it had a population of one million and was the second largest city of the Roman Empire, an important seaport, and the empire's greatest cultural and educational center. It had a Jewish population of about four hundred thousand in the northeast part of the city. They were Hellenistic (Greek speaking) and had produced the famous Septuagint (LXX), a translation of the Old Testament into Greek.[1]

From Alexandria to Ephesus came an eloquent Jew named Apollos (short for Apollonius, "pertaining to Apollo"). Not only was he eloquent, he was well educated, "a learned man," and powerful in his use of the Old Testament Scriptures. He had already been instructed orally in the way of the Lord Jesus, probably in his home city of Alexandria.[2] So enthusiastic was he about Jesus that "he spoke with great fervor." But Luke does not say he was full of the Holy Spirit.[3]

His teaching was detailed as well as accurate.[4] He had all the facts straight about Jesus' life and ministry, as well as about His

---

[1]The Septuagint (irregular from Lat. *septum,* "seven") is usually referred to by the Roman numeral LXX. Jewish tradition said that seventy scholars translated the Hebrew Scriptures into Greek at the behest of Ptolemy II.

[2]The Western Text inserts that he was instructed in his own country.

[3]Others take the Gk. *zeōn tō pneumati,* "fervent in the spirit [or Spirit]," to mean he preached powerfully "under the inspiration of the Holy Spirit." French L. Arrington, "Acts of the Apostles" in *Full Life Bible Commentary to the New Testament,* ed. French L. Arrington and Roger Stronstad (Grand Rapids: Zondervan Publishing House, 1999), 634.

[4]As the Gk. *akribōs* indicates.

death and resurrection. But he must have heard the facts from one of the witnesses of Christ's resurrection who, like many of the five hundred plus (1 Cor. 15:6), had not come to Jerusalem and were not present at the outpouring of the Holy Spirit on the Day of Pentecost.

> ²⁶**He began to speak boldly in the synagogue. When Priscilla and Aquila heard him, they invited him to their home and explained to him the way of God more adequately.**

He was excited about what he knew, however, and "spoke boldly [showing that Jesus is the Messiah] in the synagogue" at Ephesus.

Priscilla and Aquila were present and heard him. They did not say anything to him in the synagogue but took him aside to give him further instruction. The Greek also implies (and the NIV and others so translate) that they welcomed him and took him home with them. Then they explained God's way to him more precisely. Just what they said Luke does not go into here, but the next chapter deals with twelve disciples who were in the same position, with the same need for instruction, and details are given there.

It is interesting to note here that John Chrysostom ("John of the golden mouth"),[5] the chief pastor of the church in Constantinople about A.D. 400, recognized that Priscilla took the lead in giving this instruction to Apollos.[6] The best Greek scholars today agree. Apollos was a man of culture and education. Priscilla also must have been well educated and a very gracious woman. Paul's epistles show she was, along with her husband, a fellow worker, fellow teacher, and missionary.[7] They had a church that met in their house while they were in Ephesus (1 Cor. 16:19).

Looking ahead, we can see that Apollos must have been baptized in water on the authority of Jesus (as in Matt. 28:18–19). Then they must have prayed for him to be baptized in the Holy Spirit as in Acts 2:4.

[5]The English idiom is "silver-tongued."

[6]This is important, for the Western Text had reversed the names of the couple (e.g., see KJV).

[7]See Charles W. Carter and Ralph Earle, *The Acts of the Apostles* (Grand Rapids: Zondervan Publishing House, 1959), 264.

²⁷**When Apollos wanted to go to Achaia, the brothers encouraged him and wrote to the disciples there to welcome him. On arriving, he was a great help to those who by grace had believed. ²⁸For he vigorously refuted the Jews in public debate, proving from the Scriptures that Jesus was the Christ.**

That Apollos responded positively to the instruction is shown by the letters of recommendation the Christian brothers in Ephesus wrote for him when he wanted to go over to Greece. There also his ministry was effective. He became a channel of God's grace to help the believers. He also powerfully and utterly refuted the arguments of the unbelieving Jews, "proving from the Scriptures that Jesus was the Christ," the Messiah.[8] As Paul says in 1 Corinthians 3:6, Apollos watered what Paul had planted (but all along it was of course God who was making the church grow).

2. TWELVE DISCIPLES AT EPHESUS 19:1–7

In chapter 19 we come to an important question, posed in verse 2. Today its interpretation has become controversial. But the King James translators had no doubts about its meaning. They were good scholars and they said it well: "Have ye received the Holy Ghost since ye believed?"[9]

This is a question that still needs to be asked. These disciples had no positive answer until the Holy Spirit did come upon them. When they spoke in tongues and prophesied, then they knew by experience the right answer to the question Paul asked.

¹**While Apollos was at Corinth, Paul took the road through the interior and arrived at Ephesus. There he found some disciples ²and asked them, "Did you receive the Holy Spirit when you believed?" They answered, "No, we have not even heard that there is a Holy Spirit."**

After Paul visited the churches founded on his first journey in the cities of South Galatia, he went through the hills of the inte-

[8]Luther, Alford, Farrar, and others have suggested that Apollos may have written the Book of Hebrews.

[9]Even F. F. Bruce recognized that this question "suggests strongly that he [i.e., Paul] regarded them [i.e., the Ephesian disciples] as true believers in Christ." *Commentary on the Book of Acts* (Grand Rapids: Wm. B. Eerdmans, 1954), 385.

rior of South Galatia and Phrygia. Then he came to Ephesus—a city that in wickedness and immorality ran a close second to Corinth. It was full of magic arts, spiritism, astrology, idolatry, and all kinds of superstition. Yet in the midst of all its evil, Paul had his greatest revival and longest stay.

Paul first found "some disciples," a group of "about twelve men in all" (v. 7). Some writers believe they were disciples of John the Baptist. But everywhere else in the Book of Acts where Luke mentions disciples he always means disciples of Jesus, believers in Jesus, followers of Jesus.[10] Some believe these were converted by Apollos before Priscilla and Aquila instructed him.[11] Undoubtedly, like Apollos, they knew the facts about the life, death, resurrection, and ascension of Jesus.[12]

Though Paul sensed there was something lacking in their experience, he did not question the fact that they were believers. In fact, he recognized that they were. The question he asked shows rather that they lacked the freedom and spontaneity in worship that always characterized Spirit-filled believers. The fact he asked the question also shows Paul recognized that there could be a separation between saving faith and the experience of receiving the Holy Spirit.[13]

Modern versions generally translate "since ye believed"(v. 2, KJV) as "*when* you believed." But this translation is based on their theological presuppositions. The Greek is literally, "Having believed, did you receive?" "Having believed" *(pisteusantes)* is a Greek aorist (past) participle. "Did you receive" *(elabete)* is the main verb, also in the aorist. But the fact that they are both in

---

[10]Johannes Munck, *The Acts of the Apostles,* rev. William F. Albright and C. S. Mann, vol. 31 of *Anchor Bible Series* (Garden City, N.Y.: Doubleday & Co., 1979), 187. Acts 9:25 is an exception since it refers to Paul's followers. See Anthony D. Palma, *Baptism in the Holy Spirit* (Springfield, Mo.: Gospel Publishing House, 1999), 27–28.

[11]William W. Menzies and Robert P. Menzies, *Spirit and Power: Foundations of Pentecostal Experience* (Grand Rapids: Zondervan Publishing House, 2000), 74.

[12]E. M. Blaiklock suggests that because of new discoveries about papyrology, it could well be that the Ephesians had read at least parts of Mark's Gospel. *Acts: The Birth of the Church* (Old Tappan, N.J.: Fleming H. Revell, 1980), 183.

[13]Palma, *Baptism in the Holy Spirit,* 30; Menzies and Menzies, *Spirit and Power,* 74.

the aorist is not significant here. The fact that the participle "having believed" is in the past is what is important, for the tense of the participle normally shows its relation to the main verb. Because this participle is in the past, this normally means that its action precedes the action of the main verb. That is why the King James translators, as good Greek scholars, translated the participle "since ye believed." They wanted to bring out that the believing must take place before the receiving. This also brings out the fact that the baptism in the Holy Spirit is a distinct experience following conversion.

Some modern Greek scholars do claim that the aorist participle may sometimes indicate an action occurring at the same time as the main verb, especially if the main verb is also in the aorist as it is in Acts 19:2.[14] The examples given are not really applicable to this verse, however.

The chief example, "answered and said," is idiomatic (usually a Hebraism), a formula used to indicate the continuation of a discourse. It does not help at all in the interpretation of other passages. In the few passages where the action of the verb does seem to be coincident, the participle defines what is meant by the main verb. For example: *"This He did once for all, having offered up himself"* (Heb. 7:27). *"I have sinned, having betrayed innocent blood"* (Matt. 27:4). *"You have done well, having come"* (Acts 10:33).[15] But "having believed" is hardly a definition of what is meant by receiving the Spirit. Luke makes it clear, as in other passages, that the receiving of the Spirit involves a definite baptism in the Spirit, a definite outpouring on those who are already believers.

Many other passages in the New Testament do show that the action of the aorist participle normally precedes the action of an aorist main verb. One is: *"Having fallen asleep in Christ, they perished"* (1 Cor. 15:18). That is, after they fell asleep they perished

[14]One writer, Dunn, says that anyone who suggests that the aorist participle in Acts 19:2 indicates action prior to the receiving is only showing that he (along with the King James translators, of course) has an inadequate grasp of Gk. grammar. But Dunn later contradicts himself and admits that the aorist participle usually indicates action prior to that of the main verb. See James D. G. Dunn, *Baptism in the Holy Spirit* (London: SCM Press, 1970), 86, 158–59.

[15]Italicized passages here and in the following paragraphs are my own translation.

if Jesus did not rise from the dead. Another example is Matthew 22:25. Speaking of seven brothers, the Sadducees said of the first, *"Having married a wife, he died."* Obviously, even though the King James Version translates this, *"when* he had married a wife," it does not mean the marrying and the dying were the same thing, or even that they happened at the same time. They were distinct events and the marrying clearly preceded the dying, probably by some time.

Other examples can be found in Acts 5:10, *"Having carried her [Sapphira] out, they buried her";* Acts 13:51, *"Having shaken the dust off their feet, they came to Iconium";* Acts 16:6, *"And they went through the Phrygian and Galatian region having been forbidden by the Spirit to speak the Word in Asia";* Acts 16:24, *"Having received the orders, he threw them into the inner prison."* In these cases and many more the action of the participle clearly precedes the action of the main verb.

Therefore, though there are some cases in which the aorist participle is coincident with the aorist main verb, this is not the rule. The whole impression of Acts 19:2 is that since these disciples claimed to be believers, the baptism in the Holy Spirit should have been the next step, a distinct step after the believing, though not necessarily separated from it by a long time.

The disciples' reply, "No, we have not even heard that there is a Holy Spirit," may be translated, *"But we have not even heard if the Holy Spirit is."* The meaning, however, does not seem to be that they had never heard of the existence of the Holy Spirit. What godly Jew or interested Gentile would or could have been so ignorant? It is more likely that the phrase compares with John 7:39. There, the condensed phrase *"it was not yet Spirit"* means the age of the Spirit with its promised mighty outpouring had not yet come.[16]

From this we see that these disciples were really saying they had not heard about Pentecost or the availability of the baptism in the Holy Spirit.[17] In fact, several ancient manuscripts and ver-

[16]See Stanley M. Horton, *What the Bible Says About the Holy Spirit* (Springfield, Mo.: Gospel Publishing House, 1976), 116; Everett F. Harrison, *Interpreting Acts: The Expanding Church* (Grand Rapids: Zondervan Publishing House, Academie Books, 1986), 307.

[17]See J. H. E. Hull, *The Holy Spirit in the Acts of the Apostles* (London: Lutterworth Press, 1967), 110. See also Palma, *Baptism in the Holy Spirit,* 31.

sions of the New Testament[18] actually read, "We have not even heard if any are receiving the Holy Spirit." Obviously, they had not been taught about this when they were converted.

> [3]So Paul asked, "Then what baptism did you receive?" "John's baptism," they replied. [4]Paul said, "John's baptism was a baptism of repentance. He told the people to believe in the one coming after him, that is, in Jesus."

Paul then inquired further and found that these disciples had been baptized only into John the Baptist's baptism.[19] This, Paul explained, was only preparatory, "a baptism of repentance" (i.e., *because of* repentance).[20] John himself told the people that they should believe in the Coming One, Jesus. This means, of course, that they would not only accept Him as Messiah and Savior but also obey Him, following His directions to ask for and receive the Spirit (see Luke 11:9,13; 24:49; Acts 1:4–5; 11:15–16).

> [5]On hearing this, they were baptized into the name of the Lord Jesus. [6]When Paul placed his hands on them, the Holy Spirit came on them, and they spoke in tongues and prophesied. [7]There were about twelve men in all.

Because of Paul's explanation, the men were baptized into the name (into the worship and service) of the Lord Jesus.[21] Then, after they were baptized in water, Paul "placed his hands on them" and "the Holy Spirit came on them" with the same evidence given on the Day of Pentecost (Acts 2:4). They began to speak (and continued to speak) in tongues (languages) and prophesied. Though Luke does not say "other" tongues here, it is clearly the same gift as was given on the Day of Pentecost and exercised in the Corinthian Church.[22]

It needs to be emphasized, therefore, that their baptism in the Spirit here came not only after they believed, but in this case

---

[18]Including Codex Bezae (D), p[38] (a papyrus from the third or fourth century A.D.), p[46], plus Syriac and Sahidic versions originating in the second and third centuries A.D.

[19]This probably indicates they were Palestinian Jews. Thus, the giving of the Spirit here was not just to break down ethnic barriers, as some say.

[20]See Horton, *What the Bible Says*, 84.

[21]See comments on Acts 2:38.

[22]Horton, *What the Bible Says*, 229–30.

after they were baptized in water.[23] Paul also laid hands on them, but as at Samaria, the laying on of hands did not cause them to receive the Spirit. Rather, it encouraged their faith and preceded, or at least was distinct from, the Spirit's coming upon them. Then the speaking in tongues gave them further assurance that the Holy Spirit's presence and power were real.[24] That they also prophesied indicates they were energized by the Spirit to build up and encourage the group.

STUDY QUESTIONS

1. What shows that Apollos was a genuine Christian when he arrived at Ephesus?
2. How did Priscilla and Aquila respond to Apollos and why?
3. How was the ministry of Apollos affected by the counsel of Aquila and Priscilla?
4. What evidence is there that the twelve disciples Paul found at Ephesus were Christians?
5. What was significant about their receiving the Holy Spirit?

C. Revival And Riot In Ephesus 19:8–20:1

1. TWO YEARS OF TEACHING 19:8–10

8Paul entered the synagogue and spoke boldly there for three months, arguing persuasively about the kingdom of God.

Starting with the Jew first as always, Paul went to the syna-

---

[23]As Shelton points out, this was "a subsequent visitation of empowerment, not a delayed salvation experience." James B. Shelton, review of *Power From on High: The Spirit in Israel's Restoration and Witness in Luke-Acts* by Max Turner, *Pneuma* 21, no. 1 (spring 1999): 167.

[24]See Everett F. Harrison, *Introduction to the New Testament,* rev. ed. (Grand Rapids: Wm. B. Eerdmans, 1982), 289. Some also see here an "echo effect" that shows Luke intends us to interpret this passage in the light of Acts 2:4 and 10:46 and see "a prescribed paradigm." Douglas A. Oss, "A Pentecostal/Charismatic View," in *Are Miraculous Gifts for Today?* ed. Wayne A. Grudem (Grand Rapids: Zondervan Publishing House, 1996), 262.

gogue when he arrived in Ephesus. In this case also, he was fulfilling his promise to return (Acts 18:21). For three months he was able to speak boldly and freely, "arguing persuasively about the kingdom [rule, authority] of God" (as revealed in Jesus, now ascended to the right hand of the Father [Acts 2:30–33]). Perhaps the quiet ministry of Priscilla and Aquila had prepared the way. Whatever the case, the Jews at first were unusually receptive to the gospel.

> **9But some of them became obstinate; they refused to believe and publicly maligned the Way. So Paul left them. He took the disciples with him and had discussions daily in the lecture hall of Tyrannus. 10This went on for two years, so that all the Jews and Greeks who lived in the province of Asia heard the word of the Lord.**

Opposition in Ephesus grew more slowly than in other places, but eventually some of the unconverted Jews "became obstinate" (hardened, unyielding) and disobedient (rebellious). They showed their rebellious spirit "publicly," speaking evil of "the Way," that is, of the Christian faith and way of life, in front of the crowds who packed the synagogue expecting to hear the gospel.

The opposition did not discourage Paul. He had learned to anticipate it. "So Paul left them." He found a separate place for the disciples to meet, in the "lecture hall," or schoolroom, of Tyrannus. There, instead of meeting only on the Sabbath, Paul preached and taught the gospel "daily" for two years.[1]

As Paul later indicates (Acts 20:34), he continued his usual practice. He worked at his tentmaking trade from dawn until about 11 A.M. in order to support his evangelistic party. Then, after Tyrannus finished his lectures, Paul from 11 A.M. to 4 P.M. (as stated by Codex Bezae and other ancient manuscripts) taught those whom his fellow workers brought in. They had been witnesses, going among the crowds on the streets and in the marketplaces all morning, and they brought in their converts for further teaching.

In the evenings (after 4 P.M.) Paul would go to various homes to teach and establish the believers and to help win their friends

---

[1]The three months (Acts 19:8) plus the two years (v. 10) plus "a little longer" (v. 22) is summarized as three years in Acts 20:31.

and neighbors to the Lord (see Acts 20:20).

The result was that "all . . . who lived in the province of Asia heard the word of the Lord"; the whole of this Roman province was evangelized, both Jews and Gentiles. As Paul wrote to the Corinthians, "I will stay on in Ephesus until Pentecost, because a great door for effective work has opened to me, and there are many who oppose me" (1 Cor. 16:8–9). There is no evidence that Paul himself left the city of Ephesus during this period. Yet, it is evident that the seven churches of Asia mentioned in the Book of Revelation were founded at this time. Many other churches were established too. Since Ephesus was a great center, people from all over the province came there for business or other reasons. Many of them were converted, filled with the Spirit, and taught by Paul. Then they went back to their home cities and towns where they became powerful witnesses for Christ. In this way it appears the revival spread and churches grew up around Paul's converts.

2. Special Miracles 19:11–16

11God did extraordinary miracles through Paul, 12so that even handkerchiefs and aprons that had touched him were taken to the sick, and their illnesses were cured and the evil spirits left them.

An important factor in this spread of the gospel in Roman Asia was the fact God did "extraordinary miracles through Paul." The Greek really means the Lord made miracles an everyday occurrence. So powerfully was the Lord working through Paul that people did not want to wait for him to minister to them in the lecture hall of Tyrannus. They would come to his workroom where he was busy at his tentmaking and would carry off handkerchiefs (actually, the sweat cloths he used to wipe away perspiration while he was working) and work aprons that had been in contact with his body (his skin). These they laid upon the sick, who were then freed from their diseases. Even evil spirits came out of those who were possessed. The use of these sweat cloths and work aprons was exceptional, not normative, and shows that their faith was imperfect. But in these exceptional circumstances, God chose to honor their faith and do extraordinary miracles.

¹³Some Jews who went around driving out evil spirits tried to invoke the name of the Lord Jesus over those who were demon-possessed. They would say, "In the name of Jesus, whom Paul preaches, I command you to come out." ¹⁴Seven sons of Sceva, a Jewish chief priest, were doing this.

All this caught the attention of a group of Jewish exorcists, who went about claiming to be able to cast out evil spirits. These seven were sons of Sceva,² "a Jewish chief priest" (one of the chief priests associated with Annas and Caiaphas in Jerusalem). Possibly following the example of other Jewish exorcists, they took it upon themselves "to invoke the name of the Lord Jesus" in a sort of formula: "'I adjure you by Jesus whom Paul preaches'" (v. 13, NASB). But they had no right to do this. To use the name of Jesus means to identify yourself with Him and His Word and to put yourself at His disposal for Him to do His will. No unbeliever can do this.³

¹⁵[One day] the evil spirit answered them, "Jesus I know, and I know about Paul, but who are you?" ¹⁶Then the man who had the evil spirit jumped on them and over-powered them all. He gave them such a beating that they ran out of the house naked and bleeding.

Confronting its would-be exorcists, the evil spirit answered, "Jesus I know [Gk. *ginōskō*, "I recognize" who He is]; and Paul I know about [Gk. *epistamai*, "I understand" who he is], but as for you, who are you?"⁴ Then the demon-possessed man "jumped on them"⁵ and "overpowered them all."⁶ In fact, he was so vio-

---

²Probably a variant of the Lat. *Scaeva*, "left-handed."

³Formulas for exorcism became popular among Jews in the intertestamental period, as Tobit, the Dead Sea Scrolls, and the Apocryphal "Prayer of Nabonius" show.

⁴My translation.

⁵Gk. *ephallomenos*, "leaping." Because LXX uses this of the leaping of the Spirit of the Lord (1 Sam. 10:6; 11:6; 16:13), Luke T. Johnson sees this verb expressing irony. *The Acts of the Apostles* (Collegeville, Minn.: Liturgical Press, 1992), 341.

⁶Some ancient manuscripts have *amphoterōn*, which in earlier Gk. usage (before NT times) meant "both." In NT times, however, it was often used in everyday speech to mean "all." Many ancient Gk. papyrus manuscripts confirm this.

lent with them that the seven brothers "ran out of the house naked[7] and bleeding." They had the words but not the power.

3. Many Believe 19:17–20

17When this became known to the Jews and Greeks living in Ephesus, they were all seized with fear, and the name of the Lord Jesus was held in high honor.

The news of this soon spread throughout Ephesus and a "fear," an awe inspired by the supernatural, seized Jews and Gentiles alike. This caused them to honor highly "the name of the Lord Jesus," His character, person, power, and authority. From what the demon had done to the sons of Sceva they learned that using the name of Jesus is not a magical formula. "Only those with a personal relationship with Christ and who invoke his name in humble faith are in the correct position to see God act to drive out demons."[8]

18Many of those who believed now came and openly confessed their evil deeds. 19A number who had practiced sorcery brought their scrolls together and burned them publicly. When they calculated the value of the scrolls, the total came to fifty thousand drachmas.

All this had an important effect on the believers also. They began to see that the holy name of Jesus demands a holy people. Many of them came and "openly confessed," publicly reporting, their "evil deeds" (including the attempts to cast magic spells to control people). The Greek indicates they now turned from their sin, with a total commitment to the Lord. They realized their need for righteousness as well as for salvation.

Another result was their realization that the true power over evil was only in Jesus. Ephesus was also a center for the practice of magic arts, especially the putting of spells on people or things. A considerable number of the new believers had practiced magic, including attempts at foretelling or influencing the future. Most of them still had the books they used. (Some of the

---

[7]The Gk. may mean either that they were stripped of their outer garments or that they were bare.

[8]William J. Larkin, Jr., *Acts* (Downers Grove, Ill.: InterVarsity Press, 1995), 277.

books of this kind have been discovered by archaeologists.)

Now the believers saw that these books with their formulas, spells, and astrological forecasts were of no value whatsoever. In fact, they were purely pagan, even demonic, in their origin. So they "brought their scrolls together," and, as an act of faith, "burned them publicly." Books were very expensive in those days, and when the price of these books was calculated, it came to fifty thousand pieces of silver. This was as much as two hundred day laborers or soldiers would earn in a year.

20In this way the word of the Lord spread widely and grew in power.

With this Luke concludes the story of the success of the gospel in Ephesus. But it was the "word of the Lord" (the Word concerning Jesus) that "spread widely and grew in power." The mention of power indicates that miraculous healings, signs, and wonders continued to confirm the Word. The later report (Acts 20:17) of a number of elders in the church at Ephesus indicates that there were many house churches and that the whole church had continued to grow in a healthy way.

4. Paul's Purpose To Visit Rome 19:21–22

21After all this had happened, Paul decided to go to Jerusalem, passing through Macedonia and Achaia. "After I have been there," he said, "I must visit Rome also."

Paul himself felt that these things brought not just an end, but a fulfillment to his ministry in Ephesus. "After all this had happened" is literally "When these things were fulfilled" and indicates he had carried out the ministry he came to accomplish (cf. NKJV). The tremendous growth of the church and the training of the people and their leaders meant that he could leave them now with confidence and go on to another place of ministry.

Paul's epistles show there had been problems. He says he fought with "wild beasts" at Ephesus (1 Cor. 15:32). This probably means he risked his life opposing "beasts" in human form, men who acted like beasts.[9] He also says he suffered such hard-

---

[9]Some also take Paul's question as hypothetical. However, Ignatius in his epistles to the Ephesians writes in a similar way of real beasts.

ships in the province of Asia (that is, in Ephesus) that he "despaired even of life" but was delivered by God (2 Cor. 1:8–10). Luke says nothing about this since, apparently, it affected only Paul, not the church.

The Greek is not clear about whose spirit is involved in Paul's firmly set purpose: *his own* spirit or the *Holy* Spirit (e.g., NIV, NASB, RSV). "In the spirit" (as in NASB) usually does mean in the Holy Spirit. (In NT times the Gk. did not distinguish between capital and small letters.) We can be sure also that Paul's own spirit was in harmony with, and submissive to, the Holy Spirit. His purpose therefore was a holy purpose, a God-planned purpose.

His statement "I must visit Rome" further confirms this. The Greek indicates a divine necessity was laid upon him. It is the same sort of expression as is found in John 4:4, where Jesus felt the divine imperative to go through Samaria. That Paul's purpose to go to Rome was indeed pleasing to the Lord was confirmed later by Jesus himself (Acts 23:11) and by an angel (27:23–24).

So we see Paul was being led by the Spirit and was given a vision of the next step in God's plan for his ministry. However, it was not a full vision. He did not yet know how God was going to get him to Rome. But because of the "divine 'must'"[10] from this point to the end of the Book of Acts, Rome is the objective in view.

Paul did not go to Rome directly, however, because he felt a responsibility to visit the churches in Macedonia and Greece again and also to take their offering to the church in Jerusalem (Acts 24:17; Rom. 15:26; 1 Cor. 16:1–4).

Later he wrote to the Roman believers, recognizing there was an established church in Rome, but one which obviously had never been visited by an apostle (Rom. 1:10–13).[11] By the time he wrote Romans, he hoped to go on from Rome to Spain (Rom. 15:28).

22He sent two of his helpers, Timothy and Erastus, to Macedonia, while he stayed in the province of Asia a little longer.

[10]Gerhard Krodel, *Acts* (Philadelphia: Fortress Press, 1981), 10.

[11]Some take "Babylon" in 1 Pet. 5:13 to mean Rome. However, Peter was the apostle to the circumcision, and the largest group of orthodox Jews outside of Palestine was in Babylon, where the Babylonian Talmud was later written down. It would be logical for Peter to go there. There was no reason before Nero's burning of Rome to call Rome "Babylon." Nothing indicates Peter founded the church there.

To prepare the churches in Macedonia for his visit, Paul sent Timothy and Erastus[12] on ahead. But he himself stayed "a little longer" in Ephesus. As he told the Corinthians, a great door for effective work was still open to him, but there were many who opposed him (1 Cor. 16:8–9).

5. SILVERSMITHS STIR A RIOT 19:23–20:1

a. Silversmiths' Wrath Affects The City 19:23–29

23About that time there arose a great disturbance about the Way. 24A silversmith named Demetrius, who made silver shrines of Artemis, brought in no little business for the craftsmen.

Just how many opponents there were in Ephesus soon became apparent. Luke speaks of it literally as "not a small" disturbance concerning the Pentecostal Christian way of life that Paul preached. A silversmith named Demetrius started the "disturbance."[13] His chief product, like that of most silversmiths in Ephesus, was a miniature silver shrine of Artemis containing a miniature image of this many-breasted fertility goddess of Ephesus.[14]

The Ephesian goddess actually had no relation to the other Artemis, the Artemis of Greece known as the maiden huntress and identified by the Romans with their goddess Diana. The Artemis of Ephesus was worshiped primarily by its citizens (in spite of their claims, v. 27) and was not at all like the Roman goddess Diana. The names were the same, but the goddesses were different.

However, the immense, splendid temple of Artemis was known as one of the Seven Wonders of the World[15] and was visited by multitudes of worshipers. Consequently the demand for

[12]Erastus was the city treasurer of Corinth. See Rom 16:23; 2 Tim. 4:20.

[13]Archaeological studies show that these silversmiths were not a commercial guild. They belonged to a religious guild attached to the temple of Artemis. They were temple silversmiths, directly connected with the worship of the goddess. See T. D. Proffitt, III, "Mycenaen Tablets and Demetrius the Silversmith, Acts 19:23–28," *Near East Archaeological Bulletin* 14 (1979): 59–62.

[14]Some believe that what looked like many breasts were "clusters of grapes or dates, symbols of the goddess's function as the nourishing spirit of nature." E. M. Blaiklock, *Acts: The Birth of the Church* (Old Tappan, N.J.: Fleming H. Revell, 1980), 188.

[15]The marble temple was 425 feet by 220 feet and 60 feet in height, with 127 columns (each weighing 150 tons) supporting its roof.

these shrines ordinarily kept the silversmiths quite busy and brought them "no little business" (gain, or profit). Luke calls them "craftsmen" (Gk. *technitais*, "skilled workers," "artists").

> **25He called them together, along with the workmen in related trades, and said: "Men, you know we receive a good income from this business. 26And you see and hear how this fellow Paul has convinced and led astray large numbers of people here in Ephesus and in practically the whole province of Asia. He says that man-made gods are no gods at all.**

Now sales were falling. So Demetrius gathered all these skilled craftsmen together "with the workmen [Gk. *ergatas*, "laborers"] in related trades," involved in some way in the temple businesses, and made a speech pointing out that Paul's message had spread throughout "practically the whole province of Asia." Demetrius knew what Paul's message was, but rejected it and scornfully called Paul "this fellow." Because Demetrius was losing much of his income he considered Paul as a false teacher, having "led astray large numbers of people." But he recognized how effective Paul's ministry was. Multitudes were believing the truth "that man-made gods are no gods at all." (Cf. Isa. 10:11 where "idols" translates the Heb. *'elilim*, "nothings," "worthless nonentities.")

> **27There is danger not only that our trade will lose its good name, but also that the temple of the great god-dess Artemis will be discredited, and the goddess her-self, who is worshiped throughout the province of Asia and the world, will be robbed of her divine majesty."**

As a result, the sales of the shrines were diminishing and the trade of making them looked as if it would "lose its good name" and be rejected. Not only so, Demetrius claimed that the temple of the goddess Artemis would also "be discredited." The goddess herself was also in danger of having her "divine majesty," or magnificence, diminished or destroyed. Demetrius also claimed that not only the whole province of Asia, but also the entire (inhabited) world (that is, the entire Roman Empire as they viewed it) worshiped her.[16]

---

[16]The goddess was worshiped in Masilia and Carthage and *may* have been "worshiped over much of the Roman world." Brian Rapske, "Acts Travel and

²⁸When they heard this, they were furious and began shouting: "Great is Artemis of the Ephesians!" ²⁹Soon the whole city was in an uproar. The people seized Gaius and Aristarchus, Paul's traveling companions from Macedonia, and rushed as one man into the theater.

Demetrius unwittingly bore witness to the great spread of the gospel. He also succeeded in his purpose of touching his hearers with respect to both their livelihood and their civic pride in the temple of Artemis. This, as he hoped, brought an outburst of wrath from the silversmiths. They cried out with passion, "Great is Artemis of the Ephesians!" The Greek indicates they kept up this chant, filling the whole city with confusion and disturbance. The result was that they all "rushed . . . into the theater" (a Greek-style amphitheater or arena open to the sky with room for over twenty thousand people).[17]

First, however, they "seized Gaius and Aristarchus," Macedonians who were among Paul's traveling companions. Aristarchus was from Thessalonica (Acts 20:4). Their presence shows Paul had more companions on this third missionary journey than on his earlier travels. They were seized and dragged into the amphitheater, more for their association with Paul than for anything they themselves had done.

b. Total Confusion 19:30–34

³⁰Paul wanted to appear before the crowd, but the disciples would not let him. ³¹Even some of the officials of the province, friends of Paul, sent him a message begging him not to venture into the theater.

When Paul wanted to go in among the tumultuous crowd,[18] "the disciples would not let him." He probably wanted to support Gaius and Aristarchus and hoped to use this as an opportunity to proclaim the gospel. But "even some of the officials"

Shipwreck," in *The Book of Acts in its Graeco-Roman Setting,* ed. David W. J. Gill and Conrad Gempf, vol. 2 of *The Book of Acts in Its First Century Setting,* ed. Bruce W. Winter (Grand Rapids: Wm. B. Eerdmans, 1994), 332.

[17]Ibid., 348.

[18]Gk. *dēmon,* "body of citizens" of a Greek city.

(Asiarchs)[19] connected with Roman worship in the province of Asia who were among his friends urged him not to venture into the amphitheater. No doubt they thought the crowd might tear him to pieces.

> **32The assembly was in confusion: Some were shouting one thing, some another. Most of the people did not even know why they were there.**

In the crowd some were "shouting one thing, some another." The assembly (Gk. *ekklēsia*, the same word usually translated "church") was in a state of total confusion; the majority did not know why they had come together.

> **33The Jews pushed Alexander to the front, and some of the crowd shouted instructions to him. He motioned for silence in order to make a defense before the people. 34But when they realized he was a Jew, they all shouted in unison for about two hours: "Great is Artemis of the Ephesians!"**

At this point the Jews pushed to the front Alexander (one of their own whom we don't know much about) with the intention of instructing them. That is, they wanted him to explain that the Jews were not responsible for what the Christians were doing. He came down to the front and waved his hand to get their attention and give his defense before the crowd. "But when they realized he was a Jew," the whole crowd went wild. They knew the Jews worshiped one God and denied the reality of their gods and goddesses. With one voice they kept crying "for about two hours, 'Great is Artemis of the Ephesians!'" The possession of this image and temple was a source of great civic pride for the people of the city.

c. The Crowd Quieted 19:35–41

> **35The city clerk quieted the crowd and said: "Men of Ephesus, doesn't all the world know that the city of Ephesus is the guardian of the temple of the great Artemis and of her image, which fell from heaven?**

---

[19]Gk. *Asiarchōn*, "chiefs of [the Roman province of] Asia." Only outstanding, wealthy, aristocratic citizens were made Asiarchs. In this high office they financed public Pan-Ionian Games and religious events.

36Therefore, since these facts are undeniable, you ought to be quiet and not do anything rash.

Finally, the city clerk[20] "quieted the crowd" and asked them, "Who is there of humankind who does not know that the city of Ephesus is the templekeeper [lit. "templesweeper"] of the great Artemis, even the one fallen from the sky [or, "from the sky gods"]?"[21] (The image may have been carved from a meteorite.) The city clerk in this way argued that there was no reason to be so upset and excited since these things, in his opinion, could not be denied. Therefore, it was their duty to quiet down. It would be wrong to "do anything rash."

37You have brought these men here, though they have neither robbed temples nor blasphemed our goddess.

The town clerk also pointed out that the men they had brought into the amphitheater were neither temple robbers (or sacrilegious), nor were they blasphemers of their goddess. It is important to note here that Paul had been nearly three years in Ephesus, and there was no evidence that either he or the Christians ever said anything against the temple or Artemis. They were not iconoclasts. They simply kept preaching the good news of Jesus Christ in a positive way, and the sale of the images and shrines automatically dropped.

38If, then, Demetrius and his fellow craftsmen have a grievance against anybody, the courts are open and there are proconsuls. They can press charges. 39If there is anything further you want to bring up, it must be settled in a legal assembly.

The clerk also called for law and order. The court days were kept regularly in the marketplace; the proconsuls were available.[22] That is, the governor appointed by the Roman Senate would be there to give judgment. If Demetrius and his fellow craftsmen had a case against anyone, let them bring their charges against one another (in the lawful way). Then, if anyone wanted

---

[20]Or "chancellor," a citizen of Ephesus who was their official contact, or liaison, with the Roman government officials in Ephesus. He acted as mayor.

[21]My translation.

[22]The plural is general and does not mean there was more than one at a time.

to seek anything beyond that, it should be explained and settled in "a legal [duly constituted] assembly" (Gk. *ekklēsia*, the word usually translated "church"), that is, not in a riotous gathering (also *ekklēsia*) like this.

> **⁴⁰As it is, we are in danger of being charged with rioting because of today's events. In that case we would not be able to account for this commotion, since there is no reason for it." ⁴¹After he had said this, he dismissed the assembly.**

Actually the clerk was upset about the mob because it put the city "in danger of being charged with rioting" (or revolution). The Romans used their armies to ensure peace and order. In the Roman rulers' eyes there would be no reason or excuse for the events of this day; the Ephesians could give no account for this crowd, which the Romans could take as a seditious meeting or a conspiracy. The city risked losing the privileges of self-government that the empire had given it. The people understood the city clerk's reasoning. They quickly dispersed when the clerk "dismissed the assembly" (Gk. *ekklēsia*).

The use of the Greek *ekklēsia* for this assembly is an important help to understanding the word as it was used in New Testament times. It shows that the word had lost its old meaning of "called out" and was used of *any* assembly or gathering, including an illegal assembly or a spontaneous gathering such as this one in the amphitheater. Therefore the word *ekklēsia*, usually translated "church," is properly translated "assembly," having the connotation that it was any assembly of citizens. It is used in this passage of an assembly of the citizens of Ephesus. When it is used of believers, the proper translation is also "assembly," having the connotation that it is an assembly of believers who are "fellow-citizens with God's people [the saints]" (Eph. 2:19).[23]

d. Paul Leaves For Macedonia 20:1

> **¹When the uproar had ended, Paul sent for the disciples and, after encouraging them, said good-by and set out for Macedonia.**

[23]It should be noted also that the word *ekklēsia* in the NT is never used of a building or an organization as such. It always refers to people.

Part of the pressure on Paul in Ephesus was his care and deep concern for all the churches. His letters to the Corinthians show he was especially concerned about the assemblies in Macedonia and Greece (see 2 Cor. 11:28; 12:20; 13:6). He had already sent Timothy and Erastus to Macedonia. Now it was time for Paul to go too.

After the riot and all the noise ceased, Paul "sent for the disciples" (the Ephesian believers) and encouraged them (to live holy lives and to be faithful to the Lord, as the practical sections of his epistles show). Then, after farewell greetings, he went to Macedonia. This was probably the last time he would see this body of believers. When he passed by Ephesus on the way to Jerusalem later, he saw only the elders of the church.

STUDY QUESTIONS

1. What was extraordinary about Paul's ministry in Ephesus?
2. What happened to the seven sons of Sceva and why?
3. What caused the uproar in Ephesus and with what results?

D. Paul's Third Journey Concludes 20:2–38

1. MACEDONIA AND GREECE REVISITED 20:2–5

2He traveled through that area, speaking many words of encouragement to the people, and finally arrived in Greece, 3where he stayed three months. Because the Jews made a plot against him just as he was about to sail for Syria, he decided to go back through Macedonia.

It is probable that Paul went to Macedonia by way of Troas hoping to find Titus there (2 Cor. 2:13). Not finding him, he went on to Philippi (2 Cor. 2:12–13). There Titus did come with good news (2 Cor. 7:6–7).

During the summer and fall Paul "traveled through that area" (i.e., Macedonia, v. 1) and visited the various churches "speaking many words of encouragement" (or, as the Gk. says, he encouraged them with "much discourse"). Probably he also visited the cities west of those visited on the previous journey, since in Romans 15:19 he says he fully preached the gospel "all the way around to Illyricum" (Dalmatia, Yugoslavia), on the northwest side of Macedonia on the Adriatic Sea. During this time, about A.D. 56, he wrote 2 Corinthians, probably from Philippi.[1]

Then he went down into Greece "where he stayed three months," no doubt the three winter months of A.D. 56, 57. Most of this time was probably spent in Corinth (see 1 Cor. 16:6). Tradition says Paul stayed with Gaius (Rom. 16:23) and wrote the epistle to the Romans there just before he left. He also finished taking up the collection for the believers in Jerusalem, and the churches chose representatives to go with him (Rom. 15:25–28; 2 Cor. 8:18–23; 9:3–5). They would assure the churches of Greece and Macedonia "that the offering would be administered in a way that would honor the Lord, giving Him the glory."[2]

Just as he was about to go to Syria, the unbelieving "Jews made a plot against him." So Paul changed his plans. Instead of taking a ship from Greece he decided to return through Macedonia.[3]

[4]He was accompanied by Sopater son of Pyrrhus from Berea, Aristarchus and Secundus from Thessalonica, Gaius from Derbe, Timothy also, and Tychicus and Trophimus from the province of Asia. [5]These men went on ahead and waited for us at Troas.

Seven men who were accompanying Paul into Asia apparently took the ship as originally planned. They "went on ahead" of him to Troas and waited for him there. These seven were Sopater (also called Sosipater, Rom. 16:21) of Berea, Aristarchus and Secundus of Thessalonica, Gaius of Derbe, and Timothy, and Tychicus,[4] and Trophimus[5] of Asia (Ephesus). Many writers believe they were the representatives of the churches that contributed to the offering for the poor among the Jerusalem Christians. They had the responsi-

[1]Stanley M. Horton, *I and II Corinthians* (Springfield, Mo.: Logion Press, 1999), 173.

[2]Ibid., 225.

[3]The Western Text adds that he was guided by the Holy Spirit—which was certainly true.

[4]"Lucky."

[5]"Healthy."

bility to see what was done with the money and report back to their home churches. The Early Church was very careful to keep good financial accounts and just as careful to make them known to the members of the congregation.

The word "us" (v. 5) indicates Luke went back with Paul through Macedonia. Note the increased amount of detail in the following passage.

2. Eutychus Raised From The Dead At Troas
20:6–12

6But we sailed from Philippi after the Feast of Unleavened Bread, and five days later joined the others at Troas, where we stayed seven days.

Paul apparently celebrated Passover in Philippi. Then after the seven days of the Feast of Unleavened Bread in April, he sailed from Philippi with Luke. At Troas they met the others and remained there for seven days.

7On the first day of the week we came together to break bread. Paul spoke to the people and, because he intended to leave the next day, kept on talking until midnight. 8There were many lamps in the upstairs room where we were meeting.

At Troas Paul probably went to the synagogue on the Sabbath, as was his custom. Then, on the day following, "the first day of the week," the believers gathered with Paul and his companions to "break bread." This means they all brought food, shared a fellowship meal, and concluded with an observance of the Lord's Supper. This is the first clear indication that Christian believers met to worship on Sunday (cf. 1 Cor. 16:2; Rev. 1:10).

Paul took the opportunity to preach. Since he was going to leave the next day, he prolonged his discourse "until midnight." He could do this, for there was plenty of light from the "many [olive-oil] lamps" in the upper room of the home where they were meeting. That the upper room was a third story (v. 9) indicates a large home and a wealthy homeowner. The room could probably hold two or three hundred people.

9Seated in a window was a young man named Eutychus, who was sinking into a deep sleep as Paul talked on and

on. When he was sound asleep, he fell to the ground from the third story and was picked up dead.

A young man, Eutychus,[6] was sitting on a window sill listening. About midnight he was "sinking into [gradually overpowered with] a deep sleep." Everyone's attention was on Paul, so no one noticed. As Paul kept on preaching, the young man, when sound asleep, fell from the third story "and was picked up dead." This was a literal not a figurative description; Luke, as a physician, would have been able to determine this.

10Paul went down, threw himself on the young man and put his arms around him. "Don't be alarmed," he said. "He's alive!"

Immediately, Paul went down (probably by an outside stairway), fell on him, and put his arms around him tightly. We can be sure he prayed as he did so. (Cf. 1 Kings 17:21; 2 Kings 4:34, where Elijah and Elisha had similar experiences.) Then Paul said, "Stop your uproar, for his life is in him."[7] That is, his life had returned to him.[8]

11Then he went upstairs again and broke bread and ate. After talking until daylight, he left. 12The people took the young man home alive and were greatly comforted.

After that Paul went back up, broke bread, ate ("tasted" with enjoyment), and kept on talking with the believers "until daylight." Then he left. The boy was also taken home alive (and fully recovered), and they were very greatly encouraged.

3. SAILING BY EPHESUS 20:13–16

13We went on ahead to the ship and sailed for Assos, where we were going to take Paul aboard. He had made this arrangement because he was going there on foot. 14When he met us at Assos, we took him aboard and went on to Mitylene. 15The next day we set sail from there and arrived off Kios. The day after that we crossed over to Samos, and on the following day arrived at Miletus.

[6]"Good Luck."
[7]My translation.
[8]"Life" is the Gk. *psuchē*, which also means "soul" or "person" but which here does mean physical life.

Luke and the rest of Paul's companions did not stay until daylight. They went on ahead to the ship and set sail for Assos, in Mysia, south of Troas, where they expected "to take Paul aboard." He had directed them to do this. The ship would go a longer distance (about forty miles) around a peninsula (Cape Lectum) while Paul walked the shorter distance (about twenty miles) to Assos by land.

Luke does not tell us why Paul did this; for some reason he wanted to be alone. A little later he told the Ephesian elders that in every city the Holy Spirit warned him that prison and persecution awaited him in Jerusalem (Acts 20:23). No doubt Paul needed this time alone to come to grips with going to Jerusalem (20:24).

Then by sailing along the coast of Asia Minor, stopping at Mitylene, the capital of the island of Lesbos, and passing over by Kios and the island of Samos, they came to Miletus on the coast of Asia about thirty miles south of Ephesus.

16Paul had decided to sail past Ephesus to avoid spending time in the province of Asia, for he was in a hurry to reach Jerusalem, if possible, by the day of Pentecost.

Paul did not want to take too much time in the province of Asia. He had indeed settled it with God, and now he was "in a hurry to reach Jerusalem" by the next great pilgrimage feast, the Day of Pentecost (in May), if possible.[9] This would be a time when the Jewish believers in Palestine would be together and the offering from Greece and Macedonia would be most helpful.

4. Farewell To The Ephesian Elders 20:17–38

a. Paul's Faithful Service 20:17–21

17From Miletus, Paul sent to Ephesus for the elders of the church.

Paul did not bypass Ephesus because he lacked concern for the church there. In fact, he "sent . . . for the elders of the church"

---

[9]The Law called for three "pilgrimage" feasts to be celebrated in Jerusalem: Passover, including Unleavened Bread; Harvest, also called Weeks or Pentecost; and Ingathering or Tabernacles (Exod. 23:14–17; 2 Chron. 8:13). Paul was still faithful to those Jewish traditions that did not interfere with his devotion to Christ.

to meet him at Miletus. These would be the presidents[10] of local congregations meeting in house churches. This was a very serious occasion for Paul because he believed it would be the last time he would ever see them. His farewell address to them "is the only example in Acts of an address by Paul to a believing audience."[11]

[18]When they arrived, he said to them: "You know how I lived the whole time I was with you, from the first day I came into the province of Asia. [19]I served the Lord with great humility and with tears, although I was severely tested by the plots of the Jews.

He began, therefore, by reminding them how all the time he was with them he served the Lord "with great humility."[12] Paul often called himself the Lord's slave (Rom. 1:1; 12:11; Gal. 1:10; Phil. 1:1; Titus 1:1). He served[13] also "with tears" because of his love for people he wanted to see saved, and with testings brought on "by the plots of the [unbelieving] Jews."

[20]You know that I have not hesitated to preach anything that would be helpful to you but have taught you publicly and from house to house. [21]I have declared to both Jews and Greeks that they must turn to God in repentance and have faith in our Lord Jesus.

At the same time, Paul did not let danger cause him to shrink from telling them anything that was beneficial, teaching them both publicly and in their homes. To both Jews and Greeks he declared their need to "turn to God in repentance" (a change of mind and attitude that caused them to hate sin and love Him for who He is) and "have faith in our Lord Jesus" (accepting His salvation provided by the shedding of His blood on the cross). See 1 Thessalonians 1:8–10, where faith in God involves turning "to God from idols to serve the living and true God, and to wait for his Son from heaven, whom he raised from the dead—Jesus, who rescues us from the coming wrath."

---

[10]See 1 Tim. 3:1–7; 5:17; Titus 1:6–9 for their qualifications.

[11]F. F. Bruce, *Acts: Greek Text,* 429. Luke was present and heard it, as the use of "we" indicates.

[12]Gk. *tapenophrosunēs,* includes his willingness to work with his hands (v. 34).

[13]Gk. *douleuōn,* "kept serving as a slave serves his master."

b. Willing To Die 20:22–24

22"And now, compelled by the Spirit, I am going to Jerusalem, not knowing what will happen to me there. 23I only know that in every city the Holy Spirit warns me that prison and hardships are facing me.

Paul then told the elders that he was going to Jerusalem not of his own will but "compelled by the Spirit." That is, the Spirit had made it clear to Paul that divine necessity was still upon him to go to Jerusalem. He did not know what he would encounter there, except that the Holy Spirit in city after city gave solemn warning (undoubtedly through the gift of prophecy) that "prison" (chains) and "hardships" awaited him (see also Rom. 15:31). Further warnings would be given at Tyre and at Caesarea (21:4, 11). In this way, the Holy Spirit was preparing Paul for the persecution and distress God purposed for him.

24However, I consider my life worth nothing to me, if only I may finish the race and complete the task the Lord Jesus has given me—the task of testifying to the gospel of God's grace.

These warnings of the Holy Spirit were not intended to stop Paul from going, for he was still compelled by the Spirit to go. In fact, he was willing to go. On no account did he consider his life valuable when compared with finishing his race,[14] accomplishing the task (the ministry) he had been assigned by the Lord Jesus: giving serious testimony to the good news of the grace of God. Other passages show Paul was always willing to risk his life for the gospel's sake (Phil. 1:20–24; 2:17; 3:8; 1 Thess. 2:8–9; cf. 2 Cor. 12:10). To the end of his life he kept before him the purpose of finishing his race. Then he wrote "I have finished the race, I have kept the faith" (2 Tim. 4:7). He had indeed followed God's plan for his life and ministry.

c. Challenging By Example 20:25–35

25"Now I know that none of you among whom I have gone about preaching the kingdom will ever see me again. 26Therefore, I declare to you today that I am inno-

[14]See 2 Tim. 4:6–7.

cent of the blood of all men. ²⁷For I have not hesitated to proclaim to you the whole will of God.

Paul next let the elders know that this was a final farewell. He did not think that they would ever see him again.[15] He planned to visit Rome and Spain, never expecting to return to Ephesus (Rom. 15:24,28). For this reason he bore witness that he was "innocent of the blood of all." Ezekiel was appointed a watchman for, and an admonisher of, the people of Israel who were in exile by the Chebar Canal in Babylon. If he failed to warn the people and they died in their sins, he would be accountable for their blood (Ezek. 3:18,20; 33:6,8). Paul recognized he had the same heavy responsibility for the people to whom the Lord sent him to minister.

No one could say Paul had failed to give warning. Even more important, he never shrank from telling "the whole will [Gk. *boulē,* plan, wise purpose] of God." Nor did he stop now.

²⁸Keep watch over yourselves and all the flock of which the Holy Spirit has made you overseers. Be shepherds of the church of God, which he bought with his own blood.

Paul warned the elders to "watch over" (give attention to) themselves. At the same time he expected them to exercise the office of overseer (Gk. *episkopous,* superintendent, ruling elder, president of the local congregation—the same term usually translated "bishop" in the KJV) of the local congregation, to be its executive or administrative head. Although Spirit-filled people who were led by the Spirit (as Acts 14:23 shows) had elected the elders to the office, the Holy Spirit had really given it to them. More important, they were dependent on Him for the gifts of administration (governments) and ruling necessary to carrying out the office (1 Cor. 12:28; Rom. 12:8).[16] Through the Holy Spirit they could give wise counsel, manage the business affairs of the church, give spiritual leadership, and show the people the

[15]In 1 Tim. 1:3, which was written after the events of Acts 28, Paul told Timothy, "Stay there in Ephesus." Then in 1 Tim. 3:14 Paul expressed the hope to come to Timothy soon. See also Philem. 22. It seems that God did not reveal to Paul or to Luke what would happen after the Roman imprisonment.

[16]See Horton, *What the Bible Says,* 279, 281; *I and II Corinthians,* 123.

kind of love, concern, and care that Jesus had shown His disciples when He was on earth. He required service of them, not domineering leadership (cf. Mark 9:35; 10:42–45; 1 Pet. 5:1–3).

In addition, Paul expected the elders to "be shepherds" of the church. The chief duty of the shepherd was to lead the sheep to food and water.[17] The elders therefore needed to have the Christ-given, Spirit-anointed, Spirit-gifted ministry of pastor and teacher. This was a great responsibility. They were not simply leading and teaching *their* church but "the church of God,"[18] the Lord's assembly (Gk. *ekklēsia,* "assembly," as in 19:41), an assembly made His own at a tremendous price, the precious blood of Jesus. (See NRSV; see also Eph. 1:7; Titus 2:14; Heb. 9:12,14; 13:12–13.) His blood is the ground of the new covenant (Mark 14:24; Luke 22:20), and the shedding of His blood put the new covenant into effect and brings believers into right relationship with God (Rom. 5:9; Col. 1:20; Rev. 5:9).

> **29I know that after I leave, savage wolves will come in among you and will not spare the flock. 30Even from your own number men will arise and distort the truth in order to draw away disciples after them.**

Another part of the work of a shepherd was to protect the sheep from enemies. The shepherd's staff guided. The shepherd's rod broke the bones of the wolves that came to destroy the sheep. Paul therefore warned these elders that after his departure "savage wolves" would come in among them, "not spar[ing] the [little] flock,"[19] but injuring them severely.

Not all of these wolves would come in from the outside (see Matt. 7:15). "Even from [their] own number," even from among

---

[17]See E. Glen Wagner, *Escape From Church, Inc.: The Return of the Pastor Shepherd* (Grand Rapids: Zondervan Publishing House, 1999), 112–54, for a discussion of what it means to be a pastor-shepherd.

[18]Several ancient manuscripts read "the assembly of the Lord [Jesus]." But "assembly of God" is the better reading. Note that Paul moves from God the Father to God the Son in this sentence. See Richard B. Rackham, *The Acts of the Apostles* (1901; reprint, Grand Rapids: Baker Book House, 1964), 393. Note also that the terms "elder" and "overseer" (bishop) are used interchangeably in this passage (vv. 17,28), and Paul expects them to exercise a ministry as shepherd, or pastor.

[19]See Luke 12:32 where the same term is used of Jesus' disciples.

the elders themselves, some would rise up. By "distort[ing] the truth," that is, by using half-truths or by twisting the truth, they would seek "to draw away disciples," a following, for themselves from the members of the local assemblies. This indicates that their real purpose would be to build up themselves rather than the assembly. They would also attempt to draw away disciples who were already believers; they would have little interest in winning the lost for Christ, nor would they desire to build up the churches that were already established (cf. 2 Cor. 11:13–14).

[31]So be on your guard! Remember that for three years I never stopped warning each of you night and day with tears.

The elders needed to be on their guard against wolves such as these (cf. 1 Tim. 1:19–20; 4:1–10; 2 Tim. 1:15; 2:17–18; 3:1–9; Rev. 2:2–4). Paul then challenged them to remember his example in this too.[20] For the three-year period he was with them, "night and day" he "never stopped warning" each one of them "with tears." That is, he was ready in season and out, and was always moved by tender love for them (2 Tim. 4:2). From what we read in Paul's epistles,[21] we see also that during those years he was opposed by many wolves and false brothers (people who claimed to be Christians).

[32]"Now I commit you to God and to the word of his grace, which can build you up and give you an inheritance among all those who are sanctified.

Paul always did more than warn. He also entrusted them "to God and to the word of his grace," the gospel, which was able to "build . . . up and give . . . an inheritance among all those who are sanctified" (made holy, set apart to follow Jesus, treated as a holy people, consecrated saints of God). They had been an unclean people. Now they were made clean and needed to be nur-

---

[20]"Remember," Gk. *mnēmoneuontes,* implies a call to action, that is, to follow his example.

[21]See 1 Cor 15:32, "If I fought wild beasts in Ephesus..."; 2 Cor. 1:8, "...the hardships we suffered in the province of Asia. We were under great pressure, far beyond our ability to endure, so that we despaired even of life." See Horton, *I and II Corinthians,* 156, 182–83.

tured "according to God's redemptive plans."[22]

**33I have not coveted anyone's silver or gold or clothing.
34You yourselves know that these hands of mine have supplied my own needs and the needs of my companions.**

Paul also set them an example of selfless service.[23] He did not
desire, he did not even want, anyone's silver, gold, or clothing.
They well knew that by his own hands he had supplied not only
his needs but also the needs of those who were with him. As Paul
told the Thessalonians, he worked night and day that he might
not be a burden to any of them (1 Thess. 2:9).

He did tell Timothy that elders who rule well should be given
a double honorarium, for the laborer is worthy of his hire
(1 Tim. 5:17–18). But this applied to established, growing, well-
taught churches. When Paul came into a new area he was careful to show them that he was not preaching the gospel in order
to gain material benefits. Christ's love, imparted by the Holy
Spirit, was his compelling motivation (Rom. 5:5; 2 Cor. 5:14).

**35In everything I did, I showed you that by this kind of
hard work we must help the weak, remembering the
words the Lord Jesus himself said: 'It is more blessed to
give than to receive.'"**

Paul worked with his hands, also, to set an example for all.
The object of every believer should be to give, not just to receive.
We should become mature and strong, and work hard so we can
give to help the weak (including the physically sick or weak, as
well as those who are spiritually weak).[24] Hard work also
includes mental effort, teaching, promoting the gospel in order
to help others. In doing this they would be remembering the
words of Jesus: "It is more blessed to give than to receive."

This saying of Jesus is not recorded in any of the Gospels.
Paul, in Galatians, says he did not receive his gospel from men

[22]Robert W. Wall, "'Purity and Power' According to Acts of the Apostles,"
Pneuma 21, no. 2 (fall 1999): 227. He sees the mention of sanctification here and
in 26:18 "to form an inclusio within which to interpret the real purpose of Paul's
mission according to Acts which is to make the unclean people clean."

[23]Cf. the example of Samuel on his departure from office (1 Sam. 12).

[24]Cf. Eph. 4:28 where Paul urges working with one's hands in order to be able
to give to those in need. See also 2 Thess. 3:10,12.

but directly through revelation by Jesus Christ (Gal. 1:11–12). That is, even the sayings of Jesus were given him by Jesus himself. In a number of instances in his epistles, he indicates he has a word or saying of Jesus to confirm what he says (e.g., 1 Cor. 7:10). He had taught these sayings of Jesus during his stay in Ephesus. Here to reinforce his counsel to these Ephesian elders he reminds them of one of these sayings.

d. A Sad Farewell 20:36–38

36When he had said this, he knelt down with all of them and prayed.

When Paul finished speaking "he knelt down with all of them and prayed." Praying on the knees was common in the Early Church (Acts 9:40; 21:5). But believers also prayed standing, sitting, or prostrate.[25] Paul probably prayed for the elders individually and brought their needs and requests to God.[26]

37They all wept as they embraced him and kissed him. 38What grieved them most was his statement that they would never see his face again. Then they accompanied him to the ship.

After prayer there was a considerable amount of weeping from them all as they embraced Paul (pressed on his neck) and kept kissing him (probably on both cheeks). They were filled with acute pain and sorrow, most of all because Paul said "that they would never see his face again." Then, as a mark of their affection and respect, they escorted him to the ship.

STUDY QUESTIONS

1. On what day of the week did Paul meet with the believers at Troas, and what happened there?

---

[25]Kneeling was characteristically Roman; lying prostrate, Semitic.

[26]Simon J. Kistemaker, *Exposition of the Acts of the Apostles* (Grand Rapids: Baker Book House, 1990), 739. See also Robert L. Brandt and Zenas J. Bicket, *The Spirit Helps Us Pray: A Biblical Theology of Prayer* (Springfield, Mo.: Logion Press, 1993), 262–63.

2. What did Paul emphasize to the Ephesian elders at Miletus?

VI. THE ROAD TO ROME 21:1-28:31

A. Paul Goes To Jerusalem 21:1-26

The farewell at Miletus must have been very hard for Paul. Nor did things get easier as he continued his journey toward Jerusalem. There were sad farewells all along the way. This was another turning point in the ministry of Paul. No longer does he establish new churches. He is on the road to Rome, though Jerusalem, not Rome, continues to have the central attention.[1]

1. PROPHECY AT TYRE 21:1-6

¹After we had torn ourselves away from them, we put out to sea and sailed straight to Cos. The next day we went to Rhodes and from there to Patara. ²We found a ship crossing over to Phoenicia, went on board and set sail. ³After sighting Cyprus and passing to the south of it, we sailed on to Syria. We landed at Tyre, where our ship was to unload its cargo.

It was not easy for Paul and his companions[2] to leave the Ephesian elders, nor was it easy for the elders to let them go. The first day after they left took Paul and his company to the island of Cos, next to the island of Rhodes, then they went on to land at Patara on the coast of the Roman province of Lycia. There they changed to a ship going to Phoenicia, which took them to Tyre. At Tyre the ship unloaded cargo, and they had seven days to wait before it was ready to continue its journey.

⁴Finding the disciples there, we stayed with them seven days. Through the Spirit they urged Paul not to go on to Jerusalem.

Paul did not know where the Christians were in Tyre, so he sought them out to spend the time with them. This is another

---

[1]Robert L. Brawley, *Luke-Acts and the Jews: Conflict, Apology, and Conciliation* (Atlanta: Scholars Press, 1987), 34.

[2]See Acts 20:4.

indication of how extensively believers were scattered by the martyrdom of Stephen (Acts 8:4). At Tyre, as in many places earlier (20:23), the Spirit warned of what was going to happen to Paul in Jerusalem. The Bible does not say how the Spirit did this, but from what happened a little later when Agabus came to Caesarea, we can be sure the warning came through a prophecy.

We read that the believers "urged" (kept repeatedly telling) Paul "through the Spirit" to give up his trip to Jerusalem. This does not mean, however, that the Spirit did not want Paul to go to Jerusalem. The word "through" (Gk. *dia*) is not the word used in previous passages for the direct agency of the Spirit. (See Acts 13:4, where the Gk. is *hupo*, a word used for direct, or primary, agency.) Here the Greek is better translated "in consequence of the Spirit," that is, because of what the Spirit said. The Spirit himself definitely did not forbid Paul to go on.[3] The Spirit was compelling Paul to go (Acts 20:22). Paul knew the Holy Spirit does not contradict himself.[4] It was not the Spirit but the believers' love and concern for Paul that made them keep saying he should not go.[5] In other words, because of a matter-of-fact prophecy about chains and imprisonment the people voiced their feeling that he should not go.[6] But Paul refused to let them force their feelings on him. So he still obeyed what the Holy Spirit directed him personally to do, that is, "go on to Jerusalem."

[5]But when our time was up, we left and continued on our way. All the disciples and their wives and children accompanied us out of the city, and there on the beach we knelt to pray. [6]After saying good-by to each other, we went aboard the ship, and they returned home.

[3]See F. F. Bruce, *Commentary on the Book of Acts* (Grand Rapids: Wm. B. Eerdmans, 1954), 385; also J. A. Alexander, *A Commentary on the Acts of the Apostles,* 3d ed. (1875; reprint, London: Banner of Truth Trust, 1956), 222. Cf. NEB, "They, warned by the Spirit, urged Paul to abandon his visit to Jerusalem." For a contrary opinion see James M. Boice, *Acts* (Grand Rapids: Baker Book House, 1997), 355–62. (Cf. CEV, Beck.)

[4]Jesus himself confirmed this later (Acts 23:11).

[5]David Thomas, *Acts of the Apostles* (1870; reprint, Grand Rapids: Baker Book House, 1956), 359.

[6]"They did not understand the purpose of Paul's future sufferings." Simon J. Kistemaker, *Exposition of the Acts of the Apostles* (Grand Rapids: Baker Book House, 1990), 745.

Within only a week the whole church, including "wives and children," came to know and love Paul. Reminiscent of the farewell at Miletus, the believers were reluctant to say goodbye. They escorted Paul to where the ship lay at anchor in the harbor; on the beach they knelt and prayed. How he must have been encouraged by their send-off!

2. PROPHECY AT CAESAREA 21:7–14

⁷We continued our voyage from Tyre and landed at Ptolemais, where we greeted the brothers and stayed with them for a day. ⁸Leaving the next day, we reached Caesarea and stayed at the house of Philip the evangelist, one of the Seven. ⁹He had four unmarried daughters who prophesied.

Stopping at Ptolemais (OT Accho mentioned in Judg. 1:31, now called Acre or Akka, across the bay from Haifa), midway between Tyre and Caesarea, they spent the day with the Christians. Then the ship brought them to Caesarea. There they stayed at the home of Philip the evangelist, "one of the Seven" (see Acts 6:5). He now had four virgin daughters who prophesied.[7]

The mention of these daughters seems to be significant. It shows that Philip's family served the Lord and that he encouraged them to seek and exercise gifts of the Spirit. It seems also that their ministry in this gift of prophecy must have brought encouragement and blessing to Paul (cf. 1 Cor. 14:3). At Miletus he had been anxious to hurry on his way (Acts 20:16). But here the blessing of the Lord was so rich that he stayed a considerable number of days, this despite having already spent a week at Tyre, with the Day of Pentecost approaching. It is probable also that Philip gave Luke much information concerning the early days of the Church at Jerusalem.

¹⁰After we had been there a number of days, a prophet named Agabus came down from Judea. ¹¹Coming over to us, he took Paul's belt, tied his own hands and feet with it and said, "The Holy Spirit says, 'In this way the Jews of

---

[7]The church historian Eusebius (A.D. 260–340) quotes Polycrates as saying that these daughters moved to Asia, lived long lives, and continued to minister and witness to the Early Church. See Bruce, *Commentary,* 424.

Jerusalem will bind the owner of this belt and will hand him over to the Gentiles.'"

Then the prophet Agabus, the same one who had prophesied famine "during the reign of Claudius" (Acts 11:28), "came down from Judea."[8] Taking Paul's belt (probably one made of a long strip of linen cloth that could be wrapped around the waist several times), he bound his own feet and hands as an object lesson. Then he gave the prophecy from the Holy Spirit that the Jews would bind (or be the cause of binding) Paul and "hand him over to the Gentiles" (that is, the Roman rulers; see Acts 21:30-33).

12When we heard this, we and the people there pleaded with Paul not to go up to Jerusalem.

Because of this prophecy, those who were meeting in Philip's house along with Luke and all Paul's companions kept begging him "not to go up to Jerusalem." This was undoubtedly like what had happened at Tyre: The people, upon hearing the Spirit's straightforward message, expressed their feelings about it.

13Then Paul answered, "Why are you weeping and breaking my heart? I am ready not only to be bound, but also to die in Jerusalem for the name of the Lord Jesus." 14When he would not be dissuaded, we gave up and said, "The Lord's will be done."

Paul, however, asked them what they were trying to do, "weeping and breaking my heart," making him feel crushed. Crushing the heart was a phrase used to mean breaking the will, weakening the purpose, or causing a person to "go to pieces" so that he could accomplish nothing (cf. NEB, JB). To get them to stop their weeping Paul declared he was ready "not only to be bound, but also to die in Jerusalem" for the sake of the Lord Jesus. He knew it was God's will for him to go (20:22; cf. 9:16). Then the others finally accepted the will of the Lord (cf. Luke 22:42), though it was hard for them to recognize it as the Lord's will for Paul to go to Jerusalem.

It was actually very important for the churches to know it was God's will for Paul to be bound. There were still a number of

[8]See 311, n. 82.

Judaizers around who opposed the gospel Paul preached. They were still trying to demand that Gentiles become Jews and be circumcised before they could become Christians. In effect, they were saying the Gentile believers would lose their salvation and would never inherit the future blessings God had purposed for them.

Had Paul gone to Jerusalem without all these warnings that let believers know what was going to happen, the Judaizers would have been quick to take his arrest as the judgment of God. They would have said, "See, did we not tell you? Paul's preaching is all wrong." This could have brought great confusion to the churches. But the Holy Spirit bore witness to Paul and the gospel he preached through these prophecies. (This was also in keeping with the original word given to Ananias for Paul [9:16].) At the same time, the Church itself was protected from forces that could have caused division. Truly, the Holy Spirit is the Guide and Protector we need.

3. WELCOMED AT JERUSALEM 21:15–19

15After this, we got ready and went up to Jerusalem. 16Some of the disciples from Caesarea accompanied us and brought us to the home of Mnason, where we were to stay. He was a man from Cyprus and one of the early disciples.

"We got ready" probably means they saddled up horses.[9] Then Paul and his companions along with some of the disciples from Caesarea went up to Jerusalem. These brothers from Caesarea knew a believer, Mnason,[10] who, like Barnabas, was from Cyprus and "one of the early disciples," that is, one of the 120. Like Barnabas also, he would be sympathetic to Paul's ministry and not object to entertaining Gentile believers.[11] He was known as one who delighted to entertain strangers (foreigners). The Western reading has Mnason's house between Caesarea and

[9]Some writers, however, believe it means they packed their bags (their luggage; see NEB). Perhaps both meanings are included.

[10]Probably a Gk. form of Manasseh.

[11]Some translations indicate that Mnason was visiting in Caesarea at the time Paul was there and came up with them to Jerusalem. But it is more likely that the Caesarean believers simply brought Paul and his company to Mnason's house in Jerusalem.

Jerusalem. This indicates the journey "was broken at least once, and this is certainly more credible for a journey of at least sixty miles."[12]

> **17When we arrived at Jerusalem, the brothers received us warmly. 18The next day Paul and the rest of us went to see James, and all the elders were present.**

At Jerusalem "the brothers," including Mnason, welcomed them "warmly" (Gk. *asmenōs,* "joyfully"—they were very glad to see them) and, as the Greek indicates, entertained them hospitably. The next day Paul took Luke and the rest of his companions to see James, the brother of Jesus. "All the elders" of the Jerusalem church were also present. But it is worth noting that the apostles are not mentioned. Probably, as much Early Church tradition says, they were already scattered, spreading the gospel to many different locations.[13]

> **19Paul greeted them and reported in detail what God had done among the Gentiles through his ministry.**

After greeting these elders, Paul gave them what must have been a rehearsal of his second and third missionary journeys. Specifically, he told them everything that had happened since his being with them at the Jerusalem Council of Acts 15.

4. Encouraging Jewish Believers 21:20–26

> **20When they heard this, they praised God. Then they said to Paul: "You see, brother, how many thousands of Jews have believed, and all of them are zealous for the law.**

James and the other elders "praised God" because of all He was doing among the Gentiles. But there was another matter of deep concern that was affecting the Jerusalem church. "Many thousands," literally tens of thousands (Gk. *muriades*), among

---

[12]W. A. Strange, *The Problem of the Text of Acts* (Cambridge, England: Cambridge University Press, 1992), 42. Cf. Acts 23:31–32; going from Jerusalem to Caesarea, they overnighted at Antipatris, halfway between the two cities.

[13]Peter was probably already in Babylon (1 Pet. 5:13). John went to Ephesus. Andrew may have gone to Scythia or Greece. Strong tradition says Thomas was martyred in India.

the Jews in the Jerusalem area had believed on Jesus as their Messiah, Lord, and Savior. Yet they were still "zealous for the law": eagerly devoted to the law of Moses. They considered themselves Jews who had found the true Messiah. (See the epistle to the Hebrews for addressing their position, showing that Christ is superior to Moses and that a better covenant and a better priesthood replaced the old law and priesthood.)

21They have been informed that you teach all the Jews who live among the Gentiles to turn away from Moses, telling them not to circumcise their children or live according to our customs.

False teachers, probably Judaizers or else unconverted Jews from Asia Minor, Macedonia, or Greece, had come among the Jewish Christians in Jerusalem. They had been telling the Jerusalem believers that Paul was teaching "all the Jews who live among the Gentiles" (the nations outside Palestine) not to circumcise their children. They also had said that Paul taught them to stop conducting their lives according to their (Jewish) customs. This was nothing but slander. Paul had had Timothy circumcised (Acts 16:3); he had recently taken and fulfilled a vow himself (18:18) and had observed Jewish feasts (20:6,16). He had even now traveled far to observe the Feast of Pentecost (20:16). His letters show he did not ask Jewish Christians to stop observing their customs.

22What shall we do? They will certainly hear that you have come, 23so do what we tell you. There are four men with us who have made a vow. 24Take these men, join in their purification rites and pay their expenses, so that they can have their heads shaved. Then everybody will know there is no truth in these reports about you, but that you yourself are living in obedience to the law.

The elders recognized that these accusations were false. But everyone in Jerusalem had heard them again and again. Now, since all in Jerusalem would surely hear that Paul had come, what should be done? James and the elders had a suggestion that they hoped would avoid a split in the Church. They saw a way to stop the rumors and show they were false. Four of the Jewish believers had taken a vow upon themselves, obviously a temporary

Nazirite vow. By this vow any Israelite man or woman could declare their total dedication to God and to His will. Usually the vow was taken for a limited period of time. At the close of the period they had chosen, they would offer rather expensive sacrifices, including a male and female lamb, a ram, and other offerings. Then they would shave their heads as a sign that the vow was completed (Num. 6:14–20).

Paul did not have to take the vow himself. But he was asked to go through ceremonies of purifying himself along with them and pay for the sacrifices so they could complete the vow and shave their heads.[14] This would show the believers and everyone in Jerusalem that Paul did not teach Jewish believers to go against the customs of their fathers.[15] It would also answer all the false things said about Paul and would demonstrate that Paul himself was "living in obedience to the law" (cf. 1 Cor. 9:19–23).

25As for the Gentile believers, we have written to them our decision that they should abstain from food sacrificed to idols, from blood, from the meat of strangled animals and from sexual immorality."

Then James and the elders confirmed the decision of the Jerusalem Council of Acts 15, a decision Paul had already carried to the Gentile believers. That is, though they wanted Paul, as a Jewish believer, to show he did not ask Jews to live like Gentiles, they were still willing to accept Gentile believers without asking them to become Jews.

26The next day Paul took the men and purified himself along with them. Then he went to the temple to give notice of the date when the days of purification would end and the offering would be made for each of them.

The next day Paul took the four men and did as he was asked to do, "to give notice" (Gk. *diangellōn,* "spreading the news") about completing the days of purification until the sacrifice was brought for each of them. It was important for both Jews and

---

[14]It is also possible that these four had defiled themselves in some way and were now undergoing seven days of purification (Num. 6:9). See Bruce, *Commentary,* 430–31.

[15]See comments and notes on 18:18.

Christians to know what Paul was doing.

Paul was not compromising here. As he told the Corinthians, to the Jews he became as a Jew and to those under the Law he became as one under the Law (1 Cor. 9:20).[16]

STUDY QUESTIONS

1. Why did the believers at Tyre urge Paul not to go to Jerusalem?
2. Why was it important that Agabus and other prophets give a prophecy concerning Paul?
3. Why did Paul go to the temple in Jerusalem?

B. Paul's Arrest 21:27-23:35

1. ASIAN JEWS CAUSE A RIOT 21:27-30

27When the seven days were nearly over, some Jews from the province of Asia saw Paul at the temple. They stirred up the whole crowd and seized him, 28shouting, "Men of Israel, help us! This is the man who teaches all men everywhere against our people and our law and this place. And besides, he has brought Greeks into the temple area and defiled this holy place." 29(They had previously seen Trophimus the Ephesian in the city with Paul and assumed that Paul had brought him into the temple area.)

When the seven days of purification were almost completed, Jews from the Roman province of Asia were in Jerusalem for the Feast of Pentecost. They may have been among those who "became obstinate; . . . refused to believe and publicly maligned

---

[16]H. B. Hackett, *A Commentary on the Acts of the Apostles* (Philadelphia: American Baptist Pub. Soc., 1882), 249, 251. Paul knew that these Jewish ceremonies had no value as far as our salvation is concerned. But he did recognize that they had a symbolic or teaching value for Jewish believers. They carried out these things not to gain salvation, not to get in right relation with God, but to express a dedication to God that was already settled in their hearts through Christ and their acceptance of His work on the cross.

the Way" (Acts 19:9). Paul had been "'severely tested'" by their plots (20:19). They saw Paul in the temple and threw the whole crowd into confusion. Then they "seized" him and shouted that he taught everyone everywhere "against our people and our law." Finally, they accused him of having "defiled this holy place" by bringing in Greeks (i.e., Gentiles). "Holy place" meant the inner courts of the temple. Greeks could go only as far as the Court of the Gentiles (see comments and footnote on 3:2).

They had seen Paul in the city with Trophimus, a Gentile believer from Ephesus. They jumped to the conclusion that Paul had brought him into the temple.[1]

30The whole city was aroused, and the people came running from all directions. Seizing Paul, they dragged him from the temple, and immediately the gates were shut.

At this "the whole city" of Jerusalem was stirred up. (Most of them were probably already in the temple at this time.) The Jews ran together "from all directions," seized Paul, and "dragged him from the temple," beating him as they did so. Immediately the great doors to the temple Court of the Women were shut so the mob would not desecrate the temple. No one seemed to notice or care that Paul had no Gentiles with him, however.

2. PAUL RESCUED BY THE ROMANS 21:31–40

31While they were trying to kill him, news reached the commander of the Roman troops that the whole city of Jerusalem was in an uproar. 32He at once took some officers and soldiers and ran down to the crowd. When the rioters saw the commander and his soldiers, they stopped beating Paul.

The mob was already trying to kill Paul when word came to

[1]Archaeologists have found two of the inscriptions that warned Gentiles not to go any farther than the Court of the Gentiles. They read (in Gk.): "No foreigner may enter within this barricade which surrounds the Temple and enclosure [its inner courts]. Anyone caught doing so will have himself to blame for his ensuing death." See John Rutherford, "Partition, the Middle Wall of," in *The International Standard Bible Encyclopedia* (Grand Rapids: Wm. B. Eerdmans, 1943): 4:2253. See F. F. Bruce, *Commentary on the Book of Acts* (Grand Rapids: Wm. B. Eerdmans, 1954), 34.

the Roman commander (Gk. *chiliarchos*, "leader of one thousand," the Gk. equivalent of the Lat. *tribunus militum*, "military tribune"), the officer over six hundred to a thousand men stationed in the Fortress of Antonia on the northwest overlooking the temple area.[2] They told him that all Jerusalem was "in an uproar." Immediately he took soldiers and centurions (officers in command of one hundred infantrymen) and with an unmistakable show of force ran down to them.[3] The sight of the commander and all the soldiers made the mob stop beating Paul.

> [33]The commander came up and arrested him and ordered him to be bound with two chains. Then he asked who he was and what he had done. [34]Some in the crowd shouted one thing and some another, and since the commander could not get at the truth because of the uproar, he ordered that Paul be taken into the barracks.

That the Roman commander rescued Paul from the Jewish mob was an answer to prayer. Paul had written to the Romans, "Pray that I may be rescued from the unbelievers in Judea" (Rom. 15:31). It may not have been everything that Paul had hoped for. He did not anticipate being arrested. But it was all in God's plan as the first step in getting him to Rome.

After having Paul bound "with two chains,"[4] the Roman commander asked the Jews who he was and what he had done. Everyone began shouting different things at once. There was no way the Roman commander could be sure of what was being said "because of the uproar." So he ordered the soldiers to take Paul into the barracks (in the Fortress of Antonia).

> [35]When Paul reached the steps, the violence of the mob was so great he had to be carried by the soldiers. [36]The crowd that followed kept shouting, "Away with him!"

The soldiers had to carry Paul up the two flights of steps from

[2]The fortress was built on a seventy-foot-high rock and had turrets one hundred feet high, from which the temple area and much of the city could be viewed.

[3]The quick intervention and arrest shows how seriously the Roman government regarded riots.

[4]Cf. Agabus's prophecy (Acts 21:11). Paul's feet were probably bound later when they stretched him out to flog him (22:25). The Jews were the cause of the binding, though Roman soldiers did it.

the temple area into the Fortress of Antonia because of the pressure of the crowds. They were following the soldiers trying to pull Paul away and "kept shouting, 'Away with him!'" By this they meant they wanted him killed (cf. NLT, NCV), just as an earlier crowd had wanted Jesus killed (see Luke 23:18). In fact, they would have pulled him apart if the soldiers had not lifted him up and surrounded him.

37As the soldiers were about to take Paul into the barracks, he asked the commander, "May I say something to you?" "Do you speak Greek?" he replied. 38"Aren't you the Egyptian who started a revolt and led four thousand terrorists out into the desert some time ago?"

The crowd dropped behind as the soldiers came to the top of the steps and were about to enter the fortress. So Paul spoke in Greek to the commander. He seemed surprised that Paul knew Greek and asked Paul if he were not the Egyptian "who started a revolt and led four thousand terrorists" (Gk. *sikariōn,* "dagger men"), who were known to assassinate their opponents. (Egyptians at that time spoke Greek from childhood.) One duty of the commander was to keep peace in the temple area. He evidently thought Paul must be an insurrectionist.

39Paul answered, "I am a Jew, from Tarsus in Cilicia, a citizen of no ordinary city. Please let me speak to the people." 40Having received the commander's permission, Paul stood on the steps and motioned to the crowd. When they were all silent, he said to them in Aramaic:

Paul answered by identifying himself as a Jew, a citizen of the prestigious city of Tarsus.[5] This implies that he was "a noble person from a sophisticated place."[6] Then he asked permission to

---

[5]Tarsus enjoyed "political, economic and intellectual prominence. An inscription proclaims 'Tarsus, the first and greatest and most beautiful metropolis.'" Brian Rapske, *The Book of Acts and Paul in Roman Custody,* vol. 3 of *The Book of Acts in Its First Century Setting,* ed. Bruce W. Winter (Grand Rapids: Wm. B. Eerdmans, 1994), 73. Its population was about half a million (a large city for the time; Rome was one million). It boasted a university, and its location commanding the Cilician Gates gave it strategic importance.

[6]Bruce J. Malina and Jerome H. Neyrey, "First-Century Personality: Dyadic, Not Individual," in *The Social World of Luke-Acts: Models for Interpretation,* ed. Jerome H. Neyrey (Peabody, Mass.: Hendrickson Publishers, 1991), 87.

"speak to the people." When this was given, he was allowed to stand on the stairs. Signaling his desire to speak, he got the attention of the crowd and there was sudden quiet. Then Paul began to speak.

The language he spoke (Gk. *Hebraidi*) is generally taken to be Aramaic,[7] the language the Jews brought back from Babylonia after their exile there in the sixth century B.C. But there is considerable evidence from inscriptions, coins, apocryphal documents, and pseudepigraphal writings that Jerusalem Jews took pride in being able to use the old (biblical) Hebrew. All Jews also read the Bible first in Hebrew in the synagogues every week, so they would all be familiar with the biblical Hebrew. The Dead Sea Scrolls also show that the people did know Hebrew. By using the biblical Hebrew, Paul gained the attention of the crowd.

3. A WITNESS FOR CHRIST 22:1-21

1"Brothers and fathers, listen now to my defense." 2When they heard him speak to them in Aramaic, they became very quiet. Then Paul said:

This defense on the stairs was the first of five that the Romans would permit Paul to make. In it Paul emphasizes his heritage as a Jew and his encounter with Christ.

He began by respectfully calling them "brothers and fathers." When the crowd recognized Paul was speaking in Hebrew, they "became very quiet" (not because Heb. was a sacred language, but because it made them realize he was a Jew, not a Gentile, for Gentiles carried on all their business with the Jews in the Greek language).[8]

3"I am a Jew, born in Tarsus of Cilicia, but brought up in this city. Under Gamaliel I was thoroughly trained in the law of our fathers and was just as zealous for God as any of you are today.

Paul then proceeded to identify himself as a Jew born in Tarsus

---

[7]John uses a related word, *Hebraisti,* for terms that are Aramaic (John 5:2; 19:13,17,20). However, he also uses it for the Heb. *Abaddon* (Rev. 9:11; as in Job 26:6; 28:22; Prov. 15:11), showing that it is not limited to Aramaic.

[8]Note the chiastic pattern of the defense that follows in vv. 3–21.

but brought up in Jerusalem under Gamaliel.[9] That is, his schooling was under that famous rabbi. Gamaliel trained him with strict attention to every detail of the "law of our fathers" (the law of Moses with the addition of all the traditions of the scribes and Pharisees). He was also a zealot,[10] eagerly devoted to God, just as all his audience were (cf. Rom. 10:2). He told the Galatians, "I was advancing in Judaism beyond many Jews of my own age and was extremely zealous for the traditions of my fathers" (Gal. 1:14).[11]

[4]I persecuted the followers of this Way to their death, arresting both men and women and throwing them into prison,

Clearly, Paul was not blaming them for beating him. Once, in his zeal for God, he would have done the same thing. In fact, Paul "persecuted the followers of this [Christian] Way" up to the point of causing the death of believers, "arresting [Gk. *desmeuōn,* "binding with chains"] both men and women," and having them put in prison (see Gal. 1:13; Phil. 3:5–6). Again Luke draws attention to the faith of women who were believers.

[5]as also the high priest and all the Council can testify. I even obtained letters from them to their brothers in Damascus, and went there to bring these people as prisoners to Jerusalem to be punished.

The high priest was a witness to this (cf. 9:1–2; probably Caiaphas, who was now dead and replaced by Ananias [see 23:2],

[9]This indicates Paul came to Jerusalem in his early youth, probably in his early teens. See H. B. Hackett, *A Commentary of the Acts of the Apostles* (Philadelphia: American Baptist Publication Society, 1882), 256; R. N. Longenecker, *Paul, Apostle of Liberty* (1964; reprint, Grand Rapids: Baker Book House, 1976), 27.

[10]The noun *zēlōtēs* may indicate not merely the Zealot movement or zealotry directed against the Romans but rather a zeal "against any group that posed a threat to Torah observance." Mark R. Fairchild, "Paul's Pre-Christian Zealot Association: A Re-examination of Gal. 1:14 and Acts 22:3," *New Testament Studies* 45, no. 14 (October 1999): 526.

[11]Paul's education gave him "a thorough knowledge of Scripture (Paul *quotes* the Old Testament over ninety times)." Simon Légasse, "Paul's Pre-Christian Career According to Acts," in *The Book of Acts in Its Palestinian Setting,* ed. Richard Bauckham, vol. 4 of *Acts in Its First Century Setting,* ed. Winter (Grand Rapids: Wm. B. Eerdmans, 1995), 375.

but his records were available), as were "all the Council" (the elders of the Sanhedrin). From them he received letters to the Jews of Damascus and went there to bring the believers in chains "to Jerusalem to be punished."

> ⁶"About noon as I came near Damascus, suddenly a bright light from heaven flashed around me. ⁷I fell to the ground and heard a voice say to me, 'Saul! Saul! Why do you persecute me?'

Then Paul told how he experienced the light from heaven and heard the voice of Jesus asking why he kept persecuting Him. In this account Paul adds the detail that it happened "about noon."

> ⁸"'Who are you, Lord?' I asked." 'I am Jesus of Nazareth, whom you are persecuting,' he replied.

Probably because Paul realized the light that shone around him was "from heaven" (v. 6), he felt the One speaking was supernatural and called him "Lord," though wanting to know who He was. The speaker identified himself as "Jesus of Nazareth," for the Jews knew Him by that name, and again stressed that Paul was persecuting Him.

> ⁹My companions saw the light, but they did not understand the voice of him who was speaking to me.

The Jews traveling with Paul saw the light and heard the sound of Jesus' voice but did not understand what was said (cf. John 12:28,29). Such a brilliant light must have reminded them of the Shekinah glory that once was in the Holy of Holies of the temple.

> ¹⁰"'What shall I do, Lord?' I asked." 'Get up,' the Lord said, 'and go into Damascus. There you will be told all that you have been assigned to do.' ¹¹My companions led me by the hand into Damascus, because the brilliance of the light had blinded me.

Paul's question recognized Jesus as both Lord and Master. He wanted to do what Jesus desired him to do (cf. Acts 2:37). But Jesus did not explain. He just sent Paul into Damascus to receive instructions about what God had appointed for him to do. Because the "brilliance" (Gk. *doxēs*, "glory"; cf. 2 Cor. 4:6) of the light blinded Paul, the Jews with him had to lead him as he walked into the city. They too must have recognized that something supernatural had taken place.

> 12"A man named Ananias came to see me. He was a devout observer of the law and highly respected by all the Jews living there. 13He stood beside me and said, 'Brother Saul, receive your sight!' And at that very moment I was able to see him.

Paul then drew attention to the fact that Ananias of Damascus was "a devout [God-fearing, godly] observer of the law," that is, in the way he was careful to keep the Law. All the Jews who lived in Damascus "highly respected"[12] him. Paul at this point does not mention that Ananias was a believer in Jesus.

Ananias called him "brother," accepting him as a believer. His command for Paul to receive his sight brought immediate healing.

> 14"Then he said: 'The God of our fathers has chosen you to know his will and to see the Righteous One and to hear words from his mouth. 15You will be his witness to all men of what you have seen and heard.

Paul then gave more details of what Ananias said to him after restoring his sight. Ananias told him that the God of their fathers (Abraham, Isaac, and Jacob) had chosen him "to know [come to know, realize] his will and to see the Righteous One [the righteous Servant, that is, the Messiah] and to hear words from his mouth," not from a distance but face-to-face. God did this so Paul could be "his witness to all men" (all humankind) of what he had seen and heard. That is, Paul became a first-hand witness of the fact that Jesus was resurrected and glorified. That Paul was chosen to hear words from Jesus' mouth indicated Jesus would give him the facts of the gospel (as recorded in our four Gospels), which Jesus must have done during the three years Paul was in Arabia (Gal. 1:17–18).

> 16And now what are you waiting for? Get up, be baptized and wash your sins away, calling on his name.'

Ananias was quick to encourage Paul to be baptized and wash away his sins, calling on Jesus' name. This was a command to

---

[12]Gk. *marturoumenos,* "having borne witness," i.e., to his godly character and obedience to the Law.

express faith. The sins would be washed away through calling on the Lord's name, however, not by the water of baptism.[13] As 1 Peter 3:21 brings out, the waters of baptism cannot wash away any of the filthiness of the flesh (that is, of the old nature).[14] Rather, they are an answer (appeal, pledge) of a good conscience that has already been cleansed by faith in the death and resurrection of Christ (1 Pet. 3:20–21; see also Rom. 10:9–10). Peter also compares this to Noah. That is, the fact that Noah came through the flood was a witness to the faith that caused him to build the ark before the flood (see Heb. 11:7). So coming through the waters of baptism bears witness to the faith of those who believed in Christ and received the cleansing of His blood and of His Word before the baptism.

> [17]"When I returned to Jerusalem and was praying at the temple, I fell into a trance [18]and saw the Lord speaking. 'Quick!' he said to me. 'Leave Jerusalem immediately, because they will not accept your testimony about me.'

Paul then skipped over his experiences in Damascus and told how he had returned to Jerusalem. There, praying in this very temple, he was in a trance. This was not a trance in the modern or pagan sense, but a state where his mind was disturbed by the circumstances (cf. Peter's experience, Acts 10:10). Then he saw Jesus, who told him, "Leave Jerusalem immediately," for the people of Jerusalem would not receive Paul's witness to Him.

> [19]"'Lord,' I replied, 'these men know that I went from one synagogue to another to imprison and beat those who believe in you. [20]And when the blood of your martyr Stephen was shed, I stood there giving my approval and guarding the clothes of those who were killing him.'

Paul tried to argue that the Jerusalem Jews knew what he had done in connection with the death of Stephen and his relentless persecution of the believers. He apparently felt that his audience would surely listen when they saw what a change had taken place in him.

[13]Hackett, *Commentary on the Acts,* 258.

[14]Gk. *apothesis rhupou,* "a putting away of filth," is taken by most contemporary translations to mean "removal of dirt from the flesh" (NASB). However, *rhupou* can mean moral filth, or uncleanness.

21"Then the Lord said to me, 'Go; I will send you far away to the Gentiles.'"

But Jesus again commanded him to leave. His purpose was to send him (as an apostle) far away "to the Gentiles" (the nations).

This appearance and command of Jesus was not included in chapter 9. There we read that the Jerusalem leaders, because of a Jerusalem plot to kill Paul, sent him to Tarsus. But now it is clear that it took this appearance of Jesus to make him willing to go.

4. SAVED FROM SCOURGING 22:22–29

22The crowd listened to Paul until he said this. Then they raised their voices and shouted, "Rid the earth of him! He's not fit to live!"

The Jews in the courtyard below listened to Paul until he spoke of the command to go to the Gentiles. The truth that God cares about the Gentiles is clear in the Old Testament (e.g., Gen. 12:3; Isa. 11:10; 42:4). But Roman oppression had blinded the minds of this generation of Jews. Gentiles in their eyes were dogs, scavengers. Consequently, in their prejudice, they began crying out again for Paul's death. He was violating what they had wrongly come to consider as the purity and integrity of the Jewish people.

23As they were shouting and throwing off their cloaks and flinging dust into the air,

While they were shouting this, they were also throwing off their outer garments and shaking out the dust from the folds of their robes as an expression of their anger and as a symbolic mourning of what they considered to be blasphemy (cf. Neh. 5:13). Thus, they expressed their rejection of Paul and his message.

24the commander ordered Paul to be taken into the barracks. He directed that he be flogged and questioned in order to find out why the people were shouting at him like this.

This uproar caused the Roman commander to have Paul brought into the Fortress of Antonia. To find out why the Jews shouted so against him, the commander (who would not have understood Hebrew) also told the soldiers to flog and question him. That is, they were to question him as they flogged him (using a whip of leather thongs with pieces of bone and metal sewn in them).

Paul had already been whipped by Jews five times and beaten with rods by Romans three times (2 Cor. 11:24–25). But this punishment by a Roman scourge was worse and often crippled or killed its victim.

To prepare Paul for the scourging, the soldiers made him bend over and stretch forward. They bound him in that position with thongs (leather straps) to receive the flogging. (Some commentators believe the meaning is that he was hung by the thongs with his feet a few inches above the ground.)

25As they stretched him out to flog him, Paul said to the centurion standing there, "Is it legal for you to flog a Roman citizen who hasn't even been found guilty?" 26When the centurion heard this, he went to the commander and reported it. "What are you going to do?" he asked. "This man is a Roman citizen." 27The commander went to Paul and asked, "Tell me, are you a Roman citizen?" "Yes, I am," he answered.

At this point Paul asked the centurion who was supervising the preparations for the flogging if it was legal to flog a citizen of Rome whose case had not even been tried. This the centurion reported to the commander—who came at once, asking Paul if he was a Roman, which, of course, he was.

28Then the commander said, "I had to pay a big price for my citizenship." "But I was born a citizen," Paul replied.

The commander then remarked that he had had to "pay a big price" for his Roman citizenship.[15] But Paul replied that he was Roman born. His father or grandfather must have given unusual service to the Romans in Tarsus and been rewarded by Roman citizenship for himself and his family.[16]

[15]Roman citizenship was often sold in the reign of Emperor Claudius (A.D. 41–54), especially by his wife and other court favorites. It apparently became a means of personal gain. Apparently the commander had used it as a means of gaining a higher commission in the Roman army.

[16]Some older commentaries say that the entire city of Tarsus was given Roman citizenship, but the historical evidence does not confirm this. Fairchild notes that

²⁹Those who were about to question him withdrew immediately. The commander himself was alarmed when he
realized that he had put Paul, a Roman citizen, in chains.

The soldiers who were about to question (and torture) Paul
quickly left. The commander "himself was alarmed." He knew
that Paul, as a Roman citizen, had a right to bring charges
against him for putting him in chains.

5. FACING THE SANHEDRIN 22:30–23:10

³⁰The next day, since the commander wanted to find out
exactly why Paul was being accused by the Jews, he
released him and ordered the chief priests and all the
Sanhedrin to assemble. Then he brought Paul and had
him stand before them.

The commander kept Paul in protective custody (without the
chains no doubt). The next day, because he wanted to know
exactly why the Jews were accusing Paul, he brought him out
and "ordered the chief priests and all the Sanhedrin to assemble." Paul, who was once a member of the Sanhedrin and had
cast his vote to stone Stephen, now had to face this highest court
of the Jews. Their council chamber had been west of the temple
area, but the Jerusalem Talmud says it was relocated south, within the Royal Stoa, in the midst of the shops. The Roman commander brought Paul there and "had him stand before them."

¹Paul looked straight at the Sanhedrin and said, "My
brothers, I have fulfilled my duty to God in all good conscience to this day."

Paul showed no fear or hesitation. He knew he was in the will
of the Lord, and he had learned to depend on the Holy Spirit.
Fixing his eyes on the council, he called them brothers, implying
he was still a faithful Jew. Then he declared that he had lived his
life and fulfilled his duties before God conscientiously up to that
day. His conscience was clear (see 1 Cor. 4:4; Phil. 3:6,9).

Jerome traced Paul's parents to Gischala (Gush Halav) in upper Galilee. The
Romans deported them to Tarsus, selling them as slaves. They were later freed
and granted Roman citizenship (as many freed slaves were). Fairchild, "Paul's Pre-
Christian Zealot Association," 516–19.

2At this the high priest Ananias ordered those standing near Paul to strike him on the mouth. 3Then Paul said to him, "God will strike you, you whitewashed wall! You sit there to judge me according to the law, yet you yourself violate the law by commanding that I be struck!"

At this the high priest, Ananias, ordered those standing by Paul to hit him on the mouth. Paul reacted to this because his sense of justice was aroused: "God will strike you [cf. Deut. 28:22], you whitewashed wall!"17 Paul took him to be one of the members of the council that was sitting there to judge him according to the Law. Yet he had commanded him to be struck contrary to the Law. The oral law treated a man as innocent until he was proved guilty (cf. Lev. 19:15).

4Those who were standing near Paul said, "You dare to insult God's high priest?" 5Paul replied, "Brothers, I did not realize that he was the high priest; for it is written: 'Do not speak evil about the ruler of your people.'"

Those who had struck Paul rebuked him for insulting God's high priest. Paul quickly apologized. He did not know the one who gave the command was the high priest. Herod of Chalcis made Ananias high priest in A.D. 47.18 Paul had been in Jerusalem since then only a few times and for short periods, so it is not strange that he had not seen the high priest before. It is probable also that since the Roman commander had convened the Sanhedrin on this occasion, the high priest was sitting among the other members of the court instead of presiding.

17That is, a wall whitewashed to hide the fact it was crumbling or decaying. Some see also a reference to what Jesus said about whitewashed tombs (Matt. 23:27). See Hackett, *Commentary on the Acts,* 263. Paul used the term to mean that despite the high priest's appearance, he had a corrupt heart and mind.

18Ananias was a very greedy and disgraceful high priest. In A.D. 66 he was put to death by the Jews themselves. See Bruce, *Commentary,* 449–50. Some believe Paul knew that Ananias was the high priest but was using irony here. That is, they take it that Paul meant no true high priest would do what Ananias did. See J. W. Packer, *Acts of the Apostles* (Cambridge, England: Cambridge University Press, 1975), 187; Johannes Munck, *The Acts of the Apostles,* rev. William F. Albright and C. S. Mann, vol. 31 of *Anchor Bible Series* (Garden City, N.Y.: Doubleday & Co., 1979), 223. It seems more likely that he actually did not know, for Ananias was a recent appointment.

But though Paul did not know who the high priest was, he did know the Scriptures. His quotation of Exodus 22:28 shows the genuine humility of his spirit and his willingness to submit to the Law that his accusers claimed he had defied.[19] In any case Jesus' followers were to remember to turn the other cheek (Luke 6:28–29).

> **6Then Paul, knowing that some of them were Sadducees and the others Pharisees, called out in the Sanhedrin, "My brothers, I am a Pharisee, the son of a Pharisee. I stand on trial because of my hope in the resurrection of the dead."**

Then Paul realized that there was an issue he could declare. As he already knew, but now noticed again, part of the Sanhedrin were Sadducees, part Pharisees. Paul had a background as a Pharisee. He told the Philippians he was "a Hebrew of Hebrews; in regard to the law, a Pharisee" (Phil. 3:5). The Pharisees believed the hope of the resurrection was fundamental to the hope of Israel and necessary to the full realization of God's promise. The Sadducees rejected the idea of any resurrection.

Paul, therefore, took advantage of that situation with courage. It was an opportunity to witness to the truth of resurrection in general and to the fact of the resurrection of Jesus in particular; he was not out of order in this.[20] Even before his conversion, as a Pharisee he realized how significant the doctrine of future resurrection is. Crying out that he was "a Pharisee, the son of a Pharisee,"[21] he declared that it was with respect to the hope and resurrection of the dead that he was being called into question.[22]

---

[19]The Heb. of Exod. 22:28 refers to government leaders, not spiritual leaders such as priests or prophets. However, ever since the late Persian period, the high priest had acted as a de facto governor or liaison between the Jews and their Gentile overlords.

[20]Some think he later regretted taking things into his own hands (24:20–21).

[21]Though he was not as strict as some, he could still consider himself a Pharisee. See Longenecker, *Paul, Apostle of Liberty,* 261–62. This put Paul "in the center of a revered sphere of Judaism," and Brawley takes this as exonerating Paul's "mission among gentiles." Robert L. Brawley, *Luke-Acts and the Jews: Conflict, Apology, and Conciliation* (Atlanta: Scholars Press, 1987), 99. See, however, Phil. 3:7.

[22]The pseudepigraphal book 1 Enoch promised resurrection. Its discovery among the Dead Sea Scrolls shows that first-century Jews had a strong belief in

(Though the riot broke out because of the charge of Paul's bringing a Gentile into the temple and recurred when he declared God had sent him to the Gentiles, this was not the real problem. That Jesus rose from the dead and guarantees the resurrection of believers was the heart of his message.)

7When he said this, a dispute broke out between the Pharisees and the Sadducees, and the assembly was divided. 8(The Sadducees say that there is no resurrection, and that there are neither angels nor spirits, but the Pharisees acknowledge them all.)

This split the assembly into two camps. As they contended with one another, the discord grew. They even went beyond the idea of resurrection and began arguing about the existence of angels and spirits, which the Sadducees also denied.[23]

9There was a great uproar, and some of the teachers of the law who were Pharisees stood up and argued vigorously. "We find nothing wrong with this man," they said. "What if a spirit or an angel has spoken to him?"

The result was "a great uproar" as they clamored against each other. Some of the experts in the interpretation of the Law (scribes) who were on the side of the Pharisees stood up and "argued vigorously" on Paul's behalf. They found "nothing wrong" (nothing bad) in him. They suggested that an angel or spirit might have spoken to him.

10The dispute became so violent that the commander was afraid Paul would be torn to pieces by them. He ordered the troops to go down and take him away from them by force and bring him into the barracks.

The mention of "angel" and "spirit" must have stirred up the

---

resurrection. The Jewish Mishnah (the traditions of the Pharisees, written down about A.D. 200 and made a basic part of the Talmud) states that those who deny the resurrection of the dead will have no part in the age to come. This became the orthodox Jewish belief and the doctrines of the Sadducees were rejected. See Jacob Neusner, trans., *The Talmud of Babylonia* (Atlanta: Scholars Press, 1992), 18.C: Gittin, 164. See Bruce, *Commentary*, 454.

[23]Ancient rabbis spoke of "ministering angels." Neusner, *The Talmud of Babylonia*, 14.B: 156.

Sadducees. Things grew "so violent" that the Roman commander became afraid that Paul might be torn apart. So he ordered the soldiers to go down and pull him from the crowd and take him back to the Fortress of Antonia.

6. ENCOURAGED BY THE LORD 23:11

11The following night the Lord stood near Paul and said, "Take courage! As you have testified about me in Jerusalem, so you must also testify in Rome."

It had been a hard day for Paul. But during the night, the Lord Jesus suddenly stood by[24] him and said, "Take courage! [cheer up and don't be afraid]." As Paul had given a clear witness for Christ in Jerusalem, "so" (Gk. *houtō,* "in just the same way") must he also witness in Rome (also as a prisoner). Paul's desire to go to Rome[25] had seemed impossible after his arrest. But Jesus now made it clear that a witness in Rome was still God's will for him. This encouragement upheld Paul in the sufferings, trials, and difficulties that were still to come.

7. A JEWISH PLOT DISCOVERED 23:12-22

12The next morning the Jews formed a conspiracy and bound themselves with an oath not to eat or drink until they had killed Paul. 13More than forty men were involved in this plot.

The next morning over forty Jews held a meeting to plot Paul's death. In doing so they "bound themselves with an oath" (Gk. *anathematisan heautous,* "invoked a curse on themselves"), saying they would neither eat nor drink until they had killed Paul. This desire to assassinate shows how much they hated Paul.

14They went to the chief priests and elders and said, "We have taken a solemn oath not to eat anything until we have killed Paul. 15Now then, you and the Sanhedrin petition the commander to bring him before you on the pretext of wanting more accurate information about his case. We are ready to kill him before he gets here."

---

[24]Gk. *epistas,* "standing over." See F. F. Bruce, *Acts: Greek Text,* 467.
[25]Cf. Rom. 15:23.

Then they went to the chief priests and elders and explained their plan. These elders were, no doubt, Sadducees who did not like what Paul said about the resurrection. The conspirators asked these leaders to get the Sanhedrin to make an official request to the Roman commander to bring Paul down, as if they intended to determine more precisely the facts concerning him. Before he got near, they would be waiting, prepared to kill him. That is, they would ambush him on the way, so the Sanhedrin would not be held responsible for his death.[26] But they needed the Sanhedrin to make the request. It was the only way to get Paul out of the safety of the Roman garrison.

16But when the son of Paul's sister heard of this plot, he went into the barracks and told Paul. 17Then Paul called one of the centurions and said, "Take this young man to the commander; he has something to tell him."

Paul's sister's son happened to come on the scene just at this time and he heard their plot.[27] So he went immediately to the Fortress of Antonia and told Paul. Paul then called a centurion and asked him to take the young man to the Roman commander.[28]

18So he took him to the commander. The centurion said, "Paul, the prisoner, sent for me and asked me to bring this young man to you because he has something to tell you." 19The commander took the young man by the hand, drew him aside and asked, "What is it you want to tell me?"

When the soldier took Paul's nephew to the commander, he referred to Paul as "the prisoner." The commander received the boy courteously, took him "by the hand," and "drew him aside" so they could talk privately. Then he asked what he had to tell him.

20He said: "The Jews have agreed to ask you to bring Paul before the Sanhedrin tomorrow on the pretext of wanting more accurate information about him. 21Don't give in

[26] *The Message* in v. 15 has "'Before he gets anywhere near you, we'll have killed him. You won't be involved.'"

[27] Some writers believe he had come to Jerusalem from Tarsus to be educated, just as Paul had. See Bruce, *Acts: Greek Text,* 457. Others think Paul's parents had returned to live in Jerusalem while their children were still young (cf. 22:3).

[28] Since Paul was a prisoner in protective custody and a Roman citizen not yet condemned, friends and relatives would be allowed access.

to them, because more than forty of them are waiting in
ambush for him. They have taken an oath not to eat or
drink until they have killed him. They are ready now,
waiting for your consent to their request."

The boy told the commander of the plot and warned him not
to be persuaded by their request for "more accurate information"
about Paul. The men who had "taken an oath" were prepared,
just waiting for the commander's "consent to their request."

**22The commander dismissed the young man and cau-
tioned him, "Don't tell anyone that you have reported
this to me."**

The commander then let Paul's nephew go, after making him
promise not to tell anyone that he had reported these things to him.

8. PAUL TAKEN TO CAESAREA 23:23–35

**23Then he called two of his centurions and ordered
them, "Get ready a detachment of two hundred soldiers,
seventy horsemen and two hundred spearmen to go to
Caesarea at nine tonight. 24Provide mounts for Paul so
that he may be taken safely to Governor Felix."**

The commander knew he would be held accountable for a
Roman citizen in his custody: If Paul was assassinated the commander would be executed. He was taking no chances—two
hundred foot soldiers, along with "seventy horsemen and two
hundred spearmen."[29] Horses also were to be provided for Paul
to ride so that he might be taken safely to Felix, the Roman governor of the province.[30] Paul was probably given a military cloak
to wear, so that if any Jew happened to see this military sortie go
by they would not suspect he was among them.

**25He wrote a letter as follows: 26Claudius Lysias, To His
Excellency, Governor Felix: Greetings. 27This man was
seized by the Jews and they were about to kill him, but I**

---

[29]That they were spearmen is debatable. The Gk. *dexiolabous* refers to something taken by the right hand, so it could refer to small weapons such as short
spears. Others say it refers to their authority rather than their weapons.

[30]Marcus Antonius Felix was procurator of Judea from before A.D. 52 until
A.D. 59.

came with my troops and rescued him, for I had learned that he is a Roman citizen.

The commander also wrote a letter to explain to the governor why he was sending Paul. Acts says it was "as follows" (Gk. *periechousan ton tupon touton,* "having this form"). Probably what is meant is that this is an actual copy of the letter.[31]

In the letter the commander named himself, Claudius Lysias. (Lysias was a Greek name, indicating his Greek background.) Then he explained how he had rescued Paul from the Jews who had been about to kill him. He put himself in a better light than was actually the case, however. He implied that he rescued Paul because he had learned Paul was a Roman citizen; we can give him credit, though, for trying to put Paul in a good light.

28I wanted to know why they were accusing him, so I brought him to their Sanhedrin. 29I found that the accusation had to do with questions about their law, but there was no charge against him that deserved death or imprisonment.

He explained that the accusations were based on questions of Jewish law and that he had found nothing worthy of death or of being chained as a prisoner.

30When I was informed of a plot to be carried out against the man, I sent him to you at once. I also ordered his accusers to present to you their case against him.

Because of the plot, he sent Paul to the governor, commanding his accusers to bring their charges against Paul to him in Caesarea also.

One wonders if word of this came to the forty-plus conspirators before Paul was taken out of the city. Picture Paul, surrounded by four hundred soldiers and seventy cavalry, leaving Jerusalem at nine o'clock in the evening. Such a troop movement, even at night, must have attracted attention. Though it may not have been known that Paul was in the midst of them, someone surely must have investigated. In any case, the commander made sure that they had no chance to do anything to him.

[31]Gk. *tupon* can also mean type, pattern, or copy.

The Bible does not tell us what the conspirators did about their vow. Obviously they had to eat and drink before long. Probably they found some way to offer a sacrifice or offering to atone for their failure to keep the vow. The Jewish Mishnah indicates there was such a provision. The Talmud also provides grounds for the absolution of vows.[32]

> **[31]So the soldiers, carrying out their orders, took Paul with them during the night and brought him as far as Antipatris. [32]The next day they let the cavalry go on with him, while they returned to the barracks. [33]When the cavalry arrived in Caesarea, they delivered the letter to the governor and handed Paul over to him.**

That night the soldiers brought Paul as far as Antipatris (where there was a Roman colony and military station), about halfway to Caesarea. Since they were out of the hill country and somewhat safer, in the morning the foot soldiers returned to the Fortress of Antonia. The cavalry conducted Paul the rest of the way to Caesarea, delivered the letter, and brought Paul before the governor.

> **[34]The governor read the letter and asked what province he was from. Learning that he was from Cilicia, [35]he said, "I will hear your case when your accusers get here." Then he ordered that Paul be kept under guard in Herod's palace.**

After reading the letter, Felix asked Paul "what province he was from," probably because only if Paul came from a Roman province could he, as a Roman, take charge of him on his own authority. Then he ordered that Paul be kept in "Herod's palace" (Gk. *praitōriō*, Lat. *praetorium*), the palace built by Herod the Great where the governor now had his residence and kept his soldiers.

STUDY QUESTIONS

1. What were the results of Paul's visit to the temple and why?
2. What did Paul emphasize in his message from the steps of the Fortress of Antonia?

[32]Neusner, *Talmud of Babylonia*, 15.B: 10.

3. Why did Paul say he was a Pharisee, when he faced the Sanhedrin?
4. What caused the commander to transfer Paul to Caesarea?

C. Paul's Appeal To Caesar 24:1-26:32

1. PAUL ACCUSED BY THE JEWS 24:1-27

a. Tertullus Presents Their Case 24:1-9

[1]Five days later the high priest Ananias went down to Caesarea with some of the elders and a lawyer named Tertullus and they brought their charges against Paul before the governor.

Only once did the Jews bring formal charges against Paul. On this occasion they hired a "lawyer" (Gk. *rhētoros,* "orator, professional public speaker, speaker in court") to act as counsel for the prosecution.

After five days[1] the high priest, Ananias, with some of the members of the Sanhedrin (undoubtedly those who were his Sadducean friends), arrived with the orator-lawyer Tertullus[2] and reported to the governor against Paul. Paul was then called, and Tertullus was given opportunity to present his accusation against him.

[2]When Paul was called in, Tertullus presented his case before Felix: "We have enjoyed a long period of peace under you, and your foresight has brought about reforms in this nation. [3]Everywhere and in every way, most excellent Felix, we acknowledge this with profound gratitude. [4]But in order not to weary you further, I would request that you be kind enough to hear us briefly.

Secular history shows that Felix was actually a violent, unfair man. Josephus records that the Jews hated him. Nevertheless,

---

[1]The Gk. probably means on the fifth day.

[2]Probably a "diminutive of *Tertius,* 'Third.'" Margaret H. Williams, "Palestinian Jewish Personal Names in Acts," in *The Book of Acts in Its Palestinian Setting,* ed. Richard Bauckham, vol. 4 of *The Book of Acts in Its First Century Setting,* ed. Bruce W. Winter (Grand Rapids: Wm. B. Eerdmans, 1995), 103. He was probably a Hellenistic Jew with some education in Roman law.

Tertullus began by flattering the governor. He declared that through him the Jewish nation had experienced "a long period of peace"; his forethought had "brought about reforms"; these things the Jews accepted in all ways and in all places "with profound gratitude." But that he might not "weary [the governor] further," Tertullus begged him to listen briefly "'by [his] kindness'" (v. 4, NASB; consideration, fairness).

> **5"We have found this man to be a troublemaker, stirring up riots among the Jews all over the world. He is a ringleader of the Nazarene sect 6and even tried to desecrate the temple; so we seized him [and wanted to judge him according to our law].**

Tertullus then belittled Paul, calling him "this man," and falsely accused him of being a "troublemaker" (Gk. *loimon,* "a dangerous plague or pestilence"), one stirring up "riots" (insurrection, revolution) among the Jews who are "all over the [inhabited] world" (that is, in the Roman Empire). Then he implicated all the Christians by calling Paul a ringleader of the "sect" (Gk. *hairesos,* "party," "school") of the Nazarenes (Gk. *nazōraiōn,* the followers of the Man of Nazareth).

Finally, after this general accusation, Tertullus gave the specific charge. Paul, he said, tried to "desecrate the temple." But they had caught him in the act, stopping him before he could do so. This, of course, was false. Moreover, Tertullus did not tell how they had seized Paul—as a mob bent on beating him to death, without benefit of a trial.

> **7[But the commander, Lysias, came and with the use of much force snatched him from our hands 8and ordered his accusers to come before you.] By examining him yourself you will be able to learn the truth about all these charges we are bringing against him." 9The Jews joined in the accusation, asserting that these things were true.**

Instead, (as the Western Text and most other ancient New Testament manuscripts indicate here)[3] Tertullus pretended that Paul was being judged properly by their Law when the Roman

[3]The Western Text adds the bracketed words in vv. 6–8; see NIV note. This may be a place where the Western Text (Codex D) is correct.

commander intervened with "much force" and commanded his accusers to appear before the governor.

Tertullus also confidently declared that by examining Paul himself the governor would be able to find out that these accusations against Paul were true.[4] The Jews then joined in pressing charges against him, saying again and again that these things were so.

b. Paul Answers 24:10–21

10When the governor motioned for him to speak, Paul replied: "I know that for a number of years you have been a judge over this nation; so I gladly make my defense.

When the governor nodded to Paul, indicating that he should speak, Paul addressed him courteously, stating facts, but without the flattery of Tertullus. Since Felix had been some years a judge of the Jews, Paul felt he could make his defense "gladly" (Gk. *euthumōs*, "cheerfully").[5]

11You can easily verify that no more than twelve days ago I went up to Jerusalem to worship. 12My accusers did not find me arguing with anyone at the temple, or stirring up a crowd in the synagogues or anywhere else in the city. 13And they cannot prove to you the charges they are now making against me.

Then he presented the facts that the governor could "easily verify" for himself. It was at that time "no more than twelve days" since Paul had come to worship in Jerusalem.[6] That is, he had been there only a week before he was seized by the mob. During that time they had not found him arguing with (or preaching to) anyone. Nor did he stir up a crowd in the temple, in the synagogues, "or anywhere else in the city." In no way could they prove any of their accusations.

[4]Some ancient manuscripts of the NT indicate that Tertullus meant Lysias the tribune should be examined rather than Paul.

[5]The corresponding verb can mean "to cheer up or encourage," so a few commentators consider that Paul made his defense "with confidence" (see NEB, JB; cf. NLT).

[6]Worship was an important part of Paul's purpose for coming to Jerusalem. See Acts 24:14. See Richard N. Longenecker, *Paul, Apostle of Liberty* (1964; reprint, Grand Rapids: Baker Book House, 1976), 262–63.

¹⁴However, I admit that I worship the God of our fathers as a follower of the Way, which they call a sect. I believe everything that agrees with the Law and that is written in the Prophets,

Paul then proceeded with a public declaration of his faith. "As a follower of the Way," called a "sect" (Gk. *hairesin,* "party," "school," the same term used of the Pharisees and Sadducees),⁷ he maintained that he continued to serve the God of his fathers (his ancestors, Abraham, Isaac, and Jacob). He also maintained that he was still faithful to his Jewish heritage, still a believer in "everything that agrees with the Law and that is written in the Prophets." Tertullus was wrong. Paul also "implicitly rejects the label of a 'school' . . . because for him Christianity is now the only way and not simply one of choice."⁸

¹⁵and I have the same hope in God as these men, that there will be a resurrection of both the righteous and the wicked. ¹⁶So I strive always to keep my conscience clear before God and man.

By the Law and the Prophets, Paul also had a hope in God, a hope that these Jews shared. This hope was for "a resurrection of both the righteous and the wicked" (Dan. 12:2; John 5:29).⁹ For this reason Paul exercised himself continually to have a conscience free from causing offense to God and people.

¹⁷"After an absence of several years, I came to Jerusalem to bring my people gifts for the poor and to present offerings. ¹⁸I was ceremonially clean when they found me in the temple courts doing this. There was no crowd with me, nor was I involved in any disturbance.

⁷Gk. writers used the term for philosophical schools. Josephus regarded the term as equivalent to *philosophia.* Charles H. Talbert, *Reading Acts: A Literary and Theological Commentary on the Acts of the Apostles* (New York: Crossroad Publishing, 1997), 5.

⁸Steve Mason, "Chief Priests, Sadducees, Pharisees and Sanhedrin in Acts," in *Acts in Its Palestinian Setting,* ed. Bauckham, 154.

⁹Other texts make it clear that the Millennium comes between the resurrection and judgment of the righteous and the resurrection and judgment of the unrighteous. See Stanley M. Horton, *Our Destiny: Biblical Teachings on the Last Things* (Springfield, Mo.: Logion Press, 1996), 52–53, 77, 81, 87, 187–89, 222–24.

After this discourse on the resurrection, Paul returned to the facts of his case: "After an absence of several years" he had come back to Jerusalem with "gifts for the poor and . . . offerings" to God (see 1 Cor. 16:1–3; 2 Cor. 8:1–24). It was while he was presenting these offerings that they had found him in the temple—not defiling it but ritually purified, with "no crowd . . . nor . . . any disturbance."

19But there are some Jews from the province of Asia, who ought to be here before you and bring charges if they have anything against me.

But there were certain Jews from Asia who had falsely accused him (see Acts 21:27–28). They were the real accusers, and it was really their duty to be the ones to come before Felix and make their accusation if they had anything against Paul.

20Or these who are here should state what crime they found in me when I stood before the Sanhedrin— 21unless it was this one thing I shouted as I stood in their presence: 'It is concerning the resurrection of the dead that I am on trial before you today.'"

Paul here was taking advantage of the Jewish law's demand for witnesses to make the accusation (Num. 35:30; Deut. 17:6–7,15). Then he made it clear that none of these priests and elders present were witnesses of what went on in the temple. There was really only one thing they had witnessed. They were present when he had stood before the Sanhedrin and cried out that it was with respect to the resurrection of the dead that he was called into question. He would willingly let them accuse him of that.

c. Felix Postpones Making A Decision 24:22–27

22Then Felix, who was well acquainted with the Way, adjourned the proceedings. "When Lysias the commander comes," he said, "I will decide your case."

Felix then "adjourned the proceedings." He had been governor long enough to have a more accurate knowledge of the teachings and lifestyle of the tens of thousands of Christians in Judea than Tertullus and the Jews present gave him credit for.[10] So he post-

---

[10]Perhaps Cornelius the centurion or Drusilla, the Jewish wife of Felix, encouraged such knowledge. (See note 11).

poned his decision, saying that when the commander Lysias came down he would learn the details of the things that concerned them. There is no evidence, however, that he ever sent for Lysias.

23He ordered the centurion to keep Paul under guard but to give him some freedom and permit his friends to take care of his needs.

Felix then commanded the centurion to guard and protect Paul. He was to also allow Paul a considerable amount of freedom, not forbidding his friends from visiting him, bringing him food, and giving him whatever else he needed.

24Several days later Felix came with his wife Drusilla, who was a Jewess. He sent for Paul and listened to him as he spoke about faith in Christ Jesus.

After some days Felix, with his Jewish wife Drusilla,[11] came, summoned Paul, and listened to him tell of the "faith in Christ Jesus" (lit. the "in Christ Jesus" faith, that is, the gospel).

25As Paul discoursed on righteousness, self-control and the judgment to come, Felix was afraid and said, "That's enough for now! You may leave. When I find it convenient, I will send for you."

Paul not only presented the facts and the theology, but as he did in all his epistles, he went on to discuss practical matters of "righteousness, self-control, and the judgment to come." At this, Felix became terrified and told Paul to go for now. (He was not ready to leave his dissolute life.) At a convenient time he would call him again. He was using procrastination to excuse his unwillingness to repent.

26At the same time he was hoping that Paul would offer him a bribe, so he sent for him frequently and talked with him.

[11]She was the daughter of King Herod Agrippa I (Acts 12:1) and the sister of King Herod Agrippa II and the princess Bernice. Felix had seduced Drusilla from her former husband, King Azizus of Emesa (modern Homs in western Syria). She was the third wife of Felix. They had a son, Agrippa III, who died in the Vesuvius eruption that destroyed Pompeii in A.D. 79. The Western Text adds that Drusilla was the one who wished to see Paul and hear his message, so Felix summoned Paul to satisfy her.

At the same time Felix greedily hoped that Paul would give him a great deal of money (Gk. *chrēmata,* "riches"). He knew Paul had many friends and probably expected them to present a bribe for his release.[12] Therefore, he sent for him "frequently and talked with him."

27When two years had passed, Felix was succeeded by Porcius Festus, but because Felix wanted to grant a favor to the Jews, he left Paul in prison.

This continued over a two-year period. Then Porcius Festus, who arrived in A.D. 59 and remained in office until his death in A.D. 61, replaced Felix. The date of Paul's arrest was thus A.D. 57.

Because Felix still wanted to curry favor with the Jews, he "left Paul [chained] in prison." Even so, that did not help Felix. After he was removed, the Jews sent accusations to Rome against him. Nero would have punished him except that his wealthy, influential brother M. Antonius Pallas interceded for him.[13]

2. TRIAL BEFORE FESTUS 25:1–8

1Three days after arriving in the province, Festus went up from Caesarea to Jerusalem, 2where the chief priests and Jewish leaders appeared before him and presented the charges against Paul.

The Jews in Jerusalem had not given up. They still considered Paul their archenemy and wanted his death. So they took advantage of the new governor, Festus, with the intent of seeking a new opportunity for carrying out their plots.

After Festus took office in Caesarea he rested a day and then went up to Jerusalem.[14] Immediately the chief priests and chief men of the Jews informed him of their charges against Paul.

3They urgently requested Festus, as a favor to them, to have Paul transferred to Jerusalem, for they were preparing an ambush to kill him along the way.

[12]Some writers believe Paul received an inheritance about this time, but this has not been proven.

[13]Josephus *Antiquities of the Jews* 20, 182.

[14]According to the Jewish way of counting, "after three days" means on the third day. See R. C. H. Lenski, *The Interpretation of the Acts of the Apostles* (Minneapolis: Augsburg Press, 1961), 987.

Then the Jewish leaders "urgently requested" (Gk. *parakaloun*)[15] Festus to send for Paul and have him brought to Jerusalem. Again there was a plot to ambush and kill him along the road.

4Festus answered, "Paul is being held at Caesarea, and I myself am going there soon. 5Let some of your leaders come with me and press charges against the man there, if he has done anything wrong."

Festus must have been informed of their previous plot, so he replied that Paul was held (guarded) in Caesarea where Festus would soon be going. He then suggested that leaders (Gk. *hoi dunatoi*, "persons of power or ability," probably members of the Sanhedrin) go to Caesarea with him. Then if there was anything wrong (Gk. *atopos*, "out of place," "improper") in Paul, let them accuse him.

6After spending eight or ten days with them, he went down to Caesarea, and the next day he convened the court and ordered that Paul be brought before him. 7When Paul appeared, the Jews who had come down from Jerusalem stood around him, bringing many serious charges against him, which they could not prove.

After eight or ten days, Festus did go down to Caesarea. The next day he sat on the judgment seat (Gk. *bēma*, the judge's throne, the tribunal). That is, he called for a new official trial and had Paul brought in.

The Jerusalem Jews then stood around Paul, making "many serious charges" against him—none of which they could prove. Luke does not give any details here, but the charges were undoubtedly similar to those Tertullus had brought before Felix two years earlier.

8Then Paul made his defense: "I have done nothing wrong against the law of the Jews or against the temple or against Caesar."

---

[15]The Gk. is stronger than simply asking "a favor" (NCV, NLT). William J. Larkin, Jr., translates the verb as "persistently implored." *Acts* (Downers Grove, Ill.: InterVarsity Press, 1995), 345. They kept urging or begging him (CEV; v. 2, TEV).

Luke also merely summarizes Paul's defense here. Paul contended that he had not sinned in any way "against the law of the Jews or against the temple or against Caesar" (that is, against the Roman government). Later Festus shows that Paul bore witness to Christ's death and resurrection as well (v. 19).

3. Festus Agrees To Send Paul To Caesar 25:9–12

9Festus, wishing to do the Jews a favor, said to Paul, "Are you willing to go up to Jerusalem and stand trial before me there on these charges?"

Festus, desiring to gain favor with the Jews like Felix before him, asked Paul if he would be willing to go up to Jerusalem for another trial before him. Paul, of course, knew what this would mean. Like the first time, he had gotten wind of the new plot to ambush him. Unlike the first account, however, Luke does not go into detail; perhaps it would have gotten his source in trouble.

10Paul answered: "I am now standing before Caesar's court, where I ought to be tried. I have not done any wrong to the Jews, as you yourself know very well. 11If, however, I am guilty of doing anything deserving death, I do not refuse to die. But if the charges brought against me by these Jews are not true, no one has the right to hand me over to them. I appeal to Caesar!"

Paul knew he had one recourse to keep out of the clutches of the Jewish leaders. Every Roman citizen had the right to appeal to Caesar. Paul recognized that the authority behind the judgment seat where Festus sat belonged to Caesar. As a Roman citizen Paul was where he had a right to be judged. He had done no harm or injury to the Jews, as Festus well knew.

Paul then stated his case for his "appeal to Caesar."[16] If he was unjust and had done anything worthy of death, he would not "refuse to die" (that is, he would not object to the death penalty). But since there was nothing to the accusations, "no one [had] the right" (or authority) to turn him over to the Jews as a favor to them.

---

[16]Nero was the Caesar. Up to this point Nero had good advisers, and Paul had every reason to be confident he would get a fair trial in Rome.

12After Festus had conferred with his council, he declared: "You have appealed to Caesar. To Caesar you will go!"

Festus talked this over with his provincial council. But there was really nothing he could do. Paul had appealed to Caesar; to Caesar he must go. Probably Festus was glad the case was now out of his hands.

4. Festus Presents Paul's Cause To Agrippa 25:13–22

13A few days later King Agrippa and Bernice arrived at Caesarea to pay their respects to Festus. 14Since they were spending many days there, Festus discussed Paul's case with the king. He said: "There is a man here whom Felix left as a prisoner.

Some days later, King Agrippa (Herod Agrippa II, also known as M. Julius Agrippa II, son of the Herod of Acts 12), with his widowed sister Bernice, came to Caesarea to pay his respects to the new governor of Judea. Agrippa II had been made king of Chalcis, between the Lebanon and Anti-Lebanon Mountains, in A.D. 48. Later (A.D. 53) he became king of the tetrarchy of Philip, east of the Sea of Galilee, and of Lysanius, west and northwest of Damascus. In A.D. 56, Nero added cities around the Sea of Galilee to his territory.

Since they were there "many days" Festus laid Paul's case before Agrippa, desiring to consult with him about it, possibly for political reasons, or because Agrippa followed Jewish customs religiously and would be able to evaluate Jewish accusations (see 26:3).

15When I went to Jerusalem, the chief priests and elders of the Jews brought charges against him and asked that he be condemned. 16"I told them that it is not the Roman custom to hand over any man before he has faced his accusers and has had an opportunity to defend himself against their charges.

After relating how the Jews in Jerusalem brought charges against Paul and asked for a sentence of condemnation, Festus told how he refused to give them Paul as a favor and how he brought them together and put Paul on trial, giving him the customary "opportunity to defend himself."

17When they came here with me, I did not delay the case, but convened the court the next day and ordered the man to be brought in. 18When his accusers got up to speak, they did not charge him with any of the crimes I had expected. 19Instead, they had some points of dispute with him about their own religion and about a dead man named Jesus who Paul claimed was alive.

Then, as a Roman he was surprised, for they had not charged Paul with any of the crimes he had supposed they would. Instead, they took issue with him about "their own religion" (or, "their . . . superstition," KJV)[17] and a dead man named Jesus—alleged by Paul to be alive.

20I was at a loss how to investigate such matters; so I asked if he would be willing to go to Jerusalem and stand trial there on these charges. 21When Paul made his appeal to be held over for the Emperor's decision, I ordered him held until I could send him to Caesar."

Festus, however, did not admit that it was because he wanted to seek favor with the Jews that he had asked Paul to go to Jerusalem. Instead, he told Agrippa he was "at a loss [at his wits' end] how to investigate such matters." Then, because Paul refused to go to Jerusalem and appealed "to be held over" for a decision by the emperor (Gk. *tou Sebastou*, "the Augustus," a title meaning "worthy to be reverenced," used here of the emperor Nero), Festus commanded that he be kept under guard until he could "send him to Caesar."

22Then Agrippa said to Festus, "I would like to hear this man myself." He replied, "Tomorrow you will hear him."

Agrippa responded by saying he himself had been wanting to hear Paul (for a long time, as the Gk. implies). This pleased Festus, and he set the time for the next day.

---

[17]Gk. *deisidaimonia* can mean "system of religion" or "superstition." Since Festus is talking to Agrippa, who was a practicing Jew, "religion" is the better translation.

5. Paul Before Agrippa 25:23–26:32

a. Festus Presents His Case 25:23–27

23The next day Agrippa and Bernice came with great pomp and entered the audience room with the high ranking officers and the leading men of the city. At the command of Festus, Paul was brought in. 24Festus said: "King Agrippa, and all who are present with us, you see this man! The whole Jewish community has petitioned me about him in Jerusalem and here in Caesarea, shouting that he ought not to live any longer.

The next day Agrippa and Bernice arrived "with great pomp," that is, in all their royal robes and with all their attendants. The chief army officers and the prominent men of Caesarea came too.

After Paul was brought in, Festus addressed King Agrippa and the others who were present, calling on them to look at "this man" about whom "the whole Jewish community . . . in Jerusalem" had petitioned him, crying out that he "ought not to live any longer."

25I found he had done nothing deserving of death, but because he made his appeal to the Emperor I decided to send him to Rome.

Again Festus declared he found that Paul had done nothing worthy of death. But since he appealed to Caesar, Festus decided to send him.

26But I have nothing definite to write to His Majesty about him. Therefore I have brought him before all of you, and especially before you, King Agrippa, so that as a result of this investigation I may have something to write. 27For I think it is unreasonable to send on a prisoner without specifying the charges against him."

His problem was he had "nothing definite" (reliable, trustworthy) to write to Caesar (Gk. *tō kuriō,* "the lord"). He hoped that after this examination before Agrippa he would have. It seemed "unreasonable" (Gk. *alogon,* "irrational," "absurd") to send a prisoner without a letter identifying his alleged offense.[18]

---

[18]Waverly Nunnally pointed out to me that "this again seems contrived, and because of the 'pomp' it appears to be a Roman 'spectacle' (i.e., entertainment)

b. Paul Answers 26:1–23

(1) Paul The Pharisee 26:1–11

¹Then Agrippa said to Paul, "You have permission to speak for yourself." So Paul motioned with his hand and began his defense: ²"King Agrippa, I consider myself fortunate to stand before you today as I make my defense against all the accusations of the Jews, ³and especially so because you are well acquainted with all the Jewish customs and controversies. Therefore, I beg you to listen to me patiently.

This is Paul's final hearing in Acts, and the third account of his conversion, giving new details.

With Agrippa's permission to speak for himself, Paul "motioned with his hand" (Gk. *ekteinas tēn cheira*, "stretched out his hand," in the manner of a Roman orator) and proceeded to make his defense. He counted himself fortunate to appear before Agrippa because he was "well acquainted with all the Jewish customs and controversies." (Being a Jew by religion, Agrippa could be expected to have a concern about these things.) Therefore Paul begged him to "listen . . . patiently."

⁴"The Jews all know the way I have lived ever since I was a child, from the beginning of my life in my own country, and also in Jerusalem. ⁵They have known me for a long time and can testify, if they are willing, that according to the strictest sect of our religion, I lived as a Pharisee.

Paul pointed out first that all the Jews had known him "for a long time," his manner of life in Tarsus as a child as well as in Jerusalem as an adult. They knew he "lived as a Pharisee," publicly following the teachings of this strictest of Jewish sects. (See 2 Cor. 11:22; Gal. 1:13; Phil. 3:5.)

---

vs. a judicial proceeding. In what follows, no new or better understanding results." Lewis Foster writes, "This was not an official trial but a special hearing to satisfy the curiosity of Agrippa and provide an assessment for Festus." "Acts," in *The NIV Study Bible*, ed. Kenneth Barker (Grand Rapids: Zondervan Publishing House, 1995), 1698. It would enable him to include in his report a record of this additional attempt to ascertain a more substantial charge—having consulted Agrippa, who was credited with being familiar with such matters.

6And now it is because of my hope in what God has promised our fathers that I am on trial today. 7This is the promise our twelve tribes are hoping to see fulfilled as they earnestly serve God day and night. O king, it is because of this hope that the Jews are accusing me. 8Why should any of you consider it incredible that God raises the dead?

Now Paul stood there being judged "because of [the] hope in what God . . . promised" the patriarchs (Abraham, Isaac, and Jacob, and possibly other ancestors of Israel). This promise, Paul said, "our twelve tribes"19 in earnestness served (worshiped) God day and night "hoping to see fulfilled" (to reach as their God-given destination). The Jews' accusation against Paul concerned this hope. Why would the king judge it incredible if "God raises the dead" (that is, especially now that God has raised Jesus from the dead [cf. 1 Cor. 15:12–20])? Paul thus declares that Christ's resurrection and ours is the fulfillment of prophecy and is central to our worldview and to our view of life after death.

9"I too was convinced that I ought to do all that was possible to oppose the name of Jesus of Nazareth. 10And that is just what I did in Jerusalem. On the authority of the chief priests I put many of the saints in prison, and when they were put to death, I cast my vote against them. 11Many a time I went from one synagogue to another to have them punished, and I tried to force them to blaspheme. In my obsession against them, I even went to foreign cities to persecute them.

Paul, like so many of the great witnesses to Christ, openly confessed what Christ had saved him from. He had thought it necessary to do "all that was possible" against Jesus of Nazareth (His character, nature, and authority); he had "put many of the saints [the believers set apart for God] in prison."20 When they were put to death, he had "cast [his] vote against them."21 Going from syn-

19Note that Paul recognized that the Jews of his day included all twelve tribes. He himself was of the southern tribe of Benjamin. The prophetess Anna was of the tribe of Asher (Luke 2:36), one of the ten northern tribes. The Jews at that time knew what tribe they belonged to. The ten tribes were obviously never "lost."

20The Gk. is plural, "prisons" (NASB).

21It is on this basis that we must believe Paul was a member of the Sanhedrin. He did more than hold the clothes of the witnesses against Stephen. He had cast

agogue to synagogue, he had often punished the believers, trying to compel them to "blaspheme" (that is, "to call Jesus accursed"[22]). The Greek implies (as the NIV brings out), however, that he was not successful. Nevertheless, by his violent persecution of believers he was trying to destroy the Church (Gal. 1:13).

So exceedingly and madly enraged had he been against them that he had pursued them "even . . . to foreign cities." (In 1 Tim. 1:13, Paul points out that he had acted in ignorance of the truth.)

(2) Paul Converted And Commissioned 26:12–18

> [12]"On one of these journeys I was going to Damascus with the authority and commission of the chief priests. [13]About noon, O king, as I was on the road, I saw a light from heaven, brighter than the sun, blazing around me and my companions.

Paul then recounted the story of his conversion on the road to Damascus, where he was going with "the authority and commission" the chief priests had given him. Comparing the "light from heaven" with the noonday sun, he emphasizes its brightness.

> [14]We all fell to the ground, and I heard a voice saying to me in Aramaic, 'Saul, Saul, why do you persecute me? It is hard for you to kick against the goads.' [15]"Then I asked, 'Who are you, Lord?'" 'I am Jesus, whom you are persecuting,' the Lord replied.

As before, Paul told how Jesus asked why he kept persecuting Him. The saying "It is hard for you to kick against the goads" was a common phrase used to express opposition to God.[23] Jesus then identified himself.

> [16]'Now get up and stand on your feet. I have appeared to you to appoint you as a servant and as a witness of what you have seen of me and what I will show you.

---

his vote against him, and many other Christians, a vote that called for the death penalty.

[22]F. F. Bruce, *The Book of Acts,* rev. ed. (Grand Rapids: Wm. B. Eerdmans, 1988), 465.

[23]This identified the voice from heaven as divine. See Longenecker, *Paul, Apostle of Liberty,* 98–100.

Beginning at verse 16, Paul gave Christ's commission in greater detail. Jesus said he appeared to Paul to appoint him to the important task of being a "servant" (Gk. *hupēretēn,* "helper," "assistant," "attendant") and a witness "both of what you saw [of me] and of what I shall appear [personally continue to reveal] to you."[24] Later, Paul humbly calls himself a slave (Gk. *doulos*) of Jesus (Rom 1:1; Titus 1:1). This shows he responded by giving himself completely to the Lord's service.

> **[17]I will rescue you from your own people and from the Gentiles. I am sending you to them [18]to open their eyes and turn them from darkness to light, and from the power of Satan to God, so that they may receive forgiveness of sins and a place among those who are sanctified by faith in me.'**

Jesus promised to rescue Paul from his "own people" and from "the Gentiles" (the nations) He was sending him to (cf. Jer. 1:7–8). Paul would be Jesus' agent "to open their eyes" and to "turn them from [the] darkness" of sin and ignorance to the "light" of the gospel, and from the authority of Satan to the (true) God, so that they might receive "forgiveness of sins."

With that forgiveness they would also receive "a place" (Gk. *klēron,* "an inheritance"); that is, they would be recipients of God's grace and His promises among those who are "sanctified" (made holy, set apart to God as His people to do His will)[25] "by faith in me" (that is, the kind of faith that is fixed in Christ).

Thus Paul showed that Jesus himself gave him a commission to carry out His work, as Isaiah prophesied of the Messiah in 42:6–7 and 61:1–2. That is, Paul would be sharing in the work of Christ and carrying it on. "Paul did not simply know about Christ; he knew Christ. Until the fact of the *risen Christ becomes part of our lives, something motivating and empowering us,* we have little to say, even if we know the facts."[26]

---

[24]My translation. Jesus would make him a firsthand witness of the gospel message (see Gal. 1:12,16).

[25]See Acts 20:32.

[26]William H. Willimon, *Acts* (Atlanta: John Knox Press, 1988), 181, Willimon's emphasis.

(3) Paul's Faithful Witness 26:19-23

¹⁹"So then, King Agrippa, I was not disobedient to the vision from heaven. ²⁰First to those in Damascus, then to those in Jerusalem and in all Judea, and to the Gentiles also, I preached that they should repent and turn to God and prove their repentance by their deeds. ²¹That is why the Jews seized me in the temple courts and tried to kill me.

Paul then declared that he had not been "disobedient to the vision from heaven." The word "vision" here does not mean a dream-type vision, but an actual appearance, in which Jesus in person spoke to him.

His obedience was shown in the way he declared to the Jews at Damascus, Jerusalem, all Judea, and also to the Gentiles that "they should repent" (change their minds and fundamental attitudes), "turn to God," and then "prove their repentance by their deeds." It was because of this message (which included blessings for the Gentiles) that the Jews seized Paul in the temple and attempted to kill him.

²²But I have had God's help to this very day, and so I stand here and testify to small and great alike. I am saying nothing beyond what the prophets and Moses said would happen—²³that the Christ would suffer and, as the first to rise from the dead, would proclaim light to his own people and to the Gentiles."

Then Paul again began to bear witness to Christ. By the help of God he was still alive and was standing "to this very day," testifying "to small and great alike." The great, of course, included King Agrippa.

Paul's witness was not limited to his own experience, however. Everything he said was only "what the prophets and Moses [had already] said would happen." In other words, Paul's total message was based on the Scriptures: They declared that the Messiah must suffer; they showed how He, "as the first to rise from the dead," would proclaim light to the people (the Jews) and to the Gentiles (the nations). His resurrection was and is the central assurance of the gospel, the pledge of our resurrection (John 14:19).

c. Festus And Agrippa Reject The Gospel 26:24–29

24At this point Festus interrupted Paul's defense. "You are out of your mind, Paul!" he shouted. "Your great learning is driving you insane."

This was a powerful defense of the gospel. Festus felt its conviction and reacted against it by interrupting Paul. Shouting out, he said, "You are raving mad, Paul. Your great learning is turning you into a raving madman."[27] "Great learning" (Gk. *polla grammata*) can also mean "many writings," that is, the Scriptures Paul had been talking about.

25"I am not insane, most excellent Festus," Paul replied. "What I am saying is true and reasonable.

Paul gently and courteously replied, "I do not speak as a madman, most excellent Festus, but I utter forth [anointed by the Spirit, as in 2:4,14; 10:44] words [Gk. *rhēmata*] of truth and sound good sense."[28]

26The king is familiar with these things, and I can speak freely to him. I am convinced that none of this has escaped his notice, because it was not done in a corner. 27King Agrippa, do you believe the prophets? I know you do."

Paul told Festus that Agrippa was "familiar with these things." Paul could "speak freely" (and boldly) to him, for he was persuaded that none of these things had "escaped his notice," for they (the facts of Christ's death and resurrection, the events of the gospel) had not been "done in a corner"; they were done publicly and were publicly known. With this, Paul turned his attention again to the king. Addressing Agrippa, Paul asked him if he believed the prophets. Without waiting for an answer, he added, "I know you do."

28Then Agrippa said to Paul, "Do you think that in such a short time you can persuade me to be a Christian?"

Suddenly, and with surprise, Agrippa realized Paul was trying to convert him. By saying Agrippa believed the prophets, Paul

---

[27]My translation.
[28]My translation.

was implying that he would therefore have to believe what they said about the Messiah, and this should cause him to believe what Paul said about Jesus. But it seems Agrippa was not willing to say he did believe the prophets; neither was he willing to say he believed Paul.

Agrippa's reply has been translated and interpreted in a number of ways. Some ancient manuscripts read literally, "In [by] a little, you seek to persuade me to become a Christian" (cf. RSV). The King James Version takes this to be an admission that he felt the force of Paul's arguments and Paul was almost persuading him to be a Christian.[29]

Other ancient manuscripts read, "In [by] a little, you seek to persuade me to act a Christian," that is, act the part of a Christian. Many writers take this as a rejection. He did not want Paul to use him to corroborate the gospel.

"In [by] a little" could mean "in brief" or "in a few words." Or it may mean "in a very short time." Consequently, some say Agrippa meant "In brief, you are seeking to persuade me to become a Christian" (cf. NIV, NCV), and they interpret this simply as an expression of surprise. Others interpret the reply as irony: "In so short a time do you really think you can persuade me to become a Christian (or act, or live, like a Christian)?" (cf. LB). Still others take it to be a sharp rejection, "In brief, you are trying to persuade me to act (play the part of) a Christian" (cf. NAB).[30] It may be better to take it as noncommittal, but, whatever the translation, it is clear Agrippa was rejecting Paul's efforts to convert him.

29Paul replied, "Short time or long—I pray God that not only you but all who are listening to me today may become what I am, except for these chains."

Paul, however, refused to be discouraged. He replied, "I pray to God that both in brief or at length [or in a great degree], not only you, but all who are listening to me today might become

---

[29]David Thomas, *Acts of the Apostles* (1870; reprint, Grand Rapids: Baker Book House, 1956), 435, upholds this view, citing Rudolf Stier, *The Words of the Apostles*, trans. G. H. Venable (1869; reprint, Minneapolis: Klock & Klock Christian Publishers, 1981). (Cf. NASB, JB.)

[30]F. F. Bruce says the idiom is, "In short, you are urging me to act the Christian." *Acts: Greek Text,* 506.

what I am [that is, a fortunate servant of Christ like me], except for these chains."[31] It is possible that Paul held up his hands to show the chains on his wrists at this point.

d. Agrippa Recognizes Paul's Innocence 26:30–32

[30]The king rose, and with him the governor and Bernice and those sitting with them. [31]They left the room, and while talking with one another, they said, "This man is not doing anything that deserves death or imprisonment." [32]Agrippa said to Festus, "This man could have been set free if he had not appealed to Caesar."

King Agrippa had heard enough. By standing up, he indicated the hearing was over. Then he and those with him went out and discussed the hearing. All agreed that Paul had done nothing worthy of death or imprisonment; nothing in Roman law could hold him guilty. Then Agrippa told Festus that Paul might have been set free "if he had not appealed to Caesar."

It is implied also that the emperor would see Paul's innocence and would have to set him free. Though Nero was the emperor in A.D. 59, he had not yet embarked on any campaign against the Christians. Under Roman law at this time it was not a crime to be a Christian. Not until Paul's second imprisonment, which is reflected in 2 Timothy, did it become dangerous under the Romans to be a Christian.

STUDY QUESTIONS

1. How did Paul answer the charges against him brought by Tertullus?
2. Why did Paul appeal to Caesar?
3. What did Paul emphasize in his defense before King Agrippa?

---

[31]My translation.

D. Paul's Voyage To Rome 27:1-28:15

1. CONTRARY WINDS 27:1-8

¹When it was decided that we would sail for Italy, Paul and some other prisoners were handed over to a centurion named Julius, who belonged to the Imperial Regiment. ²We boarded a ship from Adramyttium about to sail for ports along the coast of the province of Asia, and we put out to sea. Aristarchus, a Macedonian from Thessalonica, was with us.

This account of Paul's journey to Rome gives us one of the most interesting and factual accounts of a sea voyage and a shipwreck to be found anywhere in ancient literature. Luke uses "we" throughout the passage, so it is clear he was an eyewitness.

For the trip from Caesarea to Italy, Paul and other prisoners were turned over to a centurion named Julius "who belonged to the Imperial Regiment," or "Augustan cohort"[1] (v. 1, NASB). They first took passage on a ship belonging to Adramyttium, a port of Mysia, southeast of Troas. It was headed up the coast of Asia Minor.

Luke took passage on this ship to be with Paul. So did Aristarchus, a Macedonian believer from Thessalonica (also mentioned in Col. 4:10 and Philem. 24). They went along to help him and serve him in every way they could. Thus, Paul did not travel as an ordinary prisoner. He had friends.[2]

³The next day we landed at Sidon; and Julius, in kindness to Paul, allowed him to go to his friends so they might provide for his needs. ⁴From there we put out to sea again and passed to the lee of Cyprus because the winds were against us. ⁵When we had sailed across the open sea off the coast of Cilicia and Pamphylia, we landed at Myra in Lycia.

[1]A cohort directly responsible to the emperor. "Cohort I Augustus" had its headquarters in Batanea in northeast Palestine, east of the southern end of the Sea of Galilee, in the territory of Agrippa II.

[2]Sir William Ramsay in *St. Paul the Traveler and the Roman Citizen* (London: Hodder & Stoughton, 1895), 345-46, speculates that Luke and Aristarchus took passage as Paul's slaves, thus giving Paul more prestige in the eyes of the centurion. Cited by F. F. Bruce, *Book of Acts*, rev. ed. (Grand Rapids: Wm. B. Eerdmans,

Julius, like many of the centurions mentioned in the Gospels, was a warm-hearted officer, sympathetic to Jew and Christian alike. The next day at Sidon, Julius, treating Paul with humanitarian kindness, permitted him to go to his Christian friends there to obtain care for his needs. Then, battling contrary westerly winds, they sailed east and north of Cyprus along the southern coast of Asia Minor to Myra, an important city in Lycia, the southernmost part of the province of Asia.

> **⁶There the centurion found an Alexandrian ship sailing for Italy and put us on board. ⁷We made slow headway for many days and had difficulty arriving off Cnidus. When the wind did not allow us to hold our course, we sailed to the lee of Crete, opposite Salmone. ⁸We moved along the coast with difficulty and came to a place called Fair Havens, near the town of Lasea.**

At Myra, the centurion transferred Paul and his friends to a ship from Alexandria that was sailing for Italy with a cargo of grain (see v. 38). Egypt was the chief source of wheat for the city of Rome, and ships that carried wheat were considered very important.

The winds continued to be contrary, and they sailed very slowly trying to reach Cnidus on the coast of Caria in southwest Asia Minor. But the northwest winds did not let them get there. They were driven "to the lee of Crete," that is, along the east coast of the island of Crete. Then they struggled along its south coast until they reached Fair Havens (the Gk. can mean "good harbors").

2. Caught In A Storm 27:9–20

> **⁹Much time had been lost, and sailing had already become dangerous because by now it was after the Fast. So Paul warned them, ¹⁰"Men, I can see that our voyage is going to be disastrous and bring great loss to ship and cargo, and to our own lives also."**

1988), 501. But it is more likely that they joined Paul as friends. "At Acts 24:23 Felix grants Paul the privilege of being attended by his friends. Nothing in the texts suggests the circumstances have changed." Brian Rapske, *The Book of Acts and Paul in Roman Custody,* vol. 3 of *The Book of Acts in Its First Century Setting,* ed. Bruce W. Winter (Grand Rapids: Wm. B. Eerdmans, 1994), 378.

Because considerable time had passed, including "the Fast" (the Day of Atonement, the tenth of Tishri, which in A.D. 59 was on October 5),[3] Paul recognized that it would be dangerous to continue their voyage. He had been in three shipwrecks already (2 Cor. 11:25), and he knew how dangerous winter storms could be. So he went to those in charge of the ship and advised them of the certainty of injury and "great loss" to the ship and its cargo, as well as of their lives if they continued.

11But the centurion, instead of listening to what Paul said, followed the advice of the pilot and of the owner of the ship. 12Since the harbor was unsuitable to winter in, the majority decided that we should sail on, hoping to reach Phoenix and winter there. This was a harbor in Crete, facing both southwest and northwest.

The centurion, however, was persuaded by both the pilot and the owner of the ship to keep going. "The harbor was unsuitable to winter in," so the majority counseled trying to reach Phoenix (modern Phinika), a harbor farther west that was better located, whether the winds came from the northwest or the southwest.

13When a gentle south wind began to blow, they thought they had obtained what they wanted; so they weighed anchor and sailed along the shore of Crete. 14Before very long, a wind of hurricane force, called the "northeaster," swept down from the island. 15The ship was caught by the storm and could not head into the wind; so we gave way to it and were driven along.

A gentle south wind reinforced the thinking of the centurion and the others that they could make it to Phoenix, so they sailed west, keeping close to the south coast of Crete. It was not long, however, before Paul's prediction came true. A vehement, turbulent, typhoon-like wind called "the 'northeaster'"[4] suddenly rushed against them from the east-northeast. It caught the ship in

---

[3]The only fast prescribed by the Law (Lev. 23:27).

[4]Gk. *eurakulōn*. This is the correct reading. Brian Rapske, "Acts Travel and Shipwreck," in *The Book of Acts in Its Graeco-Roman Setting,* vol. 2 of *Acts in Its First Century Setting,* ed. Winter (Grand Rapids: Wm. B. Eerdmans, 1994), 38. Some manuscripts, however, have *eurocludōn,* "the southeast wind that stirs up waves."

its grip and drove it away from the shores of Crete. The sailors tried to face it into the land, but the wind was too strong. So they had to give way and let the wind carry the ship where it would.

> **16As we passed to the lee of a small island called Cauda, we were hardly able to make the lifeboat secure. 17When the men had hoisted it aboard, they passed ropes under the ship itself to hold it together. Fearing that they would run aground on the sandbars of Syrtis, they lowered the sea anchor and let the ship be driven along.**

The lee (south side) of a small island, Cauda or Clauda, gave them only temporary relief. Even then it was with difficulty that they were able to secure the lifeboat, a small boat that normally was towed. After they hoisted it onto the deck, they used ropes (Gk. *boētheiais,* "helps") to undergird the ship. That is, they fastened cables vertically around the ship to try to keep the timbers from straining too much or giving way.[5]

Then, afraid they would be driven off their course into Syrtis, a quicksand off the coast of North Africa west of Cyrene that was a well-known graveyard of ships, "they lowered the sea anchor" to act as a brake (or possibly the topsail to moderate the wind; see NEB, NCV, CEV) and so were carried along by the wind.

> **18We took such a violent battering from the storm that the next day they began to throw the cargo overboard. 19On the third day, they threw the ship's tackle overboard with their own hands.**

The next day, because they were still in the grip of the storm, they began to throw things overboard to lighten the ship. Usually this would mean throwing part of the cargo overboard. But this ship's cargo of grain was so important to Rome that it was the last thing they would get rid of (see v. 38). They probably began with personal baggage and cabin furniture.

Then, on the "third day" (i.e., according to their way of counting, the day after they began throwing things overboard), "with their own hands"[6] they tossed overboard the ship's tackle

[5]The Western Text adds that they furled the sails (see KJV).

[6]"We cast out with our own hands" (v. 19, KJV). The size and weight of the main yard would probably need both passengers and crew to help toss it overboard. Bruce, *Book of Acts,* 486–87.

(probably including the main yard).

²⁰**When neither sun nor stars appeared for many days and the storm continued raging, we finally gave up all hope of being saved.**

The storm continued "many days" (probably eleven, see v. 27). Without any sighting of the sun, moon, or stars, they had no way of knowing where they were. Finally, as this great winter storm continued to press upon them, it stripped away all hope of rescue.

3. PAUL'S VISION AND COURAGE 27:21-37

²¹**After the men had gone a long time without food, Paul stood up before them and said: "Men, you should have taken my advice not to sail from Crete; then you would have spared yourselves this damage and loss. ²²But now I urge you to keep up your courage, because not one of you will be lost; only the ship will be destroyed. ²³Last night an angel of the God whose I am and whom I serve stood beside me ²⁴and said, 'Do not be afraid, Paul. You must stand trial before Caesar; and God has graciously given you the lives of all who sail with you.'**

For a long time the men on the ship (see v. 37) "had gone . . . without food." The Greek word could mean they lacked food, but in verses 34-36 we see they still had food on board. The word can also mean abstinence from food because of a loss of appetite or because of seasickness. The storm must have made many seasick. Even if a person is not seasick himself, the sight and odor of seasickness in others is enough to cause a well person to lose his appetite.[7]

Then one night an angel appeared and encouraged Paul by telling him to stop being afraid. It was necessary (by the divine plan) for him to come before Caesar, and God also had graciously given him "the lives of all" those who were sailing with him. There would be no loss of life (a significant number—276, according to v. 37), only of the ship.

Before Paul told the others of this God-given assurance, he reminded them of his warnings given before they left Crete. He

---

[7]I speak here from experience.

was not simply saying, "I told you so!" He remembered that they had refused to listen to him before; he wanted to be sure they would listen to him now. So he caught their attention by getting them to admit (in their minds) that he was right. Then he gave the glory to God "whose I am and whom I serve."

25So keep up your courage, men, for I have faith in God that it will happen just as he told me. 26Nevertheless, we must run aground on some island."

Notice also that he began by encouraging them to be of good courage and keep up their spirits (v. 22). He concludes in the same way. But the ground for their courage was Paul's faith in God.

What a picture this was! Paul the prisoner communicating his faith: "Men, . . . I have faith in God." But he added they "must" (Gk. *dei*—as a necessary part of God's plan) be shipwrecked on an island. How different this was from Jonah's experience in a storm on the same sea (Jon. 1:3–17)!

27On the fourteenth night we were still being driven across the Adriatic Sea, when about midnight the sailors sensed they were approaching land. 28They took soundings and found that the water was a hundred and twenty feet deep. A short time later they took soundings again and found it was ninety feet deep.

On the fourteenth night they were still being driven by the wind, in whatever direction it blew, "across the Adriatic Sea" (actually, the Mediterranean Sea southeast of Italy, which was then considered part of the Adriatic Sea). About midnight the sailors "sensed" (had a suspicion) they were approaching land.[8] So they threw out a weighted rope to sound the depth and found it 120 feet. A little later, possibly after about a half hour, they sounded again and found the depth to be 90 feet.

29Fearing that we would be dashed against the rocks, they dropped four anchors from the stern and prayed for daylight.

Afraid the ship might run aground on the rocks and break up

---

[8]Some ancient manuscripts read that the land was resounding. In other words, they thought they could hear waves breaking on the shore.

before they could escape, they tossed out four sea anchors from the stern and "prayed for daylight." That is, they prayed that day would come before the ship ran aground.

> 30In an attempt to escape from the ship, the sailors let the lifeboat down into the sea, pretending they were going to lower some anchors from the bow. 31Then Paul said to the centurion and the soldiers, "Unless these men stay with the ship, you cannot be saved." 32So the soldiers cut the ropes that held the lifeboat and let it fall away.

The sailors decided it would be dangerous to wait any longer, so they made "an attempt to escape from the ship." When they were discovered, they had "let the lifeboat down into the sea" under the pretext of "going to lower some anchors from the bow" of the ship. Paul then told the centurion that unless these sailors stayed with the ship he and his men could not be saved. As it turned out, the sailors were needed to get the ship aground in the best place.

The soldiers under the centurion then cut the small boat adrift. Paul the prisoner, because of the need, had taken command of the situation.

> 33Just before dawn Paul urged them all to eat. "For the last fourteen days," he said, "you have been in constant suspense and have gone without food—you haven't eaten anything. 34Now I urge you to take some food. You need it to survive. Not one of you will lose a single hair from his head."

Still in command of the situation, Paul encouraged everyone to take food for their own bodily health and welfare. He assured them that not "a single hair" would be lost from anyone's head. Not only would they be saved, they would experience no injuries.

> 35After he said this, he took some bread and gave thanks to God in front of them all. Then he broke it and began to eat. 36They were all encouraged and ate some food themselves. 37Altogether there were 276 of us on board.

Paul then set them an example by taking a loaf of bread, giving thanks to God "in front of them all," and beginning to eat. At that, all 275 of the others took courage, and inspired with hope, "ate some food themselves."

4. THE SHIPWRECK 27:38–44

38When they had eaten as much as they wanted, they lightened the ship by throwing the grain into the sea.

After they were all satisfied with food, they threw out their cargo of wheat so the ship would ride as high as possible. This would help them get closer to the shore.

39When daylight came, they did not recognize the land, but they saw a bay with a sandy beach, where they decided to run the ship aground if they could. 40Cutting loose the anchors, they left them in the sea and at the same time untied the ropes that held the rudders. Then they hoisted the foresail to the wind and made for the beach. 41But the ship struck a sandbar and ran aground. The bow stuck fast and would not move, and the stern was broken to pieces by the pounding of the surf.

Despite the coming of daylight the coastland was not familiar. But they did notice "a bay with a sandy beach" and decided that "if they could" they would run the ship aground there. St. Paul's Bay (as it is known today) on the island of Malta (28:1) fits exactly the things recorded in this chapter.

"Cutting loose the anchors, they left them in the sea," because this also would lighten the ship. At the same time they unfastened the rudders (or steering paddles), raised the foresail (set on the bow) to catch the wind, and headed for the beach.

Instead of reaching the beach, they accidentally came to a place between two seas, a narrow, shallow channel. The bow of the ship ran aground in mud and clay, while the stern began breaking up because of "the pounding of the surf."

42The soldiers planned to kill the prisoners to prevent any of them from swimming away and escaping. 43But the centurion wanted to spare Paul's life and kept them from carrying out their plan. He ordered those who could swim to jump overboard first and get to land. 44The rest were to get there on planks or on pieces of the ship. In this way everyone reached land in safety.

If the prisoners escaped in the confusion of shipwreck and the disagreeableness of foul weather (28:2), the soldiers knew that they would have to pay with their own lives. So they conferred among themselves and decided to kill the prisoners. "But the centurion wanted to spare Paul's life" and he prevented them from carrying out this purpose. Then he commanded all who could swim to jump overboard first and get to the land. The rest followed, some on ship's planks and others on whatever they could find that would float. Thus all "reached land in safety." But, as Paul had warned, the ship was a total loss.

5. MIRACLES AT MALTA 28:1–10

¹Once safely on shore, we found out that the island was called Malta. ²The islanders showed us unusual kindness. They built a fire and welcomed us all because it was raining and cold.

The Lord had assured Paul that he must go to Rome. He had also promised to give him the lives of all the 275 others who were on board. He did as He had promised.

After arriving safely on land they found out the island was called Malta (Phoenician or Canaanite for "refuge"). It was south of Sicily and its people were descended from Phoenician colonists who settled there about 1000 B.C., and who probably spoke a dialect closely related to Hebrew. Rome had conquered the island in 218 B.C.

The islanders received them graciously. Throughout this passage Luke uses the Greek term *barbaroi* to refer to the "islanders." *Barbaroi* is translated variously, including "natives" (NASB), "rough islanders" (NEB), and "barbarous people" (KJV). But Luke does not mean that they were degraded or uncivilized. To the Greeks any foreigner who could not speak Greek was a barbarian. Later they gave the Romans a certain level of inclusion by redefining "barbarian" as one who could not speak Greek *or* Latin.

It is easy to see that the citizens of Malta were good, friendly people even if they could not speak Greek. Their kindness went beyond the ordinary. They lit a fire and welcomed all 276 of these strangers who had escaped the shipwreck. Because of the rain[9] and the cold, the fire was an act of great kindness and must have been a welcome sight to all from the ship.

---

[9]The Gk. perfect tense, *ephestōta*, may mean that it threatened to rain, or more likely, that it had been raining and everything was still wet.

³Paul gathered a pile of brushwood and, as he put it on the fire, a viper, driven out by the heat, fastened itself on his hand. ⁴When the islanders saw the snake hanging from his hand, they said to each other, "This man must be a murderer; for though he escaped from the sea, Justice has not allowed him to live."

Paul was not satisfied just to warm himself. He appreciated the kindness of these pagans and responded by helping gather more brushwood for the fire. The heat brought out a "viper" (or a female adder) that had been picked up with the wood, and it "fastened itself on his hand" (that is, bit him). Many writers take notice of the fact that there are no vipers on Malta today. But it is a small island and the people eventually got rid of them after Paul's day.

When the people of Malta "saw the snake hanging from his hand," they jumped to the conclusion that Paul must be a murderer, whom, though he escaped safely from the sea, "Justice" had not let live. By "Justice" (Gk. *dikē*) they probably meant "Lady Justice," their pagan goddess of justice.

⁵But Paul shook the snake off into the fire and suffered no ill effects. ⁶The people expected him to swell up or suddenly fall dead, but after waiting a long time and seeing nothing unusual happen to him, they changed their minds and said he was a god.

Paul simply "shook the snake off into the fire" and suffered no harm; Jesus' promise was fulfilled (see Mark 16:18; Luke 10:19). The local people had seen others bitten by the same kind of vipers, so they expected Paul to swell up or drop dead. For "a long time" they waited and watched, but nothing unusual happened to him. So "they changed their minds and said he was a god." A pagan worldview leads to wrong interpretations.

⁷There was an estate nearby that belonged to Publius, the chief official of the island. He welcomed us to his home and for three days entertained us hospitably.

Nearby was "an estate" (lands, properties) belonging to the "chief official" (governor) of the island, whose name was Publius. He welcomed them with kindness and for three days entertained the whole group with friendly thoughtfulness.

8His father was sick in bed, suffering from fever and dysentery. Paul went in to see him and, after prayer, placed his hands on him and healed him. 9When this had happened, the rest of the sick on the island came and were cured.

Then Paul learned that the father of Publius lay sick, suffering from "fever" (Gk. *puretois,* lit. "fevers," that is, a recurring fever) and dysentery (as Luke the physician easily identified). Paul came in, prayed for him, laid hands on him, and God healed him. The healing was so complete and so wonderful that the news of it soon spread throughout the island. This provided a great door of ministry and "the rest of the sick on the island" came one after another and all were healed.

10They honored us in many ways and when we were ready to sail, they furnished us with the supplies we needed.

We can be sure Paul kept ministering to them during the three winter months (v. 11) that followed. As a result, the people honored Paul and his friends "in many ways" (probably including gifts of money to help them stay alive during the winter months). When Paul and the others set sail in the spring, the people placed on board the things they needed for the journey. Apparently they provided not only for Paul but also for all the rest of the shipwrecked, all having arrived with nothing but the wet clothes they were wearing.

6. FROM MALTA TO ROME 28:11–15

11After three months we put out to sea in a ship that had wintered in the island. It was an Alexandrian ship with the figurehead of the twin gods Castor and Pollux. 12We put in at Syracuse and stayed there three days. 13From there we set sail and arrived at Rhegium. The next day the south wind came up, and on the following day we reached Puteoli. 14There we found some brothers who invited us to spend a week with them. And so we came to Rome.

They took another Alexandrian grain ship that had wintered in Malta, possibly at the good harbor of Valetta. The figurehead that identified it was the "twin gods [Gk. *Dioscourois*] Castor and Pollux." Greek mythology said they were sons of the Greek chief god Zeus and of Leda, the wife of the king of Sparta. Pagan Greeks considered them patrons and protectors of sailors.[10] The ship stopped three days at Syracuse in southeastern Sicily, then tacked against the wind (probably due to a change in wind direction) and came to Rhegium, at the "toe" of Italy's boot. After another day the wind changed, coming from the south, and it took them only one more day to reach Puteoli (modern Pozzuoli), the port city on the north side of the bay of Naples. There they found Christian brothers who prevailed on them to stay seven days. Clearly, the centurion who was responsible for Paul recognized that God was with him and did not oppose anything Paul desired.[11] He trusted Paul, for he saw also how Paul lived (cf. Phil. 1:2,7). "And so"[12] they proceeded toward Rome.

15The brothers there had heard that we were coming, and they traveled as far as the Forum of Appius and the Three Taverns to meet us. At the sight of these men Paul thanked God and was encouraged.

After a week of rest and good Christian fellowship they went from Puteoli to Rome on foot, taking the famous Roman road the Appian Way. At the "Forum ["Market," NASB] of Appius," about thirty-nine and a half miles[13] south of Rome, and again at the village of the "Three Taverns" ("Three Shops," Beck; "Three Inns," TEV, NKJV, NCV), about thirty miles south of Rome, delegations of Roman believers met Paul and proceeded with him and his friends back to Rome in a procession whose numbers would have done credit to a visiting monarch. (It was a custom when an emperor visited a city for the citizens to go out and meet and escort him back into the city.)

---

[10]The constellation Gemini ("the twins") is named after them.

[11]Some commentators speculate that the centurion had business in Puteoli that kept him there a week.

[12] "So" (Gk. *houtōs*, "thus," "as follows").

[13]The town was at the forty-third milestone on the Appian Way, but these milestones measured the Roman mile, equal to 1,620 yards as opposed to the 1,760 yards of the English mile. (Measured metrically, the overall distance would have been about 63 kilometers.)

Each time the delegations met Paul, there must have been a time of shouting and rejoicing. All this was an unexpected surprise to Paul. When he saw them he "thanked God and was encouraged." Surely God would give him a ministry in Rome as he desired (Rom. 1:11–12). Though Luke does not mention it, we can be sure also that the church had received Paul's epistle to the Romans, studied it with appreciation, and felt like they already knew Paul.[14] It is clear also in Romans that no apostle had visited them before this time. There is no evidence that Peter had visited them. The church in Rome was probably founded by some who were in Jerusalem on the Day of Pentecost (Acts 2:10).[15]

STUDY QUESTIONS

1. How did Paul show wisdom and leadership during the sea voyage that ended at Malta?
2. Why did the people of Malta honor Paul and provide supplies for the continuing journey toward Rome?
3. How did the Roman believers show their appreciation for Paul?

E. Paul A Prisoner, Yet Free 28:16–31

1. PAUL UNDER HOUSE ARREST 28:16

16When we got to Rome, Paul was allowed to live by himself, with a soldier to guard him.

At Rome Paul was handed over to the commander of Nero's Praetorian Guard, that is, the general in charge of the court guard of the emperor. But he was "allowed to live by himself," lightly chained by the wrist to a soldier who guarded him.[1] As

---

[14]The services in Rome were conducted in Gk. until some time in the third century A.D.

[15]Everett F. Harrison, *Interpreting Acts: The Expanding Church* (Grand Rapids: Zondervan Publishing House, Academie Books, 1986), 63.

[1]These soldiers from the Praetorian Guard served in four-hour shifts. Josephus *Antiquities of the Jews* 18.169.

verse 30 indicates, he was able to rent a large apartment and keep it at his own expense[2] for the two years he was in Rome. Luke and Aristarchus also remained in Rome to help him during this period (Col. 4:10,14; Philem. 24). Fortunately, the apartment was large enough for a considerable number of people to gather, as verses 23–25 indicate. In v. 23 it is called a *xenian,* a term meaning both "hospitality" and "guest room." It reminds us of the large upper room of Acts 1:12–14.

2. PAUL MEETS ROME'S JEWISH LEADERS 28:17–22

[17]Three days later he called together the leaders of the Jews. When they had assembled, Paul said to them: "My brothers, although I have done nothing against our people or against the customs of our ancestors, I was arrested in Jerusalem and handed over to the Romans. [18]They examined me and wanted to release me, because I was not guilty of any crime deserving death. [19]But when the Jews objected, I was compelled to appeal to Caesar—not that I had any charge to bring against my own people.

Paul had already reminded the Romans that the gospel was given to the Jew first (Rom. 1:16). So they were not surprised when after only three days Paul "called together" (invited) the Jewish leaders in Rome to his apartment. Ancient Roman inscriptions show there were several Jewish synagogues in Rome at this time.[3] As Paul began to speak he called them "brothers," hoping to get them to respond to the gospel. He then told them how he came to be in Rome as a prisoner. He emphasized his innocence and explained why he had appealed to Caesar, being careful not to put any blame on the Jewish nation ("people") as a whole.

[20]For this reason I have asked to see you and talk with you. It is because of the hope of Israel that I am bound with this chain."

Paul's purpose, however, was to do more than explain why he was there. He wanted them to know he was a faithful Israelite

[2]As *en idiō misthōmati* (v. 30) means. See F. F. Bruce, *Acts: Greek Text,* 542.
[3]Brian Rapske, *The Book of Acts and Paul in Roman Custody,* vol. 3 of *The Book of Acts in Its First Century Setting,* ed. Bruce W. Winter (Grand Rapids: Wm. B. Eerdmans, 1994), 180.

who had endured arrest and chains rather than forsake "the hope of Israel."

21They replied, "We have not received any letters from Judea concerning you, and none of the brothers who have come from there has reported or said anything bad about you. 22But we want to hear what your views are, for we know that people everywhere are talking against this sect."

The Jewish leaders replied that no letters had come from Judea, nor had anyone brought a report of Paul's trial or spoken anything bad concerning him. Then they expressed a desire to hear Paul tell what he had on his mind.

The Jewish leaders were not complimentary to the Christians, however, for they called Christianity a "sect" that people everywhere were "talking against" (opposing, debating about). Paul's epistle to the Romans shows that the church in Rome was already well established by A.D. 57, and probably long before that. Apparently, these Jewish leaders had listened to the critics and had never bothered to investigate for themselves.

3. Paul Preaches To Jews In Rome 28:23–29

23They arranged to meet Paul on a certain day, and came in even larger numbers to the place where he was staying. From morning till evening he explained and declared to them the kingdom of God and tried to convince them about Jesus from the Law of Moses and from the Prophets.

The Jewish leadership set a date among themselves and then came with their followers in considerable numbers to Paul's apartment.[4] To these "he explained and declared[5] . . . the kingdom [rule] of God." As he always did in the synagogues, he used

---

[4]Of Rome's one million inhabitants over forty thousand were Jews. Pompey brought many of them to Rome as slaves in 63 B.C. Andrew D. Clarke, "Rome and Italy," in *The Book of Acts in its Graeco-Roman Setting*, ed. David W. J. Gill and Conrad Gempf, vol. 2 of *Acts in Its First Century Setting*, ed. Winter (Grand Rapids: Wm. B. Eerdmans, 1994), 465–66.

[5]Gk. *exetitheto diamarturomenos*, "kept expounding, fully testifying [including solemn warning; cf. 20:23]."

the books of Moses and the prophets to teach the gospel and to try to persuade them that Jesus is truly the Messiah. He continued teaching, preaching, and warning the people from early morning until evening.

²⁴**Some were convinced by what he said, but others would not believe.**

"Some were convinced." That is, they believed and obeyed Paul's message and exhortation. We can be sure they became followers of Christ. But some disbelieved and continued to disbelieve.

²⁵**They disagreed among themselves and began to leave after Paul had made this final statement: "The Holy Spirit spoke the truth to your forefathers when he said through Isaiah the prophet: ²⁶"'Go to this people and say, "You will be ever hearing but never understanding; you will be ever seeing but never perceiving." ²⁷For this people's heart has become calloused; they hardly hear with their ears, and they have closed their eyes. Otherwise they might see with their eyes, hear with their ears, understand with their hearts and turn, and I would heal them.'**

Because they were in disagreement they left, but not before Paul had one final word. He quoted for them what the Holy Spirit in Isaiah 6:9–10 said to their ancestors.

As Isaiah said, the message would make the heart of the people (Israel) "calloused"—even more unwilling to receive God's message; their ears too dull or deaf to hear. They would close (Heb. *hasha'*, "smear over" or "stick shut") their eyes so they could not see the truth being presented. Instead of making them realize their hardened condition, they would be hardened further.⁶ The message was not unsound. The problem was in the hearers' sinfulness.

²⁸**"Therefore I want you to know that God's salvation has been sent to the Gentiles, and they will listen!"**

Because the unbelieving Jews (in fulfillment of prophecy) were closing their hearts and minds to God and His plan, Paul

⁶See Stanley M. Horton, *Isaiah* (Springfield, Mo.: Logion Press, 2000), 93–94.

added that "God's salvation has been sent to the Gentiles" (a reference to his own call). "They" is emphatic: The Gentiles would listen (and obey).[7] This does not imply, however, that God has no more place for the Jews in His plan. (Cf. Jer. 23:6; Acts 5:31; 10:42–43; 13:26,38; Rom. 11:26.)[8]

²⁹[After he said this, the Jews left, arguing vigorously among themselves.]

This verse is from the Western Text. It fits the situation. That is, the discussion among the Jews continued as they were leaving and probably after they left (see v. 25).

4. TWO YEARS OF OPPORTUNITY 28:30–31

³⁰For two whole years Paul stayed there in his own rented house and welcomed all who came to see him. ³¹Boldly and without hindrance he preached the kingdom of God and taught about the Lord Jesus Christ.

This was not Paul's last opportunity. For two whole years he was able to preach and teach "boldly" (Gk. *parrēsias,* see 4:13) and freely, welcoming all who came into his apartment. Neither Jews nor Romans hindered his witness to Christ. This was an answer to his requests for prayer sent to some of the churches he had founded (Eph. 6:19–20; Col. 4:3–4). Even some from Caesar's household were converted (Phil. 4:22). This probably came about through the witness of soldiers to the whole "palace guard" (Phil. 1:13).[9]

No doubt, drawing duty to be chained to a prisoner was not something soldiers enjoyed. Most prisoners would be difficult. But Paul was different. Not only was he full of the joy of the Lord, the soldiers were a captive audience and listened to all his teaching and preaching about Jesus and the Kingdom. We can be sure Paul encouraged them to accept Jesus as Savior and Lord

[7]The listening of the Gentiles was implied in Ezek. 3:6.

[8]Dennis M. Sweetland, "Luke the Christian," in *New Views on Luke and Acts,* ed. Earl Richard (Collegeville, Minn.: Liturgical Press, 1990), 59.

[9]"Praetorian guard" (NASB), the emperor's own guard and its officers, who would be in contact with Paul on the emperor's behalf when his appeal was presented.

and that they became effective witnesses for Jesus. Some believe Paul was released after two years when he was called before the emperor because the Jews had sent no accusation. Others believe the case was automatically dismissed at the end of the two years because no charges were presented. Philemon 22 shows Paul expected to be released; 1 Timothy shows he was indeed released and went to the Roman province of Asia. Ancient tradition says he did go to Spain also. This was followed by Paul's second imprisonment and death.[10]

Luke breaks off suddenly. There is no formal conclusion to this book. The Book of Acts goes on today.

STUDY QUESTIONS

1. How did the Jewish leaders in Rome respond to Paul and why?
2. What was Paul able to do during the two years he was a prisoner in Rome?

---

[10]Second Timothy 4:13 indicates he left his cloak and books at Troas, possibly because of a sudden arrest. Second Timothy also shows conditions in Rome during Paul's second imprisonment. Nero was blaming the Christians for the fire in Rome, and it had become a crime to be a Christian. See E. H. Trenchard, "The Acts of the Apostles," in *A New Testament Commentary,* ed. G. C. D. Howley (Grand Rapids: Zondervan Publishing House, 1969), 339.

Appendix:
Maps

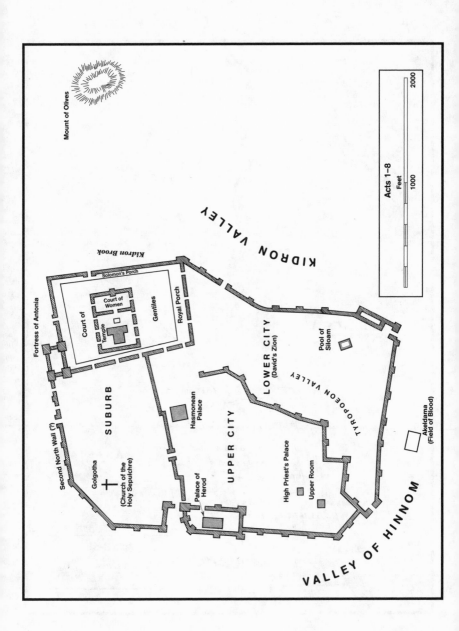

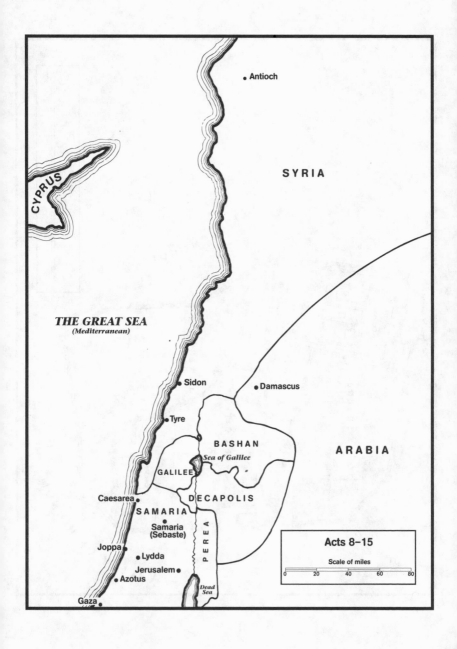

Acts 8–15

Scale of miles

0   20   40   60   80

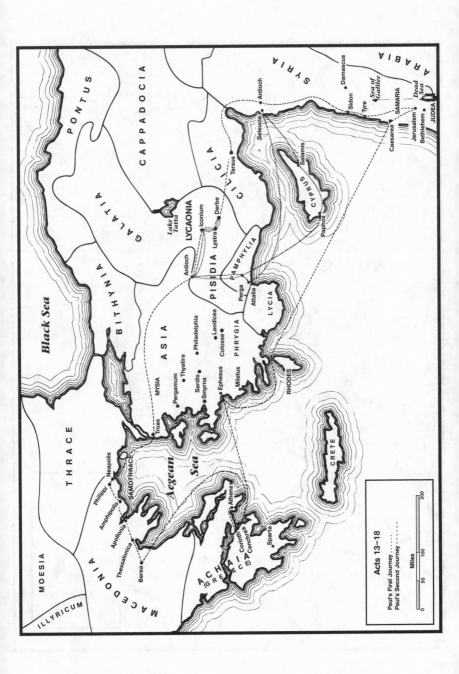

Acts 13–18

Paul's First Journey ··········
Paul's Second Journey --------

Miles

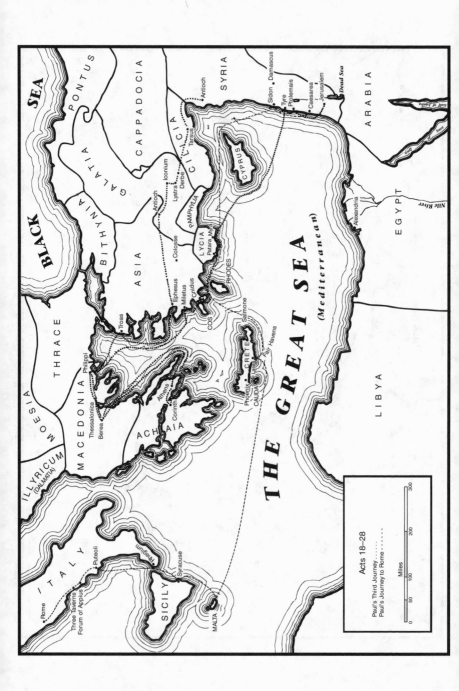

SELECTED BIBLIOGRAPHY

Alexander, J. A. *A Commentary on the Acts of the Apostles.* 3rd ed. 1875. Reprint, London: Banner of Truth Trust, 1956.

Arrington, French. *The Acts of the Apostles.* Peabody, Mass.: Hendrickson Publishers, 1988.

Barclay, William. *The Acts of the Apostles.* 2d ed. Philadelphia: Westminster Press, 1955.

Bauckham, Richard, ed. *The Book of Acts in Its Palestinian Setting.* Vol. 4 of *The Book of Acts in Its First Century Setting,* edited by Bruce W. Winter. Grand Rapids: Wm. B. Eerdmans, 1995.

Blaiklock, E. M. *Acts: The Birth of the Church.* Old Tappan, N.J.: Fleming H. Revell, 1980.

Boice, James M. *Acts.* Grand Rapids: Baker Book House, 1997.

Brawley, Robert L. *Luke-Acts and the Jews: Conflict, Apology, and Conciliation.* Atlanta: Scholars Press, 1987.

Bruce, F. F. *The Acts of the Apostles: The Greek Text With Introduction and Commentary.* 3d ed. Grand Rapids: Wm. B. Eerdmans, 1990.

———. *The Book of Acts: English Text with Introduction, Exposition, and Notes.* Grand Rapids: Wm. B. Eerdmans, 1975.

———. *Commentary on the Book of Acts.* Grand Rapids: Wm. B. Eerdmans, 1954.

Carter, Charles W., and Ralph Earle. *The Acts of the Apostles.* Grand Rapids: Zondervan Publishing House, 1959.

Dunn, James D. G. *The Acts of the Apostles.* Valley Forge, Pa.: Trinity Press International, 1996.

Earle, Ralph. *The Acts of the Apostles.* Kansas City, Mo.: Beacon Hill Press, 1965.

Fee, Gordon D. *Gospel and Spirit: Issues in New Testament Hermeneutics.* Peabody, Mass.: Hendrickson Publishers, 1991.

Gill, David W. J., and Conrad Gempf, eds. *The Book of Acts in Its Graeco-Roman Setting.* Vol. 2 of *The Book of Acts in Its First Century Setting,* edited by Bruce W. Winter. Grand Rapids: Wm. B. Eerdmans, 1994.

Green, Joel B., and Michael C. McKeever. *Luke-Acts and New Testament Historiography.* Grand Rapids: Baker Book House, 1994.

Grudem, Wayne A., ed. *Are Miraculous Gifts for Today?* Grand Rapids: Zondervan Publishing House, 1996.

Guthrie, Donald. *The Apostles.* Grand Rapids: Zondervan Publishing House, 1975.

Hackett, H. B. *A Commentary on the Acts of the Apostles.* Philadelphia: American Baptist Publication Society, 1882.

Harrison, Everett F. *Interpreting Acts: The Expanding Church.* Grand Rapids: Zondervan Publishing House, Academie Books, 1986.

Hewitt, F. S. *The Genesis of the Christian Church: A Study of Acts and the Epistles.* London: Edward Arnold, 1972.

Howley, G. C. D., ed. *A New Testament Commentary.* Grand Rapids: Zondervan Publishing House, 1969.

Johnson, Luke T. *The Acts of the Apostles.* Collegeville, Minn.: Liturgical Press, 1992.

Jones, Gwen, ed. *Conference on the Holy Spirit Digest.* 2 vols. Springfield, Mo.: Gospel Publishing House, 1983.

Juel, Donald. *Luke-Acts: The Promise of History.* Atlanta: John Knox Press, 1983.

Kee, Howard Clark. *To Every Nation Under Heaven: The Acts of the Apostles.* Harrisburg, Pa.: Trinity Press International, 1997.

Kistemaker, Simon J. *Exposition of the Acts of the Apostles.* Grand Rapids: Baker Book House, 1990.

Krodel, Gerhard. *Acts.* Philadelphia: Fortress Press, 1981.

———. *Acts.* Minneapolis: Augsburg Publishing House, 1986.

Ladd, George E. *A Theology of the New Testament.* Grand Rapids: Wm. B. Eerdmans, 1983.

Larkin, William J., Jr. *Acts*. Downers Grove, Ill.: InterVarsity Press, 1995.

Lenski, P. C. H. *The Interpretation of the Acts of the Apostles*. Columbus, Ohio: Wartburg Press, 1940.

Levinskaya, Irina. *The Book of Acts in Its Diaspora Setting*. Vol. 5 of *The Book of Acts in Its First Century Setting*, edited by Bruce W. Winter. Grand Rapids: Wm. B. Eerdmans, 1996.

Longenecker, Richard A. *Paul, Apostle of Liberty*. 1964. Reprint, Grand Rapids: Baker Book House, 1976.

Lüdemann, Gerd. *Early Christianity According to the Traditions in Acts*. Minneapolis: Fortress Press, 1984.

Ma, Wonsuk, and Robert P. Menzies, eds. *Pentecostalism in Context*. Sheffield, England: Sheffield Academic Press, 1997.

Marshall, I. Howard. *An Introduction to Acts*. Sheffield, England: JSOT Press, 1992.

————. *Luke: Historian and Theologian*. Enl. ed. Grand Rapids: Zondervan Publishing House, Academie Books, 1989.

Menzies, Robert P. *The Development of Early Christian Pneumatology: With Special Reference to Luke-Acts*. Sheffield, England: Sheffield Academic Press, 1991.

Menzies, William W., and Robert P. Menzies. *Spirit and Power: Foundations of Pentecostal Experience*. Grand Rapids: Zondervan Publishing House, 2000.

Munck, Johannes. *The Acts of the Apostles*. Revised by William F. Albright and C. S. Mann. Vol. 31 of *Anchor Bible Series*. Garden City, N.Y.: Doubleday & Co., 1979.

Neyrey, Jerome H., ed. *The Social World of Luke-Acts: Models for Interpretation*. Peabody, Mass.: Hendrickson Publishers, 1991.

O'Collins, Gerald, and Gilbert Marconi, eds. *Luke and Acts*. Translated by Matthew J. O'Connell. Mahwah, N.J.: Paulist Press, 1993.

Packer, J. W. *Acts of the Apostles*. Cambridge, England: Cambridge University Press, 1975.

Palma, Anthony D. *Baptism in the Holy Spirit*. Springfield, Mo.: Gospel Publishing House, 1999.

Parr, John, ed. *Sowers and Reapers*. Nashville: Abingdon Press, 1994.

Parsons, Mikeal C., and Richard I. Pervo. *Rethinking the Unity of Luke and Acts*. Minneapolis: Fortress Press, 1993.

Puskas, Charles B. *An Introduction to the New Testament.* Peabody, Mass.: Hendrickson Publishers, 1989.

Rackham, Richard B. *The Acts of the Apostles.* 1901. Reprint, Grand Rapids: Baker Book House, 1964.

Rapske, Brian M. *The Book of Acts and Paul in Roman Custody.* Vol. 3 of *The Book of Acts in Its First Century Setting,* edited by Bruce W. Winter. Grand Rapids: Wm. B. Eerdmans, 1994.

Richard, Earl, ed. *New Views on Luke and Acts.* Collegeville, Minn.: Liturgical Press, 1990.

Roth, S. John. *The Blind, the Lame, and the Poor: Character Types in Luke-Acts.* Sheffield, England: Sheffield Academic Press, 1997.

Sanders, Jack T. *The Jews in Luke-Acts.* Philadelphia: Fortress Press, 1987.

Shepherd, William H., Jr. *The Narrative Function of the Holy Spirit as a Character in Luke-Acts.* Atlanta: Scholars Press, 1994.

Squires, John T. *The Plan of God in Luke-Acts.* Cambridge, England: Cambridge University Press, 1993.

Stott, John R. W. *The Spirit, the Church, and the World: The Message of Acts.* Downers Grove, Ill.: InterVarsity Press, 1990.

Strange, W. A. *The Problem of the Text of Acts.* Cambridge, England: Cambridge University Press, 1992.

Strauss, Mark L. *The Davidic Messiah in Luke-Acts.* Sheffield, England: Sheffield Academic Press, 1995.

Stronstad, Roger. *The Charismatic Theology of St. Luke.* Peabody, Mass.: Hendrickson Publishers, 1984.

———. *The Prophethood of All Believers: A Study in Luke's Charismatic Theology.* Sheffield, England: Sheffield Academic Press, 1999.

Talbert, Charles H. *Reading Acts: A Literary and Theological Commentary on the Acts of the Apostles.* New York: Crossroad Publishing, 1997.

Turner, Max. *Power From on High: The Spirit in Israel's Restoration and Witness in Luke-Acts.* Sheffield, England: Sheffield Academic Press, 1996.

Tyson, Joseph B. *Images of Judaism in Luke-Acts.* Columbia, S.C.: University of South Carolina Press, 1991.

Villafañe, Eldin. *The Liberating Spirit.* Grand Rapids: Wm. B. Eerdmans, 1993.

Wagner, C. Peter. *Lighting the World: Book 2, Acts 9–15*. Ventura, Calif.: Gospel Light, Regal Books, 1995.

————. *Spreading the Fire: Book 1, Acts 1–8*. Ventura, Calif.: Gospel Light, Regal Books, 1994.

Weatherly, Jon A. *Jewish Responsibility for the Death of Jesus in Luke-Acts*. Sheffield, England: Sheffield Academic Press, 1994.

Williams, David John. *Acts*. Peabody, Mass.: Hendrickson Publishers, 1990.

Willimon, William H. *Acts*. Atlanta: John Knox Press, 1988.

Winter, Bruce W., and Andrew D. Clarke, eds. *The Book of Acts in Its Ancient Literary Setting*. Vol. 1 of *The Book of Acts in Its First Century Setting*, edited by Bruce W. Winter. Grand Rapids: Wm. B. Eerdmans, 1993.

SCRIPTURE INDEX

OLD TESTAMENT

NEW TESTAMENT

SUBJECT INDEX